The End Crowns All &

The End Crowns All ❧

CLOSURE AND CONTRADICTION IN

SHAKESPEARE'S HISTORY

Barbara Hodgdon

PRINCETON UNIVERSITY PRESS

PRINCETON, NEW JERSEY

LIBRARY OF CONGRESS CATALOGING-IN-PUBLICATION DATA

HODGDON, BARBARA, 1932–

THE END CROWNS ALL : CLOSURE AND CONTRADICTION IN SHAKESPEARE'S

HISTORY.

P.   CM.

INCLUDES BIBLIOGRAPHICAL REFERENCES (P.

INCLUDES INDEX.

ISBN 0-691-06833-X (ALK. PAPER)

1. SHAKESPEARE, WILLIAM, 1564–1616—HISTORIES.   I. TITLE.

PR2982.H56   1991   822.3'3—DC20   90-7616

FOR DICK ❧

WITH LOVE AND GRATITUDE

When Pooh saw what it was, he nearly fell down, he was so pleased. It was a Special Pencil Case. There were pencils in it marked "B" for Bear, and pencils marked "HB" for Helping Bear, and pencils marked "BB" for Brave Bear. There was a knife for sharpening the pencils, and india-rubber for rubbing out anything which you had spelt wrong, and a ruler for ruling lines for the words to walk on, and inches marked on the ruler in case you wanted to know how many inches anything was, and Blue Pencils and Red Pencils and Green Pencils for saying special things in blue and red and green. And all these lovely things were in little pockets of their own in a Special Case which shut with a click when you clicked it. And they were all for Pooh.

"Oh!" said Pooh.

"Oh, Pooh!" said everybody else except Eeyore.

"Thank-you," growled Pooh.

But Eeyore was saying to himself, "This writing business. Pencils and what-not. Over-rated, if you ask me. Silly stuff. Nothing in it."

—A. A. Milne, *Winnie-The-Pooh*

"Oh, look the last act be the best in the play."

—Romelio in *The Devil's Law Case*, John Webster

The relation between what we see and what we know is never settled. . . . The way we see things is affected by what we know or what we believe. History always constitutes the relation between a present and its past.

—John Berger, *Ways of Seeing*

Men make their own history, but they do not make it just as they please; they do not make it under circumstances chosen by themselves, but under circumstances directly found, given and transmitted by the past. The tradition of all the dead generations weighs like a nightmare on the brain of the living. And just when they seem engaged in revolutionising themselves and things, in creating something entirely new, precisely in such epochs of revolutionary crisis they anxiously conjure up the spirits of the past.

—Karl Marx, *The Eighteenth Brumaire of Louis Bonaparte*

It ain't over 'til it's over.

—Yogi Berra

CONTENTS ❧

ILLUSTRATIONS ∂

Following p. 238.

1. *King John* (John Barton; Royal Shakespeare Company, 1974): Reading John's Will—Richard Pasco (Philip the Bastard); Simon Walker (Prince Henry). Photo reproduced by permission of Joe Cocks Studio.

2. *King John* (Deborah Warner; Royal Shakespeare Company, 1988): John's Death—Nicholas Woodeson (John); Jo James (Prince Henry); David Morrissey (Philip the Bastard). Photo reproduced by permission of Joe Cocks Studio.

3. *Henry VI, The Plantagenets* (Adrian Noble; Royal Shakespeare Company, 1988): Joan la Pucelle at the Stake—Julia Ford (Joan). Photo reproduced by permission of Donald Cooper, Photostage, London.

4. *Henry VI: House of York* (Michael Bogdanov; English Shakespeare Company, 1988): Henry VI's Death—Andrew Jarvis (Richard Gloucester); Paul Brennen (Henry VI). Photo reproduced by permission of Laurence Burns.

5. *Henry VI: House of York* (Michael Bogdanov; English Shakespeare Company, 1988): York Family Portrait—Lynette Davies (Queen Elizabeth); Philip Bowen (Edward IV); Andrew Jarvis (Richard Gloucester). Photo reproduced by permission of Laurence Burns.

6. *Richard III* (Bill Alexander; Royal Shakespeare Company, 1984): The Coronation—Antony Sher (Richard III); Penny Downie (Queen Anne). Photo reproduced by permission of Joe Cocks Studio.

7. *Richard III* (Bill Alexander; Royal Shakespeare Company, 1984): Richard III's Death—Antony Sher (Richard III); Christopher Ravenscroft (Richmond). Photo reproduced by permission of Joe Cocks Studio.

8. *Richard III* (Michael Bogdanov; English Shakespeare Company, 1988): Richard III's Death—Charles Dale (Richmond); Andrew Jarvis (Richard III). Photo reproduced by permission of Laurence Burns.

9. *Richard III* (Michael Bogdanov; English Shakespeare Company, 1988): Henry VII's State-of-the-Nation Address—Charles Dale (Richmond). Photo reproduced by permission of Laurence Burns.

PREFACE ❧

THIS BOOK began as a history of conventions of ending in Renaissance drama, expanded to address the power of closural forms in Shakespeare's plays, and, finally, contracted to enclose a more manageable field, Shakespeare's histories. In that process, "closure" became an excuse, so to speak, to explore a wider textual and intertextual territory. Although many, even most, of Shakespeare's plays refuse, not only at the close but elsewhere, to prescribe their own boundaries, they remain open-ended only when waiting to be read or performed: the moment a reader, a group of theatrical practitioners, or a spectator begins to work with a text, each is constructing closure, transforming one "text" into another. Recording the names of those who assisted in shaping into a book my thinking about how endings work writes a brief history of that process.

Robert Hapgood first called my attention to the *Henry VI* plays, curbed and channeled my enthusiastic responses to *Richard III*'s theatrical politics (fueled by seeing Al Pacino play Richard in Boston's Arlington Street Church as well as by the release of Francis Ford Coppola's *The Godfather* and the Senate Watergate hearings), and reminded me that Shakespeare is and is not our contemporary. Much later, this project was initiated by several summer grants from the Drake University Research Council and the Drake University National Endowment for the Humanities Challenge Grant, both of which provided funds for research trips to Britain, not only to visit archives but to attend performances. In addition, a grant from the Drake University Center for the Humanities assisted with photographers' permission fees. My warm thanks for this institutional support as well as for a sabbatical leave, which permitted space and time for revision and rewriting.

Appropriately, since part of this project centers on the collaborative endeavors of the theater, I owe thanks to several kinds of audiences: first of all, at the Shakespeare Association of America (1982, 1986), where I presented initial drafts of the material on the *Henry VI* plays and *Richard III* in a seminar and some parts of the introductory chapter in a special session; at the Ohio Shakespeare Conference (1985), whose participants asked searching questions about an early sketch of the *Richard II* chapter; at the Modern Language Association (1986), which afforded an opportunity to rethink "performance criticism"; and, finally, at Drake University, where an early version of the chapter on *Henry VIII* was presented as the Stalnaker Lecture (1987). For several years now, my students, especially A. Paul Thompson, have patiently indulged my fascination with endings and have, on occasion, even claimed that such a preoccupation might be justifiable.

Several archives have proved indispensable. I owe warmest thanks to the Shakespeare Centre Library, where Sylvia Morris, Marion Pringle, and Mary White provided generous and gracious help, guided me through the library's resources, cheerfully supplied odd and incidental information of all kinds, tirelessly photocopied prompt copy pages, and offered an extremely congenial atmosphere in which to work. My thanks, too, to Andrew St. George, dogsbody extraordinaire, even though he has since deserted Shakespeare for Browning. I am also especially grateful to the Shakespeare Centre Library and to Levi Fox, the Director of the Shakespeare Birthplace Trust, for permission to reprint excerpts from the prompt copies of Anthony Quayle's *Henry V* (1951) and John Barton's *King John* (1974), and for putting me in touch with Angus McBean, who graciously gave permission to reproduce one of his photographs from the 1951 Festival of Britain production of *Richard II*. A similar debt is owed to Christopher Robinson, Assistant Keeper at the University of Bristol Theatre Collection, not only for his kindness but also for permission to reprint extracts from Beerbohm Tree's prompt copies for *Richard II* and *Henry VIII* and material in the extraordinary Beerbohm Tree Archive, and, at a late stage, for providing photocopies of the prompt copy of Tyrone Guthrie's 1953 revival of *Henry VIII*. In addition, my thanks to the staff at the Victoria and Albert Museum Theatre Collection, the Folger Shakespeare Library, the University of Iowa Library, and the Duke University Library, and to Liga Briedis of the Reference Department of the Drake University Library for research assistance at various stages.

Those who have read all or parts of the manuscript as well as those to whom I owe a "talking debt" have been equally helpful and perceptive: John Andrews, Bernard Beckerman, Susan Carlson, Samuel Crowl, Paul Gaudet, David Scott Kastan, Joseph M. Lenz, Joseph A. Porter, Phyllis Rackin, Carol Rutter, Virginia Vaughan, and Herbert S. Weil. Among these, I want to single out Philip C. McGuire, one of the readers for Princeton University Press, whose careful comments and attention to detail, which forced me to question many of my assumptions, are exemplary signs of an unusual intellectual generosity. In addition to those debts I acknowledge in footnotes, I also want to mention Maurice Daniels, formerly of the Royal Shakespeare Company, who kindly arranged an observership with the company; Roger Pringle, for the loan of out-of-print books at a crucial moment; Michael

Bogdanov, for granting me an interview at a particularly busy time; Sue Evans of the English Shakespeare Company, for giving me access to the company's prompt copies for several of the plays comprising its *Wars of the Roses*; and Jonathan Dollimore, for insisting on a new subtitle.

My deep thanks to Robert E. Brown, Literature Editor at Princeton University Press, for his enthusiastic support of the project and for guiding it through its initial as well as its final stages. I was also delighted to have Jane Lincoln Taylor's meticulous and consistently well-judged assistance in copyediting the manuscript.

Since in many of the plays attributed to him, Shakespeare withholds the most crucial and telling revelations until the end, it seems an appropriate principle to follow here. To Miriam Gilbert I owe a very special intellectual as well as personal debt for generously sharing her notes, both of performances I have seen and of some I have not, as well as for repeated, lengthy, consistently stimulating conversations about Shakespeare, endings, the theater, and the world. My children—Bob and Dave (the two Jacks), Rich, and Sarah—have a particular place in this story of transformations: without their understanding of themselves, it would not have been possible.

The person to whom I owe the most endless thanks, whose incisive comments have shaped and reshaped ideas, words, phrases, and paragraphs, and whose keen eye has read and reread many multiple texts—literary, theatrical, and social—is someone who, in every way, supports and shares the growth of the roses in the garden, this history, and the one we have made together. His name is Richard Abel.

The End Crowns All ❧

CHAPTER 1

"CHORUS TO THIS HISTORY"

MY SUBJECT is closure and its contradictions in the ten plays First Folio (1623) calls "Histories"—*The Life and Death of King John; The Life and Death of Richard the Second; The First* and *Second Parts of King Henry the Fourth; The Life of King Henry the Fift; The First, Second,* and *Third Parts of King Henry the Sixt; The Life and Death of Richard the Third;* and *The Life of King Henry the Eight.* Quite simply, I am interested in mapping how these plays, which close with and on sovereignty, fashion a sense of ending.[1] I also want to read their narrative structures and rhetorical figuring in such a way as to open up the relations between the plays and their past as well as present-day historical contexts and, in the process, explore how such contexts contribute to shaping closure. Moreover, since I consider that a Shakespearean play exists in multiple states—as the words constituting the playtexts, as the readings based on those texts, and as their concrete, historically particular theatrical representations, or performance texts—my project encompasses all these forms of textuality or, to put it another way, several different "Shakespeares," each an altered, provisional state of what First Folio's title page calls "the True Originall copies."[2]

Appropriately, then, I want to situate "the play" as one part of a larger intertext and to begin from a point outside its customary boundaries, with one historically particular "Shakespeare-closing." It is late evening on 31 December 1988 at the Royal Shakespeare Theatre in Stratford-upon-Avon, where the cast members are acknowledging spectators' applause for Adrian Noble's *Plantagenets—Henry VI, The Rise of Edward IV,* and *Richard III, His Death*[3]—all three performed, in sequence, throughout the day. Just moments ago, in the performance text's final image, Richmond had stood in front of Richard's body, which had been impaled on Richard's own boar-spear; Richmond had raised the crown high above his head, proclaimed the end of the war dividing Lancaster and York, united the realm, and prayed for peace. Now, the company bow reveals that Richmond's army is made up primarily of women, giving a curious spin to the play's gender economy, which intensifies when, as the audience rises to a standing ovation, Penny Downie, who has played Queen Margaret, steps forward, thanks them for coming, and invites all to sing "Auld Lang Syne." Cued by *Richard III*'s choral figure, who repeatedly and insistently reminds the play's other characters of past history, spectators take hands and sway slowly from side to side for a chorus of the familiar tune, joined together briefly at the turning of the year to commemorate their own endurance and their historical past, as remembered by a "Shakespeare" reified and remystified by a Royal Shakespeare Company production which itself looks back toward the institution's own past. In this oddly skewed but nonetheless apt coda, closure reaches beyond the play's last words, the actors' gestures and movements, their placement in stage space—beyond, too, the applause for both the play and the actors' individual contributions to its realization—to intersect with and, however briefly, reshape a wider cultural community. And if all ends, not, as in *Richard III*, with "Now civil wounds are stopped, peace lives again: / That she may long live here, God say Amen," but with "Should old acquaintance be forgot," that latter phrase also moves outward to encircle and capture spectators' assent, if not to the play's royal mythologizing, certainly to its theatrical reproduction.

While this curtain call locates one of the "Shakespeares" I will be speaking of in the recent past, such extended after-plays or memorial transactions are by no means exclusively a present-day phenomenon. Renaissance writers made distinctive, forthright claims for the capacity of plays to reach beyond their textual boundaries and so to perform similar cultural work.[4] Among them, Thomas Heywood provides testimony to the affective powers of stage performances as well as to their ability to blur the distinctions between past and present, representation and reality:

> To turn to our domestic histories, what English blood seeing the person of any bold English man presented and doth not hug his fame, and honey at his valor, pursuing him in his enterprise with his best wishes, and as being wrapt in contemplation, offers to him in his heart all prosperous performance, as if the performer were the man personated, so bewitching a thing is lively and well spirited action, that it hath power to new mold the hearts of the spectators and fashion them to the shape of any noble and notable attempt.[5]

Heywood's comments are inscribed not only within a body of writing that defines and defends the ability of poetry as well as plays to inspire and refashion ("new mold") readers and spectators but also, of course, within an extensive antitheatrical discourse of sermons, pamphlets, and official documents bearing hostile witness to the dangers inherent in theatrical representations, especially their potential to invert, interrogate, even contest, the dominant fictions of power.[6] Discussing the capacity of Shakespeare's theater to reproduce, anatomize, and so to challenge cultural practices, Louis Adrian Montrose writes, "In some members of an audience, the openness of Shakespearean drama may create a disposition to work out the potentialities of the play experience within their own world, which resumes its normal flow after the characters' final *exeunt*. . . . In the society in which Shakespeare lived, wrote, and acted, the practical effect of performing his plays may have been to encourage the expansion and evaluation of options. . . . Plays are provocations to thought and patterns for action."[7] If, for Elizabethan and Jacobean spectators, the "ends" of plays and playing could indeed call cultural prerogatives into question and if plays could not only invite but insist on the powerful metaphorical equation between stage and world, what part does closure play in such potential transformations and exchanges?

Posed in this way, the question assumes, on the one hand, a critical preoccupation with closure and, on the other, a coordinate relationship between closure and cultural practice. Both strategies of reading draw on methodologies that would have been unthinkable to, say, a Samuel Johnson. Indeed, Johnson's famous opinion on Shakespeare's endings provides a rationale for ignoring them that has, until fairly recently, functioned as an invisible critical tool: "In many of his plays, the latter part is evidently neglected. When he found himself near the end of his work, and in view of his reward, he shortened the labour, to snatch the profit. He therefore remits his efforts where he should most vigorously exert them and his catastrophe is improbably produced or imperfectly represented."[8] In drawing a line between the play as a commercial, and thus imperfectly ended, project and an ideal neoclassical form, Johnson hints at the contradictions between theatrical venturing or venues, where Shakespeare's plays were originally "published" as staged performances,[9] and their later reconsideration, as printed texts, by audiences of critical readers. Similar contradictions pertain to issues of methodological inquiry. On the one hand, a formalist model can usefully explore how narrative structures, generic signs, and rhetorical figures control the developing textual process of closure and, finally, mediate between play and audience. But that enterprise, in turn, needs to intersect with historical inquiry. It has to ask how, in plays that take sovereignty as their subject, such formal features serve to negotiate a relationship central to Elizabethan and Jacobean culture—that between ruler and subjects—in order to articulate, or rearticulate, prevailing responses to the structure of experience and so invite connections between staged representation and the everyday circumstances that lie outside Montrose's conception of the theater as a paradoxically marginal and privileged cultural space. And in yet another locus for a historical Shakespeare, it is equally pertinent to ask how present-day performance texts reinterpret these signs, structures, and conventions, recuperate their social energies, and reinscribe their fictional power to perform such cultural work. Since one of my interests is in coordinating these methodologies, I want to set them in place by sketching a series of contexts for closure, beginning with Renaissance dramatic theory.

In spite of a prevailing obsession with classical forms, Renaissance theorists take the construction of closure and completeness in poetry and drama largely for granted. At the level of language, Thomas Wilson's *The Arte of Rhetorique* and George Puttenham's *The Arte of English Poesie*, handbooks that prescribe ways of fashioning language to various purposes, do no more than list "figures of ending," such as the rhetorical formulas for *conclusio* and *peroratio* that both writers copy from Cicero and Quintillian. But even Puttenham's *epithonema*, which he calls the *surclose* or *consenting close*, applies more to discrete units of oratorical discourse, as a figure that permits a speaker or writer to design and control parts of a larger argument, than to performed drama.[10] Nor do Renaissance dramatic theorists provide anything more than a broad theoretical framework for the fundamental contribution an ending makes to a dramatic work. Classical theory, on which Renaissance writers built their structural rules—not, to be sure, consistently obeyed in practice—considers endings simply one principle contributing to an overall order. Speaking of tragedy as the "imitation of an action that is complete, and whole, and of a certain magnitude," Aristotle defines "whole" as "that which has a beginning, a middle, and an end" and an ending as "that which itself naturally follows some other thing, either by necessity, or as rule, but has nothing following it"—a definition not unlike Roland Barthes's analogy with the structure of a sentence: that closure is the site where the subject is fixed, or predicated.[11] And Donatus's threefold division of comedy into protasis, epitasis, and catastrophe—the sudden conversion of affairs to a happy ending—echoes Aristotle's beginning, middle, and end, though connections between the two writers' thinking cannot be precisely made. Renaissance theorists synthesized this scheme, first applied to Terence's comedies by Donatus and subsequent commentators, with the five-act structure prescribed by Horace in the *Ars Poetica*, producing a method of construction and analysis that could be applied to any play, whether comic or tragic.[12] But whatever structural prescriptions they may seek to enforce, such umbrella notions describe the stages of a dramatic narrative in generalized abstractions, leaving the playwright's (and his acting company's) invention relatively flexible and free. In framing his famous metaphor, the tying and loosing of a knot, Aristotle writes that "many poets tie the knot well, but unravel it ill," yet he gives no specific examples of "faulty" endings. Aside from Horace's warning, "Let no god intervene, unless a knot come worthy of such a deliverer," endings per se receive only scant attention. Seneca, for example, writing in *Epistolae ad Lucilium*, has only this to say: "Crown the drama with a fine last scene."[13]

Discussing language, usage, and style in *Discoveries*, Ben Jonson comes closer than any classical or Renaissance theorist to noting that endings require special attention: "Our composition must be more accurate in the beginning and end, than in the midst; and in the end more, than in the beginning; for through the midst the stream bears us."[14] Indeed, Jonson even inscribes his neoclassical precepts into an encounter between theory and its perception in the between-act choruses of *The Magnetic Lady*. In each, Probee, the author's boy, and the untutored spectator Damplay comment on the play's structure and progress. Through their discussion, Jonson presents his understanding of the Horace-Donatus-Terence synthesis, slightly modified by Scaliger's notion of catastasis, or counterturn, which the boy has already mentioned in the act 1 Chorus.[15] In the Chorus that bridges acts 4 and 5, Probee and the boy instruct Damplay, who longs for the play to be over, on the dramatic artistry of endings:

> DAMPLAY. Why, here his *Play* might have ended, if he would ha' let it; and have spar'd us the vexation of a *fifth Act* yet to come, which every one here knows the issue of already, or may in part conjecture.
>
> BOY. That conjecture is a kind of Figure-flinging, or throwing the Dice, for a meaning was never in the *Poet's* purpose perhaps. Stay, and see his last *Act*, his *Catastrophe*, how he will perplex that, or spring some fresh cheat, to entertain the *Spectators*, with a convenient delight, till some unexpected, and new encounter break out to rectify all, and make good the *Conclusion*.
>
> PROBEE. Which, ending here, would have shown dull, flat, and unpointed; without any shape, or sharpness, Brother *Damplay*.
>
> DAMPLAY. Well, let us expect then: and wit be with us, o' the *Poet's* part.[16]

These remarks reveal that act 4, the latter part of the epitasis, both tightens the "knots" of act 3 and shows some conclusion: Damplay knows, or can conjecture, the end. But the Boy suggests that the conclusions already reached are neither ultimate (the catastasis will "perplex" them) nor satisfactory (Probee's "dull, flat, and unpointed"). Act 5, then, has a twofold function: it springs a "fresh cheat," as well as "some unexpected and new encounter" that rectifies all, and "make[s] good the Conclusion." And even though Damplay can anticipate the play's end, he remains willing, after this explanation, to "expect"— not necessarily what happens next but how the Poet's wit will give "shape, or sharpness" to the long-awaited resolution. What Damplay learns—that endings require close attention and depend not only on knowing "the issue" but also on potential narrative surprises, enhanced by the Poet's shaping—transforms him into a neoclassically informed, newly critical spectator.

Two other theatergoers, Nell and George, the citizen-grocers of Beaumont's *Knight of the Burning Pestle*, are even more unsophisticated than Jonson's Damplay. They fail to follow the complications of either plot or character in *The London Merchant*, the play they constantly interrupt by speaking to the actors and by insisting that Rafe, their apprentice, be allowed to demonstrate his Hotspur-like specialty, "a couraging part." Structural unity eludes them; they desire only to see episodes, reprises of familiar scenes in shorthand versions that highlight spectacle and melodramatic rhetoric. But however obtuse and aesthetically naïve Nell and George may be, their Philistine reputation is somewhat undeserved; they are experts on the generic signs and rhetorical conventions of endings.[17] *The London Merchant* achieves resolution with Old Merrythought's song celebrating Luce and Jasper's love, with speeches of reconciliation and forgiveness, and with an imminent marriage. Recognizing these signs of "happy ending," George comments, "Everybody's part is come to an end but Rafe's, and he's left out." Nell then suggests, and George agrees, that Rafe "come out and die," but the players' Boy reminds them that no reason exists for Rafe's death and that dying is "unfit" in a comedy. However, George will not listen: "Is not his part at an end, think you, when he's dead?" His wishes prevail, and Rafe concludes his role as aspiring actor–wandering knight with a wildly parodic death speech in which he recapitulates a fateful romantic past, even comparing the forked arrow through his head to the cuckold's horns. This draws Nell's praise: it is all she could have hoped for, and she directs Rafe to exit. Now the players rescue their play from Rafe's death throes with a group song that reasserts comic finality; its last couplet even glances, with perhaps ironic generosity, at Rafe's death: "Hey ho, 'tis nought but mirth / That keeps the body from the earth." This celebratory song satisfies George: "Come, Nell, shall we go? The play's done." But Nell has "more manners." She knows that convention demands an Epilogue: one must thank audience members for their patience (she even invites them to her house for wine and tobacco); ask for applause, at their discretion; and seek God's blessing for them all.

Speeches framing conciliatory notions, lovers' hands joined by fathers' wishes, a death tirade, narrative recapitulation, communal songs, an Epilogue begging for applause and granting blessing: that *The Knight of the Burning Pestle* closes amidst, and almost in spite of, this boisterous jumble of generic signs and terminal conventions, each overriding its predecessor, attests to both the power and the flexibility of such forms. Some—forthcoming marriage, song—belong to comic resolution; Rafe's "last words" belong to tragedy; and Merrythought's conciliatory, "ordering" speeches, as well as Rafe's recapitulation of his history, are rhetorical conventions appropriate to the closural strategies of any genre among those listed in Polonius's famous catalogue of pure as well as hybrid forms: "tragedy, comedy, history, pastoral, pastoral-comical, historical-pastoral, tragical-historical, tragical-comical-historical-pastoral, scene individable, or poem unlimited" (*Hamlet*, 2.2.387–91).[18] And Nell's epilogue, with its final blessing, combines a Plautine tradition with those of morality plays and with the drama's origins in religious celebrations. Indeed, Beaumont's burlesque compendium amounts to a playwright's glossary of closural figures which not only distinguishes one from another but, by weaving tragic and comic markers together in a flexible interchange of signs, mocks the notion of genre as a stable, determining category.[19]

If *Knight* offers an extreme, and therefore all the more visible, instance of the tension between closural certainties associated with the broad generic markers of tragedy and comedy, and whatever narrative uncertainties (Jonson's "convenient delights") may counter the precise demands of those fictional formulas, its eventual comic enclosure also points to how genre operates as a kind of "cultural machine."[20] Described in "ideal" terms, tragedy and comedy confront opposing value systems, mediate their differences, and, in proposing solutions for the individual as well as for the larger social community, eliminate any threats to traditionally held beliefs. Each genre, then, essentially upholds those enculturated assumptions that, according to Althusser, represent "the imaginary relationships of individuals to their real conditions of existence" and by means of which, as Montrose writes, "social subjects are formed, re-formed, and enabled to perform as conscious agents in an apparently meaningful world."[21] Given this assumed cultural problem-solving function of genres, the point at which they achieve resolution constitutes a crucially privileged textual site: here, both genres invariably seek to avoid questions (and questioning) by concluding their narratives at an emotive climax—in comedy, as the lovers acquiesce to each other's demands and the community re-forms around them; in tragedy, at the protagonist's death and through the responses of the survivors. Although individual examples of both genres may explore and seek to interrogate received value systems, in each the close also reaffirms those systems and attempts to mask any loss associated with compromise, moves that reconstitute and renegotiate what Leonard Tennenhouse calls "the collective fantasy about the origin and limits of power."[22] Indeed, this hesitantly poised, plural, even paradoxical reaffirmation of communally held values constitutes not only one major source of a genre's popularity and strength but also the means through which it reconstitutes itself and renegotiates its own boundaries.

Each of these contexts—Jonson's neoclassical formulas, Beaumont's catalogue, genre as a highly institutionalized means of reproducing cultural mythologies—raises particular questions about closure in the history play, a notoriously slippery generic category.[23] Certainly in Shakespeare's practice, the history play can accede to the determined closural predictabilities of tragedy or comedy, as in *Richard III* or *Henry V* respectively; deploy imperfectly satisfactory signatures of both in conjunction, as in 2 *Henry IV*; or substitute indeterminacy and continuity for closure, as in 1 and 2 *Henry VI*. Indeed, the history play's radically variable closural form is only one sign of what has long been recognized as a genre in search of itself, one that rose to prominence in the 1590s and, except for isolated examples, such as Shakespeare and Fletcher's *Henry VIII* and Ford's *Perkin Warbeck*, disappeared after 1600. Traditionally subdivided into "serious" and "comic" or "romance" histories, the serious history has gained critical, if not actual, hegemony largely because of its connections with tragedy—the "king's play" and the privileged, if not entirely dominant, Renaissance genre.[24] Although it is facile, given Shakespeare's own practice, to argue that the history play has a tragic shape, it does, as Franco Moretti writes of tragedy, represent "a universe in which *everything has its origin in the decisions of the king*." Also like tragedy, the history play "pays the monarch an ambiguous homage." Yet however truly absolute the ruler's power may be within its representational politics, that power was, within the everyday politics of the collective institutional practices supporting that imagined absolutism, considerably compromised.[25] If, on the one hand, the history play accords the sovereign the primacy and centrality characteristic of tragedy and so demonstrates its cultural affinities with that form, on the other hand, such generic explanation cannot address the historically situated contradiction between representation and social reality, and its attendant cultural anxieties, that the plays themselves—in their various Elizabethan and Jacobean performed and published states as well as in their more recent reproductions and performances—address and recirculate.

Nevertheless, enough generic traces or "ghosts" derivative of comedy as well as tragedy cross and recross the plays that First Folio labels histories, especially at the close, that it seems useful to retain genre as a descriptive, if finally indeterminate, category. Indeed, it may be, as Tony Davies writes, "precisely this structured interaction between textual signifiers and changing historical meanings, rather than some immanent 'deep structure' of narrative components, that actually constitutes a genre as a historical and formal entity."[26] Rather than circumscribing and constraining the history play, such a framework assumes that it remains elastic and flexible, theoretically free to invent and reinvent its own form, including its sense of ending. Moreover, in keeping with the notion of genre as a historically determined cultural practice, it suggests positioning the histories as plays that, in both corresponding to and challenging the representational strategies of comedy and tragedy, demarcate a more inclusive cultural territory, one that cannot be explained by a single myth of ideological or formal construction[27] or, for that matter, by a single historical methodology.

Not only were there multiple ways of conceptualizing history in the Renaissance; there was more than one way of writing and interpreting it, as the broad range and variety of historical texts and heterogeneous, fragmented, and contradictory historiographical approaches illustrate. Indeed, the monolithic construction of history represented by E.M.W. Tillyard's Elizabethan World Picture and Tudor Myth, which for many years imposed a unified grid on Shakespeare's histories, achieving the force of an aesthetic ideal, has recently been absorbed and demystified within a complex of other voices, those of Shakespeare and his predecessors and contemporaries as well as those of historical and literary scholarship.[28] Although Tillyard's historical Shakespeare still constitutes one of his many guises, other, less overdetermined methodologies of reading, more alert to the need to negotiate between Renaissance historiography and present-day discursive practices, discover a more provisional Shakespeare, one who resists conforming to such static templates. As Graham Holderness suggests, Shakespeare's historical writing occurs in a transitional period between medieval and modern times and intersects with reformulations of the very idea of history— including the chronicle-compilation with its providential theory and encyclopedic practice; the didactic political science of humanism; and the "new history," with its discovery of the pastness of the past.[29] Positioned within the context of this plural discursive practice, Shakespeare's plays represent no single, clear-cut historiographical strategy but instead encompass a Shakespeare who is, by turns, a providential chronicler, a humanist historian, and a practitioner of the new history, whose historical project represents, as Holderness and others argue, a contribution to and intervention in the Elizabethan cultural debate on reconstructing the past.[30] Such an enterprise, of course, constructs a version of the past that engages with the Elizabethan present, a kind of history writing that, in constructing a series of shifting, fluid confrontations between chronicle and popular materials, between chronicle narrative and preexisting dramatic texts, also confronts the difference between cultural ideals and practice and so constitutes a discourse where multiple, contradictory positions can interact.

The single constant in this fluid exchange of texts and methodologies of historical discovery is the figure of the ruler. But just as the history play inscribes the *idealized* dominance of the institution of kingship, it also interrogates that ideal by representing alternative values, meanings, and practices capable of contesting its hegemony, thus inviting, by its continuing reproduction, the potential redefinition of the relations between sovereign and subjects.[31] Among the other discourses that enforce or destabilize the legitimacy of kings and kingship and subjects' obedience—the 1559 *Homily on Obedience*, parliamentary debates, political pamphleteering, lawsuits—the drama offered, as Marie Axton writes, "the freest forum for speculation about the succession to the throne and the issues related to it."[32] And the theater, positioned as a marginal institution that nevertheless forms one central term in the pervasive metaphor equating world with stage, was ideally suited to recuperate and mediate the conditions as well as the contradictions endemic to power relationships. To the extent that the history play displaces the succession debate—from Henry VIII to James I, a principal focus of political instability and unease—by representing alternative constructions of the idealized, potentially coercive hierarchical model of kingship,[33] the formal flexibility characteristic of the genre well serves the enterprise and the issues it addresses, and nowhere more explicitly than at the close. If expressed in "ideal" terms, closure equates dramatic form with social order, blurring the distinctions between the two. And this assumed resemblance between dramatic and social functions of endings endows closure with the potential power to establish a relational model of social legitimacy, one that may center on, or decenter, the figure of the king.

Two premises, then, anchor my study: that the representation of sovereignty on the stage closes with and addresses the immense prestige and power of the monarchy and that closure in the history play constitutes a territory that generates and seeks to legitimize new kings, operating as a magnification mirror for the values and ideology of absolutism as well as for the incoherence of those beliefs. Through conventions of containment, closure can also act as a monitoring device for such contradictions and variance, for the insubordinate, seditious, and transformational energies released by playing, en-closing their threats. And because the history play inscribes and reinscribes, either explicitly or implicitly, one particular spectator, the sovereign, within the close, anatomizing closure invites rereading the cultural impact of such terminal features as royal compliment (however masked or qualified by the dramatic voice that speaks it) not as an afterthought but as the climax and final embodiment of royalty's "master fiction."[34] This is not to assume that either Shakespeare's representational politics or his signatures of closure in these plays submit unquestioningly to that fiction. To sketch just one point I argue later in more detail, when one or several terminal discourse conventions do evoke institutionalized forms of belief and circumscribe them within rather rigidly conceived verbal formulas, they exert a double power: that of cultural imperative and that of convention. Since the history play articulates its ending in relation to those of the dominant genres of tragedy and comedy, in which both large and small units of design are strongly anticipated, when any one feature is exaggerated or highly stylized, is displaced from its usual position, is present in a highly truncated form, is reworked, or is suppressed entirely, such alteration disrupts the expected mechanisms and signals a shift in meaning. These structural as well as rhetorical transformations and transgressions, which forge a closural design that can be thought of as an increasingly self-conscious process and as play-specific rather than genre-specific, make it possible to contest as well as to celebrate, through the power of the convention, the power of the Crown. Indeed, reading closure in Shakespeare's histories reveals how one particular textual site is traversed by and mediates the competing ideologies of its time-bound cultures to produce an Elizabethan, a Jacobean, or a present-day "Shakespeare."

To conclude this swift overview of methodological problems and reading strategies, I want, finally, to include theatrical performance within the particular textual domain of my project. Arguing for the historical particularity of texts, Leah Marcus writes, "texts can have—perhaps always have—embedded local identities of their own."[35] Certainly, among the various Shakespeares I speak of, performances not only have the most "local identity" but occupy the most marginal territory and so require a fuller explanation. Intensely ephemeral, and dependent on particular theatrical circumstances, such as casting decisions, economic conditions, and the shape and size of and the degrees of naturalism or illusion possible in specific theaters, performances are invariably geared to historically determined cultural or critical preoccupations. In reproducing or reconstituting the play's social meanings as theatrical meanings, performances rework these elements in terms of variable processes of theatrical production and consumption. Peter Brook, a director who claims no interest in history, only one in the aesthetic relations between performances and their audiences, expresses this fleeting moment well: "A production is only correct at the moment of its correctness, and only good at the moment of its success. In its beginning is its beginning, and in its end is its end."[36] And even after a number of voices, John Russell Brown and the late Bernard Beckerman most prominent among them, have consistently and forcefully argued for study of the performed play, its status remains highly indeterminate as a means of "real"—that is, *textual*—knowledge.[37] To come to terms with the voiced as well as the unvoiced assumptions that performances lack textual authority is in itself to perform, and write against, a kind of history.

In 1964, T. S. Eliot outlined in *Elizabethan Essays* a view of the relationship between play and performance that remains influential and so affords a starting point: "I know that I rebel against most performances of Shakespeare's plays because I want a direct relationship between the work of art and myself, and I want the performance to be such as will not interrupt or alter this relationship any more than it is an alteration or interruption for me to superimpose a second inspection of a picture or a building upon the first."[38] Eliot's desire for a "direct relationship" with Shakespeare's art, one that a performance "will not interrupt or alter" (except by, presumably, slight superimposition), views the play as a vehicle through which he can listen to "Shakespeare" and to himself—an essentially private communication in which performance represents a public interference. A similar position, cautiously modified to acknowledge the collaborative nature of performance, informs Helene Keyssar's description of what, for many, constitutes the ideal relationship between text and performance:

> In speaking specifically of the strategy of drama, there are two separate but interrelated strategic processes: the strategy of the text as designed by the playwright and the strategy of performance as commanded by the director, actors, and designers. While it is not always the case, the latter should be dependent upon the former; that is, part of the importance of the notion of

strategy to drama is that the director's knowledge of the strategy of the text should be the basic resource for production decisions of every kind.[39]

Arguing for a strategy that any staging should follow, Keyssar conceives of the relationship between text and performance as dependent and derivative, a stance Maynard Mack in observing that "what we notice in peformance . . . includes all we have learned from reading and discussion," extends to encompass spectators.[40] Mack's "we" (in itself a questionable construct) approaches performance not only armed with understanding but in search of the familiar—that is, those elements of the text already discovered, dissected, and unpacked. For Mack as well as for Eliot and Keyssar, a performance *should* exhibit (relative) familiarity, *should* recall an informed spectator's own previous readings, *should* bring to consciousness as many *known* connections—whether critical, historical, or sociocultural—as possible.

Such a knowing spectator desires neither discovery nor surprise but textual fidelity—whether in terms of Eliot's undisturbed direct line of communication, Keyssar's ideal of dependency, or Mack's thoroughgoing foreknowledge—and so seeks a control over the play's theatrical realization that will generate the illusion of a unified voice as well as a unified subject. Performances, however, fracture such ideal constructs into multiplicity, diversity, heterogeneity, and, often, discontinuity, especially when they venture into unknown territory that may shatter readers-turned-spectators' notions of textual integrity. Committed to the known, this spectator not only sees and hears selectively but rejects whatever makes it impossible to, in Eliot's phrase, "superimpose a second inspection . . . on the first" as a disturbance of what Keyssar calls the "strategy of the text." Often used to justify the "ideal" performance of critical desire (never yet, I think, achieved for any of Shakespeare's plays), this phrase, especially in a present-day critical climate that embraces and celebrates textuality, fosters an oppositional, adversarial relationship between text and performance.

Perhaps the most articulate recent advocate of this position, Harry Berger, Jr., claims that the "play as a script for performance" limits the latent textuality of the "play as a text" because it "diverts us with perceptible embodiments that conceal their true nature by their very form and existence as embodiments." Time-bound, unfolding quickly before spectators' eyes and ears, performance not only gives the text an exclusively "local" identity but co-opts spectators who, in submitting to its theatricality and ritual power, become complicit with its strategy and "impose on [them]selves the fictions [they] want to believe in." Such "embodiments," Berger argues, displace, through repression, an "antitheatrical" text, one that contains an inbuilt critique of the play's theatrical status. Only reading (the "play as text") can demystify the "coercive power of [theater's] visible illusion"[41] (what Eliot succinctly describes in a line from "The Dry Salvages" as "you are the music / While the music lasts"), call its "shaping fantasies" into question, and so not only recuperate its "true" metaphoric and psychoanalytic signs but expose the "fair designs" of theatricality as a sham.

Although I agree with Berger that readerly and spectatorly experience do constitute separate and distinct modes of knowing, I am unwilling, on theoretical as well as historical grounds, to accept a hierarchy that locates performance as an inferior form of textual production. Indeed, to question this premise is to question others. Berger couples the "true nature" of textuality with the skills of a highly informed reader, alert to a wide range of critical strategies, and contrasts this knowing specialist with a spectator whose powers of audition and cognition falter and whose critical faculties cease to operate once the lights go down and the (circumscribed and constrained) staged representation begins. Moreover, by avoiding references to specific performances, he opposes unequal categories and sets "performance," used as an abstract noun, against specific "plays as texts" (*Macbeth*, *King Lear*, and *Richard II*). By assuming that the theater cannot perform a critique of its own mimetic processes, Berger's post-Lacanian methodology slips strangely into a pre-Brechtian phase where it is both theoretically and practically impossible for either a staged representation or its spectators to perform such deconstructive moves. Yet recent work in cultural studies has shown that no cultural practice ever achieves absolute "coercive power" but, rather, constitutes a site of continual struggle in which the production and framing of meaning are constantly open to negotiation and renegotiation, including critique and resistance.[42] In terms of present-day theatrical practice, a case in point is Michael Bogdanov's 1986 *Romeo and Juliet* for the Royal Shakespeare Company, which closes as Prince Escalus, standing before the star-crossed lovers' golden statues, holds a press conference that demonstrates how power exploits personal tragedy to display and consolidate itself and so reveals the conditions of our present-day "enslavement," not only to the spectacle of the political but to the theater's own "fair designs."[43]

Yet another issue at stake here concerns rereading or, more precisely, the economics of reading versus watching performances. Once purchased, a playtext is literally "free" for repeated rereadings, whereas seeing a particular performance more than once—a practice that allows a spectator to reexamine, if not to stop, the text—may, at present-day ticket prices, cost the spectator quite a bit of money. But a more basic distinction exists: on the one hand, there is a self-individuated private project, resulting in a text (the critical reading) that replaces the play with another text; on the other hand, a collectively understood and collectively mediated performance, a public project that re-*places* the play within a theatrical and cultural space. Although the final *products* (the critical reading, the performance) do indeed differ, the *processes* that generate each text, each "performance," so to speak, share more similarities than differences. Indeed, alteration, interruption, and intervention are features endemic to imagining and creating both sorts of texts. To focus on one example, alteration, critical practice regularly makes cuts, additions, and digressions that may be not only more considerable but, often, more drastic than those found in the theater; furthermore, in the process, whole sections of the "play as text" go by even more rapidly than in the theater—if indeed they are cited at all. Berger himself, in a subtle and insightful reading of the initial scenes of the *Henriad*, "excavates" a psychoanalytic narrative of Gaunt and Bolingbroke's father-son relations, basing his case on approximately 145 full or partial lines drawn from a number of speakers and so reproducing more "text" than most critical discourse, much of my own included.[44] Such surreptitious interpretive practice, however, is not called cutting; it is called constructing an argument. By contrast, even performances of *Richard II* that omit, say, the scenes pertinent to another "family romance," those detailing the Aumerle conspiracy and the Duchess of York's efforts to exonerate her son, account for more of the text than the fifteen- to thirty-page critical reading.[45]

When directors and actors engage in such interpretive acts, the terms applied to the resulting product change: in the theater, reading strategies accorded critical license elsewhere are renamed "directorial interference." Yet *Hamlet* and *A Midsummer Night's Dream* specifically authorize such practices.[46] When the players come to Elsinore, Hamlet takes the First Player aside, saying "Can you play 'The Murder of Gonzago'? . . . You could for a need study a speech of some dozen or sixteen lines which I would set down and insert in't, could you not?" "Ay, my lord," answers the Player; with his consent, Hamlet tailors a pre-existing text ("extant . . . in very choice Italian") to make it "speak / With most miraculous organ" to a particular audience at a particular time, to represent not a specific historical occasion but "something like the murder of my father" (*Hamlet*, 2.2.525–29, 579–80). And, like Hieronimo's play in *The Spanish Tragedy*, Hamlet's newly adapted "piece of work" depends on a typically Tudor premise, that the play was an "image" whose action could decisively alter the course of real events.[47] Similarly, the alterations Peter Quince and his fellows make during rehearsals of *The Most Lamentable Comedy and Tragic Death of Pyramus and Thisbe* are designed to suit the play to its performance space, occasion, and audience, and result from casting limitations as well as (probably) economic constraints. Quince's original script names two characters—Thisbe's mother and Pyramus's father—who are transformed during the course of rehearsals: one into a moon, a technical effect that glances at all of *Dream*'s actual and implied virgin queens; one into a wall, a stage property that literalizes Egeus's function as a blocking parent. These radical changes require newly written material for both Moon and Wall; additional worry over frightening the ladies prompts another Prologue announcing that Lion is Snug the Joiner. And in both instances, the resulting performances depend on a view of the play as a flexible, unfixed entity, open to a process of adaptation and cocreation in the theater as well as in the mind.

Furthermore, recent reexaminations of Elizabethan and Jacobean theater practice suggest that the staged representation not only preceded but certainly had primacy over the "play as text." Indeed, Hamlet's famous instructions to the players—that "the purpose of playing . . . is, to hold, as 'twere, the mirror up to nature" (*Hamlet*, 3.2.19–21)—privilege neither the written text, which Hamlet has changed and reinterpreted to suit his own personal and political designs, nor the reader, but *playing*. Even once a play reached printed form, many early quarto title pages carefully assured potential consumers that what they were buying was the play "as it was sundry times acted," often by a particular company, on one or another of London's public stages.[48] Like present-day writers of film scripts and the scenarios deriving from them, Shakespeare and his fellow dramatists wrote within and against a system of performance texts that was, it appears, at least co-privileged with the published texts, which attempted to reproduce the staged representation for an emerging audience of readers.[49] To recuperate such claims (which, after all, are the Elizabethan equivalent of present-day advertising) of a direct relationship between staged representation and purchased text is, of course, impossible as well as ahistorical. But what might at least partially recover the Elizabethan practice of privileging theatrical representation is to unmask the conceptual illusion behind the term "text." With this in mind, when I refer specifically to the words that are traditionally construed as "Shakespeare's play," I generally use the term "playtext," both to convey some sense of their indeterminacy and to differentiate them from other, more determinate, textual categories.[50] To further destabilize both the ideal of an established, authoritative text of a Shakespearean play and the notion that the written word represents the only form in which a play can possess or participate in textuality, I refer to theatrical representations as "performance texts," an apparent oxymoron that freely acknowledges the perceived incompatibility between the (infinitely) flexible substate(s) of a Shakespearean play and the (relative) fixity of the term "text."⁵¹

Certainly the present-day critical climate values the multiple, imperfect states of many Renaissance texts, challenges the notions of an inviolate canon and transcendent "authorship," and generates renewed attention for the contradictory collaborative atmosphere that gave rise to theatrical representations. Why, then, not give equally privileged attention to, in Philip C. McGuire's phrase, "radically variable and radically particular" performance texts?⁵² Although some existing forms of discourse do acknowledge such variability, particularly the so-called stage-centered reading, which attempts to create the equivalent of a performance text in rehearsal by generating multiple options for representation, the result is often just as empty and static as the fabled "Originall" architecture, uninhabited by live bodies and lacking a "local habitation and a name." If, however, specific theatrical representations can own the privileges accruing to textuality—a very distinctive and collaborative textuality, to be sure, but nonetheless perceptible as well as describable—such a project could move toward demonstrating how various textual configurations coexist, not necessarily in adversarial, but rather in complementary, contradictory tension, a relationship that is historically and culturally determined and defined. One purpose of my project is to create a discourse that will privilege this intertextual complementarity and so permit particular textual constellations—each differently perceived, each traditionally subjected to different modes of analysis—to address each other, sometimes across the space of a paragraph.

Perhaps more than most areas of textuality, closure in Shakespeare's histories encourages this free exchange. For one thing, it is impossible to know the full extent to which afterpieces, such as epilogues or jigs, may have been a regular addition to particular performances at court or even in the public and private theaters.⁵³ Even more fundamentally, *exeunt* is perhaps the most flexible of Shakespeare's stage directions. Whereas some playtexts either prescribe or imply particular effects (a dead march, for example) others remain "as you like it." In either case, however, the precise enactment and enclosure of the final spatial model of a performance text remains open. Although this "speaking picture" may, following Keyssar's dictum of desirability, depend on the director and actors knowing (and conforming to, repressing, or violating) the "strategy of the text," such features of closure, occurring after the words constituting the playtext have been spoken, cannot be associated with what Berger identifies as the "uneasiness that accompanies our feeling that we are never hearing all that is being said" over which the "shadow of textuality" falls.[54] Rather, in this "after-play," closure consists of white space that invites inhabitation and representation. Conceptualizing and reading such spatial models requires thinking of performance texts not as the realization of an ideal text that is being "brought to life," but as constituted by critical as well as production processes that stretch and, at times, even break through that textual envelope to generate a specific series of radical interventions. And writing the cultural history of such reinterpretations and interventions is crucial if the profession's newly dominant discourse, new historicism, is to separate itself from "essentialist old historicism." The new historicism, which by and large equates plays with their texts, and thus focuses on that which gives the illusion that it "abides," reproduces the assumption that only reading can yield insights about those texts. Yet the principles of the "new discipline," especially its insistence on representation, invite, if not compel, a focus on how—in appropriating the "play as text" to serve particular critical constructs (such as the notion of tetralogies)[55] or to reinterpret communally held values—present-day theatrical practice performs cultural work and so traces, intersects with, and intervenes in particular historical circumstances and re-presents or directly encounters their prevailing ideologies.[56]

In exploring the contours of closure in a number of performances *of* and performances *on* Shakespeare's histories, I do not mean to insist, or even to suggest, that all be compared on the same level or that all have equal value. None, certainly, has the status of a defended text; indeed the very existence of multiple states of Shakespeare's histories works toward confirming the plurality of a "True Originall" by demonstrating its ability to be reproduced in another form.[57] My analyses of the closural features of playtexts and performance texts are intended as partial readings of this intertextuality; together they constitute a multiplicity of "speaking pictures" for Shakespeare's historical project, a kind of "performance work" that expands "the play" to include its playtexts and performance texts as well as the readings each engenders.[58] The strategy I have chosen—to consider the so-called double tetralogies in what is commonly accepted as their order of composition[59] and to frame them with *King John* and *Henry VIII*—observes, in the case of the double tetralogies, their approximate sequence for Elizabethan spectators and, in the case of *King John* and *Henry VIII*, pays homage to First Folio's publication scheme, which presents the plays according to a historical sequence of rulers. Although I alternate between reading the playtexts, their critical reproductions, and specific performance texts, much of what I say derives from questions raised by particular stagings I have seen. Here, the experience of repeated viewings suggests that, even though individual performances will shift in microdetail, develop, and alter within the course of a production's run, the macrostructure of a performance text tends to remain stable, enabling many of its features, especially its spatial relationships, to be read like a painting.[60] Recuperating such detail requires empowering description, from individual spectators' "thick descriptions"[61] to those provided by prompt copies and stage managers' books, as a form of knowing. In choosing from among a wide range of available examples, I do not provide a comprehensive stage history of closure or a full description of all features of one performance text. Although I include some film texts, my primary focus is on stage representations, in particular those mounted by the Royal Shakespeare Company, most of which I have seen and which are well documented. For convenience' sake rather than to perpetuate the notion of a controlling *auteur* vision, I identify these with the director's name and, even though most continued over the course of two years, with the year in which each opened, usually in Stratford. Since I have only twice experienced, in the theater, a sense of a communally unified audience, rising as though one to offer a standing ovation, and since critical practice, my own included, rests largely on articulating distinctions between and differences of opinion, I try not to refer to either readers or spectators as "we" and thus to assume or enforce collective agreement among them. Ultimately, then, what I make of play, playtext, performance text, and performance work is necessarily the textual construction of a singular, historically and culturally determined reader and spectator.

CHAPTER 2

FASHIONING OBEDIENCE: *KING JOHN*'S "TRUE INHERITORS"

King John was not a good man—
  He had his little ways.

—A. A. Milne, "King John's Christmas"

MILNE'S King John—alone, without friends, receiving Christmas greetings only from himself and never getting presents—seems designed as an object lesson encouraging readers, but especially its children-listeners, to be good so as to receive gifts from Father Christmas. Reassuring himself that he will get "one present, anyhow," John asks for a "big, red India-rubber ball," but on Christmas morning, his worst fears come true: "Nothing again for me!" As he stands at his window envying the happy children playing in the snow, "through the window big and red" comes that India-rubber ball, whether by child's intent, marvelous accident, poetic fiat, or all three; the poem then closes with the narrator's blessings for Father Christmas, printed in darkened block capitals.[1] In the comforting moral sphere of Milne's poem, even bad King John receives a miraculous Christmas gift—a small globe of a world—in a perfectly powerful resolution sanctioned by a fictional figure who represents secularized religious authority.

Much like the ending of Milne's poem, the closing speech of Shakespeare's *King John* also attempts to resolve its issues—the King's legitimacy, his succession, and his "little ways," including his responsibility for the death of a rival heir, his rule by self-interest, and his subjects' disobedience—by evoking an ideal unification at least as encompassing as the complex of values Milne associates with Father Christmas and the desire for a big, red India-rubber ball, a unification that goes by the name of "England to itself."

This England never did, nor never shall,
Lie at the proud foot of a conqueror,
But when it first did help to wound itself.
Now these her princes are come home again
Come the three corners of the world in arms

And we shall shock them! Naught shall make us rue
If England to itself do rest but true!

$$(5.7.112–18)^2$$

Even if its spectators did not recall that another play, *The Troublesome Raigne of King John of England* (1591), ended with similar sentiments,[3] the convention alone would set up familiar echoes, for it combines the didactically confrontational ending of the morality play; the "last words" of the dramas of Shakespeare and his contemporaries, usually voiced by the speaker of highest rank,[4] often the play's newly authorized ruling figure; and the Epilogue, to construct, so to speak, an extremely legitimate formal close. Elizabethan spectators would also recognize, in the Bastard's appeal to national integrity, echoes of Armada pamphleteers who in turn are citing biblical watchwords.[5] While *Gorboduc*'s Eubulus argues through a similar position for one hundred lines in the final speech of that play, the Bastard's compressed phrases are shorthand signs for commonplaces so widely acknowledged as to have become the national anthem of the 1590s: a country invincible, its power derived from wholeness, from being "true" to itself. As Fredric Jameson argues, the codification of complex human experience, not in names but in proverbial tags that allude to conventional concepts or to a recognizable destiny operative at a given historical moment, can become, for a reader or spectator, a powerful schema for organizing fragmented events.[6]

Shakespeare's histories circulate many such "anthems": John of Gaunt's paean to "this royal throne of kings" (*Richard II*, 2.1.31–68), Henry V's St. Crispin's Day speech (*Henry V*, 4.3.20–77), and Bishop Cranmer's prophetic blessing of Elizabeth and James (*Henry VIII*, 5.5.15–62) come immediately to mind as key texts that, detached from their respective plays, have been mined to address cultural imperatives and read as Shakespeare's authentic voice, speaking across history.[7] While far from unique in this respect, the Bastard's words have been variously appropriated to serve cultural as well as critical myths. On 22 February 1939, with Europe on the brink of World War II, Neville Chamberlain would quote *King John*'s concluding lines to urge Britons toward an ideal social harmony that could sustain Britain's national war effort.[8] And near the end of that war, E.M.W. Tillyard and Lily B. Campbell praised its "ringing affirmation" of Tudor doctrines of order, which both saw as fundamental to Shakespeare's histories: what came to be known as "the theme of England" offered a complex of sociopolitical values that floated free of the historical moment to establish an Elizabethan World Picture, with Shakespeare at its center, as the core of British literary culture.[9] From the late 1960s forward, however, readers would describe the Bastard's words as a "piece of studied patriotism," the calculated rhetoric of a master politician designed to mask complex social realities with an ideal, unattainable order.[10] And once deconstruction, with its capacity to fault or question the ability of all language to operate except in reference to itself, became a powerful critical myth, reexamining the relations between *King John* and its concluding lines led to reading it as an instance of closure and its discontents.[11] While similar dissatisfactions pertain to many of Shakespeare's histories, since *King John* stands outside the conventional tetralogy schema imposed by critical discourse, it offers an Archimedean point from which to begin. Indeed, its particular negotiation of prior historical materials calls into question the crucial relation between king and subject that those histories address.

While those of her subjects who read Richard II, through his faults, as a figure for Queen Elizabeth could make equally damaging analogies between Elizabeth and John—especially insofar as both had been responsible for the death of a rival claimant: John for Arthur, Elizabeth for Mary, Queen of Scots—such potentially topical parallels were not only out of date by the mid-1590s but seem to have been absorbed and diffused by King John's official Elizabethan image.[12] Although his defiance of the pope and his surrender of the crown to Pandulph had been appropriated by medieval chroniclers "for the imitation of succeeding times and admonition to the faithful,"[13] Tudor historians remade the early chronicle accounts to produce a more favorable image of John as a patriot-martyr whose defiance of Rome offered proof that the universal hegemony of the church was incompatible with royal supremacy and so presaged a Protestant England, where church and state were one. Moreover, in the *Homilie against Disobedience and Wylfull Rebellion* (1571), read out weekly in parish churches, John's reign served to figure civil dissension as well as to warn against Catholic conspiracies, for in Elizabeth's time as in John's, the pope was an enemy who could, in offering to discharge Englishmen's oaths of obedience in exchange for rebellion against a heretic king, deprive subjects of their rights. Recast as Tudor ideology, then, John's history supports the twin foundational principles of monarchy's social contract: royal supremacy and civil obedience. Both Anthony Munday's *A Watch-woord to England* (1584) and the anonymous *Troublesome Raigne* mobilize this reconstructed myth to take didactic positions against Catholicism and, more specifically, against Spain. Shakespeare's *King John*, however, hollows out John's mythic Tudor identity to reveal its precarious, contradictory shape.[14] In a sense that extends beyond its intertextual relation to *Troublesome Raigne*, Shakespeare's play is "doubly written":[15] in negotiating between John's medieval and Elizabethan histories, it constructs an imaginary middle ground beneath a labyrinthine plot of betrayal and disobedience. No parable against either kingship or popery, "We speak no treason against Kings or Rome" perhaps best describes its politics of accommodation, especially in its closing scenes. And its opening moves are crucial to situating that close, particularly since the play begins, as no other Elizabethan account does,[16] not only by calling John's legitimacy into question but by engaging with the contradictory and competing perspectives that determine royal "right."

What ensures a sovereign's legitimacy? Is a usurper a lawful king? How is the succession to be determined—by genealogical right, by the terms of a monarch's will, by parliamentary fiat, by "strong possession," or by some combination of these? With two rightful claimants to the throne, what—and who—determines which one is worthiest? What relationship obtains, or should obtain, between church and state, between English kings and papal authority? What obedience do subjects owe to a tyrant, especially one responsible for the murder of a rival heir? The subject of legal as well as popular debate throughout Elizabeth I's reign, these questions, as Marie Axton argues, were also accessible subject matter for its drama: among Shakespeare's histories, *King John* confronts them more directly than most.[17] Initially, deciding England's ownership involves what seems to be a simple choice between right and possession, a dilemma the play displaces onto the Faulconbridge brothers, whose situation parallels John's relationship to Arthur: one brother in "strong possession," another claiming blood ties to Richard Cordelion that are recognizable, by Elinor as well as John, in his "accent" and "composition" (1.1.39, 86–90). In affirming Robert's right to possess the Faulconbridge lands, John confirms his own right to England's land and displaces his illegitimacy onto the Bastard, whom he then fashions in his own image, so to speak, as Richard Lackland. But although these first signs of what the Bastard later calls "commodity" conveniently settle, by royal fiat, the competing claims of de facto and de jure rights within the private realm, once the contest over "double right" shifts into a more public international arena where Philip of France supports Constance's claim for Arthur's title to the English throne and accuses John of usurping true authority, it becomes clear that a sovereign's right to rule depends not on his own voice but on proving his superiority before an audience of subjects.[18]

War, of course, offers the simplest proof of "whose right is worthiest," but John and Philip's military display results in stalemate, and Angiers's spokesman cannily declares a "both-alike" brand of loyalty (2.1.281, 331). Urged on by the Bastard, both agree to "lay Angiers even with the ground, / Then after fight who shall be king of it," until the Citizen proposes a match between Blanche and Lewis, a "fair-faced league" both Kings accept (2.1.399–400, 417). And its further compromises—John's "wedding gift" of six French provinces for Lewis and two titles, Duke of Brittany and Earl of Richmond, for Arthur—refigure the split between lands and titles marking John's earlier decision in the Faulconbridge case. While in Elizabeth's England, the discourse of courtly love could articulate an idealized image of the Queen's relation to the state, it does not succeed in feudal Europe, especially once Pandulph, the papal legate, arguing for obedience to a higher allegiance on which all form and order depend, excommunicates John for opposing him and threatens Philip with a similar curse. To the already bewildering array of strategies for ensuring legitimacy, *King John* now adds another: the power of the church to delegitimize a king and, as it later turns out, to restore that legitimacy.[19]

By circulating this range of options as well as the consequences of choosing between John's "borrowed majesty" and Arthur's "powerless hand," *King John* sketches in a history with particular Tudor resonances. Tudor monarchs had been obliged to abandon the doctrines of legitimacy and divine right largely because neither justified their own claims to the throne; indeed, had such laws been enforced, all might have been termed usurpers. Queen Elizabeth, herself once proclaimed illegitimate by an Act of Parliament, was forced to downplay hereditary primogeniture as fundamental law; in proclaiming that Parliament possessed the right to alter the succession, she was relying on the public need for unity and security.[20] But if Elizabeth's policy succeeded in masking the fault lines within Tudor genealogical imperatives, that is not the case in *King John*'s curiously skewed gender economy, where women's voices serve to undermine the myth of patriarchal succession, which assumes a direct connection between males within a blood line and so works to erase women's legal as well as biological roles. In *King John*, each competing claim for legitimacy has the support of a widowed mother's powerful, and powerfully subversive, voice. Elinor is "An Ate, stirring [John] to blood and strife" (2.1.63); Constance would change the calendar to erase the date of the political alliance between Blanche and Lewis, argues for "armed discord 'twixt these perjured kings," and defies Pandulph's law as "perfect wrong" (3.1.87–88, 111, 189). Even Philip, though without a mother, is vulnerable to Pandulph's threat that "the church, our mother, [may] breathe her curse, / A mother's curse, on her revolting son" (3.1.256–57). Moreover, Elinor and Constance interrupt the negotiations between John and Philip to accuse one another of adultery: Elinor by denying her grandson his patriarchal right; Constance by stressing Elinor's part in Arthur's blood to explain why he has been deprived of his royal birthright. And by confessing her own infidelity and so affirming the Bastard's paternity, Lady Faulconbridge supports Elinor's reading in him "a trick of Cordelion's face" (1.1.85). If women can not only bear witness to the history of their sons' breeding but publicize their own adulteries and so guarantee or defame male prerogatives, how secure is any son's title to lands or, especially, to a throne? Insofar as women can undermine what Phyllis Rackin calls the "masculine historical project," in *King John* their voices serve to call the authority of the male-centered historiographical tradition into question and so to expose the "arbitrary and conjectural nature of patriarchal succession and the suppressed centrality of women to it."[21]

In localizing the voices of its women so that all—even Blanche, the most perfectly malleable among them—speak to the issue of legitimacy, *King John* checks and contains their potentially subversive witnessing. But the question they raise—the difference between belief at the level of represented "truth" and conjectures about what actually occurred—persists to further disturb the circumstances surrounding Arthur's death, the play's most crucial and problematic event. Here it is not so much a case of "double writing," for *King John* makes no attempt to reproduce the chronicler's indecision over how Arthur died, but of "double reading."[22] Unaware that John no longer threatens him but needs him living and well in order to ensure his nobles' fealty, Arthur leaps from the walls and, with his dying words, reads the event as regicide—"My uncle's spirit is in these stones" (4.3.9)—as do the nobles who first discover his body. Conflicting opinions, accusations, and false reports have an effect on the politics of royal right similar to that the women's voices have on the issue of legitimacy. Now, however, when choice (always impossible) no longer matters, the playtext acknowledges Arthur as England's "true" king. And, as though to further stress the tenuous nature of such a commitment, the Bastard becomes its spokesman. Lost "among the thorns and dangers of this world," it is he who claims for his cousin and reads the dead heir as "all England," "The life, the right and truth, of all this realm" (4.3.139, 142, 144).[23] If legitimate, he would, at this point, be able to lay claim to England's throne; as it is, he is bound in double obedience: to the idea of a rightful king and to King John's "borrowed majesty."

King John's most ambiguous, mutable figure, the Bastard is, quite literally, a "marginal man," named only in Holinshed's margins as "Philip king Richards bastard son."[24] In one reading, he replaces Arthur as "true inheritor," a substitution that some of *King John*'s critics, moved to recreate what *Macbeth*'s Malcolm calls "the king-becoming graces" (4.3.91) in their absence, have magnified into imagining the Bastard as the king of the play.[25] The reading is attractive, for indeed the play exploits his link to John and his royally constituted legitimacy as Richard I's son to shore up kingship through a fiction of kinship. Variously positioned as illegitimate and legitimate, Chorus and protagonist, monarch and subject, the voice of the realm and the voice of the culture,[26] the Bastard's plural roles assume the absence of a single, coherent subject position—either within the play or outside its boundaries, among its spectators. Indeed, he represents a special instance of what Jonathan Dollimore calls "transgressive reinscription": marginal to the power structure, he seeks to be reinscribed within it but, once incorporated, he remains at its fringes, able to demystify and subvert its operations.[27] In another play, such a figure might be associated with the carnivalesque, capable of inverting power relations;[28] in *King John*, however, where the King himself turns kingship upside down, the Bastard serves to protect the institution he embodies from further taint.

In *King John*, the problem of rule, therefore, becomes a problem of reading. Much about the play operates like a present-day television commercial, especially those that market a product to a plurality of audiences simultaneously by creating multiple subject positions.[29] Increasingly, those characters initially constructed as marginal spectators or commentators—Hubert, John's nobles, and especially the Bastard—become fully integrated "English-speaking subjects" who not only voice kingship's ideal "truths" but, like Hubert and the Bastard, act for the King (3.3; 4.1; 4.2) and, much later, in the Bastard's case alone, ventriloquize his voice: "Now hear our English king, / For thus his royalty doth speak in me" (5.2.128–29). If this strategy figures John's insecure claim, which the play exploits as a given, it also protects the office while calling its occupant into question and so permits John's original claim before Angiers—"England for itself"—to float free of reference to specific illegitimate monarchs, usurpers, potential tyrants, or "bad" kings. And when, in spite of having been recrowned (a ceremony the playtext does not represent), John fails to gain his nobles' fealty and feels himself threatened by "subject enemies" as well as "adverse foreigners" (4.2.171–72), the play readdresses the question of his authority by downwardly displacing the self-interested behavior the Bastard calls "commodity" from the rulers onto the ruled.[30]

Put simply, from Arthur's death forward, *King John* explores the power of the ruled, in the absence of a rightful king, to reconstitute the semblance of an ideal state.[31] Contradictorily, the commodity principle, which, when exercised by subjects rather than rulers, contains the potential for subversion and deviation not only from standards set by the *Homilie against Disobedience* but also from notions of "government for the greater good," now becomes crucial in fashioning loyal subjects. Although King John himself figures in three of the play's seven final scenes, each appearance successively diminishes his authority. It is the "lawful" rebels against a supposed child-murderer, in seeking to heal the blots on their own honor with obedience to an alternative king, and the Bastard, by attempting to refashion John in a heroic, warlike image (5.1), who support and sustain notions of de jure and de facto rule or "true right."[32] While arguing that the scenes following Arthur's death all concern reversals of allegiance generates an overly schematic model of *King John*'s political economy, each scene either details a specific shift in allegiance or concerns the results of those shifts. Reacting to Arthur's death, Salisbury speaks for the nobles and "forbid[s his] soul" from obedience to John (4.3.64); later, John gives his crown to Pandulph, who immediately returns it, in a bargain to forestall French invasion (5.1). The English nobles swear fealty to Lewis, who then rejects Pandulph's truce and prepares to battle a "warlike" John who, distracted by fever, pays scant attention to the messenger's good news of the French fleet's wreck on Goodwin Sands (5.2–3). When the dying Melun tells the English nobles of Lewis's proposed betrayal (ironically, it is Lewis, not John, who would punish English rebels), they revoke their oaths to "calmly run on in obedience / Even to our ocean, to our great King John" (5.4.56–57). And Lewis, misreading natural signs, assumes victory in the ensuing scene just before learning of the English nobles' "new flight; / And happy newness, that intends old right!" (5.4.61). Throughout this sequence, however, nothing does operate according to "old right," insofar as that could be identified with any official stand on obedience and rebellion. Rather, these dizzying shifts echo not Tudor doctrine but Tudor practice.

Indeed, *King John*'s chameleonlike nature—what I have called its politics of accommodation—is particularly evident in the last third of the play, which, in alternating between English and French factions, markedly accelerates its pace and represents its events, largely through report, in a kind of shorthand, relying on allusions to omens and prophecies to supply a sense of their significance and pressure. Here, natural forces (ill winds, John's fever, a slowly setting sun, tides) and human interventions (Melun's wounding, John's poisoning by the monks of Swinstead Abbey) combine in a cause-effect pattern of chance and coincidence to generate the impression that what *King John* does not show may have at least as much, if not more, import than what it dramatizes. The classic way to account for this strategy of underrepresentation is, of course, to compare *King John* to *Troublesome Raigne*.[33] Such comparisons can also account for its curious refusal to take orthodox Tudor positions and so to engage with the anti-Catholic polemics that were the wrappings of John's official image. Two events fully dramatized in *Troublesome Raigne*—John's hesitation over yielding his crown to Pandulph and the monks' plot to poison him, which fulfills God's will by ridding the land of an evil heretic-tyrant—are, in the case of the first, only briefly sketched, and in the case of the second, simply reported. In both cases, underrepresentation[34] works to suppress precisely those events that might divide or fracture audience response—submission to Rome, the killing of a king by "monarchomach" monks[35]—and to deflect from fashioning a unified spectator position. In this regard, Tillyard's pejorative phrase for the last act of *King John*—"uncertain of itself"[36]—is precisely the point. By leaving its offstage spectator-subjects free to construct obedience as not dependent on allegiance to a particular religion, the play shifts conflict out of the realm of church politics to allow for the incoherence of and contradictions in thought governing the relations between sovereigns and subjects. And it is through such semblance of ideological neutrality, which offers the possibility of a negotiated position within hierarchical feudalism, that *King John* constructs its close.

Perhaps the most puzzling event in this elliptic representational economy is the night meeting between Hubert and the Bastard (5.6), which reports John's poisoning by monks at Swinstead Abbey. At the level of narrative, the scene functions, by providing necessary information, primarily to make John's situation at the close more credible; at the level of kingship, however, it generates the enigmatic possibility of another illegitimate succession. Before Hubert tells the Bastard that the Lords have returned with Prince Henry, the Bastard is in precisely the same situation John was in at the death of Richard I, a possible inheritor and potential usurper.[37] For those who would read him as the play's appropriate king, the Bastard's "Withhold thine indignation, mighty heaven, / And tempt us not to bear above our power" (5.6.37–38) hints that he may even have contemplated such a move. Yet *King John* not only delays fully exploiting this particular reversal but, ultimately, steps away from such an imaginary solution (however attractive) for the ideological contradictions within kingship it has put into play.[38]

For most readers, *King John*'s sense of ending is, however, at least

as imaginary as crowning the Bastard England's King. Despite being
one of the bleakest succession scenes in Shakespeare's histories,[39] it is
packed with narrative as well as rhetorical signs of resolution, as
though to validate royal genealogy by means of dramatic rules. While
some of its features (John's death and the nobles' return with Prince
Henry) are anticipated and prepared for, others (Pandulph's reported
offstage presence; the Dauphin's peace offer permitting the English
"with honor and respect . . . to leave this war" [5.7.85–86]) neatly tie
up all loose ends to restore errant English subjects to the land and to
the dying King. A brief show of allegiance confirms and celebrates
these corrected relations between monarch and subjects as, first, the
Bastard bequeaths his "faithful services / And true subjection everlast-
ingly" to the new King, and then Salisbury and the others offer their
love "to rest without a spot for evermore" (5.7.104–5, 107). Yet John,
preoccupied with his illness, not only seems unknowing but dies midway through the Bastard's report, while his successor, Prince Henry,
speaks only the briefest and most generalized elegy: "Even so must I
run on, and even so stop. / What surety of the world, what hope, what
stay, / When this was now a king, and now is clay?" (5.7.67–69).
Moreover, neither England's King nor its nobles have remained "true."
Only the Bastard, who speaks the phrase, retains that distinction, for
the play's events have consistently shown "for evermore" to be contingent on "commodity." Although *King John*'s events clearly demonstrate that "there is no sure foundation set on blood" (4.2.104), the
play, in its last riff on "right breeding," finally validates the principle
of primogeniture by producing, *principe ex machina* , an heir who, like
Arthur, is a "powerless hand," but who has no mother's voice to affirm
or deny his "miraculous legitimacy." The playtext's own phrase for
this displacement of the political by the formal comes from Salisbury,
who tells Henry he is born "To set a form upon that indigest / Which
he hath left so shapeless and so rude" (5.7.26–27). But even though
the play recuperates royal genealogy as the desired ideal and so satisfies
the "plain old form" (4.2.22), its last speaker is not its new sovereign
but his most loyal and obedient subject:

> This England never did, nor never shall,
> Lie at the proud foot of a conqueror
> But when it first did help to wound itself.
> Now these her princes are come home again
> Come the three corners of the world in arms
> And we shall shock them! Naught shall make us rue
> If England to itself do rest but true!
>
> (5.7.112–18)

Absorbing and refiguring the lessons of the *Homilie against Disobedience*, the Bastard's words translate them into renewed practice. Earlier, I called his speech an extremely legitimate close. Yet its particular bricolage of rhetorical signs of ending can also be read as a bastard form, a last figure for *King John*'s initial questions concerning plural claims on royal legitimacy. By giving the Bastard the right to "speak the kingdom," *King John* evokes a postfeudal fantasy that, in stopping short of bastardizing kingship, discloses the historical limits of subversion at the fictional limits of the play. And by having the play's most marginally historical figure, who encompasses contradictory roles, reimagine Tudor ideology, *King John* also offers, so to speak, de facto evidence that an illegitimate player can sustain the role as well as recuperate its strategies for containing unruly subjects. But, unlike many of the closural, epiloguelike speeches of the earlier drama, this one addresses neither the play's new King nor the reigning Queen but instead looks the entire realm directly in the face to figure "England" and "her princes" as celebrants of a union that substitutes, for the King's Two Bodies, the power of the body politic. At its close, *King John* moves away from its uneasy negotiation between medieval and Tudor images of its King and of kingship to take on a specifically Elizabethan configuration in which the need for security in the matter of the succession breeds a unity called "England to itself." Finally, the apparent freedom of multiple subject positions that the play allows its own "speaking subjects" extends to address all its spectator-subjects as England's new "owners." It is *King John*'s last figure for commodity—transformed, through its politics of accommodation, to offer, not a mirror for magistrates, but a complex, even refractory, mirror for subjects.

≥

Driven by somewhat similar notions of ownership, nineteenth-century theatrical producers appropriated *King John* as a means of excavating a historical past in order to empower contemporary Britons with an understanding of their own history and, not incidentally, to enhance the nation's claims to empire.[40] Kemble, Macready, and Charles Kean mounted reconstructions that established a playing style that framed individual performances, praised for their emotive power, within lavish, archaeologically detailed "pictures,"[41] a tradition continued by Beerbohm Tree's 1899 revival, which embodied "all the pomp and rude splendour of a warlike and chivalrous age" in a pageant play "gallant and glowing with colour like an old illuminated chronicle."[42] Tree married his own view of John's political acumen and heroic stature with the end-of-the-century desire to recuperate and reenvision the past in a *King John* that featured, just before John's surrender of the crown to Pandulph (5.1), an interpolated dumbshow, "The Granting of Magna Charta," based, so Tree claimed, on historical documentation and explained in the souvenir program, which quoted ten of its sixty-one articles, as "one of the most solemn moments of our history."[43] If such evidence of John's heritage could be thought entirely appropriate to late nineteenth–century Britons' pride in their liberties and rights as well as their legal system, late sixteenth–century viewers might well have found the addition somewhat anachronistic. Elizabeth and her ministers chose to deemphasize a document that laid out precise relations—specifically, economic and land-grant privileges—between sovereign and subjects, and instead to stress, in theory, the role of Parliament as a kind of proto-democratic ruling body and, in practice, to rely even more heavily on her own Privy Council in foreign as well as domestic decision making.[44] Indeed, although some of Tree's critics objected to the intrusion on precisely these grounds, others argued that a wordless tableau does not violate Shakespeare and that, considering the liberties Shakespeare himself had taken with history, it was surely admissible to redress the author's oversight, especially when it had an educational benefit.[45] Seeing the world in images had become a habit in the first half of the century; at its conclusion, pictorialism had become the dominant cultural mode. And the theater was only one among many mass spectacle attractions—illustrated magazines as well as illustrated editions of Shakespeare, panoramas, dioramas, stereoscopic views, and motion pictures—that turned London into a mosaic of simulacra.[46] Characterizing turn-of-the-century theatrical taste, Tree remarked that "the public demand absolute exactitude, they delight in photographic accuracy, and are satisfied if the thing produced exactly resembles the original without stopping to think whether the original was worth reproduction."[47]

If some material images were unworthy to be reproduced, this was not the case with Shakespeare. And recreating his plays extended beyond simply replicating, with antiquarian zeal, the architecture, objects, and costumes of a particular period; these were just one aspect of a physical realism that solidified around the central actor. In the case of *King John*'s closing scene, considered by many "the most striking of all the series of pictures in the play," it was Tree's subtle and powerfully realized performance that "sent a tremour through the house."[48] Tree staged John's death as a night scene in the orchard of Swinstead Abbey, complete with medieval cloisters and blossom-laden trees, their pink and white flowers softly glowing in the evening light. A procession of monks carrying lanterns crossed the stage on their way to vespers, and the sound of their offstage plainsong chant continued until John, dressed in a striking white robe, was carried on in a chair. In Tree's restrained and realistic performance, he spoke with great difficulty, groping blindly for the crown, which was on the arm of his chair; quickly, attendants placed it on his head and, as the Bastard gave his report, John remained upright, staring straight ahead, a dignified, regal figure. Hearing no response to the Bastard's news, a noble touched John's shoulder, and the King sank back into his chair, dead, as "the mellow lin-lan tones of evening bells"[49] sounded in the dusk. With the dead King at center stage, surrounded by his son and the nobles, the Bastard stepped forward to speak his final lines as the sun burst through the clouds, signifying a new day and a new reign, while the monks' requiem crescendoed to a last "Amen," accompanied by the peals of an organ. If this apotheosis confirmed what Tree, in a program note, had called "the greatness of [John's] fall," it was the Bastard's last words, as it turned out, that gave Tree's revival a topicality he could not have anticipated. When, on 11 October, a few weeks after *King John*'s opening, the Boer War finally broke out, a play that "bristle[d] with red-hot patriotism and lines singularly appropriate to the occasion"[50] not only fulfilled its spectators' desires for historical realism but offered, in the Bastard's rallying cry, proof of Britain's imperial destiny.

The close of Douglas Seale's 1957 *King John* for Stratford's Shakespeare Memorial Theatre[51] offers another instance in which a staged pageant of royal continuity must have evoked memories of fairly recent events: George VI's death and, in 1953, Elizabeth II's accession. Entering to a full tableau of John seated center stage, surrounded by Prince Henry and the nobles, with a number of monks and soldiers grouped in the background, the Bastard kneels to pay homage to the King, who rises with a start at the news of the army's loss, only to collapse in death, his nobles kneeling in attendance as the Bastard folds John's hands across his body. Rising to proclaim himself John's servant still, the Bastard prompts the other nobles to stand as well before again kneeling, this time to Henry, on "may your sweet self put on / The lineal state and glory of the land," a gesture the nobles repeat. To climax the repetitive patterns of kneeling and rising that articulate the shift of power from one king to another, Henry then raises the Bastard, signalling the others to rise as well; drawing his sword, Henry kneels alone by his father's body while the Bastard speaks his final lines. In a move that evokes *Hamlet* to invite reading John's story as tragedy, six soldiers raise John's body to their shoulders and, following the monks and nobles, exit in a slow procession, to leave the new King and the Bastard alone on the stage. Finally, Henry rises and extends his hand to the Bastard, who takes it, and the two exit together through a pair of massive upstage doors emblazoned with heraldic devices, which then close on this patriarchal image of loyal subject and new King to figure the beginning of Henry's reign as a nurturant partnership between a bastard "father" and a legitimate son.

While this "marriage of succession" perfectly complements *King John*'s early debates over lineal right and possession, critics of Seale's performance text, many of whom mention the close, comment only on the Bastard's final speech. For J. C. Trewin, not only did the last lines make "a declaration of faith that need not be a brag," but Alec Clunes spoke them with "plain steady truth that was in itself enough to lift the heart and stir the blood."[52] Even the often cynical Kenneth Tynan was willingly co-opted by Clunes's Bastard, "a hearty, beaming clergyman summoned to restore order to an unruly youth club: his voice, that ripe and fluent instrument, reconciled me by a hair to a reading totally at odds with the text."[53] Although Harold Hobson, pointing to the gap between John's history and Shakespeare's closing "hymn of patriotism—rising at the end to a flamboyant outburst of nationalistic fervor," thought John a most "unsuitable monarch" for revealing such sentiments and faulted Seale's production, not the play, for not resolving this contradiction, he concluded that the "deeply poetic feeling" imposed on the text makes his objection "fortunately irrelevant."[54] And for at least one critic, Rosemary Sisson, Seale's performance text mythologized history. She writes, "two great crosses outlined above the battlements emphasize, with Christopher Whelan's haunting music, the supernatural power which lies behind the ebb and flow of history—a history which, in this powerful but sensitive production, seems as vital as the happenings of our own time."[55] Such testimony to how persuasively the Bastard's speech can, in performance, join together members of one interpretive community not only reifies what I take to be its original function but illustrates how, even at the height of European cold-war politics, this *King John* could serve to enhance an equation between "Shakespeare" and "history" and so to preserve both in an ahistoric time warp of national memory.

Seventeen years later, in what was less a revival than a radical reimagining of John's history, John Barton produced, for the Royal Shakespeare Company, a *King John* constructed from Shakespeare's play, *Troublesome Raigne*, and Bale's *King Johan* that also included, much as though the name "John" carried special force in its composing, newly written material by "King Barton" himself.[56] Rereading

King John at the end of 1973, Barton saw, in its "world of outward order and inner instability, of shifting ideologies and self-destructive pragmatism," a mirror of present-day England, where corruption within the national as well as the international power elite, soaring inflation, and political hypocrisy demonstrated the inability of government to respond to people's everyday needs and resulted, in the mid-1970s General Election, in widespread disillusionment with the promises of postwar socialism.[57] Turning to *Troublesome Raigne* for possible explanations of why such parallels had not surfaced in recent performances of *King John*,[58] he decided that "a marriage of the two texts might be fruitful." An initial decision to make only limited cuts and insertions (a not unusual company practice) eventually led to more extensive textual changes that, according to Barton, "do no more than develop and clarify tendencies already in the three plays from which this version is drawn"; moreover, he argued that since "in a sense any production of a play is an adaptation of the original . . . a production cannot help creating as well as criticising, so turning the original text into something it is not by itself."[59] Indeed, at a time when the plays of Bertolt Brecht, John Arden, and Edward Bond were regularly presented on London stages, Barton's *King John* was part of a wider theatrical context in which playwrights drew on the historical past, either by creating new plays (such as Arden's *Left-Handed Liberty*, commissioned to celebrate the 750th anniversary of Magna Charta) or rewriting existing plays (such as Brecht's *Edward II* and Bond's *Lear*) so as to interrogate present-day social realities.[60] Certainly such a marriage of history with existing dramatic texts to address present-day cultural circumstances reproduces Elizabethan and Jacobean compositional methods: just as Shakespeare manipulates the King John materials to evoke connections to a Tudor cultural ethos, Barton's adaptation incorporates elements from existing discourses in a kind of "creative vandalism" that imitates *King John*'s own originating history.[61] Moreover, Barton's *King John* also reproduces the spirit of critical practice, which, by appropriating *Troublesome Raigne* as an intertextual guide, if not an actual road map, seeks to explain *King John*'s elliptic narrative as well as its representational economy.

In addition to its polemical stance, much of what *Troublesome Raigne* offers that *King John* does not has to do not only with fully dramatizing events that *King John* mentions in passing or takes for granted, but also with resolving its central issues to construct a more satisfying close. In giving special emphasis to John's dissembling with Pandulph and his poisoning by monks, *Troublesome Raigne* positions John as a proto-Protestant hero and, in permitting him to repent as well as to acknowledge his ill-rule, seems to invite spectators to forgive him. Moreover, his successor clearly reasserts royal prerogative to dismiss competing claims and eliminate the threat of foreign rule before the Bastard restores England to itself—inviolate, without schism, and poised to address the contemporary Elizabethan present. Like *Troublesome Raigne*, Barton's new *King John* invested in John's official Tudor image by fully representing his submission to Pandulph and his poisoning at Swinstead Abbey, the first of which Shakespeare's playtext represents in four lines (5.1.1–4), the second as report (5.6). The longest scenes in Barton's "triply written" *texte combinatoire*, they also demonstrate how, by defamiliarizing Shakespeare's play, Barton constructed what was perceived by most as a transgressive counterdiscourse.

In what Robert Smallwood describes as "almost certainly the most severely altered Shakesperian text ever to be delivered at the Stratford theatre,"[62] John's encounter with Pandulph became a parodic coronation, the fourth of six in the performance text.[63] Smallwood describes Barton's staging:

> John, squirming before Pandulph in hypocritical penitence, was ruthlessly stripped to a loin cloth by a squadron of well-drilled monks, made to kiss Pandulph's boot as he surrendered the crown, then, pardoned and absolved by the Cardinal, crowned with a dunce's cap and pushed onto the throne to hold a skull and bone in place of the orb and sceptre which figured in all the other ceremonies. The ceremony was completed with the old music-hall routine of a custard-pie in the face, John's promise to "hold this crown as tenant from the Pope," and, after a little necessary mopping up and the substitution of the real crown for the dunce's cap, by John being pushed down the steps of the throne, screaming, as Pandulph withdrew behind the traverse at the rear of the stage. John was left alone, seated quietly, down stage centre, as though it had only been a nightmare all along.[64]

As the first of two major additions, Barton's black-comedy spectacle, with its burlesque king, certainly clarifies John's progressive disintegration, but its derisive caricature also deepens the engima Shakespeare's *King John* carefully sidesteps: why the Bastard remains loyal to such a self-denigrating, inadequate ruler. Indeed, by increasing John's role in its second half, Barton's performance text shifts the relationship between dramatic and "royal" power, between the Bastard and John, through which Shakespeare's play negotiates its close. And making John the central figure in yet another strikingly theatrical "entertainment" further disturbs and unsettles Shakespeare's representational economy.

For John's poisoning at Swinstead Abbey, Barton condenses *Troublesome Raigne*'s two scenes (2.6 and 2.8) into a new pastiche, supple-
mented by his own additions, which pays homage to Marlowe's *Doctor Faustus* as well as to Milne's "King John's Christmas."[65]
Proclaiming " 'Tis close of day, yet I am England's King," John enters,
borne on a litter and attended by Hubert, to see a large Christmas tree
dominating the upstage area; as the monks welcome him, John recalls
that Christmas Eve is his birthday and predicts his coming death.
Then, after he exits to rest, one of the monks steps forward to catalogue John's crimes against the church and, after listing various ways
to kill him, decides "That John should end by poison, being a poison /
To England's earth and all this famous land." Later, at John's Christ-
mas-birthday feast, staged as a parody of da Vinci's "Last Supper,"
that same monk, asked by John to drink first from the wassail bowl,
falls dead across the table just as John himself drinks to the health of
England. When Hubert urges John to call on Christ,[66] the King falls to
his knees and, in a vision of hell reminiscent of Faustus's inability to
repent, damns himself for Arthur's death just before soldiers enter to
pull him to his feet, mock him as "Sir Dust," pick his pockets (empty
except for a single groat), and drag him off. Here, nearly every feature
of Barton's interpolation patterns toward completeness: John's life not
only ends on the day it began[67] but is framed by an occasion that, in
conflating Christmas and Easter, positions him as both Christlike martyr and penitent tyrant; moreover, the monk who had read Richard I's
will at the play's opening and who had played Peter of Pomfret becomes John's poisoner, a combined morality-nemesis figure once again
associated with premonitions of death. Just as John's submission to
Pandulph mocked the coronation in Barton's earlier carnivalesque
nightmare, so does appropriating "The Last Supper" as a fool's feast
to kill a King perceived as a type of Antichrist invert and debase the
Eucharist ceremony. And both the parallels with Faustus's despair and
the soldiers' callous treatment of a John Lackland who has become a
penniless nobody provide further connections with Christian mythology. Curiously doubled, Barton's overdetermined framework of connections ratifies the king's body and, simultaneously, empties it of
meaning to transform John into a symbolic representation, one familiar to morality plays but alien to Shakespeare's *King John*—a kind of
"Everyking" figure who, in confronting death, makes his office and his
mortality equally frail and contemptible.

In so refiguring John as an absurd "jingoistic clown,"[68] Barton's performance text severely dislocates the Bastard's own critique of power
politics as well as the play's last moves—his "ordering of this present
time" (5.1.77). When Hubert meets the Bastard to tell him of the ar-

my's loss in the Wash and John's poisoning (*King John*, 5.6; Barton, scene 18), Barton expands *King John*'s fugitive hints concerning the Bastard's possible succession by having Hubert report that John has changed his will: "The King," he says, "would have thee King," going on to explain that, since John's own claim is "ever doubtful, / He fears his son can but inherit doubts." But the Bastard's response—"Fie, fie, 'tis madness; what, a bastard sit / On England's throne? Let's hence and purge it"—closes off the option Shakespeare's *King John* circulates and delays answering until the end: that of fashioning the Bastard as a bourgeois king. And with succession determined at this point, Barton's Bastard becomes, in the last scene, not the arbiter of a newly reconstituted state but a figure who mediates, so to speak, between "King Barton" and *King John*.

The final scene opens with Prince Henry, flanked by monks and lords, kneeling in prayer downstage of Swinstead Abbey's Christmas tree. Offstage singing, prompting Salisbury (not Prince Henry) to remark that it is "strange that death should sing," precedes John's entrance, his figure shrouded in a white garment resembling swaddling grave-cloths and supporting himself with a long staff. Midway through his lament, the Bastard and Hubert enter together and, as the Bastard kneels to speak to him, John hands him his will just before he dies. As in Shakespeare's *King John*, the Bastard declares his obedience to John and charges the nobles to "show now your mended faiths," but with the reading of John's will, Barton's text kicks free of Shakespeare's. When urged by the nobles to read the will, the Bastard at first protests but then agrees, yet what he reads is not, as might be expected, that he is John's heir but that (with a long pause before naming him) Prince Henry is the new king (fig. 1). Did John lie to Hubert? Hubert to the Bastard? Is the Bastard reading the text of the will or improvising to exempt himself from what the play has shown to be kingship's cares and its penchant for "commodity," and so to assign the office to an Arthur-like surrogate? On the one hand, the Bastard's revelation can be read as a final sign of commodity; on the other, it can sustain the ideal of obedience through which a "true" subject, by contravening the dead King's wish, restores genealogical right and inheritance by blood as the dominant principle of succession. If either reading seems possible, the staging of John's burial and Henry's coronation, which follow, masks these questions with yet another ceremony. In a sequence that rhymes with the opening, where Richard I's will was read as monks carried in his white-shrouded corpse and lowered it into the stage-trap just before John himself was crowned, monks now lower John's body into the same trap, the Bastard throws his lionskin over the body, as though to bury the sign of his own birth and title with the dead King, and John's death-nemesis reappears from among the monks, stepping forward to speak a generalized epitaph for John that also reiterates the insecurity of states, of kings, and of life itself that Barton's performance text has consistently emphasized.[69]

As Barton's text continues, it reproduces the insistently ceremonial shape characteristic of many of *Troublesome Raigne*'s scenes as well as those in his own adaptation:

BASTARD.	Now take the crown, and wear it on thy head,
	That by succession art our lawful King.
	The LORDS *crown* PRINCE HENRY, *silently*
BASTARD.	God save the King.
ALL.	God save the King.
SALISBURY.	Long live the King.
ALL.	Long live the King.
LORDS.	May the King live for ever.
ALL.	May the King live for ever.
PEMBROKE.	To you, with all submission, on our knees
	We do bequeathe our faithful services.
PRINCE HENRY.	Then, for the love of God, look to the state of England.
	Let no enemy hold her in miserable bond;
	See you defend her as it becometh you all;
	See that you cherish her in field and hall.
	So shall she flourish in honour, lords, again,
	In peace and great plenty so you uphold my reign.
	Drums afar off. Enter MESSENGER
MESSENGER.	My lords, the Dauphin's powers make hitherwards
	And all our army standeth at a gaze,
	As wond'ring what their leaders will command.
SALISBURY.	Come, let us hence.
	Exeunt all but the BASTARD
BASTARD.	This England never did, nor never shall
	Lie at the proud foot of a conqueror,
	But when it first did help to wound itself.
	Now these her princes are come home again,
	Come the three corners of the world in arms
	And we shall shock them: nought shall make us rue,
	If England to itself do rest but true.
	Exeunt

Reading Barton's conclusion without reference to Shakespeare's *King John* yields an image of a kingdom united by obedience to its newly crowned King, its faithful servants ready, as at the play's opening, to address the fresh crisis of a foreign threat. Barton's staging, however, emphasized the emptiness of the coronation ritual: crowned by the Bastard to the familiar (and, by this sixth coronation, debased) litany of affirmation, the gold-masked King Henry seems more a puppet—"the licensed fool in a court of petty tyrants"[70]—than England's "true inheritor." Moreover, not only is it the hypocritical Pembroke who voices lines that in Shakespeare's *King John* belong to the Bastard, but all Prince Henry's lines are either cut or reassigned, and his charge, "For the love of God, look to the state of England," recited as though it were a prepared speech, reproduces the lines from Bale that John had spoken at his coronation, which opened the play. Indeed Henry's speech, with its linked rhyming couplets, sounds like the end of this inverted morality, yet the play continues and—as Salisbury and the others leave, presumably to lead an army against the Dauphin, for whom they had betrayed John and who had planned to betray them—struggles forward into history. Given this already double ending, the Bastard's last speech reads as a concession to Shakespeare's playtext, an obligatory coda. Left alone, he picks up a large book (Shakespeare's *Complete Works?*) from underneath the Christmas tree, crosses downstage center to read the last speech of Shakespeare's playtext, places the book on the floor, and exits, hands in his pockets, whistling his jaunty signature tune. In Shakespeare's *King John*, the Bastard steps away from the play and so moves into the present of its audience, but Barton's Bastard seems, instead, to turn his back in denial. His almost contemptuous detachment from these final events figures his own gift to King John as less the equivalent of Milne's "big, red India-rubber ball" than a Christmas Eve fiction read out from an authoritative text that may or may not prove "true."[71] That Barton's finale incorporates what may be a purposeful misreading of one royal text (John's will) and a cynical reading of another (Shakespeare's patriotic Epilogue to his history) seems not only an appropriate close for this de-figuring of kingship but its most perfectly self-reflexive gesture.

According to critical consensus, Barton's project served neither Shakespeare's play nor his own claims for transforming *King John* into a mirror of the failures and betrayals of mid-1970s politics.[72] Perhaps its most sympathetic critic, Michael Billington, writes, that "at times you get the feeling you're watching three different plays running concurrently," yet he also called the result "one of the best new plays we've seen this year."[73] For its 1590s audiences, *King John* would also have been a "new play," one distinctly different from *Troublesome Raigne* but one that appropriates, at the close, its patriotic moral to reconstitute the state. Barton's appropriations from prior dramatic texts are no less contradictory. In that his inversions of ritual and ceremony dismantle kingship, his reconstituted play moves *King John* in a direction it already anticipates, yet in making space within *King John* for the morality polemics it eschews, Barton's version also takes a curious step backward. He himself admits that his *King John* "fell somewhat between two stools, and that [he] should have changed the text either less or more."[74] In all likelihood, either option would have been read more as an infraction against "Shakespeare" than as a new configuration of a relatively unfamiliar play. If one of Barton's major transgressions was to refashion *King John* as an intervention in present-day politics, then certainly his most flagrant renegotiations of the "True Originall" come at the close, where his recomposed Bastard is no longer the energetic presence whom Shakespeare's *King John* invites readers and spectators to endow with imaginary royal virtue but a figure who refuses, finally, any political action to become, quite literally, only one who can read its rhetoric with disdain. In short, Barton knocked out the supports by which generations of critics had been able to position themselves as Shakespeare's man-who-might-be-king. If one abiding cultural function of Shakespeare's *King John*, with its final litmus test of loyalty, has been to transform commodity to community, what Barton's adaptation emphasized is how, in late twentieth–century Britain, commodity now lies at the heart of community. And if *King John* has, in the past, been bought and sold to sustain the twin myths of kingship and obedience, Barton's own not-so-saleable commodity reveals not so much the extent to which calling those myths into question threatens Shakespeare's playtexts as the extent to which it threatens the traditions surrounding their "true" interpretation. As an emblem for this *King John*'s reception, commodity was indeed the name of the game.

While Barton's *King John* turned Shakespeare's playtext as well as its refigured Bastard upside down, Deborah Warner's 1988 Royal Shakespeare Company performance text reproduces a more "Originall" version and, simultaneously, in terms of the close, a new configuration. In the black-box space of The Other Place in Stratford, Sue Blane's set consisted of three dozen plain ladders, used as siege instruments at Angiers, and six plain chairs—minimalist trappings that placed the play's conflicts within a cage or forest to figure power, in this metallic age, as the ability to scale heights and remain "on top." With its royalty and nobles costumed from what Paul Taylor called "a jumble sale at the Army and Navy store,"[75] this *King John* inherited some features from Buzz Goodbody's 1970 Theatregoround version, which exposed politics as a silly game for a little-boy, cartoonlike King whose crown kept falling over his ears. Warner's King John, well aware of his insecure right, guards his crown zealously: before Angiers, it hangs on a chain from his belt, and he whips it on his head as he claims to be king; cocking it over the top of one of the ladders when he asks Hubert to kill Arthur, he leaves it behind but then rushes back to repossess it. A Père Ubu or Wizard of Id figure, he wears a greatcoat and helmet several sizes too large and, at Angiers, wields an oversize sword—an image of the usurper the play claims he is, dressed in borrowed robes he cannot fill. And Warner's Bastard is no aristocrat in commoner's disguise but a young, rough, and unskilled Jack the Giant Killer, a football hooligan who wraps himself in a Union Jack to evoke, at least for British spectators, the recent violence of fans at the European championship matches.

In a performance text shaped by strong ensemble acting and with one foot still in the rehearsal room, Warner drives the spare, swift narrative economy of *King John*'s last scenes forward to a finale where only a few ladders remain and what spectacle there is condenses around the figure of the dying King. Barefoot and dressed in a white nightgown and shawl, John is carried in and laid on the floor; his manic psychotic energy reduced, he seems to have regressed to babyhood or, as Prince Henry says, to "clay." As the nobles kneel in a circle around his central figure, with Henry standing aside to oberve them, they form a kind of living crown, an emblem of the precarious instability of the new state. The Bastard, hunkering before them, speaks the play's last lines, not to rouse its spectators to nationalistic fervor, but to prop up his own position and plead with the nobles, each of whom has betrayed both King and state (fig. 2). On his final word, a rapid blackout then gives way to a brief clarion-call of drums and trumpets, a faint echo of past *King John*s and the age of empire. In turning the Bastard's speech back toward the play, Warner demystifies its sixteenth–century topicality and also, implicitly, acknowledges that it may no longer have the power to negotiate between stage and world. By so dismantling the Bastard's claims, she throws *King John*'s close into a configuration that reveals the distance between Armada and late twentieth–century politics: "England to itself" is, after all, Elizabeth I's England, not that of Elizabeth II, or even of Margaret Thatcher. But Shakespeare's "True Originall" and Warner's *King John* are also similar in that both aim to disperse the cultural orthodoxy of, respectively, previously written and previously performed texts. And if, some four hundred years after Shakespeare's play was first performed, Warner's unease with *King John*'s Elizabethan sense of ending reads as more of a negotiation, perhaps present-day "anthems" demand just such a starkly demystified compromise.

ENCLOSING CONTENTION: *1, 2,* AND

3 HENRY VI

It is shaped, sir, like itself, and it is as broad as it hath
breadth; it is just so high as it is, and moves with it own
organs. It lives by that which nourisheth it, and the elements once out of it, it transmigrates.

—Antony and Cleopatra

"EVEN SO must I run on, and even so stop," says *King John*'s Prince
Henry, marking his awareness, at his father's death, of the limits of
life and the continuity of kingship. His words, together with their sit-
uational context, suggestively describe the narrative and formal strategies that construct closure in Shakespeare's three *Henry VI* plays—
plays that "run on," like an uncontrolled sentence, beyond signs of
tragic (or comic) enclosure and then stop. Indeed, their endings constitute a formal embarrassment, prompting critical assessments that
range from "dramatically inconclusive" to the less pejorative (and seductively contemporary) "open-ended," or, as if committed to show
part of a process with neither beginning nor end, "containing Minus
Act I and Act VI."[1]

Most critics downplay the localized issue of closure or subsume it
within broader frameworks. Efforts to discover unity in each play as
well as in the three considered as a trilogy center on terms such as
"Shakespeare's plan," "design," and "plot," appropriating a vocabu-
lary of sedition that (consciously or unconsciously) reproduces and
apes one subject the plays address.[2] Some analogize disorderly narrative with the pervasive themes of dissension and disorder, widening
their discussions to claim that Shakespeare's need to develop his "great
theme"—England, triumphant as Respublica—generated modifications of dramatic form, and to praise Shakespeare's masterful com-
pression and transformation of his sources as well as his careful sub-
ordination of individual episodes to that theme.[3] By relying on theme
(here roughly equivalent to "Tudor Myth") as the controlling sign of
a new genre—with Shakespeare as its instigator—some readers bypass
the supposed closural deficiencies of the three *Henry VI* plays and supply *Richard III*'s more familiar and conclusive final signs as the appro-

priate resolution of a preplanned scheme. Not only does such a reading create a neat tetralogy and a satisfying sense of ending, but it also positions the *Henry VI* plays as a preparatory, though necessary, passing phase and, ultimately, as apprentice work prefacing a second tetralogy.[4] Others explain both their episodic characteristics and their unshaped ends by placing them in developmental relation to preexisting models, especially Greek and Senecan tragedy; the morality, divine, or salvation histories; and so-called romance histories; still others evoke nondramatic analogues, notably the epic.[5] Infinitely chameleonlike, the plays can seem to be compiled rather than composed, encompassing recognizable features (or, at the very least, traces) of all these forms. Stubbornly refractory, they also refuse, like Antony's crocodile, to conform to specifications other than their own. And even these exhibit further uncertainties: two of the plays exist in both Quarto and Folio texts, with differing titles as well as some significant rhetorical and structural differences. Finally, because textual scholars question their authenticity, their dating, and their order of composition, any "final verdict" concerning Shakespeare's (probably) initial foray into historiography remains—much like the question of ending—suspended.

Simply acknowledging these plays as "sports" within an admittedly hybrid and notoriously slippery genre provides a starting point in accounting for their endings. Although each moves toward imitating one or another familiar generic shape, each also eludes that shape at the close by putting into play a shifting, unstable conglomerate of established, if flexibly prescriptive, conventions associated with and borrowed from existing forms. The tensions between the prior stability of these conventions and their sometimes traditional, sometimes innovative—even radically subversive—deployment in the three *Henry VI* plays suggests some further questions. To what extent do these plays conform to traditional historical models and generic patterns and conventions, and to what extent do they invent permutations of these models and conventions in order to achieve a distinctive sense of ending? If they do represent a genre in the making, how do their closural strategies compare to those of other plays? If indeterminate or "failed" closure constitutes one of their hallmarks, does such instability raise questions about the stability of the historical subject—and, more precisely, what implications does it have for the crucial relations between king and subject and for the exercise of power, as well as its subversion?[6]

To address these questions, I want first to situate the formal issues surrounding closure in relation to two other texts—Edward Hall's chronicle and *Gorboduc*—and then to examine quite briefly the final rhetorical figuring of a number of pre-Shakespearean plays that appropriate historical materials. In turning to Shakespeare's plays, I discuss them in their historical order, which may or may not be the chronological order of their composition.[7] Although I consider each as a discrete entity, I assume that together they constitute a Folio trilogy, which suggests thinking in terms of closures rather than closure—one for each play, one for 2 and 3 *Henry VI* as a two-part play, one for the trilogy. Finally, I sketch the interrelations and variances within closure, as well as issues arising from representational politics, by looking at several recent performance texts: John Barton and Peter Hall's 1963 adaptation, *The Wars of the Roses*, Terry Hands's 1977 Royal Shakespeare Company production of the *Henry VI* trilogy, and Michael Bogdanov's 1988 *The Wars of the Roses*, as well as Adrian Noble's 1988 Royal Shakespeare Company *The Plantagenets*, the last two of which (like the Barton-Hall adaptation) condense the *Henry VI* plays into two performance texts.

ŝ

> The Union of the Two Noble and Illustrious Families of Lancaster and York Being Long in Continual Dissension for the Crown of This Noble Realm, with All the Acts Done in Both the Times of the Princes, Both of the One Lineage and of the Other, Beginning at the Time of King Henry the Fourth, the First Author of This Division, and so Successively Proceeding to the Reign of the High and Prudent Prince King Henry the Eight, the Undubitate Flower and Very Heir of Both the Said Lineages.[8]

Readers of Edward Hall's title page for his dynastic family history immediately confront a directive on how to read its close. This set of instructions outlines a restricted if not severely enclosed interpretation of history in which two end points—the marriage of Henry VII and Elizabeth, joining the families of Lancaster and York, and Henry VIII's succession—represent the events of most significance to Hall's contemporary Elizabethan audience. As Hall's choric Prologue further develops his narrative strategy, what emerges is the plan for a kind of English Exodus, conceived as both a reconstruction and an exorcism of a horrible, unimaginable, unwritable past.

> What mischief hath insurged in realms by intestine division, what hath ensued in countries by civil dissension, what detestable murder hath been committed in cities by separate factions, and what calamity hath ensued in famous regions by domestical discord and unnatural controversy: Rome hath felt, Italy can testify, France can bear witness, Beame can tell, Scotland may

write, Denmark can show, and especially this noble realm of England can apparently declare and make demonstration. . . . But what misery, what murder, and what execrable plagues this famous region hath suffered by the division and dissension of the renowned houses of Lancaster and York, my wit cannot comprehend nor my tongue declare neither yet my pen set fully forth.[9]

Placing England's story from Henry IV to Henry VIII within a context shared by other nations, the first sentences outline a chaos: the intestine division, depopulation, civil dissension, murder, separate factions, domestic discord, and unnatural controversy common to all realms, but especially apparent in England. As his text continues, Hall reminds readers that although "all the other discords, sects and factions almost lively flourish and continue at the present time," the "old divided controversy" has been erased—"clearly buried and perpetually extinct"—by the person of Henry VIII, the heir of the Lancaster-York matrimonial union. For the chronicler, these interrelated events develop meaning only through contrast. Since union, agreement, and concord can occur only "in respect of division," Hall proposes to reveal not only "the original cause and fountain of the same" but also the "calamities, troubles, and miseries which happened and chanced during the time of the said contentious dissension."[10] His view of this history as a series of cause-effect patterns privileges difference and conflict as essential forerunners to comic closure: a marriage resulting in a "most noble, puissant and mighty heir," an earthly equivalent to godhead. Announcing its ending before it begins, Hall's humanistic-moral project has the aura of secular divine comedy: Dantesque England reaching perfection in the person of one ruler.

Yet in spite of a predetermined focus on the results of historical process, Hall's history writing is not completely seamless. Mimicking its central theme, division, his masterplot separates into reigns measured in years, many of which, in turn, he conceives as discrete, if not self-contained, narratives, each with its sequel. But although Hall enforces time's linear rule, he does not represent England's history exclusively as a series of "kings' lives." Rather, the openings of most monarchs' reigns signal not beginning but rebeginning, often by briefly alluding to or actually replaying significant events from a previous reign—or, as in the case of Henry V, by praising his policy and "ends," so turning Henry's rule into a kind of flashback told by an omniscient narrator. Within each reign, a clear sense of the successor's preeminence balances (and in some cases overrides) an individual monarch's impending death. Thus Hall buries the conflicting rumors surrounding

Richard II's death within his retelling of Henry IV's "unquiet time," which also includes references to Henry V's succession as a kind of prologue to his "victorious acts." Similarly, Henry V's funeral opens Henry VI's "troublous season," which continues and blends into Edward IV's "prosperous reign," where Henry's death occurs. And whereas Edward V's "pitiful life" chronicles Richard III's rise to power, Richard's own history opens with his coronation and ends with his death. However loosely some of the thematic titles Hall gives to each reign anticipate familiar dramatic patterns, only Richard III's "tragical doings" specifically evoke an established genre. It is as though Hall conceives of history as a super-genre that respects and accommodates such patterns but eventually encompasses them. And by shaping consecutive reigns to subsume birth, marriage, and death into an overlapping process, Hall stresses continuity and succession as substitutes for more conventional forms of closure.

But Hall also creates a distinctive closural system for each narrative unit, one that, if only momentarily, arrests the flow of time and makes a stop. As a coda to each reign, the chronicler's voice intrudes to speak a eulogy that not only describes the king's person, traits, and qualities but summarizes and interprets his deeds. These meditative, sometimes quite detailed portraits seem designed to leave his readers with a composite subjective image, fixed in memory. Only Henry VIII escapes such epiloguelike treatment: noting Henry's death briefly, the chronicler's text ends with a substitute epitaph, a prayer for Edward VI, the living portrait who continues the line. At its close, Henry VIII's "triumphant reign"—initially the privileged end point of Hall's project—opens onto contemporary history to confront the single circumstance that makes closure within his text both impossible and potentially threatening: dynastic continuity. "The King is dead. May the King live forever": Hall's sense of ending sustains and reproduces the terms of this self-regenerative paradox of the King's Two Bodies.[11] Ultimately, closure ensures the institutional (and ideological) stability of kingship and invites Hall's readers to place themselves in some historical relation to the "king's games"[12] he describes.

An even more powerfully inclusive and confrontational sense of ending must have prevailed among audience members at Whitehall on 18 January 1562, when Queen Elizabeth commanded the second performance of a highly patterned neoclassical tragedy devoted to English politics and shaped from chronicle history materials.[13] That play, *Gorboduc*, remains remarkable chiefly for its self-consciously experimental innovations: a five-act division emphasized by introductory choruses and dumbshows; lengthy rhetorical orations substituted for action; blank verse; and an insistent symmetry, beginning at the level of the individual line and extending outward to encompass ever larger units of structure in a perfectly formal, perfectly balanced design.[14] Perfectly balanced, that is, except for its ending. In a radical departure from its Senecan models, *Gorboduc* closes, not by ending, but by reopening the division with which it began.

Sackville and Norton's play dramatizes two actions, only one of which is completed.[15] The first, *Gorboduc*'s division of the kingdom, results in the deaths of both his heirs: Ferrex kills Porrex; Queen Videna kills her remaining son. At act 4's ending, Gorboduc begs Eubulus, his counselor, to kill him, but Eubulus urges patience; following Gorboduc's exit, Marcella, the Queen's attendant, castigates her and recounts the death of Ferrex before leaving with Arostus (one of the two counselor-figures) to comfort the King. As in each preceding act, this one is securely self-enclosed, contained by the Chorus's sententious comments, which place these events in relation to mythic exempla. The dumb show that prefaces act 5, with its "company of harquebussiers and of armed men, all in order of battle," signifies the "tumults, rebellions, arms, and civil wars to follow . . . between the nobility after the death of King Gorboduc and of his issues, for want of certain limitation in succession of the crown."[16] Act 5 then opens with reports of Gorboduc's and Videna's deaths at the hands of traitorous rebels, but these events do not, as might be expected, close the play. Instead, the situation—rulerless Britain—initiates its second, incomplete action, a sequel to and a sustained meditation on the previous acts. Speaking to the assembled Dukes, the wise counselor Eubulus advises punishing the "wavering" commons: he stresses obedience and the importance of maintaining distinctions between nobility and commons, and urges battle to "repress their power." Three of the Dukes exit, leaving Fergus, the Duke of Albany (a Scot), alone to speak a "crown-catching" soliloquy. When, in the second scene, a messenger brings news of Fergus's intent to invade the kingdom, the other three Dukes prepare to join together against him in open civil war.

Rather than ending with yet another Chorus to position and interpret these events, act 5 avoids repeating this convention and its potential for enclosure. Instead, it offers not one but two lengthy orations, the first spoken by Arostus, the weak counselor, the second by Eubulus, substitute for the Chorus. But since Arostus and Eubulus have throughout functioned as both allegorical and human figures and have consistently provided choral commentary, the single-speaker convention easily expands to include two voices. Far from subverting the convention, this choice doubles its force by opposing two idiosyncratic

interpretations, two possible courses of action. Arostus effectively
elides the coming war, first by praising the nobles' desire to attack the
treasonous Fergus and then by describing the "torn estate" sure to
follow the victory. Finally, he urges that a Parliament be held after
the battle to choose the rightful heir, for he fears that foreign kings
will seize the vulnerable land. Had the nobles agreed with Arostus,
the play might have ended with their assent. But they remain silent.
Now Eubulus, predicting genealogical closure—"Lo, here the end of
Brutus' royal line"—exposes Arostus's naïveté to read their "rising
minds" and further detail war's dismemberment. "Wasted and de-
faced, spoiled and destroyed," the heirless kingdom plagued with potentially ambitious nobles cannot now be saved by a parliament "not
likely with consent to end." Crown and Parliament should together
have chosen a successor during the King's lifetime, but since that time
has passed, the only happy man is he whose "speedy death" prevents
him from witnessing the miseries, murders, and wronged justice that
will surely accompany sedition and civil war. Eubulus concludes by
evoking divine providence in a truncated prayer phrased as hopeful
command—"Yet must God in fine restore / This noble crown unto the
lawful heir"—and with a final couplet linking his perspective to the
didactic moralizing expressed by the Chorus at the close of each previous act:

> For right will always live and rise at length,
> But wrong can never take deep root to last.

> (5.2.278–79)

Although these predictive sentiments and formal pressures offer
closural comfort, the situation, and especially the nobles' silence, lend
them a conditional ring.[17] *Gorboduc* ends by balancing options—
the threat of civil war against an alternative effected by human laws
working through divine intervention—and by implicating its audience
to resolve those issues in its own present. At the performance attended
by Elizabeth, that desire for resolution implicated one audience member in particular. Eubulus's advice amounts to an urgent directive to
the Queen to name a successor in order to prevent what he sees as
certain, total social disorder.[18] His final words constitute a charge
that joins playtext and social text: at the limits of the play, the
representation addresses the historical reality. And in formal terms,
closure invites a sequel—*Gorboduc, Part 2*, which might be titled *The
Whole Contention of the Noble Kinsmen*, and which opens either onto
sedition or onto the desired ideal, a legitimated and continuous monarchy. By manipulating its own established enclosural forms, *Gor-*

boduc demonstrates that closure need not signal arrest and settlement but can inscribe within its bounds a circulation and exchange that approximate, even reproduce, continuous historical process—"endlesse worke" reaching resolution by linking past to present.

Few pre-Shakespearean plays that appropriate historical or pseudohistorical materials having to do with civil war end with such politically explicit immediacy—or, especially, with the urgency attendant on the 1562 performance before the Queen.[19] Several, such as *The Famous Victories of Henry V* (1583–1588), *The Wounds of Civil War* (1587–1592), and *Edward I* (1590–1591), privilege narrative simply by referring the close to comic or tragic patterns and concluding swiftly, either with promised marriage or death, either of which resolves a disrupted order. Robert Greene's *Friar Bacon and Friar Bungay* (1589) further formalizes this kind of narrative close with Bacon's mystical vision of England's comic apocalypse, which the play's King, Henry III, further interprets and ratifies before inviting all to a royal feast. Most, however, further contain and enclose the action with a choral frame or an Epilogue that, by implicitly or even explicitly evoking the name of majesty, connects the play with social reality. These range from a familiar praise of monarchical virtues, as in *The Misfortunes of Arthur* (1588), which closes by extolling Arthur's renown and fame, to, in *Locrine* (1591–1595), a hybrid form combining moral admonition with prayer, spoken by Ate, the goddess personifying ambition and criminal folly, as presenter. Moralizing the tragedy, she interprets its history of treason, usurpation, pride, tyranny, and civil discord as a warning, since "a woman was the only cause," and urges the audience to pray for Elizabeth—"that renowned maid, / That eight and thirty years the scepter sway'd" (ll.2276–77). And in contrast to such misogynistic anxiety, which records fugitive fears of the "woman on top,"[20] two plays—*Richardus Tertius* (1580) and *The True Tragedy of Richard III* (1588–1594)—trace (at considerable length) Queen Elizabeth's descent, transcending and replacing the threatening events of Richard's reign through juxtaposed reminders of the present monarch's beneficent succession. In yet another, *The Life and Death of Jack Straw* (1590–1593)—which dramatizes Wat Tyler's uprising so as to castigate such threats to hierarchy—Richard II's reluctant execution of the rebels in the closing sequences is countermanded by a final epiloguelike speech in which he knights the actors who have played the rebels, deflecting their fictional threat by incorporating them as members of an also fictional feudal elite.[21] And indeed, within the Elizabethan system of patronage, playing kings (or rebels) could result, if not in true nobility, in something like this representation, transforming "marginal men" into gentlemen property-owners with considerable status.[22] Strikingly, all these terminal features manipulate the boundary between play and audience to offer closing affirmations that are essentially, if not generically, comic. And most implicate the sovereign, or her princely representation, as a figure capable of transforming a threatening social reality into a hopeful future.

Situating Shakespeare's closural practice for the *Henry VI* plays within an intertextual process that includes both history and drama assumes that Shakespeare was a Renaissance *bricoleur* par excellence who used Hall as well as other chronicles not only as sources of historical information but also as a "deep structure" and who fashioned his drama from a broad range of well-known formal, as well as metaphoric and thematic, models.[23] The case of the *Henry VI* plays, however, renders the corollary premise, which positions Shakespeare more as a wholeheartedly conservative borrower than a radical lender, somewhat suspect. These plays consistently privilege what might be called chronicle closure, and selectively adopt or adapt the sign systems associated with tragedy or comedy, circumscribing, de-emphasizing, rearranging, and transforming those formal features so that they no longer function as transparent signs of dramatic or social legitimacy. Yet such a strategy does not deflect attention from generic signs; rather, these become newly privileged as what might be called areas of local attraction within each play. Placed in unfamiliar positions within the narrative strategy, they serve to further structural uncertainty and to interrogate—and renegotiate—notions of dramatic form.

Hall serves as a model for such renegotiation. Like the chronicle, the *Henry VI* trilogy opens with the death of Henry V and ends after Tewkesbury; furthermore, each play encompasses the death, or fall from power, of a ruling figure and concludes by partially dramatizing a successor's rise. In addition, the events chosen to resolve both *1* and *2 Henry VI*—the end of the French war and Henry's future marriage with Margaret; the Battle of St. Albans—are those clearly marked by Hall as turning points, but both endings delay fully developing either the marriage or the significance of the battle's aftermath until the opening of the next play. Among the three plays, only *3 Henry VI* relies heavily on formal rhetorical figuring to assert its close, deploying an ascending series of comic conventions but simultaneously undermining their closural force. In each, closure opens readings that oppose one another: some characters envision definitive resolution; others push beyond such a sense of ending to imagine, or fantasize, a future. Moreover, each close accommodates the characters' aims and intentions and foregrounds their relativity, raising questions of what it is to have intentions or aims, especially insofar as they concern the Crown.[24] In inscribing signs that connote stability—peace, a new king, a future heir—closure re-presents the past and future oppositions of its historical subject, imitating the historical process. But no Epilogues or satisfying moral interpretations enforce a choice or offer a final vision of history, nor does the ending reveal any desire to enclose the play's events, through metadramatic gestures, within either a dramatic or a historical past. If, as Hayden White argues, the demand for closure in a historic story is a demand for moral meaning[25]—a proposition reflected in Hall and *Gorboduc* as well as in the range of available dramatic templates that formalize closure—Shakespeare's closural practice in the *Henry VI* plays contests that proposition. Rather, each ending activates a desire to reopen the story, preventing its own interpretation, a responsibility the spectator or reader implicitly assumes. Such communal closure prolongs the process of history, and of interpretation, extending both into the social text of the audience.

To the extent that both play and social text interrogate the same historical subject—monarchy—the patterns marking each play's ending function to link aesthetic with political power. Closure is above all a social transaction, a space where the narrative confronts the audience (and, implicitly or explicitly, a particular member of that audience, the ruling sovereign) with an image of succession. But although each equates closure with conserving and enforcing that principle, such conservatism does not necessarily ally closure with an unquestioning, monolithic view of power. Rather, closure in the *Henry VI* plays might be defined as a textual site within which power and its principles are openly critiqued. This closural design, its powers of resolution complemented by structural as well as thematic repetitions and recapitulations and, at times, a circular return to beginnings, is not, of course, exclusively limited to Shakespeare's presentation of historical materials. But what does distinguish the endings of the *Henry VI* plays from those of non-Shakespearean plays based on historical sources as well as from Shakespeare's own tragic and comic practice is the extent to which closural emphasis rests, not on rhetorical or transactional terminal conventions, but on narrative.[26] That emphasis constitutes not a generic but an authorial system that evidences a particular preoccupation with the relationships between dramatic form and the Elizabethan social text. Although these plays obviously do not close as "naked narrative," their endings not only mediate alternative notions of social order but disclose how existing narrative generates the potential for further narrative. This, perhaps the most provocative feature of the trilogy's sense of endings, attains the force, if not of a convention, of an intense meditation on how dramatic narrative reconstitutes itself at the close. And that generative process analogizes the powerful hegemony of the myth of royal succession, which also reconstitutes itself—"The King is dead. May the King live forever"—across the gap between two sentences, signifying ending as beginning.

ଅ

From its opening with Henry V's funeral, interrupted by three messengers bringing news of English defeats in France, *1 Henry VI* develops a narrative strategy that parallels England's "intestine division" with a foreign war that further threatens to fracture a kingdom ruled by a youthful political neophyte positioned between two factions, one headed by Gloucester, the Protector, the other by Cardinal Winchester. Centered on two opposed heroic figures, the English Talbot and France's Joan La Pucelle, that war constitutes *1 Henry VI*'s structural centerpiece, played out through repeatedly juxtaposing English victory with defeat. This pattern is further complicated, late in act 4, by the rivalry between York and Somerset, a premonition of the widening Lancaster-York conflict that results in delayed reinforcements and, ultimately, in the deaths of Talbot and his son. From this point forward, the narrative moves quickly, intensifying its basic alternations by interweaving Joan's capture, Suffolk's surrogate wooing of Margaret, Princess of Anjou, for Henry VI's bride, and the conclusion of the French war with the issue of Henry's coming marriage.

Described in this way, *1 Henry VI* has the look of a comedy enclosing a heroic tragedy or, perhaps more accurately, a chivalric military history. Indeed, this seems to have been the entertainment *1 Henry VI*'s most famous spectator, Thomas Nashe, saw: "How it would have joyed brave Talbot (the terror of the French) to think that after he had lain two hundred years in his tomb he should triumph again on the stage, and have his bones new embalmed with the tears of ten thousand spectators at least (at several times) who, in the tragedian that represents his person, imagine they behold him fresh bleeding."[27] That Nashe singles out Talbot both confirms *1 Henry VI*'s popular appeal, in the wake of the 1591–1592 French campaigns, and suggests how empathetic engagement with a particular character, combined with intense patriotic fervor, can not only reshape a play in a spectator's imagination but supply a desired end—in this case, England's triumph.[28] Nashe's "review" also points to another phenomenon: how selective reading, and assumptions about what constitutes "true" Shakespeare, have reshaped *1 Henry VI* for twentieth-century readers. Disintegrators, labeling it a "drum and trumpet play," have assigned its scenes of male heroism and political spectacle to "Shakespeare" and relegated its "shameful" treatment of Joan to another, or several other, playwrights.[29] In addition, the play's seemingly irresolute ending has come under particular scrutiny. Those who posit a post-assembled trilogy argue that the uneasy peace treaty with France (5.4) constitutes the appropriate (and appropriately male) conclusion and that the final scene, which anticipates the "fatal marriage" of Margaret and Henry VI, was a later addition designed to bridge *1* and *2 Henry VI.*

But in spite of Nashe's jingoism and later readers' anxious claims for inauthenticity or faulty artistry that protect Shakespeare from authoring its troubling portrait of Joan, *1 Henry VI* is less the "Talbot play" of past critical tradition than a "Joan versus Talbot play." That central opposition not only drives the play's narrative strategy but also shapes and inflects its troubling, less than triumphant, and formally problematic close. Furthermore, the antagonism between the two plays out, through displacement, Elizabethans' anxious fantasies concerning female dominance and, in particular, the spectacle of the man-woman, the Queen who, at Tilbury's pre-Armada appearance, had worn male attire.[30] Figured remarkably like Elizabeth in many attributes, Joan represents a subversive challenge to gender as well as to the closed chivalric code owned by males. Like the Queen, she "exceeds her sex" and, as a sainted, knightly warrior who proves that one does not need to be a nobleman to perform the deeds of a noble man, threatens to undermine the secular code of indexing that sustains the social hierarchy.[31] Even as she is selectively (and expediently) inscribed within *1 Henry VI,* Joan, like the Queen whose ghosted image she echoes, functions as a spectacular, and intensely troubling, site of gender display and so condenses, as Leah Marcus argues, the prevalent skepticism concerning the Queen's claims to anomalous gender identity. Although, on the level of history, the war between France and England opposes two countries in an international conflict, at the level of representation that war constitutes a battle for the ownership of masculine gender.[32]

Early in *1 Henry VI,* Joan embodies an urgent set of religious as well as secular symbols and attributes that masculinize the weakened French and, in the early confrontations with Talbot, threaten to emasculate the English, shaming Talbot's valor, transforming his men from dogs to whelps, from lions to sheep (1.4.1–30). And precisely because she threatens to disrupt and violate gender polarities, the French as well as the English label her a strumpet, while the English further demonize her as "foul fiend of France," "hag of all despite," "devil or devil's dam," and "witch." As the narrative moves toward closure, the playtext consistently deploys these categories in order to represent her again as counterfeit, unwholesome, not holy—a hoax who taints Charles's claim to the French crown and thus ensures England's own legitimacy in France.

Although both Hall and Holinshed suppress much of Joan's history in their chauvinistic and otherwise biased accounts, in both chronicles her capture precedes Henry's coronation in Paris as well as the proposed marriage arrangements with the Earl of Armagnac's daughter, suggesting a link between English imperialism and Joan's imprisonment, the most telling sign of French defeat. By reversing this chronology, Shakespeare's *1 Henry VI* articulates a very different history. Not only does it insulate Henry by eliding the causal relation between the two events (Henry is crowned in 4.1; Joan's capture occurs in 5.3) but, more significantly, it opens the play's closing sequences to further rearticulations and revisions of the gender contract. The initial move here restores chivalry as an English attribute. Although the narrative anticipates a final confrontation between Joan and Talbot, his death and that of his son result from English betrayal, not a Frenchwoman's "sorcery," a betrayal Talbot himself attempts to mask when he urges his dead son to "imagine [death] a Frenchman, and thy foe" (4.7.26). Heavily rhetorical lament and epitaph further celebrate the Talbots' valor, situating them in relation to mythic examples, and by mocking Lucy's catalogue of Talbot's titles (4.7.60–71), Joan turns against the ideal she had appropriated as her own. The next time she appears, following a brief scene concerning Henry's proposed marriage with the Earl of Armagnac's daughter (5.1), she is revealed first as Charles's warlike compatriot (5.2), and then, when her "familiar spirits" forsake her, as the "ugly witch" both the French (in earlier asides) and the English (in forthright accusations) had argued her to be, a cursing hag in league with "the gloomy shade of death," with "mischief and despair" (5.3; 5.4). Furthermore, whereas the historical Joan derived divine power from Saint Catherine and Saint Michael, *1 Henry VI*, by linking her with "God's mother," the Virgin Mary (1.2.78–84), patterns her Catholicism to include a fugitive association with two other Catholic Marys, Elizabeth's half-sister and the Scottish Queen she executed, some alleged through witchcraft.[33]

Joan, of course, is also executed, but *1 Henry VI* does not represent what official records would recount as heresy and, later, as martyrdom, which provoked popular rebellion and disobedience and threatened to destabilize the institutionalized church. Rather, Shakespeare's playtext undertakes an extraordinary juggling act in order to contain and displace the potentially subversive cluster of signs it has put into play. As Joan is taken away, cursing, Suffolk leads on Margaret of Anjou, another prisoner-enchantress who, at first, absorbs another, more positive set of attributes associated with women—more precisely, with Joan as well as Elizabeth.[34] As "beauty's princely majesty," Margaret "daunts" Suffolk's eyes, just as Joan, by conquering Charles in single, chivalric combat at their first meeting, aroused his desire; and just as he attempted to worship her in the language of courtly love (1.2), so does Margaret "conquer" Suffolk, whose lyrical, Petrarchan phrases sound remarkably like those evoked in other dramatic as well as nondramatic texts to praise Gloriana, the Virgin Queen. Like Joan and Elizabeth, Margaret is a virginal maid, the King's obedient and chaste servant, a creature with "pure unspotted heart": precisely those attributes that histories other than Hall's and Holinshed's assemble around Joan, and which serve to define Elizabeth's iconicity, are here displaced onto Margaret, righting gender ideology by reappropriating women as "miracles," as ransomed war booty, as beautiful and therefore to be wooed, as women and therefore to be won. This process continues into the following scene, which refashions Joan's femininity, enabling the English to exploit the contradictions between maiden purity and adulterous foulness she represents.[35]

Here again, such womanly proofs—her claims to royal bastardy and pregnancy; even the names of her lovers, Alençon and Reignier, the Duke of Anjou—construct Joan in Elizabeth's image, condensing around her what Marcus calls the "dark fantasies" circulating among some subjects of the Virgin Queen.[36] Reading this conjunction of signs one way produces a *1 Henry VI* that "consumes to ashes" not only Joan but all such speculations; read in another, the play confronts the threats posed by the dominant man-woman, the Amazonian ruler, in order to eradicate the spectre of female rule, cleanse the kingdom by means of a public spectacle of ritual burning, and restore militaristic dominance to males. Intensely equivocal, the playtext suspends its contradictory images of women—the false French witch condemned to flames and the King's daughter with "virtues . . . / And natural graces that extinguish art" (5.3.192)—in uneasy tension. Indeed, the violent energies and resonant patterning that figure both women with Elizabeth's attributes spill over to taint *1 Henry VI*'s most authoritatively conclusive scene, where Cardinal Winchester mandates the terms of a treaty requiring French allegiance to the English Crown (5.4). All these signs of ending, however, enact little more than a ceremonial formula, its ritual form deflected by the imagined offstage spectacle of Joan's burning. If one function of the scene is to represent war as an exclusively male enterprise, York's phrase—"effeminate peace" (5.4.109)—

suggests how its ending remains not only contaminated by gender but, at best, a hollow ceremony.

One further motif links the events concluding the French war with Elizabeth—a prophecy, spoken by Lucy over the Talbots' dead bodies, that "from their ashes shall be reared / A phoenix that shall make all France afeard" (4.7.92–93). The mystically generative image of the phoenix, associated with the Queen as her motto, appears to counter the spectacle of Joan's sacrificial burning, together with her unborn child, with that of the Talbots, father and son dying in one another's arms, and suggests a relation between Talbot and Elizabeth. But any potential parallels between the two fade, dominated by the more powerful nexus connecting Elizabeth with Joan. The reference does, however, point, Janus-like, to several other figures, among them Henry V, whom Henry VI associates with Talbot—"I do remember how my father said / A stouter champion never handled sword" (3.4.18–19)—and who, for a time, represented both the dead hero-King and the son too young to fight. Furthermore, when viewed in retrospect, *1 Henry VI* generates its action from the need to replace Henry V, whose funeral opens the play. Yet what its ending makes clear is that Henry VI can neither emulate nor, in a sense, "succeed" to his father's kingdom. In yet another interrupted, truncated ceremony, *1 Henry VI* concludes by disrupting and subverting the genealogical bases of monarchy.

In that it functions as a betrothal, the playtext's final scene pays homage to the generic expectations of comedy, but its formal dissatisfactions and the series of replacements it dramatizes render it transgressive. As though to repeat, and further negotiate, the play between false and true images of Elizabeth, the scene focuses not on the "real" power of the King, but on that of his surrogates. Having wooed Margaret, Suffolk now woos Henry, who, in rejecting the Armagnac marriage earlier proposed by Gloucester, sets himself apart from the Protector, his surrogate father. Speaking the playtext's last words in soliloquy, and so violating the convention that these belong to the speaker of highest rank, Suffolk not only replaces Gloucester but supplants Henry as well:

> Thus Suffolk hath prevailed; and thus he goes,
> As did the youthful Paris once to Greece,
> With hope to find like event in love
> But prosper better than the Trojan did.
> Margaret shall now be queen, and rule the king;
> But I will rule both her, the king, and realm.

(5.5.103–8)

To remember Hall is to see it otherwise. Characterizing Henry's marriage with Margaret, the chronicler says it "engendered such a flame, that it never went out, till both the parties with many other were consumed and slain, to the great unquietness of the king and his realm."[37] In *1 Henry VI*, Gloucester's response to Henry's decision— "Ay, grief, I fear me, both at first and last" (5.5.102)—is the only sign of phrases that might, as in the Epilogues of other historical plays, have enclosed, and safely contained, these events, moralizing their interpretation. But Shakespeare's playtext reworks such terminal expectations, suppressing potentially satisfying recapitulatory or admonitory features in order to privilege closure as a site of exchange for a protagonist-successor whose desire for future power substitutes for the power of more conventional closural forms. In terms of the way Suffolk transcends inherited terminal conventions, he would seem the most likely figure for the phoenix. But two other figures, one in ghosted form, press to be recognized. One is Margaret, of "valiant courage and undaunted spirit / (More than in women commonly is seen)," who, Suffolk argues, will "beget more conquerors" (5.5.70–71,74). This vision of the future not only promises to carry forward the transgressive gender contract initiated with Joan but to resituate the "misrule" played out in France within England, part and parcel of its "intestine division." At least insofar as both Margaret and Joan allude to Elizabeth, some (John Knox among them) would have seen a potential image of such misrule occupying England's throne at the time of the play's first performances.[38] Yet *1 Henry VI* suspends that fugitive gloss, and its attendant cultural anxieties, by closing with a curiously apt male fantasy—apt not only because it evokes a legendary adulterous triangle,[39] but also because, in predicting (accurately, as it turns out) Margaret's rule over Henry, it reasserts male dominance: Suffolk will "rule both her, the king and realm." Suffolk's words touch on yet another troubling issue: the Queen's marriage. It was precisely in order to avoid being ruled by a man (as her sister, Mary, had been) and so to lose both her independence and her power that Elizabeth kept her suitors at bay, and represented herself as lover, wife, and husband to the kingdom.[40] Curiously and obliquely, Suffolk's fantasy almost precisely echoes Elizabeth's constructed selves, so that his final words recirculate her multiple identities and appropriate them, regendered, as his own.

❧

THE | First part of the Con = | tention betwixt the two famous Houses of York | and Lancaster, with the death of the good | Duke Humphrey: | And the banishment and death of the Duke of | *Suffolk*, and the Tragical end of the proud Cardinal of | *Winchester, with the notable Rebellion of | Jack Cade: | And the Duke of York's first claim unto | the Crown.*

The 1594 Quarto title page functions both to advertise *Contention*'s events and to map out its attractions and multiple centers of narrative privilege—three deaths, a "notable rebellion," York's bid for the crown—but without naming either the King or Queen Margaret, its most royal actors. In contrast, Folio's title—*The Second Part of Henry Sixth, with the death of the Good Duke HUMPHREY*—predicts another play, one that centers on the King and his surrogate father-Protector and, by emphasizing only Humphrey's death, hints at its particular importance. Although the texts agree on the ordering of events, Quarto's title, probably closer to that by which the play was known to its contemporaries than the Folio's more formal *Second Part*,[41] also calls attention to its two-part narrative strategy. Almost precisely like *Gorboduc*, *2 Henry VI* first dramatizes a division of the kingdom resulting in the deaths of Gloucester and Winchester before reopening, not, as in *Gorboduc*, with a dumb show signifying "tumults, rebellions, arms, and civil wars," but with a full representation of Jack Cade's May Day riot and York's attempt to reconstitute the monarchy, with himself as King, events that close the play.

But Folio's title is an equally useful guide, especially in marking what might be called *2 Henry VI*'s internal close, where power is transferred from Protector to King. As in *King John*, which constructs an alternative king in the figure of the Bastard, *2 Henry VI*'s first three acts locate kingship's authority in Gloucester: it is his power that Margaret and the nobles seek to overthrow, first by demonizing his wife; then by forcing him to yield up his office; and finally by plotting his death. In the England of Henry VI, the desire for power breeds faction and anarchy, which live so close to the surface that each of its major (and most of its incidental) characters practices a form of treason. And each instance progressively reveals how Henry's lack of authority authorizes further seditious acts; provocatively, the crimes of treason belong to the King himself. Moreover, treason—a subject on everyone's lips, circulated and recirculated in repeated accusations—presumes what Henry's passive, decentered presence almost consistently denies: that there is both a state and a king. And, as in *1 Henry VI*, gender disorder—represented in two transgressive families, Gloucester's as well as Henry's—symbolically affirms the prevalent social disorder.

The first half of *2 Henry VI* obsessively recirculates *1 Henry VI*'s anxious concern with the "man-kind woman" or "masterly wife [who] is even a monster in nature."[42] Although the succession passes from Gloucester to Henry, it is their wives' desire for "royal majesty" and their "unruly" behavior that play out that shift in power, threatening to prove true Thomas Platter's proverbial claim that, in the liberties permitted them, "England is a woman's paradise."[43] Here, however, Shakespeare's playtext shows extreme policy. Even as it reveals female aggression and assertiveness and so continues to focus on "misrule," the "Elizabethan" attributes clustered around Joan and then displaced onto Margaret in the earlier play not only diminish in intensity but are further dispersed, shared out between Eleanor, Duchess of Gloucester, and Queen Margaret. The ambitious Eleanor absorbs the most damning of these, Joan's witchcraft. Just as Elizabeth sought the advice of the "great conjuror," John Dee,[44] Eleanor, seeking the crown for her husband, consorts with black magicians, Bolingbroke and Margery Jourdain, the witch, and is accused, with them, of practicing against the state (1.4). But whereas the commoners—Bolingbroke and the two unholy priests, Hume and Southwell, together with Jourdain—pay for treason with their lives, Eleanor is required only to perform public penance and is banished—ironically enough, to the Isle of Man (2.4). Here, the law exploits and demonizes the deviancy of the ruled in order to insulate and further empower the rulers' own deviancy. Eleanor's guilt not only taints Gloucester's "honest name," so that, at Henry's request, he yields up his Protectorship, but makes him vulnerable to the further (false) charges of treason brought against him later in Parliament by the Queen, Suffolk, Cardinal Winchester, York, and Buckingham (3.1).

To the extent that Eleanor's betrayal of her husband reveals that she has "us[ed] herself dishonestly,"[45] she also absorbs some of the onus of Margaret's adulterous (and dangerous) liaison with Suffolk, and it is Gloucester, not the (apparently) cuckolded Henry, who banishes his wife from "bed and company" (2.1.191). Indeed, 2 Henry VI, like the King himself, takes Margaret's relationship to Suffolk as a given of political marriage; certainly no one moves to correct the Queen's "dishonesty." However, among a wide range of misogynist references in the Cade sequences, Contention even includes several to licensing women's adultery; one in particular glances at the Henry-Margaret-Suffolk triangle. A sergeant demands justice from Dick Butcher for ravishing his wife, to which Dick replies, "Why, my lord, he would have 'rested me and I went and entered my action in his wife's proper house": Cade's "justice" commands Dick to "follow [his] suit in her common place," cut out the sergeant's tongue, and "brain him with his own mace" (G₃ᵛ; G₃ʳ; following Pelican, 4.7.119). In carnival's inversions, authority fails to protect his own "property" and is muted, beaten with his own "sceptre." But elsewhere, Henry's political impotence figures his sexual lacks; any one of the quarreling peers, says

Margaret, "can do more in England than the king" (1.3.69). Her own "doing" takes form as transgressive mothering of both husband and lover: as Eleanor warns Henry, "She'll pamper thee and dandle thee like a baby" (1.3.143); much later, Margaret cradles Suffolk's severed head at her breast (4.2). And in yet another sign, at the familial level, of the disordered state, Henry mourns the loss of his fatherly Protector, likening himself to a dam bewailing her calf as she watches butchers "bearing it to the bloody slaughterhouse" (3.1.212–20). Unmanned and regendered by "deposing" Gloucester, Henry leaves the Parliament and, immediately thereafter, Margaret assumes an autonomous role as England's "most master."

Here, contradictory versions of Quarto and Folio mimic the realm's troubled gender economy by assigning the Queen differing degrees of authority, both in plotting Gloucester's death and in responding to the news of Irish rebellion. If these can be considered "Elizabethan" and "Jacobean" versions, what is most curious here is that while Folio seems designed to protect the reigning monarch by eliminating Buckingham, who shared the name of James I's known favorite, the "Elizabethan" text does not so protect the Queen's name. Both versions have all the remaining nobles agree that Gloucester must die and show Suffolk and Cardinal Winchester his willing executioners. But in Folio, Margaret remains mute while Winchester, speaking for the absent Protector and the King, deputizes York, voices his own part in the Gloucester plot, and breaks up the gathering (TLN 1614–31). Quarto, however, empowers Margaret. She not only authorizes York's Irish campaign but, just before a mass exit leaves York alone, reminds Suffolk and Winchester of their charge:

> Suffolk, remember what you have to do,
> And you, Lord Cardinal concerning Duke Humphrey,
> 'Twere good that you did see to it in time,
> Come let us go, that it may be performed.
>
> *(E₁ᵛ; cf. Pelican, 3.1.27–30)*

Margaret's more precise association with the death of a "false" King in Quarto seems an almost unbelievable trace of Elizabeth's execution, in 1587, of another rival "false prince," Mary, Queen of Scots. Yet in 1594, when Quarto was first printed, such a possible connection between Margaret and Elizabeth apparently troubled neither the Queen nor her censors; only the "Jacobean" Folio, by erasing her final commands, suppresses this potentially disturbing analogy together with Buckingham's name.[46]

There are differences, too, in the murder itself. Here again, Folio represses what the more sensational Quarto represents: "Then the

Curtains being drawn, Duke *Humphrey* is discovered in his bed, and two men lying on his breast and smothering him in his bed. And then enter the Duke of *Suffolk* to them" (E₂ʳ). And once again, both texts repeat *1 Henry VI*'s pattern of true and false royal images, this time by juxtaposing Gloucester's real death with Henry's momentary fainting fit to reveal, at the "father's" death, the son's powerlessness and, in Margaret's railing against him, the husband's failure to silence an outspoken wife (3.2.73–121). At this point, *2 Henry VI* imitates tragic closure in a tightly choreographed sequence of separations and deaths that, according to traditional models, should ensure Henry's "succession."[47] But far from confirming the providential verities Henry evokes, once again ceding his power to a greater will, *2 Henry VI* affirms instead Gloucester's terrible dream of a broken staff—one half topped with Winchester's head,[48] the other with Suffolk's (1.2.25–31)—and puts into play the necromantic prophecies of Bolingbroke and Jourdain: Henry's deposition of Gloucester, Suffolk's death "by water," and Somerset's death, near the alehouse sign "The Castle." By the end of this play, only one part of that ambiguous early prophecy remains unfulfilled: Henry's "deposition" by Richard Gloucester and Richard's own death.

With Suffolk's assassination as a kind of prologue, *2 Henry VI*'s second half shifts away from female misrule to another form of festival inversion: Cade's transgressive pseudosocialist commonwealth. Before Cade appears, York introduces him as a "devil" who resembles the real Mortimer, language that recirculates the notion of true and false royal images and anticipates what the play represents as a series of successions. For Cade, says York, will, "like a wild Morisco, / Shaking the bloody darts as he his bells" (TLN 1671–72), act as his substitute, test his own claim to the crown. In that Cade's rebellion parodies York's own, it functions much like a play-within-the-play or, rather, a deviant form of that usually localized convention, for Cade's Saturnalian misrule resists such formal containment and spills over its boundaries to threaten both the state and the King. "O graceless men! they know not what they do" (4.4.38) says King Henry, voicing the traditional view of rebellion. But these "graceless men" know precisely what they do; furthermore, their behavior not only grows from but reprises the earlier social disorder.

Cade's own phrase, "in order when we are most out of order" (4.2.76), perhaps best expresses the relationship of the sequence both to what has gone before and to what is to follow. Filled with fantasies of appetite, desire, and absolutist power, the Cade material discloses tensions in the social order and the ideology that sustains it, transforming the nobles' earlier infighting to visible, brutal violence.[49] 2

Henry VI records voices like those of Cade and his followers earlier:[50] the petitioners who complain of the Cardinal's man entailing the house, lands, and wife of one man and of Suffolk's enclosure of common land (1.3); the armorer who accuses his master of claiming York as England's rightful heir (1.3; 2.3); the Simpcoxes' "pure need," which makes them stage a fake miracle (2.1). Here, however, those voices trace a history of oppression, displacing the responsibility for the nobles' treasons onto a site of class struggle. Although, as Jonathan Dollimore points out, the socially deprived always constitute some threat to government, that threat becomes overt only when, as here, they are mobilized by forces higher up the feudal ladder.[51] What can be inferred about treason from the play's earlier scenes is here made patently clear: imitative of the nobility, the rebels see themselves "inspir'd with the spirit of putting down kings and princes" (4.2.31–32). But although Cade's inversions mirror those the nobles themselves use to manipulate, and later to seize, the King's power, Cade himself seeks not to depose King Henry but to replace Gloucester and become the new Protector (4.2.147). And just as its first half reprises features of *1 Henry VI*'s disordered gender contract, *2 Henry VI*'s last two acts recirculate features of the Protector's earlier history.

Gloucester's history is most fully re-represented by the rebels' "trial" of Lord Say, the King's treasurer.[52] First introduced when Henry leaves London for Kenilworth, Say offers to stay behind, in secret, in order to protect the King. But he is captured, and when Cade confronts him, he accuses Say of giving up Normandy, of traitorously corrupting youth in erecting a grammar school, of causing printing to be used, of building a paper mill, of having men about him who "talk of a noun and a verb," of appointing justices of the peace to call poor men before them concerning matters of which they are ignorant, of putting such men in prison and hanging them for not being able to read—and finally, of having his horse wear a cloak when poor men have none and of having a familiar under his tongue who speaks in God's name (4.7.23–48). Aside from the charges levelled at learning, which glance more precisely at Henry, the list reproduces almost exactly the nobles' claims against Gloucester and his Duchess.[53] And like Gloucester, Say's claims of innocence result in his speedy (offstage) death, following which his head and that of his son-in-law, James Cromer (a sheriff from Kent, Cade's own home), are placed on poles and made to kiss and part at every corner—perhaps glancing at the French custom of greeting. Like the nobles' earlier scapegoating of Gloucester, the Say incident furthers the double representation of treason as, in Dollimore's phrase, "that which power fears and also that which power works through."[54] Among the many signs of onstage as well as offstage violence, Say's "treasons" constitute 2 *Henry VI*'s most transgressive instance of the self-interested partiality that, in the eyes of the rebels, sustains aristocratic misrule.

But however much Cade's rebellion subverts the nobles' practices, it carefully insulates, even isolates, the King. It is not kingship itself but rather a contradictory *claim* to kingship that 2 *Henry VI* inverts and subjects to critique. Like York explaining his genealogy to Warwick and Salisbury (2.2), Cade outlines his heritage; although Dick the Butcher and Smith the Weaver mock him, they (like Warwick and Salisbury with York) go along with his grandiloquent claims—and hope to profit from them. Later, in claiming to be Mortimer's changeling child, Cade further ridicules the basis of all such "proofs" majesty offers of its legitimacy (4.2.119–35). And how indeed can bastardy matter when Elizabeth, once proclaimed a royal bastard, sits on the throne? It is the King's *name*, not his ancestry, that matters; as in *King John*, de facto overrules de jure: when a soldier enters shouting "Jack Cade, Jack Cade!" he is instantly killed for not using Cade's self-proclaimed title (4.6.7–8). And Cade himself is finally routed by Henry V's name, which Clifford uses to lure the rebels to fame (and name) in foreign wars (4.8).[55] Curiously contradictory, Cade's inversions protect, even conserve, the king's name.

At least in Folio. There, Cade's primary threat to Henry is a structural one, for the rebellion sequence surrounds two scenes showing the King and his officers at risk (TLN 2530–2612; cf. Pelican, 4.4; 4.5). But Folio also juxtaposes news of Cade's defeat and York's return from Ireland to show Henry "twixt Cade and York distressed" (TLN 2884; Pelican, 4.9.31), with York's "proud array" posing the greater danger to the state. Quarto, however, represents Cade as a usurper.[56] When, for example, Stafford asks if Cade will yield to the King's mercy and receive pardon, he replies, "Nay, bid the King come to me: and he will, and then I'll pardon him, or otherwise I'll have his crown"; and later, after the Staffords' deaths, Cade announces "tomorrow I mean to sit in the King's seat at Westminster" (F₄ᵛ; cf. Pelican 4.2.67–68). What Quarto records here almost precisely anticipates 3 *Henry VI*'s opening scene, where York sits on Henry's throne and, with his consent, becomes his successor. Yet Quarto much more explicitly contains the rebels' subversive energies. Brought on stage "with halters about their necks," they receive Henry's pardon, and Quarto does not anticipate York's return, or reveal, as Folio does, Henry's self-blame—"Come, wife, let's in, and learn to govern better, / For yet may England curse my wretched reign" (TLN 2902–3; Pelican, 4.9.48–49). Rather, Quarto's scene concludes more decisively, with cries of "God save the King!" and with Henry praising God for "this happy victory" (G₄ᵛ). In both versions, the politics of representation return to the question of true and false kings and, beyond that, to a "Lancastrian" versus a "Yorkist" text. In stressing Cade's link to York, Folio positions both as "false" figures of misrule while, by separating the two, Quarto implicitly records the possibility that York may be, like Henry, a "true" king. Finally, insofar as the Cade material recirculates the issue of misrule, his most telling inversion may be the accidental prescience his rebellion—and the circumstances of his death—carry beyond the boundaries of the play. For in recording the history of a man who desires to reform the country's laws and make his mouth the parliament of England, and in representing his executioner as a contented sovereign-subject, 2 *Henry VI* imagines a moment when the "good people of the nation"[57] would execute a real future King who, like the false Cade, would give up his head.

Both *Contention* and 2 *Henry VI*, however, represent York as Cade's apotheosis.[58] In the carefully patterned sequence of loyalty tests that precede the Battle of St. Albans and in the battle itself, treason, and the question of false and true kings, comes to a final trial. And again, alternative versions of the central encounter between York and Clifford suggest differing textual allegiances.[59] In both texts, the combat begins as Warwick offers to fight Clifford and then withdraws; York and Clifford address one another, fight, and York wins. Quarto's exchange represents their duel as a Lancaster-York blood feud:

> YORK. Now Clifford, since we are singled here alone,
> Be this the day of doom to one of us.
> For now my heart hath sworn immortal hate
> To thee, and all the house of Lancaster.
>
> CLIFF. And here I stand, and pitch my foot to thine,
> Vowing never to stir, till thou or I be slain.
> For never shall my heart be safe at rest
> Till I have spoiled the hateful house of York.
> *Alarums, and they fight, and York kills Clifford*
>
> YORK. Now, Lancaster, sit sure, thy sinews shrink,
> Come, fearful Henry, grovelling on thy face,
> Yield up thy crown unto the prince of York.
>
> $(H_3^v; H_3^r)$

In contrast, Folio represents two noble, chivalric adversaries:

> CLIFF. What seest thou in me York? Why dost thou pause?
> YORK. With thy brave bearing should I be in love,
> But that thou art so fast mine enemy.

CLIFF. Nor should thy prowess want praise and esteem,
      But that 'tis shown ignobly, and in treason.
YORK. So let it help me now against thy sword,
      As I in justice, and true right express it.
CLIFF. My soul and body on the action both.
YORK. A dreadful lay, address thee instantly.
CLIFF. *La fin couronne les oeuvres.*
YORK. Thus war hath given thee peace, for thou art still,
      Peace with his soul, heaven if it be thy will.

(TLN 3239–51; cf. Pelican, 5.2.19–30)

In this version, Clifford's epitaph records a lingering echo of Henry V's glorious French war, and York addresses heaven, asking peace for Clifford's soul rather than, as in Quarto, challenging a "fearful Henry" to yield his crown.

But more is at stake here than the difference between Quarto's rather blatant signs of "immortal hatred" between Lancaster and York and Folio's ironic and certainly more ambiguous rendering of the famous war's first battle, which shows chivalry still in place within the social order. For although both Quarto and Folio represent York's replacement of Henry—York and his power enter just after Margaret and Young Clifford urge Henry from the battle (5.2.90–5.3.1)—in Folio, that physical exchange of would-be king for King is the surest sign of York's takeover. At the battle's end, as throughout the action, kingship has a shifting, double persona, and Folio finally walks a narrow line in order to sustain kingship as its subject without completely subverting, and thus subject-ing, its titular King (TLN 3319–20). Quarto, however, names *Henry*, not York, a usurper:

How now, boys, fortunate this fight hath been,
I hope to us and ours, for England's good,
And our great honor, that so long we lost,
Whilst faint-heart Henry did usurp our rights.

(H_4^v)

Less hesitantly than the ambiguous "Lancastrian" Folio, Quarto relocates "true" right in York. Finally, both texts look forward to Henry's future Parliament and to another confrontation that will secure the throne: as York puts it, "we have not got that which we have" (5.3.20). And in both, Warwick, kingmaker and potential traitor, speaks the last words:

Saint Albans battle, won by famous York,
Shall be eternized in all age to come.

Sound drums and trumpets, and to London all,
And more such days as these to us befall!

(5.3.30–34)

Celebrating York's victory, Warwick imagines it set down, "eternized in all age to come." But in which "history," which "Shakespeare?" Although my reading has mobilized certain details to suggest Elizabethan-Jacobean or Yorkist-Lancastrian figurings of "Shakespeare," neither Quarto nor Folio is without contradictions. To put it in terms both *Contention* and *2 Henry VI* consistently recirculate, neither represents a "true" or "false" textual configuration. And neither, at least in printed form, speaks apparent treason. Performance, with its wider range of unrecorded (in print) bodies, accents, and gestures, might in the 1590s have spoken rather differently, but those particulars of representational politics remain unknown. Surely, however, the existence of two versions of a play that duplicates, even reduplicates, kingship constitutes one of the rarest coincidences in the strange, eventful history of Shakespeare's multiple-text plays.

ଛ

Outlining the relationship between *2* and *3 Henry VI*, Dr. Johnson, at once decisive and elusive, comes close to describing a two-part play: "This play is only divided from the former for the convenience of exhibition; for the series of action is continued without interruption, nor are any two scenes of any play more closely connected than the first scene of this play and the last of the former."[60] The 1595 Octavo title, "The true Tragedy of Richard | Duke of York, and the death of | good King Henry the Sixth, | *with the whole contention between* | the two Houses Lancaster | and York," makes a similar connection between *Contention*'s "first part" and the "whole." Although Malone's theory that Shakespeare revised an existing two-part play has long been discredited,[61] the closural Prologue—or terminal opening—of *3 Henry VI* seems an undeniable sign of a closer temporal connection between the two than that between *1* and *2 Henry VI*. The first twenty-four lines reprise *2 Henry VI*'s coda of St. Albans's aftermath through concise reports of the King's escape and the battle's final phase as well as economical, prophetic gestures: Edward points to his bloodied sword; Richard throws down Somerset's head. As before, Warwick vows to seat York on the throne, and with his next words—"This is the palace of the fearful king / And this the royal seat" (1.1.25–26)—battlefield becomes court, and York sits in Henry's place.

Blurring distinctions between beginning and ending, *3 Henry VI* opens by stressing the mutability of both, querying its own discrete form. Framed by two court spectacles, the action begins by calling hereditary, lineal right into question and interrupting the succession and then closes by restoring, but also qualifying, its generative promise. From this admittedly schematic perspective, the play, like *1 Henry VI*, resembles a comedy. If so, what became, in its 1623 printing, the last part of a trilogy is a particularly subversive revenge comedy of succession, one that recirculates and intensifies the festival inversions and transgressive family relations of the earlier plays. For *3 Henry VI* represents England's civil war as a conflict between patrilineal and matrilineal power. In its initial moves, Henry cedes the crown to York after his own death, disinheriting his son, Prince Edward. And once Queen Margaret learns of the crown's entailment, she divorces herself from Henry's bed and, as Joan's Amazonian apotheosis, puts on armor to defend her son's birthright. But although she, like Elizabeth in Cecil's phrase, continues to be "more than a man, and (in troth) sometime less than a woman," few disquieting associations link the two Queens, and Margaret's masculine dominance gives off only faint echoes of a state governed by a "monstrous" warrior-mother.[62] Rather, *3 Henry VI* focuses primary attention on the man's part in the bloody misrule of the kingdom and on masculine inversions of generation and gender. Ironically, Henry's betrayal of his son initiates a linked series of violations that, as Coppélia Kahn argues, replace patriarchal succession with a substitute grounded in similar principles: the vendetta.[63]

Opening *3 Henry VI* at almost any point discloses the severely patterned alternations between York and Lancaster shaping its narrative strategy as well as the mechanism through which each broken oath, each betrayal, each instance of blood revenge breeds the next, as though ironically imitating the generative process. As Clifford says when he kills Rutland, York's youngest son: "Thy father slew my father. Therefore die" (1.3.47). But one particular scene condenses, through metonymy, all such parricides and filicides. At the Battle of Towton, King Henry sits apart, on the same stage molehill where Queen Margaret had earlier crowned York as Carnival King, then mocked and killed him (1.4), and compares its "equal poise" to indeterminate natural changes—the clouds and light at dawn, the tide-swayed sea. Fantasizing a shepherd's life, its time shaped by nature's needs, he witnesses two recognition scenes: a son who has killed his father and a father who has killed his son.[64] Chorus to this double spectacle, Henry reads their dead faces as a prophetic emblem:

The red rose and the white are on his face,
The fatal colors of our striving houses.
The one his purple blood right well resembles;
The other his pale cheeks, methinks, presenteth.
Wither one rose, and let the other flourish.
If you so contend, a thousand lives must wither.

(2.5.97–102)

This highly ritualized, antiphonal meditation on the war's dead constitutes 3 Henry VI's only sign that Hall's unwritable history of unnatural conflict extends from rulers to ruled and threatens on all levels the patriarchal bond that grounds the social order. And its morality-inspired visual and verbal design[65] seems perfectly suited to express Henry's providential vision, as though dramatist and King together might control and order the chaos of civil war and so contain its threats.

Yet such containment occurs only at the level of form, and only at the close, with a celebratory finale that appears to end "the whole contention." While Hall marks the Yorkist victory at Towton as the end of Henry VI's "troublous season" and the beginning of Edward IV's "prosperous reign," 3 Henry VI is less decisive. For Shakespeare's play withholds confirming the Yorkist succession and instead further exploits the civil war along gender lines, opening up an oddly ambivalent critique that weaves through the closing scenes. Although the cruelly ironic subversions of family bonds characterizing the Lancaster-York vendetta substitute for and govern patriarchal relations on both sides, the Yorkists also sustain "natural" father-son relations—first through York himself, then through a surrogate father, Warwick, and finally through Edward. On the Lancastrian side, however, Margaret's "unnatural" misrule privileges mother-son relations. And, as in 1 Henry VI, a dynastic marriage focuses the gender issues surrounding both transgressive families—the one motherless, the other fatherless. Like Suffolk in the earlier play, Warwick goes to France to get Edward a Queen, the Lady Bona; meantime, Edward woos and wins Lady Elizabeth Grey (3.2). At the French court, where Margaret has sought help from Lewis, Warwick receives the news of Edward's marriage, "disinherits" his surrogate son, joins his daughter to Margaret's son, Prince Edward, and returns to England, now King Edward's "sworn and mortal foe" (3.3.257). Warwick's defection not only "corrects" Lancastrian family relations but fractures York family unity: whereas one of his daughters "fathers" him to Lancaster, the other draws Clarence, King Edward's brother, to Margaret's camp. And on the Yorkist side, Richard, in soliloquy, demeans Edward's "use" of women and mocks

his own ability to "witch sweet ladies with my words and looks"
(3.2.150), tying his deformity to feminine witchcraft:

> Why, love foreswore me in my mother's womb;
> And, for I should not deal in her soft laws,
> She did corrupt frail nature with some bribe
> . . . .
> To disproportion me in every part,
> Like to a chaos, or an unlicked bear-whelp,
> That carries no impression like the dam.
>
> (3.2.153–62)

Once Richard relocates Joan's witchcraft in his mother's womb, he not
only absorbs some of Margaret's (and Elizabeth's) more potentially
threatening attributes; he becomes her antithetical double.[66] And although she "minds to play the amazon" (4.1.106), it is "father" Warwick who commands Lancaster's forces during the shifts of power that
culminate with King Henry's capture (4.8), Clarence's return to Edward (5.1), and Warwick's death (5.2)—events that, not incidentally,
refigure the original gender opposition between motherless and fatherless families. When Margaret finally does appear, the concluding
Tewkesbury battle sequence progressively marginalizes her "monstrous" power and transforms her, so to speak, into a more "natural"
mother.

Margaret's last-minute appearance bears some faint echo of Elizabeth's at another decisive battle, Tilbury, where she spoke, as Margaret does here, of courage against great odds.[67] But although her followers praise her "valiant spirit," they also correct her Amazonian
power by co-opting it for themselves—for patriarchal relations. Both
Prince Edward and Oxford use the occasion as a loyalty test to invite
fearful soldiers to leave; then Oxford replaces Margaret with Henry V
as a model for the Prince and the assembled troops, and an entering
messenger speaks not to Margaret but to the Lords. Edward's entry
with his army further reinforces the contrast between masculine and
feminine leadership: he speaks first, with forceful surety, while Margaret, through tears, evokes Henry's name and ruined realm, justice,
and God's name in a speech that seems designed to ventriloquize the
absent King's "fatherly" voice. And, as with 2 Henry VI's final battle,
Quarto (1595) and Folio differ substantially, again sketching out,
though not so clearly as in the earlier play, "Yorkist" and "Lancastrian" versions of Tewkesbury. Here is Quarto:

ALL.   Saint George for Lancaster.

Alarms to the battle, York flies, then the chambers be
discharged. Then enter the king [Edward], Cla[rence] &
Glo[ucester], & the rest, & make a great shout, and cry,
for York, for York, and then the Queen is taken, and the
Prince, and Oxf[ord] & Som[erset], and then sound and
enter all again.

KING EDWARD.   Lo here a period of tumultuous broils,
Away with Oxford to Hames Castle straight,
For Somerset, off with his guilty head.
Away, I will not hear them speak.

OXFORD.   For my part I'll not trouble thee with words. *Exit Oxford.*

SOMERSET.   Nor I, but stoop with patience to my death. *Exit Somerset.*

KING EDWARD.   Now Edward, what satisfaction canst thou make,
For stirring up my subjects to rebellion?

PRINCE.   Speak like a subject, proud ambitious York.

(E$_4$^{r}; F$_1$^{v}; cf. Pelican, 5.4.s.d.82; 5.5.1–6, 17)

Quarto's stage directions not only define a specific sequence of action not accorded to any other battle in either text but call attention to Edward's victory, first by emphasizing the (possibly defiant) silence of Margaret and her son, and then by Edward's confrontation with the Prince, accusing him of rebellion. In contrast, Folio's stage direction— "*Alarum, Retreat, Excursions, Exeunt*"—indicates only a generic battle and, following Oxford's and Somerset's exits, includes a Henry-like comment from Margaret: "So part we sadly in this troublous world, / To meet with joy in sweet Jerusalem" (TLN 2970, 2980–81). Moreover, Folio separates mother from son, giving Edward a delayed entrance (TLN 2985), which lends additional emphasis to Henry's male heir and to the war as an exclusively male enterprise.

Or almost exclusively so, for in both Quarto and Folio, Prince Edward shows himself as more mother's son than father's child—insisting on his right, as Henry had not in the play's opening scene; taunting the Yorkists with insults similar to those Margaret had spoken to York on the molehill just before she, together with Clifford and Northumberland, killed him (1.4). And once he is killed (in Quarto, only by Edward; in Folio, by all three brothers), Margaret accuses the childless Yorkists of infanticide, and asks them, in turn, beginning with Richard, to kill her. Although Edward prevents him from killing Margaret, and he leaves for the Tower to "root them out," Margaret and Richard are here irrevocably linked through mother-son relations, through sharing complementary deprivations: Margaret, her son; Richard, his mother. And this relation between the two breeds the play's most transgressive inversion. For the following scene generates, between a Lancaster and a York, an anomalous rebirth. Here, however, both texts associate the final sign of those Margaret calls "butchers" and "bloody cannibals" with Edward, who, having just killed Lancaster's heir, anticipates the birth of his own (5.5.87–90).

More than any battle scene in any of the *Henry VI* plays, Tewkesbury's butcheries recapitulate past narrative to further link killing with generation, providing a climax to the mechanical savageries that have shaped the narrative, and condensing its ironies into a symmetrical, schematic pattern beginning with the murder of York's youngest son, Rutland (1.3), and ending with Prince Edward's, the final link in the vendetta. These circular returns also bleed into Richard's murder of Henry VI, which repeats the Rutland-York cycle—first the son, then the father, obliterating the line. On a purely schematic level, killing Henry fulfills Richard's opening vow, as he threw down Somerset's head: "Thus do I hope to shake King Henry's head" (1.1.20). And because both Henry and Richard are figures isolated from family (Henry by his removed saintliness, Richard by his deterministic self-construction), their conflict represents several ultimate oppositions—usurped King versus future usurper, martyr versus tyrant; the two faces (and bodies) of monarchy.[68] What is enacted here, at Henry's death and in Richard's verbal re-representation of his birth, which follows the killing of the King, constitutes an unnatural, perverse parody of generation and succession that not only furthers the gender critique by again displacing Richard's deformities onto the mother but also subverts the myth of succession—"The King is dead. May the King live forever"—and in so doing begins to erase Edward IV's reign. And because the King-father dies replacing, so to speak, his own lost son with an anomalous heir, he bears some part of that transgression himself, a guilty burden his Daedalus-Icarus comparisons reinforce (5.6.21–25).

Contradictorily, *3 Henry VI* protects this unnatural, illegitimate birth by making Richard dramatically legitimate: Vice and Machiavel, his threats are deflected and enclosed by native and alien forms of the same convention. And his soliloquy presence links him to another dramatic father, York, who in *2 Henry VI* vows, as Richard does, to get the crown (3.1.331–83). Here, however, Richard uses soliloquy to deny kinship and reveal his autogeny:

I have no brother, I am like no brother;
And this word "love," which greybeards call divine,

> Be resident in men like one another,
> And not in me: I am myself alone.
>
> (5.6.80–83)

Born sui generis out of self-will and dramatic convention, Richard represents neither nation nor king nor family but the self. And the tension between convention and its "unruly" use will, in *Richard III*, exchange the power relations between subject and king for those between king and actor, drawing a dangerous and subversive analogy between fashioning a king and fashioning a role. If such a transformation does not yet precisely threaten the state, it does, in the later play, threaten the limits of dramatic form by (if only briefly) exchanging England's tragedy for Richard's comedy. The final scene of *3 Henry VI* initiates that transformation by briefly imagining a conclusion for the "whole contention" that imposes a comic after-history on England's bloody civil war.

An invention without any chronicle source, that last scene embraces and intensifies a number of signs associated with comic closure. Its spectacle alone represents renewed community and dynastic continuity: a newly enthroned King, together with his Queen and his heir and surrounded by his brothers and his court, stage-manages a show of love and obedience. Not one but four terminal conventions complement this spectacle and further enforce closure: Edward recapitulates the action and proclaims war's end and the restoration of Yorkist power; all present confirm both the new King and his child; a last speech ties up loose ends of narrative and anticipates a peaceful reign; and a final call for music caps the communal harmony. Such a cluster of signs amounts to a mechanism that invites an unquestioning, uncritical acceptance of and equation between succession and closure, even to the point of containing Richard's potential threat by figuring his presence as one element among several in the overall design.[69]

At the level of language, the scene subscribes even further to overtly anxious comic artifice. Rethinking England's "slaughterhouse" state as a garden, Edward's opening speech introduces a chain of images that evoke, not the animal references consistently associated with the Yorkists, but those of seasonal cycles, exploiting the plant-Plantagenet pun to link plentiful harvest to the rebirth of a "natural" king. To further celebrate the surety of his accession, Edward lists, not the names of those in his own family, but the Lancastrian fathers and sons who have been killed in the war—including among them "father" Warwick but excluding the murdered Prince Edward and Henry VI. By reversing the terms of the usual after-battle report, which praises the deeds and valor of the winners, Edward de-forms the convention; and in omitting the names of King Henry and his heir, he not only further erases the Lancastrian claim but masks the Yorkists' own violations. As when his thought coupled killing with generation at Tewkesbury, Edward reconfirms and restores the line of patriarchal succession through hereditary right, and his colloquial address to his Queen seems to suggest a fugitive desire for a living "Bess" who could have just such a legitimate heir.[70] If so, the figure is only a trace of what a younger Elizabeth might have read as a challenge, for no further connection links *3 Henry VI*'s Queen Elizabeth to the living sovereign. Positioned as a devoted wife and doting mother, Edward's Queen represents a newly generative power, replacing Margaret's inversions with a corrected image of domestic womankind. The restored patriarchy carefully suppresses and controls all such "monstrous" female misrule: Margaret, ransomed home (ironically) by her father's offer of the lands reallocated to him by her marriage treaty, is restored to her father and returned to France. And when she reappears in *Richard III*, it is as a ghostly fiction of herself, offering bloody instruction and remembrance of things past to that play's Queens and mothers.

3 Henry VI, which has subverted and finally destroyed family bonds, ends by generating a new—and complete—family. In imposing a new dynastic line, the close circulates and repositions a number of propositions about the relations of gender and power. Central to both the family and that repositioning is Richard's tribute to Edward's family tree and to its fruit. Serpent in the garden, parricide, and filicide, the epitome of Yorkist family violence, the warrior who has made and remade himself through misusing a woman, Richard gives Edward's child a Judas kiss of betrayal.[71] His gesture denies the birth of Edward's child as well as the restored patriarchal succession, cancelling both as principles of either continuance or closure. Rather, the close regenerates in Richard a perfected emblem for the play, self-constructed outside kinship and normality, representing in his physical presence the anxious fears of deformed generation that *A Midsummer Night's Dream*'s closural blessing will later attempt to deflect and thwart.[72] Familiarized by dramatic convention yet made alien by his extremes, Richard poses potential threats to kinship and kingship that cannot be encompassed in terms of the "real." Insofar as he represents some "darker purpose," the symptom of an unspeakable, terrifying unknown, he is the next worst thing to a kingdom without a successor. And it is his ironic gaze toward the future that compromises spectators' absorption within this spectacle of comic closure. At this most contradictory and contested closural site, *3 Henry VI* flirts with identifying Richard as the representation of what is absent in the Elizabethan social text—the missing heir of the sovereign who, like Richard, was an anomaly, one with "the body of a weak, frail woman but the heart and stomach of a king, and a King of England, too."[73]

So forcefully does Richard's presence destabilize the comic signs that attempt to contain him that *3 Henry VI*'s close generates what might be called tetralogy thinking. Like Richard, who has already mapped out his own narrative strategy of succession, the playtext's commentators (myself included) tend to leap ahead to his play, as though a desire to close with Richard—and also (perhaps) with the strictly patterned inevitability of familiar tragic signs—equates formal and historical closure. In the theater, too, subsuming Shakespeare's three *Henry VI* plays within some larger design has, until quite recently, governed their limited performance history.[74]

When, for the first time in nearly three hundred years, F. R. Benson did stage the *Henry VI* plays—for his 1906 Shakespeare Memorial Theatre repertory season—they were seen together with the other histories as part of a cycle.[75] Almost half a century later, however, Sir Barry Jackson's 1952 Birmingham Repertory productions of *2* and *3 Henry VI*, to which *1 Henry VI* was added for the 1957–1958 Old Vic season, shook the plays loose from this critical-historical epic framework. Even so, Jackson reshaped *3 Henry VI*'s close to further its connection with *Richard III*. In order to strengthen "a very sketchy affair on which to end an almost melodramatic play," he left Richard alone onstage after Edward's final couplet to speak the first lines of *Richard III*'s opening soliloquy, "his voice being finally submerged by the fanfares and bells marking his brother's supposedly permanent triumph."[76] Elsewhere, however, Jackson made extensive cuts dictated by economic pressures and theatrical viability—especially by the need to fit lengthy plays into available time frames.

Driven by similar constraints, John Barton, in his 1963 Royal Shakespeare Company adaptation of the *Henry VI* plays with Peter Hall, went even further: their project not only edited but completely refashioned them, condensing three into two—entitled *Henry VI* and *Edward IV*—and adding a reworked *Richard III*.[77] To some extent, including *Richard III* was a response to Jackson's productions, which "seemed oddly incomplete." But Barton and Hall also "believed *Richard III* itself would emerge as a different and richer play if performed in such a context. . . . In order to interest audiences in the plays as a single entity, we not only decided to use the overall title of *The*

Wars of the Roses, but on occasion to play the whole cycle on a single day."[78] The playing version of the Barton-Hall tetralogy-trilogy retained a little over 6,000 lines of the original 12,350 in Shakespeare's four playtexts, to which Barton added 1,400 lines—some from other plays, some of his own.[79] Attempting to solve the theatrical problems posed by "a mass of diffuse narrative," Barton shifted lines from character to character within scenes and from one play to another, restructured whole sequences of scenes, telescoped others, and added linking passages in order to clarify narrative condensations and to give individual scenes as well as sequences stronger formal shape. Most significantly, however, their version was designed to serve Hall's conviction that "Shakespeare's philosophy of order" was equivalent to Tillyard's Elizabethan World Picture.[80] For not only did Hall embrace Tillyard's hierarchical notions of just proportion, order, and degree (ideas reflected in Barton's reworked playtexts); he also affirmed divine retribution as a controlling ideology: "even if . . . chaos is inevitable and necessary, it is still a sin, and punishment will follow the violation of natural laws. Bolingbroke . . . and his family suffer retribution for generations." Moreover, Hall saw this theory "not as a relic of medievalism but as a piece of workable human pragmatism, humanitarian in its philosophy and modern and liberal in its application."[81] But if the Barton-Hall project was essentially conservative in appropriating a feudal past as embodying a set of "universal truths" that might or could authorize an unstated social hierarchy in post–World War II Britain, its other, more radical, influence—Jan Kott's *Shakespeare, Our Contemporary*, which Hall read in proof on his way to *Wars'* first rehearsal—supported Hall's analysis of the plays as "an ironic revelation of the time-honored practices of politicians. I realized that the mechanism of power had not changed in centuries . . . [and] was convinced that a presentation of one of the bloodiest and most hypocritical periods in history would teach many lessons about the present."[82]

This double commitment to Elizabethan state propaganda and contemporary political relevance, filtered through a somewhat reductive version of Marxist thinking ("the implacable roller of history crushes everybody and everything"), generated a peculiarly hybrid and (as it turned out) eminently saleable cultural commodity. And because Barton either removed or replaced those narrative and rhetorical features that did not directly empower Hall's providential reading and rearranged others in order to achieve coherence, unity, and moral impact, his adaptation produced narrative and closural strategies more structurally and formally decisive than those of Shakespeare's originals. The newly ideologized trilogy enclosed *Edward IV*—aside from *Richard*

III, the performance text most faithful to Shakespeare's original narrative strategy[83]—between two well-shaped, if not well-made, tragedies.

Henry VI, the most heavily restructured performance text, redirects and reweights two end points, both of which Shakespeare's own narrative strategies suggest as closural markers but nevertheless avoid. The first half closes with the English-French peace treaty (*1 Henry VI*, 5.4; Barton-Hall, scene 16), reworked to strengthen the opposition between Winchester and York, to introduce Warwick as kingmaker (*2 Henry VI*, 2.2), and to connect York's loss in France with his decision to seek the crown. Positioned as a climax, the York-Warwick plot, which prepares for the Wars of the Roses, anticipates similar closural sequences in Barton's second and third plays (as well as in Shakespeare's *3 Henry VI* and *Richard III*), both of which end with battles followed by a scene that foregrounds either a usurper or a successor. Further, Barton's restructuring silently acknowledges—and evades— the alleged awkwardness of *1 Henry VI*'s hesitant comic close by conflating the two scenes concerning Henry's marriage with Margaret (*1 Henry VI*, 5.1; *2 Henry VI*, 1.1) in the opening of *Henry VI*'s second half. In this slightly regendered ending, Margaret's relation to Suffolk as well as to Henry becomes subsumed within a formal—and ideological—coherence that privileges male experience, as well as the male project called the play.[84]

For the close of *Henry VI*'s second half (made up of *2 Henry VI*, 3–4.1), Barton again refines the contradictions and ambiguities of Shakespeare's playtext, this time by appropriating its tragic signs—among them, Winchester's "deathbed confession" of his responsibility in Gloucester's murder— to make "one of the main moral points in the trilogy: that self-seeking and wickedness breed guilt in the doer, and rejection by other people."[85] But, since Winchester does not, in Shakespeare's *2 Henry VI*, straightforwardly admit his complicity, Barton's version has Warwick question him about his part in the conspiracy, to which the Bishop responds by blaming Henry for not saving Gloucester. Then, in order to make Henry voice his own guilty awareness, Barton cobbles together a speech made up of three lines from Edward's response to York's murder (*3 Henry VI*, 2.1.74–76), an invented line, and six lines spoken by Henry in response to Gloucester's death (*2 Henry VI*, 3.2.151, 141–45).[86] Moreover, an ironic coda, the result of further rearrangement, deepens the King's guilt and self-blame. When Margaret enters with Suffolk's head (Barton-Hall, scene 25), Henry urges her to embrace "sour adversity," and she replies (in lines ascribed to *Gorboduc*), "Steel thou thy heart to keep thy vexed kingdom /

Whereof both you and I have charge and care." As Henry accepts his weakness and his responsibility for his surrogate father's death— "Come, wife, let's in and learn to govern better: / For yet may England curse my wretched reign"—Barton's newly designed close unifies event with providential ideology to reprivilege Gloucester's death within Henry's self-limiting tragedy.[87]

If both *Henry VI*'s interval break and finale foreground particular characters—York, Henry—as well as repattern events (especially in the latter) to moralize Tillyard's thesis, *Edward IV*'s representational politics for both end points not only serve similar goals but also, as though to earn the play's title, reshape Edward's brief reign to intensify retrospective and predictive connections among the three performance texts. And because almost every change, whether omission or addition, either repeats a previous pattern or anticipates a future repetition, Barton's strategies work to fold Tillyard's providentialism up within Kott's Grand Mechanism, to produce history as an endless recycling of the same narratives, though with changed players. Thus, on the level of structure, the interval break celebrates the Yorkists' Towton victory, where, by reassigning Warwick's concluding speech at St. Albans (2 *Henry VI*, 5.3.29–33) to Edward, Barton's performance text formalizes his triumph and generates two potential rhymes: first, with *Henry VI*'s midpoint, the French treaty and the York-Warwick pact; and second, with *Edward IV*'s close, where Edward again calls for drums and trumpets but then rejects their warlike sound for "mirthful comic shows." And just as the opening of the second half—Edward's wooing of Lady Grey (Barton-Hall, scene 41)—creates an additional rhyme with *Henry VI*'s identically positioned midplay marriage, inviting connections between the two, *Edward IV*'s close, as though quoting *Richard II*'s structural formality, echoes Barton's almost wholly invented opening ceremonial council scene. There, after naming his son successor, Henry hears reports from Ireland and France and, threatened by Cade's rebellion, leaves the court for Kenilworth (Barton-Hall, scene 26); here, a King once more rewards obedient subjects and acknowledges his heir. Again, one particular subject threatens to compromise his security and that of his son.

Although based on the dynamic of *3 Henry VI*'s concluding scene— Edward's recapitulatory summary of Tewkesbury, his son's presentation, his brothers' fealty (including Richard's betrayal), and a final note of harmony—*Edward IV*'s close reweights these features, primarily by considerable additions to Edward's speaking role that emphasize the Yorkists' newly won power and their attempt to appropriate and relegitimate lineal descent and title. Barton omits Edward's catalogue of the Lancastrian dead that, in Shakespeare's playtext, works both to recall their threat and to displace it onto Richard's disruptive, relatively silent presence. Instead, following the central exchange of love and allegiance (Barton-Hall, Scene 53, from *3 Henry VI*, 5.7.1–4, 15–21, 25–32, 35–36), Edward is given an invented speech that substitutes a list of Yorkist heroes for the absent Lancastrians: thanking "all who help'd us to our happy throne," he finally singles out his brothers, naming Richard "our partner and our second in these wars, / And now our chiefest minister in peace." In order to further this particular irony, not only does Richard express his love and duty to his lawful King, but Edward thanks Buckingham (not present in *3 Henry VI*) and, by promising him advancement, sets up his importance as Richard's future minister in *Richard III*. Representing Buckingham, however, exchanges one ironic presence for another's absence: with no mention of the reallocated lands constituting Margaret's dowry, she is simply dismissed by Buckingham as "a trifle," subsumed by Edward under "affairs of state," suppressed even further than in Shakespeare's original, where Clarence calls the matter to Edward's attention (5.7.37–40). As in Barton's reworking of *1 Henry VI*'s ending to delay the issues surrounding Henry's marriage with Margaret, *Edward IV*'s close focuses exclusively on male business.

Curiously paradoxical, Barton's version both ends more conclusively and expands its preparatory connections to *Richard III* more fully than does Shakespeare's *3 Henry VI*. In its final moves, Edward, anticipating the language of Richard's opening soliloquy, speaks of "bid[ding] our armour rust while we do revel / In celebration of this hard-won peace";[88] and the performance text concludes with Edward's fatuous hope for "lasting joy" (as in Shakespeare's original) and with a flourish and general exit that leave Richard alone on the stage. Resolution by exaggeration seems the operative principle in this reconstructed state scene, which privileges equally the public construction of Edward's royal power and its future deconstruction from within. Whereas a number of other scenes, both in Shakespeare's plays and Barton's playing versions, conclude with a potential usurper voicing his intent to gain power, here Richard Gloucester's silent presence constitutes not only an obvious sign of his powerful difference but also, even more obviously, a sign that, especially within the Barton-Hall trilogy, all closural moves consistently allude to and anticipate a future-perfect form that rewrites ending as the beginning of England's Tudor rule.

If *Wars* sought to position *Richard III* as "the retributive culmination of a struggle for power" and to demystify Richard as "the

Machiavellian entertainer of stage tradition" in order to stress his
"bloody totalitarianism [as] the expiation of England,"[89] in retrospect
that goal not only seems to have guided Barton's reshaping of the three
Henry VI plays but to have permitted him to see himself as following
in Shakespeare's own footsteps. Indeed, he conjectured that *Richard
III* prompted Shakespeare to rework particular scenes in the "original"
Henry VI plays "to make the whole cycle reasonably cohesive and organic."[90] *Richard III*'s close, however, constitutes another story, one
that Hall's own sense of ending represents in (loosely) Kottian terms:

> Power corrupts because the needs of being in power are in themselves cor-
> rupting. A man aspires to be a king, and is then destroyed by being a king,
> whether he be a good or bad king. Therefore how do we govern? What do
> we do? Must we long to retire, like Henry VI, to the shepherd's life?
>
> The selfish instincts of men must therefore be constantly checked—by par-
> liament, democracy, tradition, religion—or else the men of ambition would
> misgovern the rest. All that Shakespeare finally gives us as a lesson on hu-
> man experience is that at the end of every life, or every cycle of misery,
> selfishness, and destruction, you can only hope to be left with a regenerative
> principle. A baby, for example; or Richmond founding a new dynasty. Or
> the hope of young love marrying. The problems are never over, but life as a
> principle goes on.[91]

Hall's oddly powerless questions about the exercise of power negotiate
between his commitment to the operations of divine providence and a
kind of universalist-existentialist despair that roots human experience
in an only slightly mitigated tragic continuity. His stance owes as much
to F. R. Leavis, as well as to 1950s literary critical traditions of character study, as to Sartre and Camus. Using cold war terminology alluding to the threats of ambitious governments (presumably other than
those shaped by "parliament, democracy, tradition, [and] religion"),
he sketches out instructions for reading Shakespearean closure that
have ghostly affinities with those of another Hall, the chronicler whose
providentialism *Wars* sought to retrieve as a key for understanding
Shakespeare's plays as a past version of present history.

As streamlined, editorialized, and ideologized Shakespeare, the Barton-Hall *Wars* reinstituted a theatrical practice common since the days
of Nahum Tate, Colley Cibber, and Charles Kean. However conservative (in its ideology) and radical (in its treatment of Shakespeare's
playtexts), their adaptation of "doubtful Shakespeare"[92]—which both
"authors" acknowledge as questionable in principle—consolidated the
achievement of the Royal Shakespeare Company in the middle 1960s
and also renewed critical interest in Shakespeare's earliest histories.

But the three *Henry VI* plays—(relatively) uncut and unadapted—did not receive a present-day premiere until 1977, when Terry Hands directed all three as a trilogy, again for the Royal Shakespeare Company.[93]

Speaking of the trilogy structure, Hands describes "three 'inner plays,' one in each part (Talbot, Jack Cade and the three York brothers) and a 'superplay' of all three parts and four main characters (Henry, Margaret, Warwick and York) that is fed by such others as Suffolk, Gloucester and Winchester."[94] Rejecting Barton-Hall's cutting practices, Hands chose to present the three plays "without any reshaping, without any tailoring, without any adapting—in fact with less than we would do with any other production."[95] Like Barton and Hall, however, Hands sought casting, design, and staging elements that would reinforce the trilogy's unity: this included using a single company of actors, with the same actors playing roles that carried over from one part to another, as well as double and even triple casting to invite further connections between particular roles and plays.[96] To achieve further coherence, Hands rehearsed the three plays as one and scheduled them to open on consecutive nights and to run thereafter in sequential order.[97] By doing the plays "simply and fully"—repeatedly Hands refers to their naïveté, as well as to his desire to reveal their dramatic and stylistic integrity—what emerged was a straightforward process of development beginning in Part One with quick, emblematic characterization through presentational means, which opened "into the full kind of richness of [Part Two's] chess game played in the English court," followed by Part Three's ritual and "terrible ceremonial where extreme savagery is balanced by extreme grief."[98] If *Wars* served Tillyard, providential ideology, and Kott's mechanistic view of history, Hands's project claimed to serve only "Shakespeare"—with an aesthetic simplicity that remained "true to the text." Recuperating the *Henry VI* plays, then, was an archaeological retrieval that expressed trust in their alleged capacity to speak for themselves, through the actors. Within this context, which shares the naïveté Hands ascribes to the plays, Hands's representational choices for each close, however, disclose the extent to which much more than "the text" is speaking.

Reading *1 Henry VI* as "a series of tableaux vivants, of emblems," Hands's performance text designed a final composite tableau that succinctly captured the gathering tensions among the past, present, and future resolutions and oppositions that inform the close. Rather than attempting to stage the play's double endings as a naturalistic sequence, Hands appropriated conventions of simultaneous staging to juxtapose the English-French peace treaty (5.4) with Suffolk's proposal that Henry marry Margaret (5.5). As York asks for allegiance, Charles, Reignier, Alençon, and the Bastard swear on his sword, holding the pose briefly; York then moves away from the group, asks the captains to dismiss their armies, and proclaims peace. These principals as well as several soldiers remain, frozen in an upstage tableau; bright lighting further redefines the downstage space for the ensuing scene, in which Suffolk convinces Henry to marry Margaret. The court— Gloucester and Exeter together at left, Suffolk on the right—frame Henry, who draws toward Suffolk to speak his assent. Given the extreme formality of the grouping, the slightest changes of position register the nobles' reactions to Henry's decision. Concluding his speech, he turns away, moves upstage center, and looks up to the bridge, a staging element that had served for the walls of Orleans and Rouen, and now reads as an empty sign of those battles;[99] as Suffolk speaks his final lines from downstage, Margaret enters on the bridge and looks down at Henry. Here, Hands's staging approximates fourteenth– and fifteenth–century narrative paintings in its collapsing of time and space and in the formal, hierarchical relationships it delineates: individual presences give way to the larger social patterns that contain them. In the background, the warriors' qualified victory presides over Henry's coming marriage with Margaret, whose presence above, and the look she and Henry exchange, suggest both Henry's image of her as an idealized romance heroine and her supremacy over him, privileging the paradox of union and opposition that marks their future relationship. Both past conquest and promised marriage seem threatened by Suffolk's strong downstage position, closest to the audience— nearly in the present of the next play.[100] Yet this fixed spectacle inscribes closure, for an instant, in a highly artificial unity that simultaneously offers an illusion of security and inscribes, within that illusion, suggestions of change.

Although it (purposefully) lacks the artifice of *1 Henry VI*'s close, Hands's final tableau for *2 Henry VI* uses stage space similarly to conflate past and future. Because the Cade rebellion is played for maximum speed, activity, and violence, St. Albans's battle, with its two quickly decisive combats (5.2), reads both as an anticlimactic aftermath and as the natural outcome of the earlier, more encompassing threat. As York, Warwick, Edward (present only in Q3's stage directions for the scene), and Richard walk downstage on the grassy carpet that covers the stage, they embrace; York's and Warwick's swords clink briefly in the exchange, a last deadened echo of past battles presaging those to come. Hardly noticing the bodies of Somerset, Buckingham, and Old Clifford—reminders of all the deaths *2 Henry VI* dramatizes or reports—the Yorkists congratulate each other on what seems an easy victory, a foregone conclusion. As the final tableau develops, Edward remains at center stage flanked by Somerset's and Buckingham's bodies, a soldier standing at his left while, slightly downstage, Salisbury and Richard frame Old Clifford's body. First York and then Warwick leave the central grouping to move far down right, apart from the other survivors and the corpses. All rests slightly askew around Clifford's centrally positioned body, a fragmentation that counterpoints Warwick's concluding hopes for future glory. And, in a final move following Warwick's last words, York crosses past Warwick to assume the downstage center position occupied by Suffolk in *1 Henry VI*'s final stage image. These last gestures and moves, which reach toward and then reject the composition of a family portrait, suggest the characters' separation and reopposition as well as their inconclusive victory and so condense narrative into a synecdochal figure. More informal than *1 Henry VI*'s tableau, this close nevertheless echoes its characters' positioning within the deep, empty stage space. Only the people have changed, not the power structure, and again the man who would be king edges toward the audience—and toward the next play; behind him, in the immediate past, lies Clifford's body; and behind the dead (and his father) stands Edward, the future King.

For the death of Young Clifford in *3 Henry VI* (2.6), Hands's performance text constructs, at the interval close, a grouping that not only echoes *2 Henry VI*'s ending but also rhymes with the trilogy's final scene. Again, a Clifford's body constitutes the centrally placed stage property; again the Yorkists celebrate a victory. Richard stretches out beside Clifford's corpse, mocking him: "Clifford, ask mercy, and obtain no grace" (2.6.69). As the Yorkists kneel around the body, Edward has a hand on Warwick's shoulder; when Richard asks to be Duke of Clarence, he moves between Edward and Warwick to reach his brother, and Warwick pushes him away—outside this newly defined family circle, an alien among a more powerful brother and surrogate father. In the performance text's closing sequences, however, Richard reasserts himself, most forcefully so from Tewkesbury onward. Hands's representational strategies shaped "the bleak ending . . . to look like the view through the wrong end of a telescope": Margaret and Edward speak their prebattle orations only to three or four followers; the battle itself is "fought in weary slow-motion by six people"; within the deep, echoing emptiness of Hands's stage space, Richard seems especially privileged. As David Daniell writes, even Queen Margaret's request to be killed after Prince Edward's murder is "almost dwarfed by the simple business of Richard's exit and his line,

'The Tower! The Tower! I'll root them out.' . . . [Richard] leaves a
sense of his absence behind him which is nearly visible."[101] Of Hands's
choices for Henry's spectacular murder, Daniell reports:

> Under the eave of a big trap down front, Henry appears; old, crouched,
> reading, wearing only a dirty white robe, chained and gyved. Richard slowly
> pushes up another trap door in the steel grating, to join him, laughing. It is
> all brightly bottom-lit and side-lit. Alan Howard gives Henry an all-know-
> ing courage and weird simplicity, not playing the saint at all, though he dies
> in a crucified position, blood streaming from his side. Richard's thirty-two
> line soliloquy is made squatting beside the body; and as he brightly chatters
> about himself and develops his plans, his dagger strikes the steel bars be-
> tween his legs, with a regular, punctuating ringing. He rolls sideways as the
> trap closes down on the falling Henry—and he is two paces from his infant
> nephew in the final court scene.[102]

Elliptically, within seconds, Tower cell becomes throne room, court
built upon prison. In reappropriating Shakespeare's stage directions as
elements of what amounts to a cinematic language, Hands's performance text edits the two spaces together, using Richard himself to energize the cut and to transform one space into the other, economically
suggesting his protean nature as well as his coming rule, which will
imprison both his brothers and, eventually, himself.

Under suddenly brilliant lights, King Edward and his Queen appear
enthroned, an admiring court in attendance, with Richard seated quite
far downstage, directly in front of the King. In turn, Clarence and
Richard approach to kiss the child, and polite applause follows each
kiss. After dismissing Margaret to France, Edward pauses before the
next lines:

> And now what rests but that we spend the time
> With stately triumphs, mirthful comic shows,
> Such as befits the pleasures of the court?

(5.7.42–44)

But now he pauses again—at length—as though trying to imagine
what further words will confirm this peace. And then he calls to the
musicians: "Sound drums and trumpets." At the familar command,
which sounds like a burden both in the final scene of 2 *Henry VI* and
in the opening of this playtext, Richard, Clarence, and the others respond instinctively: hands reach for swords; they draw and crouch,
ready to fight. Then they relax, laughing in embarrassment, and, as
Edward speaks again to the musicians—"farewell sour annoy!"—he
and Richard begin to cross toward each other, as though about to

touch. This time, the musicians respond by playing dance music, which the Yorkists attempt to follow, but no one can remember how to execute the steps. And while the others start, stop, and bump into one another, trying to dance their "lasting joy," Richard watches the lights come down in a slow fade from behind the throne.

As in the final image of his *2 Henry VI*, Hands plays off the notion of a family portrait. Here, that portrait begins to stabilize and then dissolves in randomly harmonious movement that taints the York family celebration with the impression that these warriors, raised on bloodletting, cannot exchange battle for dance—or, in Richard's words, "bruised arms" for "the lascivious pleasing of a lute" (*Richard III*, 1.1.6, 13). And Richard, self-constructed as alien to brotherhood, stands apart, a formal, stable element in the improvised design. This final comic dance, which collapses time by balancing the past memories of battle that galvanize its characters against their future desires and intentions, neatly summarizes *3 Henry VI's*—and the trilogy's—insistently repetitive devices of recapitulation and prophecy. Hands's staging invites reading *3 Henry VI's* close through Shakespeare's later comic practice, where an outsider (a Jaques, a Malvolio) excludes himself from the tightly constructed fictional artifice. Unlike either Jackson or Barton-Hall, whose performance texts privilege Richard's future dramatic history at the close, Hands's staging contains his presence within the overall composition.[103] That its harmony is subverted not just by Richard's inability or unwillingness to join the dance but by all the Yorkists represents its particular achievement, resolving the trilogy as a comedy of succession marred not exclusively by individual anarchy but also by communal failure.

As realized by Hands's performance texts, closure in the *Henry VI* trilogy articulates a worldview that progresses from the static artifice of *1 Henry VI's* emblematic final image to *3 Henry VI's* improvised celebratory dance, as though illustrating how the composed serenity of a Duc de Berri miniature might transform to a Brueghel's convulsive energy. Yet however distinctively each crystallizes the representational mode Hands saw as characteristic of individual playtexts, all share a similarly confrontational aggressiveness. Each final image sharply delineates character relationships and keys into the tensions between past and future that underlie closure, creating a spatial model that contains but does not wholly interpret their meaning. Each calls attention to, even implicates spectators in, multiple points of view and potential future oppositions—Lancaster against Lancaster (*1 Henry VI*), Lancaster against York (*2 Henry VI*), York against York (*3 Henry VI*). Hands's choice of overtly modernist stage design, and the stark, geometrical planes and volumes of individual stage images, generate an illusion of visual purity that, in turn, fosters the illusion of a "pure text," of "Shakespeare-speaking." Perhaps best described as formalist or structuralist Shakespeare, the style privileges actors' performances as integral to a transhistorical, autonomous aesthetic: Hands's claims for "put[ting] it all very crudely, very naïvely down on the stage"[104] in order to learn, in the absence of an ongoing tradition of staging the (relatively) uncut plays, how the three *Henry VI* plays work in the theater. Although there is no denying the success and value of his project, its mannered representational strategies tend, perhaps inevitably, toward what might be called an archaeology of mystification.

Contrasting views of what constitutes an archaeology—indeed, of what constitutes history—inform Michael Bogdanov's 1988 English Shakespeare Company productions of the *Henry VI* plays and Adrian Noble's 1988 versions for the Royal Shakespeare Company. Both compress the Folio trilogy into two plays; both owe, in varying degrees, a restructuring debt to Barton-Hall's 1963 *Wars*.[105] But whereas Noble's *Plantagenets*, like the *Wars*, includes *Richard III*, Bogdanov repositions the *Henry VI* materials within a larger context—a heptalogy, the double tetralogies combined into seven plays, which borrowed Barton-Hall's title, *The Wars of the Roses*, to describe not just a localized phenomenon but a wider historical process. Although Bogdanov's staging of the *Henry VI* plays preceded Noble's by less than a year,[106] in early 1989, both ran simultaneously (*Roses* in London, *Plantagenets* in Stratford), generating a situation that mimicked an earlier (1599–1608) War of the Theaters. In that each appealed to a particular set of spectatorly values, this was a quarrel over representation; on another level, it had to do with the ownership of what Pierre Bourdieu calls inherited "cultural capital."[107]

Of the two, Noble's *Plantagenets* clearly positions itself as a direct, and entirely legitimate, descendent of the Barton-Hall *Wars*: indeed, Bob Crowley's bare, steel-grid stage floor, its choice of period costume, and its recurrent use of emblematic properties signify its specific homage to the earlier production. The adaptation (credited in the program as "adapted from a version by Charles Wood," who brought to the project an expertise with recent dramatizations of war such as *Tumbledown, Veterans,* and *Dingo*) trimmed and rearranged Shakespeare's playtexts to produce a playing version based more securely on "Shakespeare-speaking" than was *Wars*—perhaps one inevitable result of Hands's "unadapted" *Henry VI*s.[108] More significantly, however, Noble's performance text, like Hands's, risks masking political analysis with aesthetics by representing history as a pictorial discourse, one that evokes the linear myth of historical movement and reifies the past as a fancy-dress pageant shot through with notable individual performances showcasing exemplary figures. In this, *Plantagenets* appropriates the nineteenth-century British (and French) tradition of "realizing" famous paintings on the stage, not by literally imitative realizations but by evoking the aura of that tradition.[109] Not only is Noble's project culturally specific in its references, as though reproduced for English eyes only, but it unquestioningly accepts Tillyard's essentialist view of fifteenth-century English history as organized by a rage for order that cleanses the kingdom to prepare a way for Tudor right. Only a few members of the interpretive community saw beyond this familiar, firmly entrenched reading of history-according-to-Shakespeare. Comparing Noble's version to the Barton-Hall *Wars* and to Bogdanov's *Roses*, Michael Coveney writes, "there is no intellectual patterning of the events"; in Michael Ratcliffe's view, "the disturbing resonances of history are not sounded. Appearances are seductive but not deceiving, and what you see is what there is."[110] Most, however, praised Noble's achievement as an exercise of pictorial imagination that generated "a sense of England itself singing the clear tunes of its history."[111]

By contrast, Bogdanov's enterprise calls such historical music as well as the staging traditions that support it sharply into question. Nicknamed "At Last—The 1399–1603 Show,"[112] Bogdanov's marathon project (a label that refers to performers' and spectators' abilities to survive seven plays over the course of one evening and two full days) appropriates Shakespeare's plays for the last two hundred years of British—and in some performance details, of Western—history, including references to colonialist discourse. In opposition to Noble's commemorative containment of English history as encoded in theatrical sign systems that can be tapped in order to achieve a kind of cultural preservation and renewal, Bogdanov views theater, through Brechtian lenses, as *making* history and locates Shakespeare's plays as initiating a dialectic with history, a process that his company, as their contemporary interpreters, attempts to continue.[113] Interviewed about his interest in providing recognizable contemporary references for the plays' social markings, Bogdanov commented, "Shakespeare himself was writing about events that took place almost 200 years before his own time and was as much concerned with modern relevance as archeological accuracy. . . . [And since] the plays deal with civil strife, conflict between Westminster and the provinces, north versus south, the Welsh culture fighting against destruction and a ruler going off to a foreign war to avoid difficulties at home . . . you don't exactly have to hunt to find parallels with today."[114] Although Bogdanov seems, here, to reproduce and extend Barton-Hall's emphases on "universal humanist" relevance and epic continuity, *Roses* clearly posits an alternative—as well as a challenge—to Barton-Hall's totalizing neo-providentialism, Hands's commitment to "Shakespearean simplicity," and Noble's pictorial photo-representationalism. In that his remaking of Shakespeare's playtexts threatens to abolish their ties to a specific historical moment, his project engages with the perceived threat that making Shakespeare our contemporary may erase the pastness of the past through dismantling its interpretation and the traditions of theatrical representation that sustain it.

Indeed, *Roses'* most significant stylistic features position Bogdanov's project firmly within the cultural dominant of postmodernism, what Fredric Jameson calls "the cultural logic of late capitalism." Depthlessness, a waning of historicity, and the random cannibalization of signs stored in global memory: these definitional facets of postmodernism, tied to the appetite for a world transformed into images of itself, into pseudo-events and pseudo-spectacles, construct a predominantly spatial logic that, by privileging a multiplicity of surfaces (from which original signifieds have been erased), denies temporality.[115] More specifically, *Roses'* status as postmodern Shakespeare is evident in Chris Dyer's set—a minimalist black box backed by an upstage grid panel and fitted with moving scaffolds and a descending bridge that invoke the age of mechanical reproduction; in eclectic costuming—loosely Elizabethan dress for Mistress Quickly, medieval armor, Victorian frock coats, Edwardian military tunics, camouflage fatigues, Teddy Boy gear, punk and motorcycle leathers; in properties—swords, shooting sticks, machine guns, bicycles and a jeep, document scrolls and personal computers; and in sound—regional accents, 1980s popular phrases and slogans, music ranging from William Byrd's *Mass for Five Voices* to "Silver Threads among the Gold" and an onstage jazz-blues combo. Such a collage of signs may seem to subsume the historical into "a glossy finish," giving the productions "the surface sheen of a period fashion reality,"[116] and thus to construct a pastiche of the stereotypical past and present that recuperates history as style. If, however, as Jameson argues, this language of the simulacrum constitutes a symptom of an inability to experience history in some active way, to fashion representations of current experience, Bogdanov's *Roses* appropriates that inability and reverses its ahistorical tendencies in order to point to (and privilege) contemporary historical change—a positive rather than negative relationship that, as Jameson writes, "restores proper tension to the notion of historical [and, I would add, social] difference."[117]

Like Barton-Hall's project, Bogdanov's *Roses* condenses *1 Henry VI* into the first half of a play entitled *Henry VI: House of Lancaster*, co-privileging ruler and family name.[118] Also like Barton-Hall, *Roses* privileges the war in France—as well as the Joan-Talbot opposition—and interweaves the issue of Henry's marriage with the narrative moves toward closure but delays its full dramatization, including Suffolk's provocative description of Margaret, so that her arrival is the center of the ceremonial occasion that opens the second half. What differs markedly, however, is that Bogdanov's performance text reprivileges the series of betrayals that result in the uneasy French peace treaty to foreground the way in which males—subjects as well as rulers—contain the threats of female power by expressing their own power through women.

Some more specific contradictions pertinent to this sense of ending arise from the Talbots' deaths, which take place in a downstage sand-bagged foxhole, amidst a son et lumiere battle that counterpoints searchlights and machine-gun fire with the strains of Byrd's *Mass*, playing, as a similar anthem does in Grigori Kozintsev's film of *King Lear* (1970), as a kind of divine chorale or providential voice: soldiers bring Young Talbot's body, laid out on a Union Jack, to his father, who dies in his son's arms. Taking the flag from the son's body, they cover Talbot's body and drag his son unceremoniously offstage just as the French arrive with Joan and as Lucy enters to claim the dead and speak Talbot's list of titles. These details of mise-en-scène, connecting Britain's late nineteenth-century colonial wars to more recent ones, call to mind—especially in Joan's undercutting phrase, "Here's a silly, stately style indeed!" (*1 Henry VI*, 4.7.72)—the notion of war as a gentleman's game, a notion dispelled by World War I, which wiped out one-third of Britain's male population.

The speaker here is, of course, both alien and other: a French, non-noble woman; Bogdanov exploits both categories by according dramatic as well as political power to the registers of such voices and silent presences as he reshapes the *1 Henry VI* materials. After Lucy's soldiers remove Talbot's body and the French exit, a peasant woman runs across the upstage area in terrified flight from several soldiers, who grab at her clothing, laughing and jeering; they finally catch her and seem about to rape her onstage but instead roughly force her off, one of them unbuttoning his trousers. It is this female figure, rather than Joan, whom Margaret replaces, and her ensuing encounter with Suffolk reprises just such a rape. Although she seems in control of, even amused at, his sonneteering terms, she is visibly startled when, as Reignier appears on the balcony, Suffolk draws his sword and lays it against her throat, threatening her until her father agrees to the match. Just after Suffolk announces, "But I will rule both her, the King, and realm," the raped woman, her clothes half torn away, stumbles onto the stage; exiting, Suffolk passes her without a second glance.

Strafing continues as Joan enters, effectively replacing both Margaret and the raped peasant woman: dressed in a man's shirt, knee britches, rough stockings, and boots, she kneels, spotlit, on the white-carpeted stage, asking her spirits for signs. Earlier—when she bested the Dauphin at swordplay and vanquished Talbot—Andean flute music suggested the spoken sign of that spiritual link; here the only sound is an occasional burst of gunfire punctuating the silence. As Joan crawls slowly forward, York appears with two bereted commandos: one carries a red gasoline can, the other an automobile tire. Although her father is absent, she speaks her genealogy as though insisting on her own history, curses York, and is finally captured in a huge net and led off, struggling. The peace that Winchester mandates between York and the French—positioned on opposite sides of the stage—is a makeshift affair in which an angry York barely conceals his contempt for the Cardinal as well as the French and says "For here we entertain a solemn peace" with considerable irony. And the performance text revoices—and reverses—that irony in its final counterpointing of sound and image. For rather than rewriting this end point, as Barton-Hall did, to presage York's rise and establish Warwick as kingmaker, *Roses* privileges what Shakespeare's playtext does not represent, foregrounds the silenced voices it represses, and so destabilizes closure.[119] In the final image, flames rise behind the upstage grid as Joan's silhouetted necklaced figure, her arms raised toward the sky, burns, evoking the incited violence of Elizabethan ritual burning as well as present-day events in Ireland and South Africa; now, the Andean flute music (taken from Peter Weir's *Picnic at Hanging Rock*, 1975), the reified sign of another disenfranchised voice, returns. Here, Bogdanov's *Roses* takes literally Edward Hall's comment that Henry's marriage with Margaret engendered "such a flame, that it never went out, till both the parties with many other were consumed and slain"[120] and represents it as the inextinguishable fire of oppressive imperialism. It is Joan (and, by association, all equally alien presences), not England, who burns in sacrificial embers. As a rhyme with the performance text's opening on Henry V's state funeral, where four red-jacketed military honor guardsmen stand at attention around a Union Jack–draped coffin topped with a spray of red roses, waiting for the figures of power to assemble, this final image privileges not those with automatic franchise but rather those whose voices are appropriated, silenced, or absorbed by power's self-reproducing dialogue.

In some respects, Noble's staging of the Joan material seems specifically indebted to Bogdanov, though both his narrative rearrangement and his representational choices differ. Absent from the English-French colloquy over the Talbots' dead bodies, which thus centers exclusively on male honor, Joan enters, picking her way among the common soldiers' corpses. As she implores aid from her spirits, they rise, one after another, to half-sitting positions and then lie down, as though forsaking her—a curious displacement of her supposed power, which links it to the ghosts of the dead English, not to "fiends" (or heavenly forces). Captured in a net, her hands painted with stigmata and her white shift with a red cross, she is bound to a ladder and raised high on an upstage scaffold (fig. 3). One soldier reaches under her shift to feel her sex while others, taunting and laughing, bring on faggots and lit torches; in response to Joan's claims of chastity and her curses, they lower the torches, and her spotlit figure "burns," surrounded by reddish smoke, while one soldier raises a cross fixed on a lance-end to her lips. Noble's staging positions Joan's execution as the literal and figurative backdrop for the diplomatic negotiations—Henry's marriage; the peace treaty—that mark the war's end. First, Henry VI and Gloucester walk downstage where, spotlit, Gloucester proposes the first, arranged marriage (5.1). Then, Winchester, holding a handkerchief over his nose to filter the smell of burning flesh, organizes the treaty, a matter summarily arranged over a stage-right table laid with wine flagons and plates of bread. As the principals exit, a figure in a dark grey hooded cloak enters up left, stops briefly to look up at Joan, and crosses swiftly to steal food and drink from the table. Following quickly, Suffolk strips away the blanketing cloak to reveal Margaret, her rich green dress an ironic fertile contrast to Joan's burning; the wooing, which culminates in Suffolk's embrace with Reignier, Margaret's father, positions her, like Joan, as a pawn of English empire. And the point is further emphasized when, after Suffolk voices his desire to rule the realm, English soldiers move forward to plant banners at the stage edge, as though claiming French territory, while upstage, a huge Cross of St. George descends to obscure Joan's figure (painted with its own crude version of that cross), still on the scaffold. English might and myth erase all signs of the dangerous female presence, first by demonizing her as a spectacle that shapes the war's conclusion, then by masking that sight with a seal of Christian approval.

Summarizing his review of Noble's cycle, Irving Wardle writes that it "is on surest ground as the family tragedy of three grieving women,"[121] a phrase that best describes Noble's *Richard III* but which also points to how both *Plantagenets* and *Roses* recuperate women's history, not by rewriting Shakespeare to include their voices but by recording their oppression and manipulation within male power structures—representational strategies that call attention to their silent or silenced presences and, beyond that, to *aporia* within Shakespeare's plays. By appropriating Joan's history for representation, both performance texts engage with the not-said as well as the not-seen of *1 Henry VI*. Another instance of such appropriation, the close of Noble's *Henry VI* and Bogdanov's *Henry VI: House of Lancaster*, offers evidence of a different mode of recuperation, one that privileges Margaret's experience equally with Henry's to shape an ending that counters, at a similar point, *Wars'* focus on Henry's guilty relationship to his surrogate father and its spoken echoes of providentialist design to re-make royal tragedy as domestic history. In both versions, Henry's banishment of Suffolk gives him control over Margaret (*2 Henry VI*, 3.2); yet both, by closing with signs of the Henry-Margaret-Suffolk triangle, also undermine that control and reveal its contradictions. In Noble's version, which omits Suffolk's death, Margaret enters just as a doctor draws a sheet over Winchester's face; she carries Suffolk's head, wrapped in bloody napkins, and murmurs "But where's the body that I should embrace?" (*2 Henry VI*, 4.4.6). Calmly, Henry crosses toward her, extending his hand—"Let us all to meditation"—and, as an offstage anthem begins, the lights fade very slowly on this incompleted gesture, tenuously linking the three together. In contrast, Bogdanov's staging makes that interrelation more brutally precise. After Winchester's death and Suffolk's assassination, dim lighting reveals Henry, in morning dress and reading a psalter, sitting hesitantly on the very edge of the throne, as though unable to inhabit it completely. Margaret, dressed in black, enters behind him, cradling Suffolk's head, wrapped in bloodied "swaddling clothes"; appearing not to see the astonished Henry, she wanders distractedly in front of him before exiting, her eyes fixed on her "child." As the lights slowly fade, Henry stares out wide-eyed, only half comprehending this vision of a childless kingdom, a dead heir, an aborted birth; in a clear soprano, an offstage voice sings Psalm 121, "I will lift up mine eyes unto the hills / From whence cometh my help." When the lights come up, Henry's throne is empty. Here, Hall's "fatal marriage" generates an image of deviant succession that turns the gender conflict expressed in the French war—and in Joan's necklacing—back on Henry, resituating those alien voices inside the royal family, privileging the singular isolation, and powerlessness, of the male ruler.

Although each rearranges the narrative sequence of Shakespeare's playtext somewhat differently, both Noble's *The Rise of Edward IV* and Bogdanov's *Henry VI: House of York* frame the ensuing battles for the crown between two scenes that dramatize a rebel's rise to power. And again, when compared to the Barton-Hall *Wars*, the choices signal different representational politics. Whereas Barton-Hall's version cobbles together a state council from *3 Henry VI*, 4.4, and invented dialogue presaging Margaret's alliance with the Cliffords to frame Jack Cade's rebellion within the rulers' voices, Noble's adaptation opens with the rebellion itself, and *House of York* with York's return from Ireland, staged as a brief dockside night scene where Warwick, not Buckingham, heads the welcoming committee. In both, repositioning the Cade material creates an implicit rhyme with the openings of the previous play and its successor, *Richard III*, each of which begins by calling a present ruler's position into question. And the opening moves of Bogdanov's *House of York* focus particular attention on the relations between rulers and ruled, between legitimate and bastard claimants: not only does Cade clearly function as York's surrogate but that relationship, and especially Cade's parodic genealogy (*2 Henry VI*, 4.2.35–69), gains an added charge through doubling the actor (Michael Pennington) who has played both Richard II and Mortimer as the charismatic, violent Cade. In Noble's as well as Bogdanov's performance texts, this initial brutality reaches a double climax, first in the stilled tableau of Henry's witness to the anonymous father and son mourning their dead (*3 Henry VI*, 2.5), and then, just before the interval break, as the York brothers taunt Young Clifford's corpse, propping it up like a dummy and pretending to ventriloquize his answers to their questions (*3 Henry VI*, 2.6). In Noble's staging of overkill, they stab the dead body, strike off the head, and play a mad game of catch, which concludes as Edward assigns his brothers dukedoms before they exit together, arms linked. Bogdanov's version, on the other hand, joins the three together in mocking Clifford but then turns Edward and Clarence against Richard: they laugh at his wish for another title, chant "Duke of Gloucester, Duke of Gloucester," knock him down, and play with him as with a football; at their exit, followed by a stumbling Richard, only Young Clifford's body occupies the stage.

The finales of both *The Rise of Edward IV* and *House of York* transform this dead threat to a living one, turning rebellion outside the reigning family to rebellion inside the newly reconstituted state—again, as at the end of both previous plays, closing on an isolated figure. In each, however, mise-en-scène functions not only, on the most obvious level, to differentiate Noble's emblematic staging from Bogdanov's collision of dislocated signs but, on another level, to refocus the interpretive debate over competing representations of history—more specifically, between Bogdanov's choices for juxtaposing assassination and family ritual, reminiscent of Francis Ford Coppola's *The Godfather* and *The Godfather, Part 2* (1972; 1974), and Noble's highly symbolic, providentially evocative representational means. In *Roses*, the penultimate scene opens with Henry VI in a white penitential gown, reading from a psalter, its text again heard over the sound system: "I will lift up mine eyes unto the hills." Dressed in camouflage battle gear, Richard enters to sit beside him on the cot; then, moving to a chair, he draws a switchblade and, keeping his eyes on the knife, plays with it while Henry talks. Very deliberately, Henry puts down his psalter before cursing Richard; as he mentions Richard's deformity, Gloucester slowly raises his eyes to look at the King, whose nearly bald head and almost skeletal features closely mirror his own (fig. 4). Then the brother who claims no brother—but who seems to face his double—strikes. As Henry falls back on the cot, Richard leaps astride him to stab once more; in a final humiliating gesture, he empties the latrine pail over the dead King's body.

In the blackout that follows, Henry's psalm recurs, this time cut off after its initial phrase, as though to mark, at Henry's death, the loss of providentialism, made available in Bogdanov's performance text as only one sign among many in its representational economy. Then the stage slowly fills as the Yorkists celebrate Tewkesbury's victory and the killing of a Lancastrian ruler (and heir) with a christening cocktail party: a jazz combo gathers around an upstage white piano; waiters pass drinks to white-flanneled male guests and ladies in delicate afternoon lawns; a nursemaid wheels on a large pram. Edward picks up his son and, to his heir, says "Once more we sit in England's royal throne"; while a photographer takes an official picture of the royal family, Richard inserts himself between Edward and Elizabeth and, as he kisses the child, the flash goes off again, capturing his manic grin and recalling Edward's wooing of Elizabeth (a similarly festive occasion, which opened the second half), where he had eavesdropped on their conversation (fig. 5). The nursemaid takes the baby off in the pram; Edward calls for "lasting joy" and dances with his Queen. While the others raise their glasses in a toast and lighting dapples the upstage area with the circling patterns reminiscent of long-ago ballrooms, Richard detaches himself from the group, and, wineglass in hand, limps swiftly downstage: gesturing toward the dancers, he speaks the first two lines of *Richard III*'s opening soliloquy, "Now is the winter of our discontent / Made glorious summer by this son of York.'

In contrast to *House of Lancaster*, where both interval break and close privilege gender oppositions, *House of York*'s structural rhymes locate future conflict exclusively in terms of male oppositions, setting it within a comic matrix. Taunted by his brothers at Towton's ceremonial mockery of dead and living bodies, Richard now mocks the others at the close—first with his overly sincere kiss and camera-conscious grin, and then by teasing offstage spectators with the initial lines of his most famous soliloquy. This particular spectacle, and Richard's position within it, simultaneously satisfies and destabilizes *House of York*'s close, exploiting and extending the features of *3 Henry VI*'s ending to advertise the next reign: much like Falstaff, who in an earlier part of *Roses* delivers his speech on sherris-sack (*2 Henry IV*, 4.3.83–119) as a television commercial, Richard becomes a hawker selling his own play to a captive audience. But another, more disturbing rhyme links *House of Lancaster* with *House of York*, inviting connections among Margaret cradling Suffolk's head, Edward holding his son and heir, and Richard, who, like Suffolk, is both would-be successor and monstrously deformed birth. Finally, Bogdanov's double close faces both past and future narrative, valorizing *Henry VI* as a two-part family play, a sixteenth-century *Dynasty*[122] that regenerates a model of linear succession and anticipates its future perversions.

Whereas Bogdanov's sense of ending is expansive, including retrospective as well as predictive connections that position closure as one point in a fluid historical process, Noble's representational strategies focus exclusively on localized effects to organize the events of *Edward IV*'s final scenes as a kind of anticipatory summary. Perhaps the most striking single difference between Bogdanov's and Noble's stagings involves the emphasis each places on actors' bodies; while Bogdanov depends primarily on reading bodies (or body parts) as registers of social and theatrical meaning, Noble privileges symbolic properties as references that not only frame actors' presences but also condense social meanings into an emblematic shorthand. Characteristic of his style is the use of upstage banners or drapes, which function much like a cinematic wipe to cut from one scene or locale to another, further coding its significance. To frame Henry VI's murder, a bloodstained white backcloth descends from the flies, masking the upstage blacks for Tewkesbury's battle. Simultaneously, the production's central machinelike organism—a high-backed golden throne mounted atop, and seemingly contiguous with, a prisonlike cage—ascends from the trap with Henry seated inside the cage; when Richard stabs the King, blood stains his gown with a red cross, linking him to Joan as well as to England's emblem, the Cross of St. George. Then, pushing Henry's body aside, Richard replaces him within the cage; his own body casts a towering shadow on the backcloth, now further painted by "the aspiring blood of Lancaster," situating him as imprisoned and victimized by his coming reign of terror. At his exit, a giant saw-edged golden sun descends, almost covering the bloody cloth, and the cage descends, leaving the throne at center stage. In pale golden twilight, the women welcome their husbands home from the wars; dropping bedrolls, packs, and armor, the men embrace their wives as Queen Elizabeth runs onstage and vaults into Edward's arms, followed by a nursemaid carrying her son. At this joyful reunion, Richard alone has no partner, but as Elizabeth and Edward share a passionate centerstage kiss, his figure, framed in a spotlight, rises from a half-kneeling position on the steps of the throne and faces the audience: his eyes widened in a fixed stare, he shouts "Now!" And the final light cue, a quick blackout, leaves the afterimage of his face, accompanied by the echoing vowel, as the ultimate signs in a cumulative series of visual replacements. The great golden sun of Edward's "sun drenched sensualist court"[123] masks the violence of Henry VI's murder as well as all the bloodshed and battles of the wars, both, in turn, giving way to another son, represented first as shadow, and then, in the brief after-close, taking on a player's insubstantial substance.

Here, as in Bogdanov's *House of York*, closure promotes the next theatrical event—which, for each project, caps the cycle. But although both performance texts make other, similar formal choices, each "speaks Shakespeare" through different representational politics, a distinction almost invariably noted by their initial interpretive communities. In the case of *Roses*, reviewers consistently mention the eclectic, cross-historical spectacle, often (especially in America, Canada, Australia, Hong Kong, and Tokyo) praising its liberating inventiveness and accessibility but, more often (especially in Britain), mourning the erasure of historical particularity—the representation of a "world poised between medievalism and modernity"[124] which seemed lost in a series of "populist productions" shot through with signs of "accessible" political and ideological currency. For *Plantagenets*, it was precisely the representation of a pictorial feudal past— what Michael Billington called a "seamless alliance between visual metaphor and verbal expression"[125]—that prompted comments such as John Peter's "the Royal Shakespeare Company has once again shaken hands with greatness."[126] Here, a kind of inherited "cultural capital" seems to invest a particular mode of theatrical representation with the power to retell "Shakespeare-history." Yet, as Bourdieu observes, "the 'eye' is a product of history reproduced by education."[127] In distinguishing between these productions, such an "educated" vision also involves situating one (Noble's) implicitly within the protective provinces of high culture and relegating the other (Bogdanov's) to a slightly lower status. Since theater is not cheap in latter-day capitalism, more than one critic feared that those who would most enjoy Bogdanov's postmodernist collage of supposed "relevance"—presumably the young, but, implicitly, nonelite spectators—could not afford the high ticket prices, either for individual plays or for the marathon project. In reviews of *Plantagenets*, however, no critic even mentioned this issue, pointing, perhaps, to the assumption that this theatrical commodity was aimed at a particular audience for whom economic considerations (and the class distinctions they reassert) disappear, subsumed within visions of "Shakespeare's" larger cultural authority. Such a move not only eliminates critique from a sphere of potential sociopolitical engagement but enables the critical community to locate "Shakespeare speaking" within an aesthetic realm, a strategy that assumes that "pure" or "classic" theatre does not constitute a political arena.

Still other circumstances operating here make intriguing tangential connections to Elizabethan history, for, in very different ways, Bogdanov's and Noble's historical projects participate in fashions of Elizabethanism. On the one hand, *Plantagenets*, with its "realized" reification of past theatrical traditions, is a specifically English commodity that reflects the insular, anxious xenophobia that characterized the later years of Elizabeth's reign. On the other, Bogdanov's representational strategies reach beyond such a circumscribed repository of cultural signs to tie into an international media discourse that brings the outside world back into England. By disrupting the traditional formulas for reproducing English history, it not only represents a very different history to the world but opens up that history to critique. And what gives that process an added ideological charge is that the English Shakespeare Company's major source of cultural (though not exclusively of financial) capital comes from outside the British Isles, where critical response, as Stewart McGill writes, "has been varied and has lacked the serious and detailed responses shown abroad."[128] Set beside each other, the two historical-theatrical projects thus analogize the binary opposition between England and other nation-states inscribed in *1 Henry VI* and in the later *Henry V*. Finally, it would seem that, of the two, Bogdanov's *Roses* specifically engages with the politics of theater as, most likely, the Elizabethans knew them. For just as the social and material conditions of Shakespeare's theater blurred distinctions between high and low art, endowing the popular with a high seriousness that recuperated the historical past as the historical present and, through anachronism and topicality, worked to make chronology invisible, so too does the postmodernist representational mode of Bogdanov's performance texts work to extend Shakespeare's playtexts beyond both their originating circumstances and the bounds of their currently authoritative cultural ownership.

CHAPTER 4

"THE COMING ON OF TIME": *RICHARD III*

And in a stage play all the people know right well that
he that playeth the sowdaine is percase a sowter. Yet if
one should can so little good to show out of season
what acquaintance he hath with him and call him by
his own name while he standeth in his majesty, one of
his tormentors might hap to break his head, . . . for
marring of the play. And so they said that these matters
be king's games, as it were stage plays, and for the
more part played upon scaffolds, in which poor men be
but lookers-on. And they that wise be will meddle no
farther. For they that sometime step up and play with
them, when they cannot play their parts, they disorder
the play and do themselves no good.

—Sir Thomas More, *The History of King Richard III*

MORE'S ACCOUNT of Richard of Gloucester's carefully staged takeover of England's crown precisely analogizes the potentially subversive relationship between social text and theatrical representation
that Shakespeare's histories nourish and, in the case of *Richard III*,
exploit.[1] Although the spectacle More describes neither convinces nor
co-opts its witnesses, who remark, "men must sometime for the manner sake not be aknowen what they know," he nonetheless suggests
that the very particular dangers of such games or scaffold-plays do not
accrue to powerful kings but to powerless spectator-subjects. Even
though they may recognize the sultan as a shoemaker, exposing his
counterfeit puts onlookers at risk: addressing the staged representation
of majesty as a familiar not only mars the play but (implicitly) threatens to erase the distinction between kings and subjects. Moreover,
those who attempt to become actors in such a fiction, to assume parts
without knowing the rules of the game, both endanger the representation and jeopardize themselves. Wisdom and safety, cautions More, lie
in separation, nonintervention, and self-effacing silence. Characteristic
of both More's narrative persona and of his own relations with displays of state power, such policy protects the representation of majesty
as well as its subjects (himself included: the "more part"), enforcing a
boundary between two realms.[2]

More's theatrical metaphor seems at first to apply specifically only to the first of the two actions *Richard III* dramatizes—Richard's sinister comedy of accession, or "The Irresistible Rise of Richard Gloucester."[3] Since my interest lies primarily in reassessing the play's second action—acts 4 and 5, or what might be called "Richmond's Homecoming"—let me summarize the first with another emblem, one which, not unlike More's, condenses several features of Richard's immensely theatrical improvisations of power, improvisations that threaten, if not to change history, at least to expose its plot as his own narrative invention.

That emblem, Bill Alexander's staging of Richard's coronation for his 1984 Royal Shakespeare Company *Richard III*, takes place in a space that resembles York Minster or Worcester Cathedral.[4] Back and side walls of perpendicular gothic tracery frame four huge, elaborately detailed marble tombs positioned right and left upstage, and some spectators lounge on top of these while others (among them Richard's already dead brothers, Clarence and Edward IV, as well as Hastings) stand in ranks on the floor. Richard, for the first time without the black steel crutches that give him the silhouette of a "bottled spider," crawls to center stage: his ermine-trimmed scarlet robe, pulled down to reveal his naked hump, trails behind him like a dragon's tail. As he and Anne kneel, Clarence's two murderers step forward to hand crowns to the Archbishop, and Hastings's two whores follow, carrying the scepter and orb (fig. 6). Impatient, Richard rises convulsively to snatch both symbols of power and to meet the descending crown, settling it on his head, crowning himself. Then, like an enormous worm, he slowly crawls to a central sedan-chair throne, where his helmeted flunkeys raise chair and King aloft. To the final soaring accolades of a "Gloria" sung by all onstage, Richard raises his torso up toward the spotlight that frames his cocky, triumphant smile at the heavens, as though again commanding the "fair sun" to reflect his narcissistic shadow back to him. And then the lights go out.

Richard III, of course, excludes such ceremony. Rather, Shakespeare's narrative strategy represents Richard's accession with two substitute scenes: Buckingham's carefully staged claims for Richard, the scene to which More refers where Richard plays "the maid's part" and reluctantly accepts the crown (3.7), and the responses of the Duchess of York, Queen Elizabeth, and Anne to the news (4.1). Both further detail his manipulative inversions of blood relations. In the first, he prompts Buckingham to infer the illegitimacy of the dead Edward IV and his son in order to secure his own right to the crown through hereditary lineal descent, a move that not only erases two Kings but suggests his mother's adultery. The second scene, however, where his mother the Duchess of York, his wife Anne, and Edward's Queen, kept from visiting the Princes in the Tower, exclaim at their powerlessness in England's "slaughter-house," records the beginnings of a rebellion against Richard that condenses around the women's outrage, their fears and curses, and Richmond's name.

Alexander's coronation scene followed this latter scene and opened onto the interval,[5] privileging Richard's self-directed play-within-the-play with a full spectacle of comic closure that not only recapitulates past narrative but reproduces, within one space, a cluster of perverse signs representing the anxious fears that Richard has turned against others to ensure his triumph. The presence of the murderers recalls Clarence's death (1.4) and Richard's manic drive to replace the males in his family; Anne's presence, Richard's sexual violence in the wooing scene (1.2); and the presence of the whores, his misogyny toward all women but especially his use of them to infer his brother's "feminine" rule, Hastings's treason, and his own alleged bewitching by Mistress Shore (3.4). Moreover, their appearance, holding the symbols of power and standing beside the Archbishop, recalls—and inverts—the image of Richard framed between two Bishops when Buckingham summons him to accept the crown (3.7). This "official" quintet establishes the usurper's social text as one interwoven with violent carnivalesque inversions of kingship, positioning criminal and marginal elements close to the seat of power. Such a confrontation between the carnivalesque and the sacred succinctly defines Richard's mockery of both the ceremony and its cathedral-like space.[6] Not only does it rhyme with the performance text's opening, which reveals Richard, his eyes closed, basking in the steadily growing spotlight illuminating his grotesque form; it also complements the playtext's unique opening strategy—Richard's dazzling self-introduction, which represents him both as the subject of his own narrative and as the primary theatrical spectacle.[7] Here, as there, the spectacle surrounding Richard's coronation situates itself concurrently within Elizabethan and present-day cultural production, driven equally by images or simulacra.[8] Moreover, it points in two directions. Although it clearly empowers Richard, the spectacle simultaneously turns against itself, its parodic construction enslaving those on stage as well as (potentially) those in the audience.

To the extent that Alexander's invented scene seems imagined by Richard himself, it reads as an homage from the theater to its King of Vices, as though the performance text responds to his desires and accords them power. But although this ceremony flaunts Richard's transgressions, its placement just before the interval also works to contain his subversive energies. More significantly, however, by making a clean break between the two actions *Richard III* dramatizes, Alexander's strategy generates a structural rhyme between two opposed images of succession: Richard's subversive coronation display and Richmond's Bosworth victory, which ends the play by replacing the deviant usurper who comes from within the society with a savior-peacemaker who comes from outside it. Viewed in retrospect, and especially by readers of the 1623 Folio, a parallel exchange occurred with Elizabeth I's death and the accession of James I, replacing a monarch some viewed as illegitimate (by birth and by sex) with a legitimate (also by birth and, especially, by sex) successor.

In his 1603 speech to the Upper House of Parliament, James reassures his new subjects of the blessings his accession brings to England: peace, perpetuity, his commitments to the true, ancient Catholic and Apostolic faith and to the power of Parliament. Moreover, he analogizes the union between Scotland and England with that between Lancaster and York, the promised event that closes Shakespeare's play:

> And therefore the second great blessing that God hath with my Person sent unto you is Peace within, and that in a double form. First, by my descent lineally out of the loins of Henry the seventh, is reunited and confirmed in me the Union of the two Princely Roses of the two Houses of Lancaster and York, whereof that King of happy memory was the first Uniter, as he was also the first ground-layer of the other [outward] Peace. The lamentable and miserable events by the Civil and bloody dissension betwixt these two Houses was so great and so late, as it need not be renewed unto your memories: which, as it was first settled and united in him, so is it now reunited and confirmed in me, being justly and lineally descended, not only of that happy conjunction, but of both the Branches thereof many times before. But the Union of these two princely Houses, is nothing comparable to the Union of two ancient and famous Kingdoms, which is the other inward Peace annexed to my Person.[9]

By confirming the importance of the event so hopefully anticipated and praised by the chroniclers, James positions himself in relation to it through language that comes close to quoting Richmond's final speech.[10] And although each of the "blessings" he mentions continues Elizabeth's own policies, with the added advantage of perpetuity, he also sets the anxieties connected with "monstrous" female rule to rest. His emphasis on patrilineal descent names no Queens; indeed, he even subsumes Elizabeth York, Henry VII's wife, to one term in a "conjunction."[11] James's politic use of the Lancaster-York union as a touchstone of cultural propaganda opens both the myth and Shakespeare's speech, which celebrates it, to other appropriative retextualizings.

Just as James fashions the newly masculine text of his kingship in relation to a mythologized historical moment,[12] critical discourse on *Richard III*'s closing action fashions its text in relation to one of several interpretative strategies. Whereas some espouse a totalizing providentialism or, alternately, a deterministic mechanism of power, others take positions more closely akin to More's ironic re-textualizing of Richard III's history as an opaque rather than a transparent political phenomenon.[13] Each reading attempts to contain or account for Richard's potentially disruptive force, either by mythologizing history, and so insulating both Elizabethan and present-day history from the threat he represents, or by mobilizing those formal, thematic, and psychological features of the playtext that contest such mythologizing in order to affirm other cultural prerogatives. To confront *Richard III*'s representational politics, I want to read acts 4 and 5 through a series of tracking movements in order to explore several interrelated issues: the representation of women's history, the elliptic underrepresentation of Buckingham's rebellion, and the final, problematic doubling of Richard and Richmond. And since Quarto and Folio record somewhat different "histories," my reading also explores how substantive and selected minor variants in the texts describe alternative relations between gender and power.[14]

§

Not only does *Richard III* sharply divide Richard's rise from his fall; its last half divides once again, in what C. L. Barber and Richard P. Wheeler describe as "something like a geological fault."[15] The first action condenses around the Princes' murder: Richard's powerful ally, Buckingham, refuses to do the deed and rises against Richard, supported by Henry, Earl of Richmond (4.2; 4.3); and with the death of his wife Anne, Richard hopes to marry Edward IV's daughter Elizabeth in order to consolidate his power (4.5). Buckingham's capture and execution, then, preface the play's final action, where Richmond's forces meet Richard at Bosworth and Richmond accedes to the throne as Henry VII and, by marrying Edward IV's daughter, unites the houses of Lancaster and York (5.1–5.5). But although both halves interweave family with national politics, the play's narrative strategy also divides along gender lines. Whereas the concluding battle sequences focus almost exclusively on males, the initial action works to align both readers' and spectators' allegiances with those of Richard's victims—especially women. Contradictorily, however, this gender rebellion against Richard records women's voices but refigures their history: their primary function, so to speak, is to engender Richmond, to name a potential successor who will, eventually, cancel the entire "monstrous regiment" of female "misrule."[16] And this distinction between voicing and history traces through Quarto and Folio as well as *Richard III*'s recent performance texts.

Although Quarto and Folio versions of act 4's initial scene—where the Duchess of York, Queen Elizabeth, and Anne, together with Dorset, Elizabeth's son, meet on the way to the Tower to greet the young Edward V and hear from Stanley (Derby) that Richard is to be crowned instead—record similar responses to the news, variants influence not only who is present but how the scene closes. Quarto ends as the Duchess of York commands Dorset, Anne, and Elizabeth to go, respectively, to Richmond, Richard and sanctuary, relegating herself to a peaceful grave; urgently, York's matriarch dictates the division of the family, wishing "good fortune" for Dorset, "good angels" for Anne, and "good thoughts" for Elizabeth. Although Quarto provides no exit directions here (H$_4$^{r}; I$_1$^{v}), the Duchess's instructions suggest, not a general exit, but a series of single exits, thus calling attention to her desire to protect Dorset before turning to her daughters-in-law, the one led to a crown which promises death, the other widowed—and both powerless. The Duchess's final lines, with their conclusive rhyming couplet—"Eighty odd years of sorrow have I seen, / And each hour's joy wracked with a week of teen" (I$_1$^{v}; cf. Pelican, 4.1.95–96)—might then be spoken either to Elizabeth as she leaves or, more pointedly, to herself, on a suddenly emptied stage.

Whereas Quarto economically reveals how Richard's accession severs the family, making them forget the imprisoned Princes in their hasty concern for their own compromised safety, Folio remembers them.[17] Following the Duchess's final couplet, Folio's Elizabeth makes a sentimental, even pathetic, appeal to the Tower:

> Pity, you ancient stones, those tender babes,
> Whom envy hath immur'd within your walls,
> Rough cradle for such little pretty ones,
> Rude ragged nurse, old sullen playfellow,
> For tender princes: use my babies well;
> So foolish sorrows bid your stones farewell. *Exeunt*

> (TLN 2580–85; Pelican, 4.1.97–103)

Somewhat elliptically, her prayer transfers the Princes, so to speak, from the family to the state; by endowing the Tower with maternal attributes, Elizabeth brings her own loss into sharp focus. Moreover, Folio's "*Exeunt*" suggests that all remain onstage to share Elizabeth's apprehensive meditation on the absent "true" successors before exiting, probably according to the Duchess's earlier directions and, possibly, at contrasting rates of speed. Most significantly, however, Folio records, in addition to the women present in Quarto, the presence of Lady Margaret Plantagenet, Clarence's daughter (TLN 2474), a potential obstacle to Richard's lineal "right" he himself recognizes in the following scene by ordering Catesby to "Inquire me out some mean poor gentleman, / Whom I will marry straight to Clarence' daughter" (4.2.51–52). Although mute, her figure can, especially if she is left alone when the others exit, further sharpen these images of women's powerlessness and their protectiveness, not of female, but of male heirs.

In recent performance texts, Quarto's final emphasis on Richard's mother, the Duchess of York, gives way to playing variants of Folio that consistently include Elizabeth's prayer but only occasionally represent Lady Margaret's silent figure. Glen Byam Shaw's 1953 Shakespeare Memorial Theatre performance text, for example, not only cuts her but deletes the Duchess of York's last speech, so the scene's end economically opposes Elizabeth and Anne, widowed Queen and future Queen: Elizabeth takes Anne's hand as she addresses the Tower and then curtseys hesitantly to Richard's new Queen before parting from her in a general exit.[18] The 1963 John Barton–Peter Hall *Wars of the Roses*, however, substitutes Queen Elizabeth's daughter, Princess Elizabeth, for Lady Margaret and so anticipates the dynastic importance of Elizabeth I's grandmother. To further explain her function, *Wars* appends a newly written coda to Queen Elizabeth's prayer in which the Bishop of Ely asks Stanley to broach the issue of the Princess's marriage with Richmond to Queen Elizabeth, and Stanley promises "secret help."[19] *Wars*'s narrative reordering, which brings forward Shakespeare's hints of the shifting allegiances surrounding Richmond's accession, serves a mythic-historical verisimilitude that later productions reject. Although Terry Hands's 1970 and 1980 Royal Shakespeare Company performance texts include Princess Elizabeth *and* Lady Margaret Plantagenet, both serve only to amplify the image of women's community and to offer comfort.[20] In the 1980 version, for instance, the Princess takes Anne's hand as she describes how she "grew captive to his honey sweet words" (4.1.79), and Margaret strokes her forehead. Similarly, at the end-of-scene exit, Lady Margaret leaves with Anne and Stanley while the Princess consoles her mother, who exchanges glances with Dorset, her son, before leaving.

And it is Dorset, not one of the women, whose solitary, mute figure registers the family's division. Shaw's image of hierarchical courtesy; Barton's insistent historicity; Hands's emphasis on women's social gestures, and then on Dorset: each staging registers women's subservience within the gender economy. Finally, Alexander's 1984 version, which eliminates Lady Margaret and the invented Princess Elizabeth, turns Queen Elizabeth into a subjected spectator much like More's "lookers-on."[21] Here, she leans against the brick proscenium wall, framed in a follow-spot, and speaks (literally) to "the Tower's" stones; then, after the others exit, she remains, witness to Richard's invented coronation procession.

Alexander's *Richard III* is unusual not only because of its aptly transgressive ceremony but because its interval point interrupts the structural illusion—generated by other recent stagings as well as by Quarto, Folio, and readers' texts—that Richard's only appearance "in pomp, crowned" (4.2) is framed by scenes that implicate and then empower women to act against him. If the first of these figures their lack of power, the second—in which the three Queens speak a ritualized litany of their woes, the Duchess of York curses Richard, and Richard seeks to marry Princess Elizabeth—gives them a generative role, so to speak, in closure. Although it would push the point to claim that setting this frame around Richard forms a womb which unmothers him to remother England, this rather precisely describes what happens. The process, however, is not without contradictions, especially in terms of Queen Margaret, a Senecan ghost of her former self transformed and regendered into a living embodiment of providential revenge. As in *3 Henry VI*, she shares with Richard a deep likeness, what Barber and Wheeler call a symbiotic relationship.[22] Just as Richard plays Prologue to the entire action, so is Margaret the presenter of its closing sequences, exchanging his "glorious summer" for "the rotten mouth of death" (1.1.2; 4.4.2). On yet another level of theatrical convention, her unhistorical presence parallels that of the Bastard in *King John*:[23] like him, she represents a vehicle through which ideology refunctions to validate a legitimate successor. Curiously, however, Margaret and the other matriarchal figures mount a challenge to Richard that follows his own deviant patriarchal strategies—his attempt to replace other men in either political or sexual roles and to use women as well as men only as currency in his "king's game."

Like Richard, who "do[es] the wrong, and first begin[s] to brawl" (1.3.324), Margaret initiates what turns into a concerted attack against Richard.[24] It is she who, like Richard, blames his mother's womb for "this carnal cur / [who] Preys on the issue of his mother's

body" (4.4.56–57); she who echoes Richard's sexual obsession in calling Hastings, Rivers, Vaughan, and Grey "adulterate"; she who, after
the three mothers catalogue their dead, calls attention to their powerlessness and lists inversions that make Richard's latent transgressions
manifest and turn Elizabeth into "nothing." First analogizing Elizabeth to a player-queen in a "direful pageant," Margaret then positions
her in relation to husbands, brothers, and sons and transforms each
title in turn: wife to widow; mother to one "who wails the name";
"one sued to" to an abject suitor; queen to "caitiff"; one who commands to one "obey'd of none"—a usurper, "York's wife," "queen of
sad mischance." And her advice—"bettering thy loss makes the bad-
causer worse"—relies on precisely the principles of exaggeration that
shape Richard's family and state politics. Like Richard, who displaces
his own deviance onto others, Margaret transfers her burden of sorrow
and wrongs to Elizabeth; momentarily, that exchange joins three generations of Queens to turn Richard's defective birth against him, exposing the obverse side of mother-son relations to punish a "bad son"
and exploit the fear and hatred Richard has engendered on both sides
of the gender economy. As it turns out, this final appearance of "monstrous regiment" shows "misrule" as simultaneously derivative of the
patriarchy and constructed outside it. And if here it is mothers who
"top" Richard, they do so through Margaret's refunctioned figure, as
the Ghost of Revenge; through an exclusively matriarchal relation not
to nature but to the supernatural, expressed most forcibly in the Duchess of York's curse on her son, a rejection that Richard immediately
attempts to reverse.[25] Seeking to marry her daughter, Richard addresses Queen Elizabeth with increasing intimacy as "dear mother"
and "good mother." In perhaps his most perverse use of women as a
medium of exchange, he attempts to undo Margaret's declension of
Elizabeth's titles and, by empowering her as Queen Mother, to remother himself.

The Elizabeth-Richard exchange not only constitutes the first of the
play's two dynastic battles but also records a confrontation between
pre-Tudor and Elizabethan inscriptions of gendered power. And in
Richard III, exclusion defines the shape of what is included: though
symbolically central to history's social text, two other Elizabeths—the
Princess who will become, not Richard's, but Richmond's Queen, and
her granddaughter, England's ruling sovereign—are absent from the
play.[26] That several contemporary Richard III–plays do include the
Princess contextualizes Shakespeare's more radically ambiguous representational strategy. Thomas Legge's Latin *Richardus Tertius*
(1579), for instance, contains not one but two wooing scenes. In the

first, Lovell approaches Queen Elizabeth to sue for her daughter's hand and receives her consent; in the second, where Richard woos the Princess, she accuses him of murder, incest, and adultery and says she prefers "to die a maid rather than to live unchaste with a tyrant as my husband, and to be abhorred by gods and men." Calling her a "stupid girl," Richard "postpone[s] this business [to] reflect on state-affairs," and the play, perhaps in deference to the reigning Elizabeth's anxious distaste at being pressed to marry, drops the issue and resolves its action solely in terms of male-centered combat.[27] This double representation effectively insulates Princess Elizabeth from her mother's "mutable mind," imagines her independent agency, and allies her, though somewhat problematically, with Elizabeth I's maiden status. In contrast, although the anonymous *True Tragedy* (1594) has no wooing scene, it punctuates Bosworth's preliminaries with anticipatory signs that favor Richmond. At his arrest, Buckingham mentions the probable match with Elizabeth; a scene later, Richard knows of it and Lovell reports Elizabeth's consent to Richard's suit. And in the following scene, Landoys, one of Richmond's men, hopes that the Queen Mother "do but keep her word . . . / Touching [Richmond's] marriage with Elizabeth" so that he can live to see York united with Lancaster. Some forty lines later, a messenger brings Richmond the Queen's greetings, and, following Richmond's victory, the Queen and Elizabeth appear on the battlefield to join in proclaiming Richmond King, after which he asks for, and receives, the consent of both the Princess and her mother to the marriage.[28]

Although the relation between Shakespeare's *Richard III* and these two plays remains uncertain, all agree on Queen Elizabeth's ambivalence concerning the marriage, an attitude grounded in chronicle sources. Hall represents an Elizabeth who is self-serving and opportunistic, conspiring with intermediaries—Richmond's physician Dr. Lewes and Stanley's wife, Margaret Beaufort—to link *either* of her surviving heirs to Richmond. Indeed, she makes an "open oath," not to Richmond but to his mother, promising the assistance of "all the friends and factors of King Edward her husband [provided that Richmond] would take a corporal oath after the kingdom obtained to espouse and take to wife the lady Elizabeth her daughter, or else lady Cecily, if the eldest daughter were not then living."[29] Then, following Buckingham's execution and delays in Richmond's campaign, Elizabeth, persuaded by Richard's messengers of "promotions innumerable and benefits . . . , promised to submit and yield herself fully and frankly to [Richard's] will and pleasure." Hall roundly condemns Queen Elizabeth as one "blinded by avaricious affection and seduced by flattering words" and links her to all women, inconstant "by the very bond of nature."³⁰

The misogynistic image of female inconstancy, especially as it figured indecisiveness, also attached to the reigning Elizabeth I, who frustrated her ministers by delaying and wavering over important state matters, among them, of course, her own marriage.³¹ Even though little in the Elizabeth-Richard situation evokes, or even approximates, the sovereign's, particularly in the 1590s, when dynastic marriage was no longer an issue, it does concern her generative history. As though to protect that history from Richard's own—even, one might say, to protect the name of Elizabeth—*Richard III* displaces those attributes the chronicler ascribes to the Queen onto Richard. He, not she, voices what Hall describes as her desire to regain power for herself and her surviving heirs; similarly, it is Elizabeth, not Richard, who harps on his "foolish fantasy to Lady Elizabeth his niece" and who brings up Anne's "quick conveyance," the issue of incest, and Richard's fear of barrenness.³² And throughout the scene, the Queen consistently mocks and ironizes Richard's appeals and oaths, using verbal strategies that are "not Elizabeth" but have previously characterized Richard's own speech. Until her final words—"Write to me very shortly / And you shall understand from me her mind"—she gives no sign of being what Richard calls her: "Relenting fool, and shallow, changing woman" (4.4.428–29, 431). Like her living namesake, Elizabeth must be sued to: Richard will write to *her*, not she to him. And by delaying mention of Elizabeth's negotiations with Richmond until after this scene, Shakespeare's narrative strategy refigures Hall's "inconstancy" to favor, and further validate, Richmond and the York-Lancaster union.

These gender inversions of voicing and power prevent the Queen Mother and her absent daughter from becoming abject victims of Richard's violently erotic fantasy of spontaneous generation, as expressed in his final vow to bury Elizabeth's dead children in her daughter's womb "where, in that nest of spicery, they will breed / Selves of themselves, to your recomfiture" (4.4.423–24).³³ Further, yet another voicing points more specifically to "the coming on of time" by alluding to Princess Elizabeth's history. But only in Folio. The second of two major substantive variants³⁴—comprising an initial exchange between Elizabeth and Richard, a long (46 lines) speech by Richard, and Elizabeth's biting response (TLN 3073–3128; cf. Pelican, 4.4.288–342)— its fifty-five lines travel beyond what Lady Macbeth calls "the ignorant present" to describe "the future in the instant," absorbing it into the play's historical present.³⁵ As though reacting to Elizabeth's claim that the only way to win her daughter is "not be Richard, that hath

done all this" (4.4.287), Richard details a series of restorative, generative reversals—from usurping her sons' kingdom to empowering her
daughter as queen; from killing to begetting; from vexation to comfort—that are precisely "not Richard" (TLN 3073–3127). Reminiscent of Queen Margaret's earlier "undoing" of Elizabeth's titles, these
reparative promises not only accurately describe the course of future
history, on which the Elizabethan present depends, but also, by positioning Elizabeth at the generative center of the kingdom, elusively
analogize Elizabeth I's own self-characterization as England's "natural
mother."³⁶ Among the inversions this scene attributes to Richard, his
voicing of Richmond's future as his own constitutes the play's most
transgressive strategy, its most radical ideological move. For what that
voicing invites—reading Richmond and Richard as doubles—not only
points forward to Bosworth and to hearing Richmond's epiloguelike
prayer of union through the time warp of this particular scene, but to
repositioning Richard not as the narrative agent of his own history but
as the object of historical narrative.

If my reading mobilizes only selected features of the Elizabeth-
Richard scene, a similar selectiveness marks theatrical practice, which
further refashions the reader's text assembled from Quarto and Folio
to a playing variant that resembles neither one nor the other. Except
for Shaw's 1953 staging, which cuts the entire scene, recent performance texts—the Barton-Hall 1963 *Wars*, Terry Hands's 1970 and
1980 versions, and Alexander's 1984 production—consistently include it, together with some portion of the long Folio variant. Among
these, *Wars* is unique in reducing 257 lines in the assembled text to 90
and using only 19 lines of Folio's "back to the future" variant.³⁷ In
conjunction with representing Princess Elizabeth in an earlier scene,
Wars' reshaping calls attention to her structuring absence much more
insistently than either Shakespeare's play or its later theatrical versions, intensifying her function as a dynastic pawn.³⁸ Although *Wars*,
like *Richard III*, locates Queen Elizabeth's change of mind in a gap
between scenes, rearrangements and interpolations not only draw focus away from her "inconstancy" but further implicate Stanley in the
marriage negotiations. Speaking to Stanley following the wooing,
Richard refers to Elizabeth as his "new-betroth'd"; *Wars* then cuts
Shakespeare's next scene, a conversation between Stanley and Urswick
that alludes to the Elizabeth-Richmond match (4.5), and, two scenes
later, Stanley brings Richmond the Queen Mother's greetings and
promises him "If thou dost thrive, her daughter shall be thine."³⁹ As
Hall and Barton admit, their adaptation supports a particular interpretation of history, one which, though not at odds either with that ac-

cepted by the chronicler or (in all probability) with Elizabeth I's own reading of her ancestor's role in the famous reconciliation, invites a kind of history-book certainty that Shakespeare's play, in Quarto as well as Folio, avoids.

Stanley's brief conversation with Urswick concerning his defection to Richmond (4.5) has similar content in both Quarto and Folio: each records his fears for his son (held hostage by Richard), Urswick's reports of Richmond's growing strength, and Stanley's mention of Queen Elizabeth's consent to her daughter's marriage with Richmond; each concludes as Stanley gives Urswick a letter "to resolve [Richmond] of my mind" (L_2^v; TLN 3368; cf. Pelican, 4.5.20). But whereas Quarto's Stanley withholds news of the marriage until the scene's end, in Folio, it follows his earlier explanations of why he "holds off his present aid" (TLN 3349–57; cf. Pelican, 4.5.1–8), as though to prove his good offices to Richmond's supporter. And by embedding the marriage issue in the middle of the Stanley-Urswick dialogue, Folio echoes its similar placement in Richmond's final speech, where he, like Stanley, appropriates it to his own political advantage. Both texts, however, generate specific links between Elizabeth's compromised situation, with her daughters in Richard's custody, and Stanley's own: in continuing the rebellion against Richard initiated by the women, he becomes their surrogate. Most significantly, Stanley's appearance at this point signals the play's move away from female-centered threats to Richard and from concern for a daughter to that for a son, a "masculine" shift that further consolidates the corrective patriarchy of Richmond's rule.

In contrast to its concise representation of Stanley's crucial role in Richmond's victory,[40] *Richard III* almost entirely suppresses Buckingham's equally historical rebellion, recording only traces of its beginning (4.3.47–48) and ending (reports that his army has "dispersed and scattered" and that he is sought as a traitor [4.4.509–17]), and dramatizing only his execution. Again, Quarto and Folio record slightly different histories.[41] In Quarto (L_2^v), Ratcliffe, Richard's flunkey, accompanies him, suggesting a totalitarian exigency that recent performance texts have adopted: in *Wars*, Ratcliffe laughs at Buckingham's Ralegh-like wordplay on All Souls' Day (5.1.12–22; "The Passionate Man's Pilgrimage"); and in Hands's 1970 and 1980 stagings, Buckingham is tethered to him with long chains, which four soldiers pull at, bringing Buckingham to his knees before they drag him offstage.[42] In Folio, however, the Sheriff (TLN 3773), an officer of the crown, supervises the execution, giving it the status of Richard's last *legal* tyrannical act, a playing variant Alexander's performance text used, giving additional emphasis as well to Buckingham's exit with a horn solo which simultaneously announces Richmond's entrance and enforces the play's economical, progressive pattern of replacement—Stanley for Elizabeth; Buckingham for Stanley; Richmond for Buckingham.

The ending of Sir Thomas More's *History of Richard III* offers an intriguing representational parallel to the fictional close of Buckingham's life in Shakespeare's play. More breaks off at a point just beyond the murder of the Princes to describe a conversation between Buckingham and Bishop Morton, who is in Buckingham's custody, and his text concludes, somewhat abruptly, with a direct quotation in which Morton remarks to Buckingham that God might have "given [Richard] some of such other excellent virtues meet for the rule of a realm, as our Lord hath planted in the person of your grace."[43] Buckingham's position in Shakespeare's play doubly analogizes the position of More, speaking as Morton, in the *History*, for in representing this treasonous temptation in 1514, when another Buckingham stood next in line for Henry VIII's throne, More as writer parallels Morton as inciter in 1483. Although in one sense his account remains unfinished, closing with what Judith H. Anderson calls the "perception that an historical cycle of compromise and corruption is endless,"[44] More's *History* perfectly completes a circle that, by situating Buckingham's rebellion in relation to Richard's usurpation, opens ambiguously onto contemporary politics. If More as narrator escapes his own treason (and that of his boyhood mentor, Morton) by silence (something that did not protect him, in 1529, from losing his head), Shakespeare, in choosing to underrepresent Buckingham's threat, remains equally tacit. Just as Elizabeth and Stanley do not openly declare themselves to Richmond, *Richard III*, in suppressing Buckingham's rebellion, speaks no treason against a crowned monarch—even a usurping tyrant. Rather, the history of that rebellion collapses into a tightly symmetrical pattern of further substitutions and replacements that points away from naming the act of treason to focus instead on representing dynastic issues as a struggle that transforms More's single scaffold to a mythic, doubly tented field of play.

No other Shakespearean play so rigorously schematizes the claims of a royal successor, constructing its close as though to mask their absence. In *Richard III*, it is not proofs of dynastic legitimacy but design that endorses Richmond's kingship.[45] On the level of structure, the playtext introduces Richmond as Richard's double by echoing Richard's opening Prologue-soliloquy; on the level of language, Richmond precisely reverses Richard's promised villainy to become a restorative force who will "reap the harvest of perpetual peace / By this one bloody trial of sharp war" (5.2.1–16). What he describes—a country with Richard at its literal geographical center, its "summer fields and fruitful vines" spoiled by a natural, animal evil (5.2.8)—constitutes initial signs of a second enclosural process that fixes Richard in space, if not in time. And from this point forward, simultaneous staging of the battle preparations insistently pairs Richmond and Richard.[46] To engender difference out of this structural similarity, the playtext opposes Richmond's communal bonds with his attendant lords to Richard's peremptory commands to his followers.[47] And while Richmond's speech rhythms, carrying his thought out to the end of the verse line, detail his assured state of mind, Richard's halting, midline breaks emphasize his deteriorating sense of self: fearing shadows, he searches out traitors in his own camp (5.3.217, 222–23). Ultimately, these patterns replace a false king with a true, analogizing the order Richmond brings to the state by appropriating and assimilating rhetorical and visual spectacle as universal categories rather than as features connected only to Richard's self-display.

That appropriation is most apparent in the vision Richard and Richmond share, which enlarges and expands the features of Clarence's earlier dream (1.4) and its concern with final things—blood-guilt, betrayal, death, judgment, heaven, hell, and conscience—to condense historical certainty within a web of curses and blessings.[48] Even before Richmond unites the white rose with the red, the Ghosts of Lancastrians and Yorkists join together to condemn Richard's tyranny and offer prayers in support of Richmond's victory (5.3).[49] Here, *Richard III* conceives and spatializes history as a theatrical spectacle of opposition that decrees succession by providential fiat, substituting ritual for genealogy to demystify Richard through Richmond's vision (it is his prayer that summons the Ghosts) and further transform him from a figure who opposes, ignores, or denies history to one who is its contested subject. As he starts out of his dream, Richard acknowledges that subjectification and almost precisely inverts his earlier self-engendering soliloquies, which exploited his defects (and especially his defective birth) in order to fashion a cocky, integrated self.[50] Naming himself murderer and nonmurderer, revenger and not-revenger, lover and hater of self, villain and not-villain, he deconstructs that persona, exposing its contradictory, self-cancelling terms. By contrast, as Richmond wakes, the playtext represents him less as a fully drawn character than an ideological function, especially insofar as his battle oration, the first of the two, shapes supernatural will into a series of naturalizing sanctions to demonize Richard as "a bloody tyrant and a homicide . . . God's enemy," and promises to restore the cultural order he has disrupted (5.3.247, 253).[51] To the extent that those promises "in the name of God and all these rights" (5.3.264) raise eerie echoes of Richard's earlier claims to protect Elizabeth's children and England's future, replacing a false tyrant with a true king simply exchanges one fiction for another, each marked by the same rhetorical mask. Contradictorily, the figuring that deconstructs Richard and mythologizes Richmond continues to hint at their similarity. Although Richard's own battle oration seems suspect in displacing the threats he represents onto his adversary, even labelling Richmond "a paltry fellow / Long kept in [Bretagne] at our mother's cost" (5.3.324–25) (the final sign of Richard's own matriarchal perversion),[52] Richmond dresses others in his armor, a curious trace of Richard's own dissembling through which the two share a theatrical identity, a counterfeit kingship.

The stage directions for *Richard III*'s two final actions condense the doubling and replacement that patterns the preceding rhetorical and spectacular display:

> *Alarum. Enter King Richard and Richmond, they fight,*
> *Richard is slain.*
> *Retreat, and Flourish. Enter Richmond, Derby*
> *bearing the Crown, with diverse other Lords.*

Although both Quarto (implicitly) and Folio (explicitly) direct Richmond's exit as well as his reentry with Stanley, Folio (TLN 3841–44, reproduced above) more clearly generates a moment where only Richard's body is onstage.[53] Not only does this invite a rhyme with the play's opening, where Richard appears alone, but Folio's white space also insists on separating Richard's death from Richmond's accession and so attempts to erase the play's insistent doubling of the two by isolating the token transfer of the crown. Almost without exception, performance texts tend to further expand these rather spare directions into a major opportunity for a final, spectacular mortal combat.

Hazlitt's description of Kean's 1814 performance in Colley Cibber's adaptation has become legendary: "He fought like one drunk with wounds: and the attitude in which he stands with his hands stretched out, after his sword is arrested from him, had a preternatural and terrific grandeur, as if his will could not be disarmed, and the very phantoms of his despair had a withering power."[54] Obsessed by the physical detail of Richard's death in Kean's performance, Hazlitt admires Richard's aspiring spirit, intellectual activity, and warlike valor and so reclaims him, at death, as the hero of his own tragedy.[55] Even the final speech Cibber creates for his Richmond in the immensely popular version performed throughout the nineteenth century praises, even as it moralizes, his fame. Cibber's Richmond bids Richard farewell and warns future kings against tyranny, but he also suggests that had Richard's "aspiring Soul but stir'd in Vertue / With half the Spirit it has dar'd in Evil," his fame might have "grac'd our English Annals."[56] To see—and applaud—Richard's moral potential and physical vitality at his death, as portrayed by a great actor, opens up a contradiction between history and theatricality that Shakespeare's play consistently exploits and, at least to some extent, overcomes. Two benchmarks of twentieth-century performance history, occurring ten years apart, suggest that the Cibber-Kean tradition of Richard's heroic defiance hovers slightly upstage of Shakespeare's original representational politics. One continues that legendary tradition; the other reappropriates *Richard III* for a different idea of history.

Acknowledging its debt to Garrick, Cibber, and others in the opening credits, Lawrence Olivier's 1955 film of *Richard III* follows its ancestors faithfully yet celebrates not just Richard's death but also the transcendent ideal of Richmond's succession.[57] For Bosworth's battle, the film, like Olivier's 1944 *Henry V* at Agincourt's battle, breaks free of its studio sets to represent a "real" England. After his horse is shot from under him, the camera follows Richard in several swift hand-to-hand combats. Then a long pan reveals him surrounded by soldiers, and the film cuts to a close-up of Richard's bloodied face before the camera dollies out as the sound track registers only his amplified heartbeat. At the last, he fights with Stanley, not Richmond, and it is finally "England," represented by the entire army, who moves in to tear at his body like animals and kill him. In a climactic high-angle shot, they all draw back in horror to frame Richard's convulsive death throes, his final "horizontal dance." Reminiscent of Kean's grandiose satanic hero, he half-rises, holding his sword aloft as though to protect himself from his own evil spirit; as he turns over and falls dead, the sound track falls silent. As it begins again, first a violin and then drums accompany Richard's processional exit. His body is thrown over a horse and lashed into place; a close-up on Richard's garter inscription (*Honi soi qui mal y pense*) then widens to pan across his body, and, in long shot, the horse is led over the hill past a solitary tree. As though in double homage to Hall's history, which describes how Richard's corpse was thrown naked over a horse, "despoiled to the skin,"[58] and to Richard's own last words—"A horse! a horse! my kingdom for a horse!" (5.4.13)—the image holds until Stanley walks into the shot, turns away from the sight, and walks toward the camera. Seeing a bush, he moves its leaves aside, and the film cuts to a high-angle close-up as the crown falls to the ground. Again in full shot, Stanley takes it up and turns toward the camera, smiling, and the shot dissolves first to a long shot of Richmond, standing on a background hill beside his tent, and then to Stanley, who raises the crown over his own head as the camera rises to frame it. In the film's final image, Stanley's arms dissolve out, leaving the disembodied crown suspended against the blue sky where, protected and isolated, it floats free of Richard, Richmond, and all potential (smiling) traitors.

Framing Richard's story between identical images, Olivier's film represents it as "an interwoven pattern of history and legend" in which the crown begins and ends all.[59] This final shift from realistic to symbolic representation neatly condenses the not altogether dissimilar transformation in Shakespeare's play from characterological to ideological fiction, a transfer that also juxtaposes two systems of legend: theater and history. But closing on the idea of the crown rather than the reality of the new King constitutes a pale, if golden, fairy-tale counterfeit to Olivier's appropriation of Richard's role. If Olivier's film text rewrites Shakespeare's own sense of ending, it also accurately identifies a major "geological fault" within that ending, a perceptual split of the King's Two Bodies into corporeal and ideological entities, one made all the more obvious by the contrast between Stanley Baker's removed, rather wooden Richmond and the attractive villainy and exaggerated demonics of Olivier's Richard. And if the major closural problem faced by any performance text of *Richard III* is to address this fracture, the major problem posed by the play also concerns actors' bodies. Just as Olivier reappropriated Garrick's and Kean's stage business to create his Richard, each actor playing the role attempts, as though aping Richard's own strategy of replacing other males in his family, to reclaim it from his theatrical forebears.

Sustained by the critical influence of F. R. Leavis and E.M.W. Tillyard, a very different reclamation was at work in Peter Hall's decision to perform *Richard III* in conjunction with the *Henry VI* plays in his reassembled 1963 trilogy, *The Wars of the Roses*.[60] In this context, *Richard III*'s final battle became not just a theatrical tour de force but the culmination of a cycle of medieval power politics. On the darkened, rusted metal stage, surrounded by swirling smoke, Richmond, armed only with a sword, fights a Richard completely encased in dark armor, wielding a spiked ball and chain as well as a sword. Blindly swinging his weapons, he resembles a trapped animal; caught by a sword-thrust through his metal visor, he finally dies, close to the audience, at the center of an empty stage. Although many reviewers clearly expected the familiar Richard, what J. C. Trewin called the "grandly theatrical double-demon,"[61] Bernard Levin, summarizing the trilogy, writes that the "last scene . . . sums up and sets the seal on all that has gone before. At the end, Richard, broken, mad and exhausted, a Hitler with only his visor for a bunker, summons up his last strength for the duel with Richmond. It is savage, primitive and horrible: so were the Wars of the Roses."[62] In the abbreviated ceremony that follows, soldiers carry off Richard's body before Richmond, accompanied by nobles, soldiers, and *citizens*, joins the standards of York and Lancaster, after which all kneel for an "Amen" and then rise quickly to exit. Alone, just as Richard was at the performance text's opening, where he stood apart from Edward IV's coronation, Richmond walks downstage to pick up Richard's fallen sword. As he lifts it, it rasps against the metal stage, drawing sparks; he pauses briefly, as though to speak, and then exits as the lights go down. Although this strategy insulates Richmond's accession from Richard's tainted body and so supports *Wars'* commitment to demonstrating the operations of Tillyard's Tudor Myth, Richmond's bleak, antiheroic stance certainly contradicts Tillyard's view of him as a divinely ordained savior. At its close, *Wars*, not unlike More's original history, faces two ways: onto the assurances of a critically endorsed, idealized past and onto modernist notions of a historical mechanism that subsumes individual agency in an endlessly recirculating "staircase of power."[63]

However conservatively biased in its analysis of power politics, *Wars* crossed past traditions of staging "Shakespeare's histories" with a loosely Brechtian aesthetic to reappropriate *Richard III* not just for an idea of history as a grand design but, by transforming such categories as historical accuracy and pageantry, for history-play-in-performance. Although later Royal Shakespeare Company "mainstream" stagings clearly reveal *Wars'* influence, each reworks the signifying possibilites of the close so that "history" dissolves away to be enfolded once again in "myth." Terry Hands's 1970 performance text,[64] for example, stages Bosworth's battle as the climax of a severely patterned masquerade dominated by a grandly psychopathic Richard, obsessed with his own deformity. In what Irving Wardle referred to as "a lurid poetic parable,"[65] Hands extended the implications of the Ghost scene—that Richard's past crimes and Richmond's alliance with supernatural forces defeat the tyrant—into a spectacular allegorical finale. As the Ghosts appear to Richard and Richmond, each remains onstage; finally, all join hands to form a circle around Richard, hoisting him into the air on the Ghost of Buckingham's final words, "Richard falls in height of all his pride" (5.3.177). Returning later to witness the battle, the Ghosts form a line upstage, and a stylized light show accompanies a slow-motion fight in which Richard finally drops his sword as the Ghosts, together with the figure of Death, move in to stab him; the final thrust comes from Death, who then faces front to speak a slightly rearranged and condensed version of Richmond's last speech.

Ten years later, Hands revised his earlier spectacle to make Richard less the victim of time's inevitable destiny and more the subject of a ritual exorcism.[66] In the final phases of Bosworth's battle, the Ghosts encircle Richard, strip him of his sword (Anne), his crutch (Clarence), his jacket (Henry VI), his shoe (Edward IV), and his left glove (Hastings). These gestures not only symbolically reenact Hall's description of how Richard's corpse was treated but attempt to erase all signs of his deformity in a violent carnivalesque scapegoating. Then, as the Ghosts hold him for Richmond to kill with a single gesture, Richard seems to fall on his own sword, and the Ghosts again circle his body in a slow dance before an oboe solo introduces Richmond's epilogue— a triumphant, but also ironic, counterpoint to the image of Richard killed by his own past crimes. On the one hand, fusing elements that Shakespeare's representational strategy keeps separate addresses the play's closural "fault lines" by acknowledging Richard's centrality and absorbing him within an overwhelmingly unified spectacle of revenge. On the other, that spectacle also exposes what Shakespeare's play both insists on and attempts to conceal: Richmond's double function as deus ex machina and Epilogue. Finally, both performance texts join director with playwright to develop a close that suits Richard's own dramatic exaggerations, deploying theatrical categories of ritual, spectacle, and convention to remystify his legendary story.

Far more economically, the close of Alexander's 1984 *Richard III* reads Richmond as Richard's moral opposite in a neomedieval salvation drama.[67] Richard, all in black save for his golden crown, struggles forward from the upstage center doors onto an empty, darkened stage, his figure silhouetted by backlighting. As he calls for his horse, Richmond, his golden armor shining in the murky gloom, appears behind him, draws his sword, and plunges it into Richard's hump. As Richard falls to his knees, he throws his arms wide in surprise, and lighting accentuates the position formed by the two figures to inscribe a huge shadowy cross on the stage (fig. 7). Richard remains on his knees, the sword protruding from his back, a scarecrow-mannequin figure, while the other nobles enter, take the crown from his head, and offer it to Richmond, who takes it but does not put it on. Simultaneously, Richard collapses, as if only the crown had held him erect. Now only an empty shell, his black shadow opposes Richmond's gleaming figure as the new King walks away from him, speaks briefly with the others, orders the captains' burial and the soldiers' pardon, and then addresses his remaining words to the audience. Compared to the carnivalesque inversions of Richard's coronation, which closed the first half, this severely limited spectacle of accession[68] attempts to counter such subversive, theatricalizing play with a conventional simplicity that confirms without question the dominant interpretation of the Lancaster-York union as a moment of "historical" apotheosis.

In that it incorporates, but also reimagines, features of all these productions, including Olivier's film, Adrian Noble's *Richard III, His Death*, the last play in his 1988 Royal Shakespeare Company trilogy, *The Plantagenets*, represents a composite performance text. Its title signals beyond all question that the most important event of Richard's life is its ending, and in advertising such significance (as Elizabethan Quarto titles often did), Noble not only invites spectators to read all else as prologue but suggests its unique dramatic as well as historical value. In Noble's staging, Richard gives his battle oration standing atop the central emblem of his reign, the prison-cage that in earlier scenes is revealed as contiguous with the throne: here, metal spikes protrude from his black battle helmet and shield, making him a grotesque sci-fi warrior, the "hedgehog" of Queen Margaret's description. He meets a silver-armored Richmond, first with swords and then with a boar spear, which Richmond picks up in an exchange of weapons, to impale Richard through his hump. As blood spurts out onto the white floor-cloth, an upstage scrim flies up, revealing all the Ghosts, their faces whitened and dressed in white bloodstained gowns. On the now brightly lit field, tainted by the tyrant's blood, Stanley retrieves the crown and gives it to Richmond, who stands downstage of Richard, transformed into the boar that was his emblem and with only the bloodied spear holding him in place, to sanction Tudor rule. On "Peace lives again," church bells ring out, music swells, and Richmond lifts the crown over his head, its title "free," its afterimage remaining after the blackout. As with Joan's ritual burning, where the Cross of St. George descended to replace her figure (*1 Henry VI*) and the shift from Henry VI's brutal murder to Edward IV's golden court (*The Rise of Edward IV*), one image masks another. Here, however, Noble's finale responds to Shakespeare's earlier simultaneous staging, sketching in the ironies of doubling and replacement with a single stroke to reveal, not hide, the costs of "true succession." Clustering signs of past, present, and future together in a symbolic tapestry, Noble's final theme park–like tableau fixes "history" within an emblematic discourse that, for late twentieth-century Britons as for Stratford's and London's tourist audiences, refigures and perpetuates a communal nostalgia that per-

mits the myth of royal transcendence full play. By encoding and trans-
mitting as many symbolic signs as possible, Noble's "history," not
unlike Shakespeare's, commemorates *Richard III*'s high moment of
cultural renewal by absorbing its contradictions into a neomedieval
icon with curiously postmodern resonances.[69]

Together with its recent theatrical ancestors, Noble's time-layered
vision of Richmond's apotheosis stands apart from the nineteenth- and
early twentieth-century tradition of "realizations," in which a "finale"
filled the stage with an entire, and entirely hierarchical, social world.[70]
It also differs, though less substantially, from the summary recorded
by the Spanish ambassador, Roderigo Consalez de Puebla, in his report
to King Ferdinand and Queen Isabella on the state of England in January 1500, nearly sixteen years after Richmond's accession:

> this kingdom is at present so situated as has not been seen for the last five
> hundred years till now, as those say who know best, and as appears by the
> chronicles; because there were always brambles and thorns of such a kind
> that the English had occasion not to remain peacefully in obedience to their
> king, there being divers heirs of the kingdom and of such a quality that the
> matter could be disputed between the two sides. Now it has pleased God
> that all should be thoroughly and duly purged and cleansed, so that not a
> doubtful drop of royal blood remains in this kingdom, except the true blood
> of the king and queen.[71]

In a rather solemn assessment, de Puebla accurately identifies the central dynastic issue: "the true blood of the king and queen." For Shakespeare as for the Spanish ambassador, little else matters: few contemporary plays so limit the close to such a confined relational model of
social legitimacy. In spite of Folio's "diverse other lords" (TLN 3844),
only Richmond and Stanley speak. And only within Richmond's closing speech do notions of communal prosperity, restored through the
new patriarchy, expand the image of dramatic order to its limits—and,
in a final contradictory, though not entirely eccentric, move, beyond it
to the social reality:

> as we have ta'en the sacrament,
> We will unite the white rose and the red.
> Smile heaven upon this fair conjunction,
> That long have frowned upon their enmity.
> What traitor hears me, and says not Amen?
> England hath long been mad and scarred herself;
> The brother blindly shed the brother's blood;
> The father rashly slaughtered his own son;

The son, compelled, been butcher to the sire.
All this divided York and Lancaster—
Divided in their dire division.
O, now let Richmond and Elizabeth,
The true succeeders of each royal House,
By God's fair ordinance conjoin together,
And let their heirs, God, if Thy will be so,
Enrich the time to come with smooth-fac'd peace,
With smiling plenty, and fair prosperous days!
Abate the edge of traitors, gracious Lord,
That would reduce these bloody days again,
And make poor England weep in streams of blood.
Let them not live to taste this land's increase,
That would with treason wound this fair land's peace.
Now civil wounds are stopp'd; peace lives again.
That she may long live here, God say Amen.

$$(5.5.18-41)^{72}$$

In Richmond's speech, Shakespeare's historical project appears most orthodox, most didactic, most committed to political and cultural synthesis. On the level of form, it submits perfectly to closure by collapsing recapitulatory statement, prayer, and moral epilogue into one discourse convention, exploiting their combined force to figure an apparently unified whole.[73] On the level of "history play," references to *3 Henry VI*'s emblematic scene (2.5) where Henry observes a father who has killed his son and a son who has killed his father, as well as explicit echoes of a terminal phrase that appears, with little variation, in all three plays—"Enrich the time to come with smooth-fac'd peace, / With smiling plenty, and fair prosperous days"—sustain and reinforce connections between *Richard III* and the *Henry VI* trilogy, endowing their "dramatic inconclusiveness" with satisfying coherence. And on the level of discourse, Richmond's obsessively mannerist rhetoric composes and recomposes the ideas of union, legitimacy, authority, peace, and prosperity into a charm of prevention that demonstrates how providential history *should* operate to displace the past with a community and integrity that can only be imaginary—what Hayden White calls "the odor of the ideal."[74] Yet even this flamboyantly coherent appeal recirculates traces of doubt and strain. Possible treason haunts Richmond—"What traitor hears me, and says not Amen?"—and no one, at least in Shakespeare's playtext, though *Wars* supplied such a response, speaks an answering "Amen." The most confrontational expression in an otherwise mediatory convention, the phrase stands curiously apart, a final sign of Stanley's "virtuous" treason to Richard prefacing Richmond's vows, which, like Richard's earlier promises (by "the time to come") to Queen Elizabeth, name her daughter as a "true succeeder."

But if Richmond's epilogue marks the limits of *Richard III*, completing and enclosing its narrative, it does not completely encompass the play's interpretation. At its very edge, *Richard III* opens up and then bridges a gap between time past and time present, between theatrical and social texts. Again, Richmond names treason, associates it with "bloody days," and seeks to render it powerless and erase it from the present. Ultimately, his final couplet transforms Richard's opening lines, "Now is the winter of our discontent / Made glorious summer by this son of York," into phrases that shift generative power from men to women, from "this son of York" to an ambiguous "she." And those last lines—"Now civil wounds are stopp'd; peace lives again. / That she may long live here, God say Amen"—also transform the fictional Queen Margaret's "misrule" into the peace associated with another Queen who resides beyond the fiction. Although the syntactic antecedent of "she" obviously refers to "peace," on another level that "she" alludes to Elizabeth I, the "true succeeder" who reigns over the present of *Richard III*'s first audiences. Bettering its ancestors, Legge's *Richardus Tertius* and the Anonymous *True Tragedy of Richard III*, which close with a genealogical review of Elizabeth's line, Shakespeare's play pays homage to a real Queen as an absent, though complicit, witness to closure.

Richard III's close valorizes two rulers, one within the play, one outside it, both equally participants in kingship conceived as theatrical spectacle. That this final prayer, the most secure ordering of religious and communal values and beliefs the play has imagined, should also critique the lack of those values in the world of its audience makes a most apt ending for a play whose central character has invoked such sanctions consistently and continuously only to mock them. As Richmond speaks for an imaginary synthesis of oppositions that only God can abate or abolish, he voices a particular interpretation of history that is not without contradictions—especially in the theater, when, as Richard rises to take a curtain call, spectators' applause acknowledges their complicity with his playing, if not with his ability to manipulate both rhetoric and history to his own advantage. One other disturbing trace of these contradictions lies in Richmond's use of Elizabeth, so like Richard's own, a positioning the play sustains but also remythologizes in the figure of Queen Elizabeth I. For it is her self-contained and self-perpetuating figure who becomes ultimately responsible for, and responsive to, the equally idealized (traitorless) future *Richard III* envisions—and contests—at the close.

The most securely enclosed of Shakespeare's histories, *Richard III* also folds out, in its closing gestures, to embrace the present. And it is this characteristically Elizabethan paradox that Michael Bogdanov's 1988 English Shakespeare Company *Richard III* exploits, remythologizing its close to encompass both past and present-day history. Condensing the play's insistent emphasis on its characters' obsessive repetition of the past, Bogdanov stages the Ghost scene to reprise Richard's crimes. Both Richard and Richmond are onstage, both in camouflage gear, their camps defined by cots positioned in the shadows, where Richmond's calm praying figure counters Richard's uneasy sleep. The Ghosts speak only to Richard, turning his own gestures against him in a series of nightmare inversions. The Princes leap astride his body, as though playfully smothering him; reversing the positions he and Richard took at his own murder, a white-gowned Henry VI sits in the cot-side chair, pulls a knife, and threatens to cut Richard's throat. Clarence pours wine into a glass from the decanter on Richard's bedside table, sits drinking it as he accuses Richard, and then splashes it on him; Rivers and Grey cross the suspended metal bridge where they had been executed; Hastings carries his head in a black shopping bag; and Anne spits on Richard's writhing body. Finally, Buckingham shines a flashlight at Richard; in the momentarily blinding light, Richard falls off the cot onto the floor, and when Buckingham shoots him, he wakes, draws his knife and, on "Guilty! guilty!" kneels, reaching his arms to heaven, "imploring pardon"—as both Richard II (at his death) and Henry V (on Agincourt Eve) had done in *Roses'* earlier plays.

Following this closely observed spectacle of providential revenge and the paired battle orations, Bogdanov's *Richard III* prepares for Bosworth's final combat by emptying the stage: only shellbursts, gunfire, searchlights, and smoke define the battle until a wounded Catesby drags himself across the empty space, shouting for rescue. Richard's deeply amplified offstage cry—"A horse! a horse! my kingdom for a horse!"—cues, not his expected appearance, but a sudden blackout, again accompanied by strafing. Then, as the lights slowly come up, huge shadows appear on the upstage wall, back- and sidelit as though to set the ensuing scene in a murky, cloud-scattered other world. Out of the smoke come Richard, in black armor, wearing a massive spiked helmet, and Richmond, in gold, both with broadswords. Their hugely aggrandized figures—anachronistic within the production's mise-en-scène—not only reach suddenly back to 1485 but also echo *1 Henry*

IV's Hal-Hotpsur combat, where both wore chain mail armor (fig. 8). Less chivalric than that, this encounter is brutal and weary, a cruel icon of feudal battle, representing that supposedly glorious past as distinctly unglorious. But that image is, in turn, given additional contradiction by the accompaniment of Samuel Barber's "Adagio for Strings," music frequently played on memorial occasions (such as John F. Kennedy's funeral) and appropriated, most recently, on the sound track for Oliver Stone's 1986 film, *Platoon*. Here, Bogdanov's representational strategy condenses what might be called the double ending of Shakespeare's pseudo-providentialist history, letting music comment on image to commemorate as well as expose the combat model of feudal succession as, at the final elegiac strains of Barber's score, Richmond plunges his sword into Richard's neck with a final thrust, kneels, draws off his helmet, and proclaims, "The day is ours; the bloody dog is dead."

While *Richard III* represents the battle aftermath and Richmond's final speech as continuous, Bogdanov ruptures that seamless discourse to replace the "pastness of the past," much as in Richmond's final couplet, with a reconstructed present. Following a momentary blackout, the lights come up on a working television studio, and when the scrim covering the scene flies out—as though lifting the veil of history—an aide welcomes Queen Elizabeth and her daughter and positions them upstage right of a centrally placed desk and chair. Now the anticipatory bustle stills as Richmond, in a grey suit (with a red Lancastrian handkerchief in his breast pocket), enters with Stanley, nods to the Queen and young Elizabeth, and, after welcoming handshakes, sits at the desk, where a makeup girl puts a final touch of powder on the power broker's image and a technician rushes forward to place a red and a white rose together in his lapel.[75] The cameraman signals, the lights fade slightly, and three monitors, suspended to form a framing triangle at right, left, and center, come alive with Richmond's face in close-up as he begins to speak: "England hath long been mad and scarred herself" (fig. 9). When he concludes, the stage lights fade, but the monitors' triple images remain lit during the fade as the national anthem plays through the final blackout.

Bogdanov's double ending serves as a perfect, and perfectly postmodern, emblem for the seven plays comprising his *Wars of the Roses*. If the first ending simultaneously celebrates and deflates the precise moment of power's transfer through contradictory tensions between image and sound, where Barber's score ironically counterpoints the image, the second reverses that process so that the commodified image of the ruler comments on the play's last words. Replicated three times, that multiple representation constitutes the new order's uninterrupted, unitary discourse about itself—its laudatory state-of-the-nation monologue. What Bogdanov's transformations make possible is less a deformation of Shakespeare's play than a contemporary authentication of its cultural function that foregrounds its own production processes. His *Richard III* translates the Elizabethan text of power to celebrate not just this particular theatrical event but those occurring elsewhere in the social text—on every occasion where the representation of power becomes an image produced and re-produced for an audience of (subjected) spectators.

"IF I TURN MINE EYES UPON MYSELF":

RICHARD II

The body is with the king, but the king is not with the
body. The king is a thing—

. . . .

Of nothing.

—*Hamlet*

ALONE among Shakespeare's histories, *Richard II* did more, in the
waning years of her reign, than address and pay obedient homage
to Queen Elizabeth's multiform image. It confronted her with a disturbing equivalence, hinted at for over twenty years by some of her
subjects, between the figure of Richard and her own royal identity.[1]
At least so the familiar story goes, which connects a 7 February 1601
performance by the Lord Chamberlain's Men of their "old" play—in
all probability Shakespeare's—about the deposition and murder of
Richard II to the Earl of Essex's quickly aborted uprising the next day.[2]
"I am Richard II. Know ye not that?" the Queen remarked to her an-
tiquary, William Lambarde, some six months following Essex's execution for treason. And his reply—"Such a wicked imagination was
determined and attempted by a most unkind Gent., the most adorned
creature that ever your Majestie made"—not only draws Richard II,
Elizabeth, and Essex together but prompts the Queen to link her "most
adorned creature" to theatrical reproduction: "He that will forget
God, will also forget his benefactors; this tragedy was played 40[tie]
times in open streets and houses."[3] To forget God was also to forget
the Queen, as William Barlow's sermon at Paul's Cross on the day of
Essex's execution had made clear,[4] and although the "tragedy" Elizabeth mentions may not refer either to Shakespeare's play or to its commissioned performance, her comment reveals some anxiety about
staged performances occurring in city spaces where—unlike either the
licensed theaters or her own pageants of state—neither she nor her
censors had control over the royal image or the circumstances of its representation.[5]

If replaying this Elizabethan scene of reading points to the potentially subversive nature of theatrical representation, it also suggests the vulnerability inherent in the ideological strategies through which Elizabeth theatricalized her own power—that they could be, and in this case were, appropriated, and by the man whose heroic image as "the embodiment of lineage, arms and honor"[6] in former years had been deliberately inscribed within such "performances" as the annual Accession Day Tilts, held on the Virgin Mary's feast day to honor the Queen.[7] And if Elizabeth's carefully fashioned image represented, through ambiguously resonant allegorical pageantry, the *idea* of worshipped divinity, the power of that image depended on her subjects' willingly loyal, absorbed gaze.[8] Certainly Essex, no less than Elizabeth, clearly understood the other side of the equation: that his image, a commodity created and sustained by royal grace and favor, depended on her eyes. Banished from her sight after his return from Ireland, Essex wrote to the Queen of his tainted subjection, expressed in terms of how he would be spoken, read, and played:

> Now, I do not only feel the weight of your Majesty's indignation, and am subject to their malicious insinuations that first envied me for my happiness in your favor, and now hate me out of custom, but as if I were thrown into a corner like a dead carcase, I am gnawed on and torn by the vilest creatures upon earth. The prating tavern haunter speaks of me what he lists; the frantic libeller writes of me what he lists; already they print me and make me speak to the world, and shortly they will play me in what forms they list upon the stage. The least of these is a thousand times worse than death.[9]

As though ventriloquizing Elizabeth's own fears of losing control over the fashioning of her image, Essex's words draw monarch and rival "royal actor" together, inextricably bound to one another's gaze; sovereignty and treason are interdependent, each read through the other's eyes. And indeed the failure of Essex's honor revolt a year later depended in part on a failure of this visual configuration: used to seeing the Lord Marshal as "the general of our gracious empress" (*Henry V*, 5 Cho., 30), positioned within the ordered obedience of Elizabeth's own spectacles, neither the City elite nor the commons understood his staged march through London as anything other than a "breach both of civil order and religious propriety."[10]

The Essex honor revolt implicates Shakespeare's *Richard II* within an elusive interplay of historical moments of closure. In the final years of Elizabeth's reign, it was the last rebellion of its kind—one that looked back toward neomedieval fealty and to a culture of honor fast disappearing in early modern Europe and, more particularly, in England, where Elizabeth, in appropriating one side of that culture to enhance her royal image, had circumscribed its emphasis on martial values by folding it up within her own representation as, variously, Diana, Gloriana, Astraea, all figures for the ruling Virgin Queen of courtly love. Indeed, one source of her quarrel with Essex involved his creation of knighthoods during the Irish campaign and his abrupt return, both of which she read as violations of her authority: complaining to her godson, Sir John Harington, she stormed, "I am no Queen. That man is above me. Who commanded him to return home? I had sent him on other business."[11] Although present-day narratives linking Essex's revolt with the February 1601 performance of *Richard II* assume a parallel between that project and a play that dramatizes the deposition and murder of the last King of England whose claim to legitimacy rested on divine right,[12] it seems entirely possible that the choice of *Richard II* by some of Essex's followers (neither he himself nor the other most prestigious conspirators were present at the February performance) had as much to do with its dramatization of the contradictions between absolutist monarchical authority and feudal power as with the deposing of a Queen. Certainly Essex himself apparently imagined his public "performance," not as radical political revolution, but as victorious reform,[13] as a material practice that would serve his own interests as well as the nation, reauthorizing his own image and so refashioning the state. Although the Privy Council proceedings concerning the Essex conspiracy made no treasonous connections between the privately commissioned *Richard II* and Essex's public performance the next day, *Richard II* nevertheless offers an uncannily perfect prologue to reproducing the past as the present and encourages submission to the "truth" of imagining Elizabeth and Richard II as similar royal images.

But however accurate or distorted that mirror may have been, *Richard II* even more precisely reflects Essex himself, and in double guises. For one, Bolingbroke—especially in the play's opening scene, where he challenges Mowbray, but also later in the gage scene (4.1.1–90)—attempts, like Essex, to put into play both the cultural conventions and the legal procedures associated with the chivalric code of martial honor. Moreover, his situation closely corresponds to what Essex saw as his grievances against the Crown: exile from court, if not from England; loss of revenue, royal favor, and title; disgraced honor. And indeed, the questions Essex poses in his 18 October 1598 letter to the Lord Keeper, Sir Thomas Egerton—a letter brought against him later as evidence of seditious intent—sound remarkably like Bolingbroke: "When the vilest of all indignities are done unto me, doth religion enforce me to sue? Doth God require it? Is it impiety not to do it?

What, cannot princes err? Cannot subjects receive wrong? Is an earthly power or authority infinite? Pardon me, pardon me, my good Lord, I can never subscribe to these principles."[14] Also like Bolingbroke, Essex rode on a wave of favorable popular opinion, especially reinforced by those who, like him, criticized the failings of the English court as proceeding "chiefly from the sex of the Queen."[15] Perhaps even more pertinently, Essex is figured in Richard as well. In prison, Essex would repudiate honor and effectively deconstruct his heroic self-image to represent himself as abjectly penitent to "the religio-providentialist view of the state on which the legitimacy of the Elizabethan regime had always rested."[16] Facing his own execution, Essex enacts a curiously inverted parody of Shakespeare's imprisoned King Richard, attempting to come to terms "with being nothing" (5.5.41).

But, however much *Richard II* resonates outward to figure a number of final events in the lives of Queen Elizabeth and Essex, the play that, in 1601, could, so to speak, overflow its limits becomes, for its later readers, much more severely circumscribed. Detached from its early seventeenth-century topical narratives, this *Richard II* sets divinely sanctioned monarch against Machiavellian "new man" whose power resides exclusively in his own will, folding history into a clash between political stereotypes or personalities.[17] And when positioned as the first play in an epic scheme of double tetralogies, it turns into a narrative that breeds guilty historical (and dramatic) heirs: six successions (and seven successive dramas) later, Henry VII joins Lancaster to York in newly shaped legitimacy.[18] In its most recent guises, which recirculate its Elizabethan narratives, the play participates in an exemplary dialectic between subversion and containment: on the one hand revealing the theater's power to subvert royal authority; on the other suggesting that the theatrical space ultimately encloses all potential threats and so reauthorizes the subversions it puts into play.[19] Despite their discrepancies, however, each of these interpretative strategies singles out *Richard II*'s most climactic events—Richard's deposition and death—and reads them, as Richard himself does, as unique spectacles in a tragedy that closes off the myth of divinely authorized kingship. Indeed, it is remarkably easy to read *Richard II* selectively, through the King's part, and so to generate a sense of ending that tells this story and excludes all others. Beerbohm Tree's 1903 production at London's His Majesty's Theatre illustrates this in its most extreme form.

"Charged with pathos from the beginning to end,"[20] the final act of Tree's *Richard II* is all catastrophe and climax: Richard's abdication (4.1), his farewell to his Queen (5.1), and his prison-soliloquy and murder (5.5). Gone is the York family drama, with the discovery of

Aumerle's conspiracy against Bolingbroke and Bolingbroke's pardon (5.2–5.3), and the final scene, with Bolingbroke facing Richard's body, which is encased in a coffin (5.6): indeed, Tree reduces Exton as well as Bolingbroke to a function—the one, Richard's assassin; the other, so to speak, Richard's successor. The abdication concludes with a stunning exit for Tree's Richard; in its carefully choreographed looking relations, he stares at the Bishop of Carlisle, each of the assembled clerics, and Northumberland, all of whom meet his glance and then turn away; finally, he turns to Bolingbroke, "seat[ed] arrogantly on the throne and slightly inclining his head to a bow" before leaving, his head held high as the curtain falls in silence.[21] For the next scene, which Tree set in a torch-lit London street, where a castle parapet and a half-timbered building frame a red-orange sun and a gallows, the curtain rise discovers a drunken man, imprisoned in the stocks and singing to himself. As the heavily guarded Richard bids the Queen and Aumerle (not present in Shakespeare's scene) farewell, swelling music accompanies a tender love scene that retains only one of Richard's references to deposition and omits any mention of Northumberland's future rebellion (5.1.55–68); when the lovers part, Richard also embraces Aumerle and hands him over to the Queen before the pair exit, followed by Northumberland and his soldiers, Richard gazing after them. Asleep during the leave-taking, the drunk now wakes to beg money from Richard, who searches his robe, finds he has nothing to give, and so graciously shakes his hand. As the prisoner points to the sun setting behind the gallows, the King looks up at it, his back to the audience; then he bows, removes his hat, and exits laughing—laughter that is taken up by the drunk as Exton and his servant enter "and follow [the] King stealthily up [the] street."

The finale takes place in a Norman-arched dungeon, where a steel-blue lime spot highlights a centrally placed cross and shines throughout on Richard's face. Cuts eliminate one-third of Richard's meditative soliloquy on time and existence (5.5.1–66) and, following the murder, all of Exton's remorseful comments; otherwise, Tree keeps the scene's overall shape, including the exchange with the groom (5.5.67–97). Attacked by Exton's men, Richard fights vigorously with a battle-ax and dagger, matching his assailants' brutality and killing several; when Exton stabs him, he falls, mortally wounded, in front of the lit cross. Tree's own stage directions sketch out the rest:

> EXTON & ATTENDANT slink off up steps. The KING continues dialogue, "Exton, thy fierce hand", etc., struggling up until he rests at the base of the column in a sitting position, and speaks [his] remaining lines. . . . At the

words, "Sinks downward here to die" he drops dying—The death bell of the
Castle now peals out in unison with plaintive music from the Orchestra;
after 3 or 4 tolls, the music changes into the Te Deum and the Choir are
ready set behind back of the Dungeon in the Coronation set, and take it up
in song—Every light fades out except one faint pencil light on the KING'S
face from the O.P. [opposite prompt, or stage right] perch, and the gauze
and black cloth are taken up. Then the limes and electrics grow, disclosing
the congregation gathered in the Abbey for the Coronation. The ceremonial
of the crown being placed on BOLINGBROKE'S head then takes place—He
rises, turns, bows to the people R. and L., and at the end of the first part of
the Te Deum the lights all fade again to blackness, leaving the KING just
sinking in his last death agony, and the Curtain falls on the end of the strain
of music from the Orchestra.

Here is tragedy par excellence, embodied as high art that equates actor-manager with King and celebrates their joined presences. Tree's
Richard belongs to a nineteenth-century tragedian's never-never land
of transcendent subjectivity, where individualized consciousness reigns
supreme, his plight coinciding with and articulated as that of the alien-
ated poet who constructs a world within, resistive to the pressures of
British (or any) late nineteenth- or early twentieth-century industrial-
ized society. His tender, protective care of his Queen, securely chaper-
oned by Aumerle; his compassionate fellow feeling for the common
man; and his mocking laughter at the setting sun exude romantic,
"gentlemanly" ironies. Moreover, his self-absorption in poetic reverie
together with his bravery in the face of death insist on his tragical-
heroical status. Like Richard himself, Tree jealously guards his kingly
role: in his directions for the double apotheosis, Richard remains
"KING" even after his dream of Bolingbroke's coronation, a reassuring
vision that not only restores the ceremonial trappings of majesty but,
ultimately, urges spectators to identify with Richard's transcendent
personal triumph over history.

   Tree's idealized revision rather accurately fulfills Aristotelian desire
by eliminating or reworking those features that contradict tragic patterning and so detract from Richard's grand pathos and tragic absolutism. Indeed, Tree's representational politics ally him with Richard,
who also consciously fashions the music of his close to mystify and
mythologize his suffering, a likeness that Tree's version insists on by
absorbing Bolingbroke's invented coronation within Richard's gaze as
his own final, King-creating vision. But such choices are not Shakespeare's. Rather, *Richard II*'s peculiarly *un*musical close, like the "sour
sweet music" (5.5.42) Richard hears in prison, breaks the time and

proportion associated with tragedy, with "the honoured spectacle of the fallen king."²² For even as the play seems to endow Richard's tragedy with transhistorical fixity as royal (or, in Tree's case, subjective) myth, it also moves toward incorporating that myth within history. Although all of Shakespeare's histories exhibit such generic tensions, the "double narrative" shaping *Richard II*'s close reveals their contradictions most acutely. Indeed, the slippage between royal tragedy and history turns Richard's tragic role and the act of tragic spectatorship into conventions that can be interrogated theatrically.

As early as his return from Ireland (3.2), Richard begins to appropriate for himself, Bottom-like, tragedy's rhetorical conventions and roles, playing chorus and prophet as well as protagonist in a sometimes parodic process of self-fashioning that culminates in what critics (silently taking the King's part) almost invariably label "the deposition scene." Here, the exchange of royal power reproduces the formula associated with closure in the *Henry VI* trilogy (considered as a three-part play) and *Richard III*: that is, each authorizes, or reauthorizes, a new king—even, as in the case of *3 Henry VI*'s last scene, in the face of latent future opposition. But although *2 Henry VI*, *3 Henry VI*, and *Richard III* also describe a midplay succession, only *Richard II* so radically calls into question the conventions of closural legitimacy surrounding such an event to emphasize, not the making, but the unmaking of a king. What Bolingbroke, York, and Northumberland would stage as legitimate succession ("I thought you had been willing to resign" [4.1.90]), Richard exposes as usurpation ("Here, cousin, seize the crown" [4.1.181]), turning the occasion that invites his "surrender" to his supposedly adopted heir into one that attempts to disenfranchise Bolingbroke's right to the crown by making his own stunningly visible.²³ Constructing kingship as a text for which he, as its Christlike priest and submissive clerk,²⁴ is both author and reader, Richard turns it upside down, speaking its hegemony as the paradoxical process of its destruction. In a ritual that takes form as a transcendent instance of festival inversion, Richard evokes the symbols of majesty—the crown, the sceptre, the balm, the sacred state and duteous oaths belonging to kings—and strips them away, thereby calling into question king as well as usurper, making both subject to the gaze of an onstage audience of traitors, among whom he finally positions himself (4.1.247–48). And when he turns to face his mirror image, substituting the "very book indeed / Where all my sins are writ" (4.1.274–75) for the articles of abdication Northumberland repeatedly urges on him, his abject self-absorption sees only "brittle glory," bankrupt power (fig. 12). "Proud majesty made a subject" (4.1.252) dismantles royal tragedy: the hollow crown and shattered glass are its crystallizing symbols; Richard's conveyance to the Tower, and then to Pomfret Castle, are its "historical" reality.

But Richard's spectacular ceremonial decoronation occurs only in the versions of *Richard II*—two Quartos (1608 and 1615) and the Folio (1623)—that appeared after Queen Elizabeth's death. Was its representation of dethroned sovereignty considered potentially seditious and so deleted from the three Quartos published during the Queen's lifetime (Q1, 1597; Q2 and Q3, 1598)? To the extent that it came under Elizabeth's 1559 proclamation forbidding plays "wherein either matters of religion or of the gouvernance of the estate of the common weale shal be handled or treated,"[25] *Richard II* might be a likely candidate for censorship, but so would other plays based on historical materials, among them Marlowe's *Edward II* (1594, 1598), which also represents the abdication and murder of an anointed king. Most commentators cite differing censorship practices for staged performances and printed books as a rationale for arguing that the Parliament scene was indeed performed,[26] and early quarto title pages do not promise, as those for other plays sometimes did, that the book represented the play "as it hath been lately acted." The 1608 Quarto, however, makes just such a guarantee,[27] but at a time, five years into James I's reign, when Richard II's history was no longer sensitive material, when a possibly disquieting match between stage and world was, at least in the case of *Richard II*,[28] safely contained by metaphor. Was this the version "lately acted" before Essex's followers in February 1601? It is impossible to know, and mobilizing such primarily negative evidence yields no sure answers. But what seems clear is that only one version of *Richard II*—without the deposition—was available to *readers* before 1608. In itself, of course, this is not unusual, for many of Shakespeare's plays exist in multiple texts, some of which describe differing representational (and political) economies.[29] But unlike the chronicle sources, which refuse to decide between versions of Richard II's death (whether he was poisoned or brutally assassinated), *Richard II*'s two texts insist on different representational economies and so invite particular attention to what might be called the politics of deposition in each.

Both *Richard II*s record Richard's progressive awareness of and his insights into rule without power well before what the 1608 Quarto title page advertises not as his deposition but as "the Parliament scene."[30] With the state poised to fall into Bolingbroke's hands, Richard meditates on "sad stories of the death of kings" (3.2.156), on sovereignty as theater—"a little scene, / to monarchize" (3.2.164–

65)—and on his own ultimate subjection to mortality (3.2.176–77). Once he hears that York has joined Bolingbroke, he discharges his followers and, later, at Flint Castle, imagines his self-deposition and loss through an exchange of symbolic objects that anticipates his catalogue of "undoing" in the Parliament scene (3.3.147–54). Indeed, as Richard descends to the "base court," he imagines himself a mythic figure— "Down, down I come, like glist'ring Phaeton" (3.3.178)—his glory already eclipsed by "Bolingbroke's fair day" (3.2.218). And just as Richard's "coming down" anticipates his abdication, so do others: the ensuing conversation between the gardeners, overheard by the Queen, assumes it is common knowledge—"Depressed he is already, and deposed / 'Tis doubt he will be; . . . I speak no more than every one doth know" (3.4.68–69, 91).

Given these preliminary figurings, readers of the three early quartos would, like the gardeners and the Queen, have little doubt about Richard's imminent deposition. Without the lines that showcase Richard's resignation (4.1.154–318), the Elizabethan quartos move from the Bishop of Carlisle's arrest for capital treason to Bolingbroke's coronation proclamation; his exit with York and the other lords then leaves Carlisle, in the Abbot of Westminster's custody, with Aumerle, the three already plotting against the new King (H_2ʳ). In these versions, Richard abdicates not only willingly but privately. York reports that "plume-plucked Richard" adopts Bolingbroke his heir and "with willing soul" yields his sceptre. Bolingbroke immediately claims the crown: "In God's name I'll ascend the regal throne," at which point Carlisle objects—"What subject can give sentence on his king?"—calls Bolingbroke a traitor and prophesies "woefullest division" (H_2ᵛ). Except for excluding Richard's resignation speech, this order of events follows chronicle accounts rather closely, though different versions of Richard's speech and descriptions of the occasion illustrate the commonly acknowledged historiographer's license to invent what was not officially recorded.[31] By locating Richard's abdication offstage, away from subjects' judging eyes, the equally inventive Elizabethan quartos invite every subject (and, potentially, one particular royal woman reader) to become her or his own historian: just as *Henry V's* Chorus urges spectators, " 'tis your thoughts that now must deck our kings" (Pro., 28), in this *Richard II*, thoughts must *undeck* a king. Insofar as textual absence requires "imaginary puissance," it comes close to inviting treason, defined in Tudor law as "*imagining* and compassing the death of a king"; indeed, the Earl of Essex was formally charged with "conspiring and imagining at London . . . to depose and then slay the Queen and to subvert the Government."[32] *Richard II's* Elizabethan quartos could be thought to encourage, not allay, sedition, for these texts do precisely what Carlisle (and Tudor law) warn against: permit "the figure of God's majesty" to "Be judged by subject and inferior breath, / And he himself not present" (4.1.125, 128–29).

In contrast to the radically flexible Elizabethan quartos, the Jacobean quartos and Folio (Q4, H$_2$^{v}–H$_4$^{v}; TLN 2075–2258) answer Carlisle's question, "What subject can give sentence on his king?" with "only the King," and re-represent what has already occurred, structuring Richard's abdication as aided soliloquy. In this "double writing" of resignation,[33] Richard's public "scene of excess" invites spectator-subjects to confront divine right as an ideal form of kingship and to assess their relation to such an absolutist solution. On the one hand, at the level of communally shared ideology, which for both Elizabethan and Jacobean subjects rested on the *idea* of divinely sanctioned monarchy if not its legitimate reality in either reigning sovereign, Richard's spectacle of state could work, not to empty the crown of meaning, but rather to expressly focus its power. Yet such a reading would (and still does) depend in some part on the royal actor, or, rather, on the playing of the King's part—even, one might add, on the playing of *both* Kings' parts. For on the other hand, and especially in the theater, the Parliament scene can also tempt its spectators to choose a king and so entertain treason. That Richard as well as Bolingbroke (and, potentially, Queen Elizabeth and King James I) may represent counterforms of kingship's ideal depends, ultimately, on the beholder's absorbed gaze and on who reads that gaze. And to the extent that staging—or, for that matter, reading, which must imagine particular theatrical effects—reveals the spectacle of majesty as "pure" theater, and therefore suspect, the Jacobean *Richard II* can be seen to glorify its "mystery" and, simultaneously, to deconstruct and hollow out its essence, showing it to be ephemeral. In its "doubly written" form, *Richard II* also moves toward locating tragedy within the self, not the institution of kingship. But theatricality taints that project as well: Richard's self-absorbed gaze at his image in the glass mirrors only the player's "shadow," only a fleetingly theatrical image of sorrow. Given a particular balance of energies on the stage that, for instance, favored Bolingbroke over Richard, the play—especially the Parliament scene—could strike deep at Queen Elizabeth's own absorption within theatricalizing images of self-perpetuating divinity as well as with the symbology of power, and could even turn spectators' thoughts toward a new ruler. As York later notes—and as Elizabeth herself well understood, especially as she became increasingly aware that her ministers' political machinations no longer revolved around her presence but were fixed on ensuring a smooth succession[34]—in Shakespeare's *Richard II* as in England's theater of state, "the eyes of men, / After a well-graced actor leaves the stage, / Are idly bent on him that enters next" (5.2.23–25).

Seductively contradictory in both its *written* forms, *Richard II* transmits its images of royal power, and of the Kings' several bodies, most precisely when, like majesty itself, it is set upon a stage, whether in the theater or in its adjacent social space. This does not, of course, fully explain the Parliament scene's absence from the Elizabethan quartos and its possible staging in the 1590s or, more pertinently, at the famous 1601 commissioned performance.[35] Certainly the Jacobean *Richard II* offers its readers an "invention" that the Elizabethan *Richard II* did not and, perhaps, could not publish. And whereas the Elizabethan quartos establish a neat symmetry between the two kings by dramatizing neither Richard's decoronation nor Bolingbroke's coronation, the Jacobean *Richard II* constructs a different closural balance between the two Kings, though not between the King's Two Bodies. Since from this point forward both playtexts are markedly similar, except for more local and far less flamboyant differences, I want to pursue a *Richard II* that, although it could be thought of as addressing James I, is more Elizabethan.

If the inversions of the Parliament scene represent the death of divine kingship, the ensuing scene, where Richard meets the Queen on his way to the Tower, meditates further on tragedy—specifically, on its hero's death.[36] Once again, an onstage audience awaits Richard's arrival; when he enters, he again becomes subjected to another's gaze,[37] appearing, to his Queen's eyes, as a living monument: "Thou map of honor, thou King Richard's tomb, / And not King Richard" (5.1.12–13). As though to enclose and commemorate his life, Richard asks the Queen to imagine him dead—"Think I am dead, and that even here thou takest, / As from my death-bed, thy last living leave" (5.1.38–39)—and to tell his story. Unlike his earlier desire to "sit upon the ground / And tell sad stories of the death of kings" (3.2.155–56), however, he contemplates not the generalized mortality of Kings but a fiction of his own sorrow: "Tell thou the lamentable tale of *me*" (5.1.44). Moralizing England's future strife, he plays Chorus to Bolingbroke's history as well as to his own and transforms his parting with the Queen into an inverted betrothal, which develops an elaborate, sonnetlike conceit of lovers exchanging hearts in a kiss, formalizing absence and sorrow to suggest a kind of double suicide. In recirculating so many closural conventions, the scene seems intensely aware of its own literary artifice; indeed, it records Richard's deposition as a melodrama that prompts the tears of "good old folks" (5.1.41)—listeners to a form of representation different from historical tragedy, with its audience of potentially judgmental spectator-subjects. And since it is Richard who insists on and controls the artifice, his self-reflexiveness seems at this point identical with that of the playtext, which, in providing this coda for a tragedy that substitutes "the deposing of a rightful king" for his death, perfectly reflects his obsession with his own ending in its manipulation of closural forms.

Later, as though obedient to Richard's desire, a tearful York frames his account of Bolingbroke's triumphal entry into London[38]—an event for which the narrative strategy substitutes Richard's privately observed procession—as part of Richard's "lamentable tale": both teller and listener are "good old folks" who "quite their griefs" with providential sentiments (5.1.43). Although York himself affirms his unquestioning loyalty to the new King—"To Bolingbroke are we sworn subjects now, / Whose state and honor I for aye allow" (5.2.39–40)—with York's discovery of his son Aumerle's role in the assassination attempt against Bolingbroke and, then, with the York family's visit to the King (5.3), *Richard II* dramatizes, or rather redramatizes, what it means to be a "sworn subject," to "allow" a ruler's "state and honor." Retesting the social contract through the poetic contract, the playtext now anatomizes allegiance with an almost condescending simplification of language that not only seems to trivialize the subject but also to displace, though not altogether mask, "real" history.

In a carefully ambiguous move, *Richard II* evades the dynastic rift created by Bolingbroke's accession, mentioning neither his attempt in the Parliament to claim right by succession nor the surviving Yorkist claim in the Mortimer family (material that shapes the central conflict in *1* and *2 Henry IV*), both of which Holinshed details.[39] But the unfolding York family comedy very deliberately alludes to Aumerle's former position as Richard's chosen successor,[40] calling attention to his lost title and his new name, Rutland. Rather than exploring either that rival claim or its corollary—that, had Bolingbroke not spared Aumerle, he would have ended the Yorkist line and thus prevented the Wars of the Roses—*Richard II* translates the issue of Aumerle's political legitimacy into domestic betrayal: as York prepares to denounce his son's treason to the new King, his Duchess assumes that he suspects her of adultery. And just as imagining Aumerle as York's bastard son expresses his status as a now illegitimated heir of "unkinged Richard" and undermines both feudal and familial honor, the new Henry IV's conversation with Harry Percy reveals that *his* legitimate heir's conduct not only taints the King's "state and honor"—"If any plague hang over us, 'tis he" (5.3.3)—but also mocks the coming "triumphs" at Oxford with his own tilting in London's stews.

Mobilizing historical material with this degree of inventiveness suggests that, in Elizabeth's England, circulating notions of legitimacy, heirs, and honor may represent potentially sensitive content that can be safely interrogated only through comic displacement.[41] In a further reappropriation of that history, *Richard II* takes literally Westminster's earlier promise that "A plot shall show us all a merry day" (4.1.334), and translates the Oxford rebellion into a play-within-the-play performed by Aumerle, York, and the Duchess for Bolingbroke, whose roles as both spectator and judge for an oddly skewed pardon tale[42] aptly translate the kingly role he would (presumably) play at the proposed Oxford tourney. Like such ceremonial tourneys—reminiscent of Elizabeth's Accession Day Tilts and Essex's central role in them—this playlet not only illustrates a spectrum of contradictory loyalties but also ends, as such pageants often did, by proclaiming the ruler "a god on earth." Structurally, the scene much resembles comedy's final trials of faith, in which threatening oppositions are masked and resolved by means of a transforming mechanism that restates the terms of the social contract and reconstructs the relationship between prince and subjects. On the level of language, the playtext renegotiates that relationship by overturning the poetic contract, which is no longer sustained and preserved by a king's verbal elegance, his fascination with symbolic icons of power, and his sense of himself as "the observed of all observers" (*Hamlet*, 3.1.154). Instead, Henry IV reads his subjects' own excesses through a popular, not a royal, text—a ballad[43] whose title, "The Beggar and the King," both accurately expresses his situation and glances at what Richard, much earlier, called "his courtship to the common people" (1.4.24).

Yet this excess attaches not to Aumerle or York—and, by association, not to male subjects—but to the Duchess. It is she who accounts for the shift in genre: her offstage voice, interrupting (and then continuing) York's formalizing couplets setting honor against dishonor, life against death, traitor against true man, prompts Henry's remark, "The scene is alt'red from a serious thing, / And now chang'd to 'The Beggar and the King'" (5.3.80). *Richard III* provides some context for this gender rebellion: at approximately this point in its narrative strategy, a similar scene occurs. There, however, as Richard argues for Elizabeth's daughter, the beggar *is* the King. Like this scene, however, it concerns legitimacy, heirs, honor, and "a happy mother's name" (5.2.93). And just as Elizabeth blunts and stalemates Richard's oaths by citing his wrongs against her, the Duchess opposes York's setting of "the word itself against the word" (5.3.122) at the level of feudal values by citing paternal love, blood, and birth—and by quite literally "outpraying" him. Indeed, her kneeling not only cues the men's kneeling, but reveals the gesture itself as parodic by reading her husband's *un*repentant refusal to kneel as hypocrisy. If the Parliament scene exposes kingship as a symbolic fiction, the York family rebellion betrays the construction of a "sworn subject" as equally problematic: as the repentant Aumerle puts it, "My heart is not confederate with my hand" (5.3.53). In Henry IV's England as in Elizabeth's (or James I's), the politics of state and those shaping its foundations, the noble family, are identical. In positioning women as actors dominated by "affection and will" who violate the public realm with private pleading,[44] *Richard II* recirculates the spectre of the unruly woman, this time as a comic inversion of the virtues of humility, mildness, and courtesy associated with ideal female rule. This time, too, *Richard II* empties "misrule" of its associations with the Queen; given the hearsay linking Elizabeth with Richard, the dangers of allusion lay elsewhere, in the figure of the Prince.

Although much about the York rebellion seems calculated to reveal Bolingbroke as not-Richard and to disclose a split within the rigidly ceremonial system of feudal loyalty that structures the play's opening opposition between Bolingbroke and Mowbray and the later exchange of gages (4.1.19–90), that system remains unchanged. Indeed, the sequence closes on yet another example of feudal loyalty: with Exton's vow to rid Bolingbroke of "this living fear" (5.4.2), the play reprises something like the vow Mowbray may have made concerning the Duke of Gloucester's murder (which Richard may have ordered), of which Bolingbroke accuses him in *Richard II*'s opening scene (1.1.100–103). But the connection between Bolingbroke and Richard is apparent only in the original Elizabethan and Jacobean quartos as well as Folio. In a move that seems designed both to blur Henry Lancaster's complicity in Richard's murder and to call attention to it, modern editors print the brief Exton scene as a self-contained unit. Although the practice of continuous theatrical performance obviously erases this distinction, so isolating Exton's vow veils its relationship to the overall narrative strategy. What the original playtexts imply, and what performance texts can reinforce—that Bolingbroke makes the comment Exton quotes on his way to order men to Oxford to seize the traitors—links Richard's death to the rebellion that threatens Bolingbroke's authority. And this, in turn, invites rereading *Richard II*'s narrative politics as representing a double substitute for that uprising and to see the comedic York family plot as a parodic inversion that anticipates, in a radical transgression (or even rebellion) of form, Richard's prison soliloquy and murder (5.5). The first of these rebellions constructs one King's power by deconstructing the loyalties that support it and then by disclosing the contradiction in his willingness to pardon Aumerle's imagined treason but to condemn others as traitors. The second recuperates Richard's absolutism twice: once, as Richard imagines, in his soliloquy, a timeless realm populated by self-generated, interchangeable subjects and kings—a vision that folds his subjection up into Bolingbroke's time—and, again, at his martyrlike death, in terms of royal myth.

If the York scenes, as well as Richard's Pomfret soliloquy, set word against word, *Richard II*'s final closural moves set King against King, scene against scene, ending against beginning in a structural pattern reminiscent of *3 Henry VI*'s ending, which also juxtaposes a king's murder in prison with the image of a successor who has "swept suspicion from our seat / And made our footstool of security" (*3 Henry VI*, 5.7.13–14). But there are important differences between the two. Although in both the killing of a king circulates blood guilt, only in *Richard II* does that guilt travel forward to taint the new King; although both recapitulate details of character and plot, only *Richard II*, just before Richard's murder, reprises such detail through an invented character, the Groom. Loyal to Richard, he figures both as an heir to the "old" Aumerle and as Exton's opposite, and his report of Bolingbroke's coronation procession and Richard's "traitorous" horse, Roan Barbary, who rode "so proudly" under Bolingbroke—a report prompting Richard's anger, and then his pardon—recirculates echoes of the earlier York pardon scene. The Groom also grounds Richard's self-conscious reversal of his earlier "Down, down I come, like glistering Phaeton" to "Mount, mount, my soul! thy seat is up on high" (5.5.111), giving the final figuring of his "lamentable tale" a peculiarly witty, and distinctly literary, spin.[45]

Richard II's final scene maps out an even more radically condensed closural economy, generating signs of ending at the level of both language and representation as obsessively as Richard himself does in his earlier farewell with the Queen. Indeed, its subject as well as its function is closure: reports of six traitors' heads en route to London and the news of Westminster's death signal the end of the Oxford conspiracy; in taciturn phrases, Bolingbroke thanks the Lords and pardons Carlisle's treason; Exton enters with Richard's body enclosed in a coffin.[46] With geometric symmetry, the situation almost exactly reprises the play's opening, where a King, surrounded by nobles (one of whom is an uncle), hears himself implicated in a kinsman's murder; only the

persons have changed. There, Bolingbroke's accusation against Mowbray, masked by the terms of feudal challenge, resulted in exile for
both; here, Exton's more forthright "From your own mouth, my lord,
did I this deed" (5.6.37) again results in double exile—Exton to "wan-
der thorough the shades of night"; Bolingbroke to a Jerusalem pilgrimage he will never (except metaphorically) complete, one far different
from those of his crusading Plantagenet ancestors in that its purpose is
not Christian conquest but expiation.[47]

So described, *Richard II* closes with almost mathematical precision
on a representation of the King's Two Bodies that exposes Bolingbroke's history to Richard's myth, showing them to be incorporate: as
in Richard's earlier promise at Flint Castle, "Your own is yours, and I
am yours, and all" (3.3.197). And when, like Richard at his abdication, the new King turns his gaze inward, he discovers himself equally
subject to and subjected by Richard's own ending. Like the chains of
axiomatic rhyming couplets that repeatedly promise but do not ensure
its finality, closure assumes paradoxical form, turns into its opposite,
and counters the stability its conventions insist on. Like the Parliament
scene, *Richard II*'s close is "doubly written." Although it records
events concerning Henry IV's succession, from the point at which Exton enters with Richard's body, it dramatizes a curious fantasy of resolution, which collapses time and space to imagine a meeting of the
King's Two Bodies that never took place and a journey that lies in the
future. The "untimely bier" to which Bolingbroke refers in the playtext's final lines is indeed untimely. And the procession he speaks of
will not happen for more than a generation, when, forty years after his
death, at Henry V's order, Richard's body is exhumed and conveyed
through London's streets "in a royal seat . . . covered all over with
black velvet, & adorned with banners and divers armes," to be buried
in Westminster Abbey.[48] At what can seem its limitless limits, *Richard
II* engages with a specific moment of memory, invites its Elizabethan
spectators to imagine England's last divine-right monarch on a journey
that parallels Bolingbroke's own, one that moves beyond the boundaries of the stage, and, in a final theatrical display, resituates Richard's
body within a sacramental space.

ಶ

"There was a silence on the stage as [Richard II's] body was carried off; there was a silence in the auditorium as the stage was left
empty, and then a thin wave of applause."[49] The occasion, opening
night for the 1951 Festival of Britain production of *Richard II* at Stratford's Shakespeare Memorial Theatre, was the first time Shakespeare's

play had been performed together with *1* and *2 Henry IV* and *Henry V* as a unified whole—a project that Anthony Quayle, its director, conceived as a radical break from theatrical tradition. Recalling Tree's finale in part explains the silence, the "thin wave of applause"; what spectators witnessed was not familiar Shakespeare: no swelling chords or closural anthem; no rearranged last words to privilege the star actor; no swelling scene, filled with three or four hundred supernumeraries; no curtain fall to mark "the end." The past practice of appropriating *Richard II*, as well as Shakespeare's other histories, as star vehicles, said Quayle, had "stealthily built a mountain of misrepresentation and surrounded it with a fog of ignorance."⁵⁰ But the Festival cycle, designed to trace common themes and structures and to emphasize character development, would release "new" meanings—in particular, those recently put forward by the best-selling scholarly studies of E.M.W. Tillyard and Lily B. Campbell, which constructed an Elizabethan World Picture as the ordering principle driving Shakespeare's historical art. Only when bound together as a tetralogy, claimed John Dover Wilson, writing in a commemorative volume, could these plays give spectators "the right to frame final conclusions about its characters."⁵¹

But however ambitious and bold its newfound coherence, the cycle did reproduce the notion of "stardom" in its controlling vision. Writes Quayle, "The true hero of the whole play [that is, the "one great play" constituted by the tetralogy] is Henry V, who personified to the people of Shakespeare's England the ideal King: brave, warlike, generous, just, and—it must be added—loving humour."⁵² Given *Henry V* as the cycle's end point, *Richard II*, the first play in the tetralogy, became virtually recoded as political drama, with Richard himself "the perfect counterpoise and prologue" to the virtuous Henry V.⁵³ Not only was Richard's "inward drama" de-emphasized in order to convey the shift from one political order to another and to sharpen the significance of the curse his death embodied, but Michael Redgrave's "historically correct" portrait of Richard—"a 'raging queer,' a dainty, feline homosexual, purring with malice and affectation [who suffers] a sea-change into something much less rich and strange, a melancholy, noble prince, making phrases out of his own disasters"⁵⁴—further demonized the character to favor, first, the manly vigor of Harry Andrews's Bolingbroke and, finally, Richard Burton's Hal and Henry V. To its initial homophobic interpretative communities, *Richard II* was Redgrave's "brilliant failure,"⁵⁵ Bolingbroke's tragedy instead of Richard's: at the end, writes T. C. Worsley, he becomes "a lonely and noble figure in the forefront of our minds."⁵⁶

Although Quayle's mise-en-scène—an expressionistically Elizabethan permanent set of rough boards—makes an austere contrast to Tree's magnificent historical realizations, like Tree he omits the York family sequence and all mention of Aumerle's treachery.[57] However, by retaining York's description of Bolingbroke's and Richard's London entry as a bridge between Richard's parting with his Queen and Exton's vow, his performance text neatly sketches in the contradictions shaping Bolingbroke's new regime. Elsewhere in the closing scenes, Quayle's prompt copy meticulously points connections to past events and rigorously obeys the playtext's implied stage directions, especially those that anticipate future events and call attention to Bolingbroke's guilt. As Exton stabs Richard, for example, the King falls to his knees and grasps Exton's hand on "Exton, thy fierce hand / Hath with the king's blood stain'd the king's own land," at which Exton wrenches free from Richard and crosses upstage to comment on his deed. Swiftly, the assassins remove the bodies, the up-center doors close, and, momentarily, a spotlight picks out the empty throne. After a brief blackout, full lighting reveals Bolingbroke about to sit on the throne, surrounded by his gathering court—a precise echo of the performance text's opening moves. Here, however, no fanfares herald the King's presence: the only orchestra cue marks Carlisle's pardon, underscoring Bolingbroke's mention of honor and so calling attention to its coming betrayal. Exton and several others precede Richard's coffin, covered with a pall and carried by six monks who place it center stage, directly under the balcony where Richard, at Flint Castle, had descended to the "base court." As he names the dead King "Richard of Bordeaux," Exton removes the pall; seeing Richard's face, York falls against Northumberland and collapses, Carlisle kneels, and Bolingbroke rises (fig. 10). Exton's "From your own mouth, my lord, did I this deed" prompts York and Northumberland to look closely at Bolingbroke, but the new King remains regally posed, sceptre in hand, as he banishes Exton, who leaves, dragging the pall behind him in a long up-center exit, during which all are silent. Bolingbroke extends the pause before he addresses "Lords, I protest my soul is full of woe" to his courtiers, crossing himself as he mentions the Holy Land; at his signal, the monks raise the coffin and carry it offstage, and, followed by Bolingbroke and the others, the procession moves offstage, leaving the space—and the spotlit throne—empty.

Compared to Tree's finale, which empowers Richard as the epitome of high romantic individualism, crowns Bolingbroke, and doubly reenslaves spectators to kingship's theatrical spectacle,[58] Quayle's choreography of gesture and look, combining symbolic and naturalistic detail, seemed to its critics not only understated but enigmatic and unsatisfying. "We would have expected," carped the *Times*'s reviewer, "that at the outset the theme [of kingship] would be stated with all possible comprehensiveness."[59] But this initial experience of loss was, after all, precisely the point of the cycle presentation—necessary in order to give precise closural value to that ideal, embodied in Henry V, and, not incidentally, to reauthenticate the story of England as well as its central institution for post–World War II Britons who, like Tudor Englishmen, were poised at a point of social change. By disclosing the contours of an ordering principle rooted in history and "Shakespeare," Tillyard's totalizing vision gave renewed cultural shape to an aggressively nostalgic desire for stability; hearing that vision, however potentially reactionary, clearly spoken from the stage had considerable political and ideological importance in articulating national-cultural experience.[60] The Festival cycle, with *Richard II* as its lyrical tragic prelude, was the postwar equivalent of Laurence Olivier's 1944 film of *Henry V*, which transformed English kingship into a celebratory commodity. To some extent, more recent performance texts of *Richard II* attempt to rediscover just such a moment of historical and cultural congruence in which kingship—or the lack of it—can be re-seen as a site of struggle.

The most strongly interpretative of these, John Barton's 1973 Royal Shakespeare Company production, reappropriated *Richard II*, not for Tillyardism but for Plowden and *The King's Two Bodies*.[61] Exceptionally formal and stylized, the performance text's most striking feature—that two actors, Richard Pasco and Ian Richardson, alternated as Richard and Bolingbroke—was echoed in the program's double-page spread juxtaposing positive with negative photographic images of both actors in rehearsal. Appropriating role-playing as a metaphor for royal as well as theatrical power, Barton's performance text rewrites both deposition and closure, subsuming the play's radical politics in radical style.[62] As Richard begins his decoronation with "Now, mark me how I will undo myself," the Lord Marshal places the golden cloak of kingship—one of several symbolic costume elements shared by both actors—over Bolingbroke's shoulders; while the other Lords pray, each object Richard mentions (including one he does not, the orb) he gives to Bolingbroke. Denying his "acts, decrees, and statutes," Richard takes a book from York, hands it to Northumberland, and leads Bolingbroke to the throne, where he sits as though at Richard's command. What happens here is less a deposition than an exchange of symbolic objects between king and usurper, or, more accurately, the transfer of necessary stage properties from one protean actor to another, "doubling" them as signs in a purely theatrical display that hollows out and abstracts social meaning. Later, in the Pomfret scene, Barton further literalizes the king's interchangeable identity: the loyal Groom who enters to Richard, dressed in a monk's cowl, is Bolingbroke and, as the two hold between them the empty mirror frame—just as, in the deposition, they had held the crown—the image articulates their double entrapment, locked in one another's private as well as public identity.

In the final scene, all on stage wear black robes, masking individual differences. Bolingbroke and York stand together as Northumberland enters with four traitors' heads, Percy with two; Bolingbroke's disgust at this display generates a context that not only motivates his pardon of Carlisle but prepares for his anguished howl[63] as Exton enters with Richard's open coffin, which, following Bolingbroke's last speech, is closed and lowered into an onstage trap. But the performance text, which began with the figure of William Shakespeare investing one of the actors as King Richard, is not over. The by now familiar drumroll and coronation fanfare heralding the king's entrance sound once again as the figure of Shakespeare enters to crown Bolingbroke. On a drum crescendo, Bolingbroke kneels, his back to the audience, to receive the golden robe and the crown-mask that mark the King. All but two of his courtiers step away, the music swells to a climax, and the royal figure turns toward the audience. As the drums suddenly cease, the two courtiers throw back their hoods to reveal themselves, one as the actor who had played Richard, one as the actor who had played Bolingbroke, standing together as they had at the opening, mirrored identities. Between them stands the glittering golden figure whose robes are empty and whose face, as Stanley Wells writes, "[is] not that of King Richard, nor of King Henry. It [is] the face of the eternal king who keeps his court within the 'mortal temples of a king.' It [is] the face of Death."[64] Barton's strategy erases any difference between kings and, finally, transforms Quayle's empty, spotlit throne and silent procession into a literal "hollow crown," subsuming historical process into a neomedieval image—the dance of death, orchestrated, if not authored, by William Shakespeare. His staging not only privileges Richard's point of view, it also remystifies royal tragedy, which, at the close, reigns supreme over the actors who have played its roles. As Miriam Gilbert writes, each is "king and usurper, king and beggar,"[65] and both stand outside of any ideology save the institution of theatrical kingship, represented by the property crown in which "Death keeps his court." But although Barton's performance text resolves both history and historical myth in a heavily stylized coup de theatre, it does invest *Richard II* with a satisfying symmetrical design appropriate to a play that relies on a cultural equation between royal hegemony and dramatic form. And in casting kingship's absent center as a politics of actorly display, this *Richard II* not only connects Elizabethan strategies of power to those of a present-day decentered monarchy but recuperates, for the gaze of late twentieth-century spectators, what Quayle's performance text had denied: the visual pleasure of the close.

If Barton's production both repositioned *Richard II* as an independent entity and absorbed the play into a timeless, transhistorical realm of pure theater, Hands's 1980 Royal Shakespeare Company performance text adopted representational strategies that detailed the shift from one "world picture" to another. "Time," wrote Michael Billington, "is the real hero here . . . even if it doesn't get a program credit": the production moved from the opulence of "a burnished copper world" to "a society of darkness, gloom, flickering torches, and of men signing documents in small back rooms," transforming "feudal rivals into broken reeds joined together by an invisible thread of sorrow."[66] By taking two intervals rather than the usual single break, Hands called attention to Richard's movement through time: the first comes after Richard's confrontation with Bolingbroke at Flint Castle (3.3); the second follows Richard's farewell with the Queen on his way to the Tower (5.1).[67] Both structural choices are not only complicit with Richard's own preoccupation with ending but turn his abdication into the play's centerpiece, staged as a self-contained action with a prologue (the gardeners' scene, 3.4) and epilogue (the farewell, 5.1). So proportioned, the play then concludes on a coda that circumscribes Bolingbroke's reign with Richard's "double" deaths and where, at the close, both space and time collapse.

As Exton and eight murderers form a line across the back of the darkened, steeply raked stage, Bolingbroke enters to stand upstage of them, not part of or witness to the ensuing action but nonetheless linked to it. Stabbed in the back, Richard breaks away from Exton and falls, dying, far downstage; Exton kneels beside his body and speaks only a single phrase of his six-line speech, "This deed is chronicled in hell." Bolingbroke then moves slowly toward Richard's body as though drawn to it along invisible lines: the severe geometry of Hands's stage picture positions dead king and usurper precisely opposite one another, central figures in a nightmare re-vision of the play's opening, where Richard displayed himself as a divine image, imperiously setting the crown upon his head as he stood before a medieval bas-relief frieze. Now, Henry Lancaster, dressed in black and holding that same crown in his hand, nears Richard's crumpled body, enveloped in chains; as the nobles enter to report the rebels' deaths, Henry seems locked in a dream, answering them mechanically (fig. 11). When he finally reaches Richard's body, he stares at it in disbelief until Exton, kneeling in obeisance to the new King, transfers Richard's blood to Henry's hand. "I'll make a voyage to the Holy Land / To wash this blood off from my guilty hand" concludes the spoken text, and, on the last word, Henry crowns himself. Then, slowly and deliberately, he turns to look at Northumberland and his son Hotspur.

Hands's *Richard II* reflects his earlier work with the *Henry VI* trilogy in its use of background and foreground space, its economy of gesture, its eloquent use of the dead. Certainly Henry's final look, which anticipates *1 Henry IV*'s coming events, alludes to one of the most eccentric closural features in the *Henry VI* plays, the voice of the character—Suffolk, Richard of Gloucester—whose desire for power compromises the resolution, driving history's plot forward. Although this speaking look can be read as Hands's own self-reflexivity, as homage or conformity to those earlier playtexts, or as both, it functions most prominently, as one additional element in Hands's anticlimactic balancing act, to make visible and exaggerate the tensions latent in *Richard II*'s close. As the scene opens, Henry already mirrors Richard in his introspective grief; his stunned reactions to the reports of carnage and death reveal his guilt even before his hand becomes literally tainted with Richard's blood. And unlike either Quayle's or Barton's finales, where, respectively, a procession and a "coronation" absorb individual as well as communal guilt within spectacle, Hands's close denies such ritual atonement. Instead, in placing the crown on his head, Henry accepts Richard's paradoxical symbol of desire and death wish and, simultaneously, in acknowledging Northumberland and Hotspur, "reads" in their figures a future threat. This Henry IV indeed seems to have usurped Richard's earlier phrase—"O that I were as great / As is my grief, or less than my name!" (3.3.136–37)—together with the King's title, and made both his own.

Each of these *Richard II*s, though in highly idiosyncratic ways—an empty, spotlit throne; a crowned death's head; an isolated ruler aware of potential opposition—represents the play's final spectacle of rule as closing with, if not on, an image of the hollow crown. Michael Bogdanov's 1988 *Richard II* for the English Shakespeare Company—the first of seven productions in his *Wars of the Roses* marathon—is no exception.[68] The informing strategy behind this cycle, however, differs markedly from that of Quayle's 1951 Festival of Britain tetralogy. Although it reproduces Tillyard's notion of structural unity linking Shakespeare's histories into two tetralogies, the first closing with

Henry V, the second with *Richard III*, *Roses* counters Tillyard's total-izing idealist assumptions and instead works at hollowing out the myth of Elizabethan order, resituating the ideological struggles the plays de-scribe in the disorders of the recent past and the present. As for the ruling figures who mark "end points" in the cycle, Bogdanov's Henry V is neither the Elizabethan chronicler's "mirror of all Christian kings" nor Quayle's "true hero," but a haunted, self-tortured, nineteenth-cen-tury imperialist conqueror, shoring up a modern proto-capitalist state through dynastic marriage; and his Henry VII is a present-day "cor-porate ruler."

As the first play in this revisionary analysis of early modern power relations, *Richard II*'s opening and closing scenes encompass a histor-ical period spanning the nineteenth century and underscore the shift from one cultural context to another, much as in Hands's performance text, at the level of mise-en-scène. A faithful copy of the Westminster Abbey throne, placed upstage center, dominates the opening stage im-age of Richard's court; a number of chairs and small tables, draped with regal velvets, floor cushions, and a velvet-draped easel stand downstage of it, in what interior decorators call intimate groupings. A length of red velvet fabric, tossed casually on the back of the throne, and a far downstage chaise longue, also covered in red velvet, complete the decor; it is the chaise, not the throne, on which Richard, dressed in a blue velvet Regency dressing gown with flowing ascot, sits with his Queen as the lights come up. Transforming throne room to drawing room immediately softens, even feminizes, royal power—signs that the unused throne, which never appears again, and the king's costume and lounging posture confirm, and to which Bolingbroke's rigid Sandhurst brace and military dress make striking countersigns.

By the final scene, all has changed: a red-leather-padded late nine-teenth-century armchair stands alone as the single property in Chris Dyer's minimalist black-box set, backed with a cyclorama grillwork, and the new King, more minister than monarch, now wears impecca-ble morning dress. Richard's coffin, covered with a black pall and set on a rough, common "cart of war" (the first appearance of a property that will travel throughout the next three plays in the cycle), is placed parallel to the front of the stage, forming a barrier behind which, after banishing Exton, Bolingbroke stands, alone save for Northumber-land's shadowed figure in the background, poised in self-reflection. Hesitantly, he starts to lift one corner of the pall but quickly drops it and stands, in silence, his hands held just above the coffin's surface, as though attempting to touch the body within. The play that began with a potential confrontation between Richard and Bolingbroke—a confrontation Bolingbroke sought—ends in an incomplete gesture, marking the gap where the King's mortal and immortal bodies remain, in spite of the myth that joins them, forever separate. Raising his eyes from the coffin, Bolingbroke hears a clear soprano voice singing an anthem—"I will lift up mine eyes unto the hills, / From whence cometh my help"—that both supports and comments on the figure of a king who, like Richard at his decoronation, turns his eyes upon himself to find there, if not treason, the shape of a historical necessity that he cannot, perhaps, yet name. Economically, Bogdanov's final image restates the Janus-faced enigma central to *Richard II*'s closural spectacle of rule: although the body may be with the king, the king is not necessarily with the body. As Hamlet's mockery suggests, the king is indeed "a thing . . . of nothing," most vulnerable when most exposed, as here, to the absorbed gaze of a historically situated beholder. In terms of Shakespeare's future history writing, the fiction of the King's Two Bodies will recur, rewritten as the father's two bodies, one of which, though fat and old, remains potentially capable of fracturing and inverting the body of the kingdom by reconstituting himself as a site of visual pleasure.

"LET THE END TRY THE MAN":

1 AND *2* *HENRY IV*

The injuries that to myself I do,
Doing thee vantage, double vantage me.

—"Sonnet 88"

Taking Falstaff's part, A. C. Bradley begins "The Rejection of Falstaff" (1902) by asking, "Now why did Shakespeare end his drama with a scene which, though undoubtedly striking, leaves an impression so unpleasant?" Eventually, he concludes that *Henry IV*'s "chief hero" is the "wild" Prince Henry, who, in order to emerge "as a just, wise, stern, and glorious King," must, together with Bradley himself, banish Falstaffian plenitude.[1] Like Bradley, Orson Welles, a later Falstaffian conjuror, also begins with the end: discussing his 1966 film, *Chimes at Midnight*, an adaptation of *1* and *2* *Henry IV* with traces of *Richard II*, *Henry V*, and *The Merry Wives of Windsor*, he comments, "I directed everything, and played everything, with a view to preparing for the last scene."[2] The close of his film, however, not only readdresses Bradley's question from a diametrically opposed position but, by staging Falstaff's body as its primary site of spectacle, turns *Henry IV*'s royal narrative, as in Hotspur's phrase, "topsy-turvy down" (*1 Henry IV*, 4.1.82).

In the cathedral space where Henry V is crowned, Welles's film articulates the rejection in a shot–reverse shot exchange consisting primarily of low- and high-angle close-ups and mid-close-ups in which two shots are especially striking. In the first, as Henry says "I know thee not, old man," he stands with his back to a Falstaff he clearly knows so well he does not even need to look at him; in the second, as the new King finally turns away from the "surfeit-swelled" old man to walk between massed banners toward the light, the film cuts to a mid-close-up of Falstaff, whose gaze registers pride in the splendid figure of his "sweet boy." When soldiers carrying lances bar his view of Hal, Falstaff moves slowly to stand alone next to a column, speaks with Shallow and, finally, moves out of the shot. As Shallow calls to him, a series of extreme long shots details his own procession as he walks away from the camera toward the darkened castle ramparts, his bulk growing smaller and smaller in the frame until, against deep, empty foreground space, his tiny silhouette disappears through a lit archway. As in Shakespeare's playtext, the Lords—here, the Bishop, Prince John, and the Lord Chief Justice—remark on the King's "fair proceeding"; but then Welles's textual rearrangements counterpose that judgment with its "fair" results: Doll is arrested, calling for Falstaff, who is ordered to the Fleet; his tiny Page, squirming through the crowd, tells Pistol that Falstaff is sick; and Bardolph comments, "The King is a good king, but it must be as it may." Before the castle battlements, Henry proclaims "Now, Lords, for France" and orders Falstaff released from prison—"We consider / It was excess of wine that set him on."

Now the camera pans right to follow Poins as he walks past the empty tavern "throne" where Falstaff and Hal had both played Henry IV and into the innyard, where he stops beside a huge coffin, resting on a rude cart: "Falstaff?" "Falstaff is dead," says the page; and, after Mistress Quickly speaks his epitaph (*Henry V*, 2.3.9–24), she watches while the three men push the enormous coffin through the innyard gates across a snow-speckled landscape bounded by the distant castle walls. The camera slowly booms up to offer an omniscient perspective that traps this procession, in a high-angle extreme long shot, between tavern and court, and Ralph Richardson's authoritatively impersonal voice speaks a pastiche from Holinshed: "The new king, even at first appointing, determined to put on him the shape of a new man. This Henry was a captain of such prudence and such policy that he never enterprised anything before it forecast the main chances that it might happen. So humane withal, he left no offense unpunished nor friendship unrewarded. For conclusion, a majesty was he that both lived and died a pattern in princehood, a lodestar in honor, and famous to the world alway." Over a slow-motion film loop of a row of soldiers, nobles, and clerics, armed and ready for war, standing against the side wall of a church, pennon lances waving in the breeze, muffled drums beat out a rhythm that replaces his words.[3]

Rejected from the court by the King and from the tavern by Death, Falstaff's body inhabits a no-man's-land between the two spaces over which the voice of "history" presides, circumscribing and displacing Quickly's report of the fat knight's death with excerpts from Henry V's chronicle epitaph. Finally, the film reconstitutes the body, and the hierarchy, of the kingdom in an image that repeats itself endlessly, like the drums that simultaneously sound Falstaff's death knell and presage the coming war. If Welles's pseudo-Aristotelian complicity with tragedy generates a "finer end" (the Hostess's phrase), it also remaps the traditional territory[4] framed by "I know you all" and "I know thee not, old man" onto Falstaff's body to call Henry V's "carefully plotted official strategy" as well as the spectacle of rule into question. Strikingly, Welles's film is responsive not only to Bradley's praise, echoed by other readers, for Falstaff and his overreaching creator, "caught up in the wind of his own genius"—"It is not a misfortune that happens to many authors, nor is it one we can regret, for it costs us but a trifling inconvenience in one scene"[5]—but also to more recent configurations of the *Henry IV* plays as an ideal testing ground for examining the relations between plebian and patrician discourses, the carnivalesque and the theater as sites of subversion that work, ultimately, to authorize the state.[6] Indeed Welles himself envisioned his film, not as a "lament for Falstaff, but for the death of Merrie England . . . a myth, which has been very real to the English-speaking world . . . the age of chivalry, of simplicity, of Maytime and all that."[7] When Steven Mullaney writes, of Falstaff's rejection, that "what surprises is not the event itself but the fact that the world being cast off has been so consummately rehearsed: so fully represented to us, and consequently, so fully foreclosed,"[8] he identifies quite precisely the rupture between "play" and "history" that shapes 2 *Henry IV*'s close, a contradiction Welles's film reveals in the disjuncture between image and sound—the one recording what history excludes to hollow out the voice of official memory.

However split between a "prodigally lavish" Falstaffian economy and one of royal legitimation, between subversion and its containment, critical narratives of the *Henry IV* plays as well as late twentieth-century theatrical practice so consistently link its two parts into one that Falstaff's banishment becomes an end that indeed "crowns all." In fact, *Henry IV*'s "master narrative" not only subsumes *1 Henry IV*'s ending but absorbs the insistently coded closural gestures of *1* and *2 Henry IV*—what Samuel Crowl, writing on Welles's film, calls "The Long Goodbye"—into a pattern that arches over both plays to (always already) expel Falstaff. Reading *1* and *2 Henry IV*'s multiple endings from a "double vantage," I want not only to raise questions concerning their late sixteenth-century representation and reception but, by looking at several of their latter-day theatrical configurations, to examine how these reproduce or refashion, arrange or rearrange, social meaning as theatrical meaning. And I want to begin by describing *1 Henry IV*'s close in a version that, complete within itself, forecloses, so to speak, on the need for a second play.

Beerbohm Tree's 1895 *1 Henry IV*[9] constructs a highly idealized resolution of the play's contradictory, oppositional father-son relations. Omitting Hal's rescue of his father, Tree cuts from Falstaff's exit, taking a quick drink from the bottle Hal has just refused, to Hotspur's entrance, effecting a double exchange: rival son for rival father, true chivalry for its lack. As Hal and Hotspur recognize one another, the prompt copy indicates a trumpet flourish, followed by a pause and "picture" before an orchestral tremolo signals Falstaff's reentry to confront the Douglas. After the fights, Hal places a battle standard over Hotspur's body, turns briefly to address Falstaff, salutes Hotspur, and, with a sigh, exits. As the stage lights dim to an "evening effect," Falstaff glances over his shield; to the offstage clashing of swords, "very piano," he slowly rises and takes another drink from his bottle; but rather than taking up Hotspur's body, he falls to his knees and is about to lie down again when, seeing Hal and Prince John enter, he tries to creep away on his hands and knees. Helping Falstaff to his feet, Hal laughs, as Hotspur had done earlier in disbelief at his own death, and willingly gilds Falstaff's lie before proclaiming "the day is ours," at which a "15th and Final Flourish" sounds, backed by "hurrahs." Tree cuts Falstaff's promise to reform and moves directly to a mass entrance that fills the stage with soldiers, who frame a central tableau in which King Henry and Prince Hal embrace, surrounded by waving banners and triumphant "Huzzahs." Not only does Hotspur's body remain on the stage to figure the rebels' defeat and Hal's victory but, since Tree himself played Falstaff and since the prompt copy indicates no exit for him,[10] this close gives Hal two fathers and celebrates his reconciliation with both amidst a splendid military spectacle.

Its pictorial realization reminiscent of eighteenth- and nineteenth-century commemorative paintings of famous battles, this sort of grand finale, its power greatly enhanced by the practice then common of playing the national anthem at the end of each performance, caps *1 Henry IV*s well into the 1950s.[11] While some performance texts, like Tree's, simply substitute military spectacle for the play's final scene, others, such as Bridges-Adams's for the Shakespeare Memorial Theatre in 1932,[12] by retaining King Henry's sentence of Worcester and Vernon, punish treason against the state and heal filial "treason" with the image of a Hal who kneels to his father at the final victory declaration. So transformed into moral myth, closure becomes a nostalgic fantasia in which rebellion has indeed lost its sway, mastered by heroism and military might embodied in a unitary spectacle that authenticates the relations between past and present cultures along a trans-historical continuum of idealized national and familial values.

In taking on such contours, these *1 Henry IV*s push to extremes the resolution of a story familiar to Elizabethans—the parable of the prodigal son, one well-known through two models, the biblical narrative and the equally mythologized tales, dramatized in the anonymous play, *The Famous Victories of Henry V*, of what Henry IV calls his son's "vile participation" (3.2.87).[13] In both versions, it is an exclusively male narrative directed toward working through father-son antagonisms and, in the case of the parable only, those between a dutiful elder son and his wastrel brother. Also in both, it is not the prodigal son's legitimacy that is in question but the need to establish his authenticity in relation to patriarchal law. Drawing on these paradigms as well as on chronicle materials, Shakespeare's play constructs a highly mythologized economy, structured through binary oppositions—court/tavern, honor/dishonor, time/timelessness, everyday/holiday, word/body, serious history/comic–popular discourse—in which the first term represents the desirable ideal, the second its inversion. As the only figure who can move flexibly between their boundaries, Hal encompasses their contradictions, for which Shrewsbury—represented on the one hand as history, and on the other as a purely theatrical invention—is the ideal testing ground.

Unlike Shakespeare's earlier histories, where conflict centers on genealogical descent in a struggle for the crown's rightful ownership, *1 Henry IV* positions the Percy-Northumberland rebellion against the state so that it serves Hal's mimetic rivalry with Hotspur as well as that between his authentic and counterfeit fathers, Henry IV and Falstaff.[14] In this extremely limited gender economy, structured by a desire for the male other that takes the form of aggression, women are positioned at history's margins: unnecessary to prove or deny Hal's or Hotspur's legitimacy (as, for instance, in *King John*), they simply delay historical time. Only the rebel leaders—Hotspur and Lord Mortimer—have wives, whose presence functions primarily to separate public from private domains and, by proving their husbands' heterosexuality, deflects the homoerotic into the homosocial; says Hotspur, "This is no world / To play with mammets or to tilt with lips" (2.3.87–88), nor has he time to listen to the Welsh lady sing (3.1.234). In their resistance to the male chivalric project, Kate Percy and Glendower's daughter are kin to Falstaff, a more substantial image of feminine "misrule," who lies within the tavern space, together with thieves, swaggerers, a Hostess-landlady, and "gentlewomen" who, it is said, "live honestly by the prick of their needles" (*Henry V*, 2.1.31–32). Although within the Oedipal narrative, Falstaff figures as Hal's surrogate father, he is coded in feminine, maternal terms:[15] his fat belly is the masculine counterpart of the pregnant woman; his Rabelaisian excesses of food and drink make him the Carnival antithesis to Henry IV's ascetic Lenten identity and his world of religious penance, bent as Henry IV is on expiating personal as well as national guilt with a crusade. It is Falstaff who accuses Hal of being the king's bastard son, and Hal, too, imagines him as female when, just before baiting Falstaff about his Gadshill cowardice and with Hotspur circulating in his mind and in his talk, he thinks himself into playing Percy and "that damned brawn" into "Dame Mortimer his wife" (2.4.104–5). That "play extempore" is then transformed into one where the roles of king and son become interchangeable, shared between Falstaff and Hal, and where women have no place: Falstaff's first "command" as "father-king" is "convey my tristful queen" (2.4.375).

But perhaps the most telling of Falstaff's multiform female guises of misrule is his association with Queen Elizabeth's virgin identity: "Let us be Diana's foresters, gentlemen of the shade, minions of the moon; and let men say we be men of good government, being governed as the sea is, by our noble and chaste mistress the moon" (1.2.23–27).[16] Desiring to undertake something like Essex's role in the annual Accession Day Tourneys that celebrated Elizabeth's powerfully mythic, theatricalized presence, his fantasy of social order would steal and invert Essex's chivalric image—echoed in Hotspur's "easy leap / To pluck bright honor from the pale-faced moon" (1.3.201–2)—in order to recode his own body. Chivalry's daytime, however, cannot admit an aging, corpulent "squire of the night's body," whose 2 *Henry IV* counterpart, mentioned in passing, is Shallow's "bona roba," Jane Nightwork (3.2.188). Even Hal, "a truant to chivalry" and the "shadow" of his father's succession (5.1.94), must transform himself to look the part of a May lord, "Ris[ing] from the ground like feathered Mercury . . . / As if an angel dropped down from the clouds," in order to confront Hotspur, a "Mars in swaddling clothes," the "king of honor" (4.1.106–8; 3.2.112; 4.1.10).[17] And although Sir John's body is also capable of metamorphosis, his transformations, and the codes he serves, work precisely to expose such glorious disguises.

Elizabethan spectators would have still other figures for Falstaff, and for his fluid gender identity, including his guise of eternal youth, that are distant from present-day readers and spectators. Spectators at *1 Henry IV*'s first performances, when Falstaff was called Oldcastle, would connect him not only with the character of the same name in *The Famous Victories* but also with a historical Sir John Oldcastle, a martyr celebrated in Foxe's *Actes and Monuments* and sentenced to death for treason by Henry V. Certainly some observers, the sixteenth-century Oldcastle descendants, Sir William Brooke and his son, the seventh and eighth Lord Cobhams, objected to such libel of the family name. And their objections had considerable weight, for Sir William was the Lord Chamberlain, with oversight responsibilities for the Master of Revels and the licensing of plays: given such sensitivity in high places, Shakespeare changed the name, and though traces of it remain in *1 Henry IV*, *2 Henry IV*'s Epilogue offers a public disclaimer that "Oldcastle died martyr, and this is not the man" (Ep., 27–28).[18] The subject of anecdotes, letters, and rivàl plays, the Oldcastle-Falstaff issue may well have been fueled by the character's impersonator, the famous clown, Will Kemp, whom Nashe described as "jest-monger and Vice-gerent general to the ghost of Dick Tarlton" and who "succeeded" Tarlton as a favorite of Queen Elizabeth as well as the general public.[19] David Wiles argues persuasively that the Oldcastle-Falstaff role was written with Kemp in mind and that Kemp's particular skills helped to shape it, especially his ability to produce the illusion, in speaking scripted words, of spur-of-the-moment improvisation. And the conventions that coded a clown's role—ambiguous social status and semi-androgynous identity, freedom to separate himself from the play's role and plot structure, metamorphosis and final exclusion[20]—rather precisely figure the attributes of Falstaff, who is both thief and knight, gentleman and marginal reveller, mother as well as father and giant "Power Baby,"[21] separate from but also central to the historical rebellion, protean liar, the excluded other. Throughout, but most especially at Shrewsbury, all of these images of his theatrical abundance come into play.

To "thrust in clowns by head and shoulders"[22] or, in this case, belly first, at Shrewsbury is, of course, Shakespeare's invention. The official chronicle sources record a battle in which the chief actors are Henry IV, Hotspur, and the Douglas, and position Hal simply as his father's helper, "a lusty young gentleman" who, though wounded, refuses to withdraw and continues to "fight where the battle was most hot."[23] And it is entirely possible to extract, from Shakespeare's own fictional account in *1 Henry IV*—in which his major additions to its royal plot are Hal's offer to oppose Hotspur "in single fight," his rescue of his father, his combat with Hotspur, his freeing of the Douglas, and the presence of Prince John—a "decent" version of Shrewsbury that avoids the "mingling [of] kings and clowns" that Sidney so deplores.[24] Indeed, these particular alterations are sufficient to reshape the chronicle record as a test of feudal and familial values, similar to those dramatized in the closing battles of the *Henry VI* plays. Selectively retold, such a decorously perfected narrative might begin as the King, with unexpected concern for his wounded son, begs him to retire; following Hal's refusal, both Henry IV and Hal praise John's valor in "hold[ing]

Lord Percy at the point"—an event that gives Hal a second rival, his "true" brother. And when Hal's "fair rescue" of his father "redeem[s] his lost opinion, he dispels his "loose behavior" and supposed treachery—and with it the filial aggression dramatized in *The Famous Victories*[25]—as a rumor perpetrated by others: "they did me too much injury / That ever said I heark'ned for your death" (5.4.50–51). So prepared for, the Hal-Hotspur combat—what Graham Holderness calls "a vivid poem of feudal romance and chivalric adventure"[26]—is an exchange of "glorious deeds" for "indignities" that, with the death of the rival (rebel) son, ensures Hal's place as Henry IV's "authentic" heir. Finally, in the play's last scene, with the rebels vanquished and punished, Henry IV acknowledges that authenticity: Hal, granted leave by his father to dispose of the Douglas, not only redeems his prisoner, and so takes on the Hotspur-like qualities his father had so admired, but, in recognition of John's valor, transfers the "honorable bounty" to his brother just before his father, for the first time, and in the play's concluding speech, calls him "son Harry" (5.5.39).

In that Falstaff is kept apart from his kingly other, Shakespeare's fiction of Shrewsbury approaches this decorous ideal: during the battle, he appears only with Hal or alone on the stage and, in conformity with convention, is absent from its final "official" ending. Yet, curiously enough, Shakespeare's "double reading" of the chronicle takes license for Falstaff's appearance at Shrewsbury from details that, in keeping with his fictional status as a Lord of Misrule, are introduced as hearsay:

> (as some write) the earl of Douglas struck [Henry IV] down, and at that instant slew sir Walter Blunt, and three other, apparelled in the kings suit and clothing, saying: I marvel to see so many kings thus suddenly arise one in the neck of an other. The king in deed was raised, & did that day many a noble feat of arms, for as it is written, he slew that day with his own hands six and thirty persons of his enemies. The other on his part encouraged by his doings, fought valiantly, and slew the lord Percy, called sir Henry Hotspur.[27]

In *1 Henry IV*'s Shrewsbury, many also walk in the King's coats: indeed, Shrewsbury begins by killing the king, later recognized by Hotspur as Blunt, and so recirculates the question of the true king's identity, the central issue behind the Hotspur-Northumberland rebellion (5.3). Having others march in the King's armor represents the King's body both as powerfully doubled and redoubled in his subjects and as an empty lie; it also questions whether counterfeiting, dying as one's self or in another's guise, is honorable when put at the king's service, dishonorable when put into play by a Falstaffian subject.

For in *1 Henry IV*, it is Falstaff, not the King, who "rises," and the ambiguous "other on his part" becomes Hal who, as in Daniel's *Civil Wars*, saves his father's life.[28] While Holinshed represents the king-father's body as a multiform illusion, in *1 Henry IV*, it is Falstaff— whose "lying" nature the play codes in his body as well as his voice— who calls such illusion, and the omnipresence of fatherly law, into question. If, like the Douglas, the play's first, or first-time, spectators assume that, in killing Blunt, he has killed the king, they could also imagine that the Douglas does indeed kill Falstaff, especially since their attention is, so to speak, doubled, for the encounter occurs at the same time as Hal's mythic combat with Hotspur, Shrewsbury's most heroic event for which Falstaff is, at first, an observer:

> *They fight. Enter Falstaff*
> FALST. Well said, Hal, to it Hal. Nay you shall find no boys' play here I can
> tell you.
> *Enter Douglas, he fighteth with Falstaff, he falls down as if he were dead,*
> *the Prince killeth Percy.*
>
> (5.4.74–75)

When, later, Hal speaks double epitaphs—one for Hotspur's "stout" heart, one over Falstaff's stout body—the conventions alone dictate resolution, neatly rounded off in perfect, and perfectly accidental, closure that dispenses with both rival son and rival parent, throwing the rivals into relationship, joining antithetical perspectives on honor that the play has kept separate but parallel, restoring order in the play's most politically significant systems: father-son relations, the threatened division of the kingdom, and Hal's authenticity. Indeed, since the last six lines of Hal's eulogy on Falstaff even fall into rhyme, it is possible for spectators as well as readers to hear these "last words" as the end of the play. In present-day theatrical configurations of the scene, the pause that invariably follows Hal's exit certainly invites spectators to believe in both deaths: even when "Falstaff riseth up" to fals-ify the illusion, it is only his ability to speak, proclaiming himself "no counterfeit, but the true and perfect image of life indeed," that codes the moment as something other than a curtain call where, eventually, the two other bodies onstage—the players of Hotspur and Blunt, dressed in armor that counterfeits the King—would also rise to acknowledge spectators' applause.

Most present-day critical configurations of this moment claim that Falstaff's resurrection invites readers and spectators, first, to be complicit with him, welcoming his surprise return from death, and then reject him when he stabs Hotspur and leaves to claim Hal's glory as his own.[29] But in fact the playtext makes none of these moralistic judgments; rather, the only "moral work" is Falstaff's own, and it constitutes a riff on the infinite possibilities of theatrical dying (5.4.114–17). Here again, *1 Henry IV*'s Elizabethan spectators would have other options. For those who knew the character as Oldcastle, the fat knight's "rising" might take on specific topical resonances and be read as a lampoon on Oldcastle's alleged dying promise that he would "rise from death to life again, the third day."[30] And when his "killing" of Hotspur is read through the conventions associated with the clown, Falstaff's weapon takes on particular meaning. His sword first appears at Gadshill as a property that figures him as both Vice and adolescent, for the Vice's traditional weapon was a dagger of lath, similar to the wooden "waster" used by apprentices in the Sunday evening fights allowed them by their masters.[31] "Hacked like a handsaw" by Falstaff himself after the robbery, it is clearly a toy sword as well as a figure for his name—a "false staff" that, in figuring his lack of a potent phallus, is an emblematic weapon well chosen to represent his ineffectiveness in chivalry's, so to speak, metallic world. And it is this same child's toy with which he gives Hotspur a "new wound in [his] thigh" (5.4.127), an injury Shakespeare seems to transfer from the chronicler's Douglas—who "brake one of his cullions" in a fall and, having so lost his manliness, was pardoned by Henry IV[32]—to Hotspur. For all its insistent mythologizing of the heroic, Shrewsbury's battle is, finally, just what Falstaff claimed it was not: "boys' play."[33] And what gives it the lie and refutes its chivalric signs, making them serve his own interests, is the clown's interventionary presence. A creature who draws his own authenticity from the suspect realm of theatrical shadows, he, more than any other, is well aware that the counterfeit—the reproduced image of the authentic—has no value until it is put into circulation and exchanged.[34]

Curiously enough, it is the rupture within Hal's own chivalry—his failure to take favors from Hotspur and, instead, to give him his own—that enables Falstaff to recirculate Hotspur's body and claim for himself the father's honor. While it is usual to displace Hal's "fault" onto Falstaff and to read Falstaff as one who takes meaning from Hal, present-day theatrical configurations in which Hal demonstrates less than chivalric tactics in the fight show him sharing in Falstaff's brand of honor, a choice that can turn his gilding of Falstaff's lie into a kind of self-justification. Even more important, however, is Falstaff's ability to steal meaning from Henry IV. As he leaves the stage to "follow . . . for

reward" (5.4.158), promising dietary reform, it looks as though Carnival will indeed yield to Lent and so, perhaps, create a new fiction of
a Falstaff who can insert his transformed body into history. His words
sound final—sound, that is, like the end of his role—and *1 Henry IV*'s
final scene excludes him from its image of a reconstituted, rebellion-
free royal hierarchy. Elizabethan spectators would recognize these
moves as entirely "decorous," for the clown's final metamorphosis and
his absence from the play's last scene were conventions of his role, and
he would, in most cases, return to perform the traditional jig finale.[35]
In the play's representational economy, convention works to dismantle
narrative closure. By the last scene, Shakespeare seems to revert to
reading the chronicle "straight": Henry IV never has knowledge of
precisely which "other on his part"—whether Hal or Falstaff—has
killed Hotspur. It is only Falstaff who, at least in some sense, has witnessed the event and turned it to imagined future advantage. And
when, at the close, the King looks forward to "such another day," he
reads into Shrewsbury's official account what *2 Henry IV* will, at first,
record as a lie destined for the ears of Hotspur's "crafty-sick" father
and, then, as the means to reinstate a newly costumed, newly titled
"valiant Jack Falstaff," and so to further transform *1 Henry IV*'s "mingle" of king and clown.

≈

From the mid-1950s forward, theatrical configurations of *1 Henry
IV*'s close for the most part avoid the seamless, unitary discourse of
spectacle characteristic of late nineteenth- and earlier twentieth-century versions and so not only "play out the play" but extend its boundaries, though not, except in one case, in order to say more on Falstaff's
behalf (2.4.460–61). In that it so clearly articulates patterns of substitution and replacement among rival sons and fathers, Terry Hands's
1975 Royal Shakespeare Company *1 Henry IV* draws the closing
scenes into what might be called a structuralist's dream.[36] In the Hal-
Hotspur combat, Hotspur disarms Hal, who then seizes Hotspur's
sword and aims two blows at his shield and a third at his stomach,
which brings him to his knees; Hal then removes Hotspur's helmet and
slashes his face with a dagger. On "I better brook the loss of brittle
life," Hotspur grabs Hal and slowly stands, to die in his arms. To further cement their brotherhood, Hal lays Hotspur's body down and,
kneeling beside it, enacts a series of ceremonial gestures: after wiping
Hotspur's blood onto his own face, he places Hotspur's sword on his
chest, crosses the dead hands over it, takes a red cloth from his own
dagger to cover Hotspur's eyes, and finally stands and removes his own

helmet while he praises his dead rival. In contrast, he pauses just long enough to see Falstaff and speak his epitaph but does not touch his body. When Falstaff returns to life, he not only performs a sequence of actions—speaking a few lines before rising to his knees and, finally, standing—that echo Hotspur's but repeats Hal's tactics by stabbing Hotspur with his own sword; linking him to both, his mimicry also calls the value of such gestures into question and, when he drags Hotspur's body offstage, subverts them completely. To further the transformed value of Hotspur's body, Hands repeats the image—not once but twice. As Falstaff exits, Hal reenters with John[37] and registers surprise at seeing neither Hotspur nor Falstaff; then Falstaff returns, dragging Hotspur's body behind him to hear a bemused Hal "gild" his lie. Left alone after Hal and John exit together, Falstaff again drags Hotspur's body out, undercutting his final promise to "live cleanly as a nobleman should do." Although this staging replaces Falstaff with John as Hal's companion, neither Hal's bond to Falstaff nor his to Hal is severed: indeed, this Hal seems to accept Falstaff's lie in order to accept his own counterfeiting self.

Hands's final stage images trace a further range of substitutions. Led in on ropes, Worcester and Vernon flank King Henry's central figure, while Westmoreland stands directly upstage of Henry, with Clarence and Humphrey at either side of him. Deliberately enforcing military justice, Henry drops, first, Worcester's rope and, after a pause, Vernon's. When Westmoreland and Humphrey exit with the prisoners, Henry moves downstage where, as Hal kneels at his right, asking for leave to dispose of the Douglas, and John moves to his father's left, both sons replace Worcester and Vernon, the traitors. On "ransomless and free," Hal stands, as Hotspur had earlier when Henry questioned him about his prisoners (1.3); and the echo of one son replacing another persists when Henry calls Hal "son Harry," puts an arm on his shoulder, and draws him toward a prominent downstage position before, pausing as though in doubt, he speaks his final line, "Let us not leave till all our own be won," which cues music filled with expectant drumbeats.[38] Hands's staging reconstitutes the initial image of Henry surrounded by roped prisoners as a Plantagenet family portrait: Clarence and John stand in Vernon and Worcester's positions, Humphrey directly upstage of King Henry, Westmoreland up left, and Hal, now the "authentic" heir, directly downstage of Henry. As in Hands's closing images for the *Henry VI* plays, this final tableau figures a hard-won stability and predicts the "true" successor. And if replacing traitors with sons and cousins also refigures rebellion as a family matter, freeze-framing the close not only suppresses such potential contradictions but makes them unreadable, masked by an image of exclusive familial hierarchy that perfectly expresses the self-regarding gaze of legitimated royal power.

While the formal satisfactions of Hands's close fix Shrewsbury's moment within time, the close of Trevor Nunn's 1982 *1 Henry IV*, again for the Royal Shakespeare Company,[39] goes beyond its limits to reread its victory through Henry IV's eyes. The final image rhymes with the opening spectacle, where a flickering candlelight procession of monks, all in white robes and cowls, moves slowly downstage, while the rest of the company fills the dimly lit boxlike rooms, walkways, and turrets of the set—watchers as well as participants assembled to sing a haunting *Te Deum*. There, the King, dressed in a gold-embroidered ceremonial white cope, emerges from the procession to stand at its head, encompassed by the symbolic weight of his costume; here, the close diminishes the full panoply of that opening tableau. Bare to the waist and wearing a large crucifix, King Henry kneels in a tunnel of light, a shadowy kingdom of men and women standing in darkness behind him to observe his solitary, agonized penance. Drawing on Henry's opening wish to undertake a pilgrimage, Nunn's ending positions Shrewsbury's victory as a tainted substitute for and displacement of Henry's desire to lead a crusade that will expiate his guilt. It is an image that can be doubly read. If read backwards through *Richard II*'s ending and forward through the King's speech on the crown (*2 Henry IV*, 4.5.178–219), the image sharply focuses Henry's private angst and, by showing him surrounded by onstage spectator-subjects, all eyes turned toward the King, enhances his vulnerability and, as in *Richard II*'s close, figures not royal power but its lack. But the image can also be read through the schematic opposition of rival fathers: although it is Falstaff who promises reform, here it is Henry IV who performs his Shrewsbury penance.

Only once in *1 Henry IV*, at the parley just before Shrewsbury's battle (5.1), do King Henry and Falstaff share the stage, within a context that flirts with equating carnival and rebellion. When the King asks Worcester how he came to rebel, Falstaff answers for him, "Rebellion lay in his way, and he found it," and Hal quickly silences him—"Peace, chewet, peace!" (5.1.27–28). Whether Henry IV either does not hear or simply chooses to ignore Falstaff's remark, he never addresses him; Falstaff himself does not speak again until, following Hal's offer to "Try fortune with [Hotspur] in a single fight" and the King's offer of amnesty for the rebels, he is alone with Hal and asks for "friendship": "Hal, if thou seest me down in the battle . . ." (5.1.121). But although the playtext denies the support of language to the moment, this does not rule out the possibility of a silent exchange between Falstaff and the King, and both Hands's and Nunn's performance texts took this opportunity to sketch in their rivalry. In Hands's staging, both the King and Falstaff start to leave, and when Falstaff turns back to plead with Hal, the King pauses to watch their encounter, as though to satisfy himself that Hal will indeed keep his promise to "redeem all this on Percy's head" rather than revert to playing holiday with Falstaff. And Nunn's Henry IV, caught between envy and contempt for Falstaff, turns away, his shoulders sagging in defeat as Hal jokes with Falstaff.[40] Emrys James, who played Henry IV in Hands's production, remarked in an interview with Michael Mullin that "one can conceive a marvellous scene being written about [Henry and Falstaff]—a meeting between them."[41] Two other performance texts—Welles's *Chimes at Midnight* and Michael Bogdanov's 1987 English Shakespeare Company *1 Henry IV*—provide such a meeting, though not, perhaps, the one James may have had in mind.

Welles's film extends Hands's and Nunn's exchange of speaking looks to read Shrewsbury's victory as a record of personal loss and, by including Falstaff in its final moves, changes the relations between history and carnival, between the official version of Shrewsbury and Falstaff's account. When Falstaff throws Hotspur's body to the ground, Hal kneels in the mud and turns the body over on its back; in a mid-long shot of Hal, seen across Hotspur's body, a figure enters the frame at left, only the bottom of his robe visible, and the camera, rising with Hal, moves left to reveal King Henry, facing his son, his back to the camera. In a tightly edited sequence of close-ups—Henry's anguished face; Hal's look, caught between his two fathers; Falstaff's glow of self-pleasure; Hal meeting his father's gaze—the film links the three figures in an ambiguous web of doubt, betrayal, and dishonor in which Falstaff's expectant "I look to be either earl or duke, I assure you" cancels what Hal wants to say but cannot: that he has killed Hotspur. In a long shot, father and son face each other across the dead body before the King walks past Hal, strides into the background, and, in the next several shots, mounts his horse, collapses over the saddle in anguish, and, recovering, raises his arm in salute as the camera pans right to follow rows of horsemen. The next sequence reveals Falstaff, surrounded by his entire crew of ragged soldiers, a huge wine keg in the background; as though the previous confrontation had not occurred, he speaks a truncated version of his dissertation on sherris-sack (*2 Henry IV*, 4.3.83–119) and offers a tankard to Hal, who takes it and drinks, his forced smile suddenly becoming serious as he turns away from Falstaff, not sharing in the general laughter. As Falstaff's own smile turns quizzical and disappears, Hal, seen in an extreme long shot, walks away across the smoke-filled battlescape, dropping the tankard: the sound track registers only the wind's empty roar, and the shot fades out. Restating father-son oppositions, Welles's film deepens and sharply triangulates them to entrap a doubly orphaned Hal between his rival fathers—cut off by his father's gaze and rejecting Falstaff's sack-nurturing maternity himself—and, in eclipsing the image of Falstaff's bulk with that of Hal's receding figure, points forward to Sir John's ultimate rejection.

Deliberately quoting Welles's film, Michael Bogdanov's *1 Henry IV* not only reorders the play's final events but figures a more radical disjuncture between historical event and Falstaffian intervention than either *Chimes at Midnight* or Shakespeare's play.[42] In this eclectically dressed production, where costume ranges from Hal's blue jeans and open-necked shirt to nineteenth-century military uniform for Henry IV to commandolike garb for the rebels and camouflage gear for Falstaff, Hal and Hotspur wear tabards and chain mail for their mythic combat on a bare stage—bare, that is, except for the rounded hill of Falstaff's body. Toward the end of a long fight with heavy broadswords, Hal loses his and curls into a fetal position, as though overcome with infantile fear. With a grin, Hotspur slides the sword across to him; recovering immediately, Hal comes at him, slices across his gut in an ugly sweep, and then plunges the sword down from the shoulder, crosswise under the tabard, to his heart. Standing behind Hotspur and cradling his body, he stabs him once more, this time from the rear, on Hotspur's "And food for . . ."—an unnecessary overkill, this Hal's deliberate revenge on his father's obvious preference for Hotspur, as well as a coup de grace in tribute to Hotspur's bravery. As Hal returns his sword to the scabbard, he starts to exit, and then, seeing Falstaff, dismissively speaks his epitaph. When, after removing a NO ENTRY sign from his shirt, Falstaff rises, he uses a child's toy sword to saw at Hotspur's thigh before heaving him onto his back as he leaves the stage.

Now the King, Worcester, Westmoreland, Prince John, and Hal return for the play's final scene, but as Henry concludes his last speech, Falstaff enters with Hotspur's body and unceremoniously plunks it down center, in front of Hal (fig. 13). His "I look to be either earl or duke, I assure you" is spoken half to Henry IV, half to Hal; positioned between the two, his bulk separating father and son, he recounts his version of Shrewsbury. Henry IV crosses to the body, looks down at it and then up at Hal, silently accusing him, before turning away to exit upstage center; after a self-righteous smirk at his brother, John follows his father, and an angry Hal smashes his sword to the floor with both hands. Pulling a cart piled with dead bodies, a soldier enters to circle the stage, weaving around Hal and Falstaff, stopping briefly at Hotspur's body before he exits. Now Hal bends over Hotspur's body, takes back the neckerchief he had worn in the earlier tavern scenes and had tied around the dead Hotspur's neck, and replaces it jerkily around his own—a mark of his kill through which he reaccepts the rivalry separating father and son. As though attempting to placate him, Falstaff delivers his promise to leave sack and live cleanly to a Hal who, without looking at him, orders him to "bring your luggage *nobly* on your back," an irony this Falstaff shrugs off as he exits, once again bearing Hotspur's body. Alone, Hal raises his sword with both hands straight over his head, turns upstage, and, his back rigid, exits toward his father into the gathering dark to the accompaniment of crashing brasses.

Like Welles's ending for Shrewsbury, Bogdanov's rewritten close sharply focuses Hal's entrapment. Although similar to Welles's strategy in catalyzing Hal's guilt through an exchange of gazes to turn him back into an unredeemed son, Bogdanov's close also more sharply calls the limits of counterfeiting into question. This *1 Henry IV* not only restores the father-son opposition but refuses to exclude a Falstaff who imagines his lie a Shrewsbury joke not unlike Henry IV's "shadows" marching in armor. By omitting Hal's gilding of Falstaff's lie, Bogdanov's rearranged ending permits Falstaff to take revenge for Hal's exposure of his Gadshill cowardice. And its final emphases rest not on Hal's rejection of Falstaff but on Hal's own exclusion, his need to prove himself once more and also, perhaps, to seek revenge against the father who, doubting his true son, believes the boastful lie of another, counterfeit, father. The close of Bogdanov's *2 Henry IV* will further transform, and interrogate, this finale to read Henry V's rejection of Falstaff as his final, bitter revenge on all such fatherly lies.

❧

Rising to the surface at Shrewsbury, Rumor becomes embodied in *2 Henry IV*, first as a choral figure who calls Shrewsbury into question, and then, from within the play proper, as messengers bring news of King Henry's defeat and Hal's death to Northumberland. History, this opening intimates, is made up of misreport, facts told by imperfect eyewitnesses who—like the messenger who reports Hal's death in Nunn's opening scene—may have left before the battle's turning point. Just as one function of Hal's "I know you all" soliloquy (*1 Henry IV*, 1.2.183–205) is to erase the Hal of another play, *The Famous Victories*, so do Rumor and the messengers' news unsettle *1 Henry IV*'s account of Shrewsbury and invite its reinterpretation.[43] Yet far from forgetting Part One, Part Two remembers and reworks its oppositional economy, reprising some scenes in particular, though in a random order. Part 1's tavern scene, for instance, recurs twice, once when Hal returns to the Boar's Head (2.4) and again in Falstaff's rejection (5.5); the Gaultree incident (4.1–4.3) replays a diminished Shrewsbury, a second rebellion that ends with apparent surrender, prompted by Prince John's politic lies, and the traitors' arrest. Once again, Falstaff expects reward for capturing a rebel—Sir John Coleville, who apparently yields to his rumored reputation as a "famous true subject" (4.3.61); once again a member of the royal family—this time, Prince John—promises to speak better of him than he deserves (4.3.82). And perhaps most unexpectedly, the Gadshill robbery, where Falstaff and Hal stole crowns (*1 Henry IV*, 2.2), and Falstaff's counterfeit death, as well as Hal's earlier confrontation with his father, are all echoed in Henry IV's death in the Jerusalem chamber (4.5). But *2 Henry IV* also consumes and subsumes its historical subject matter by positioning Falstaff, not Henry IV or Hal, as the play's central figure. As much as, if not more than, the royal succession, it is his dramatic succession that is at issue: though excluded from *1 Henry IV*'s finale, he reappears in, so to speak, reinstitutionalized form, to demonstrate how Carnival's "double vantage," though it may threaten to unseat kingship and usurp genre, ultimately reauthorizes both.[44]

Critical as well as theatrical configurations of the *Henry IV* plays almost invariably point to their interdependency; only rarely do critics (myself included) refer to one without the other, and isolated productions of *2 Henry IV* are less common in the late twentieth century than in its earlier decades.[45] When so paired in either critical or performance discourse, the closing scenes of *2 Henry IV* tend to fall into a pattern that is exclusively dictated by and subservient to history's royal narrative. Indeed, *2 Henry IV*'s traditional constellation is a story of authorial failure in which, by delaying Henry IV's death and Hal's accession, the playwright is forced to flesh out historical lack with a fictional Falstaff and so, though only coincidentally, capitalize on the character's dramatic and—judging from the number of published quartos of *1 Henry IV*—commercial success.[46] In such readings, the King's death and Hal's appearance as Henry V become the "true" or "appropriate" climax of an action centered on the education of the Prince in which Falstaff's rejection, and that of the "sick" body of the kingdom he is thought to figure, is a moral as well as a dramatic necessity for England's health.[47] Even if it does not strictly obey neoclassical rules, this configuration of the play does at least mimic the pattern of Shakespeare's earlier histories by anatomizing the institution of kingship and affirming its strategies of legitimation at the close. But 2 *Henry IV* can also be read as a critique of Shakespeare's earlier historical practice, first in that it exposes history as possible misrepresentation, and then in that it embeds those events that articulate closure in the other histories—generating a new King to ensure the succession—within a primarily Falstaffian representational economy.[48] Both views of the play, of course, insist on a similarly "unpleasant" close. In a special sense of that term, 2 *Henry IV* is a multiple-text play—one refigured by readings that insist on privileging its royal narrative and Hal's "double reformation" into a much less radical entity than its doubled closural economy would suggest. And in terms of the play's performance history, it can become re-formed to neutralize or repress Falstaff's presence and so to manage the anxieties he represents.

One of the most inherently conservative versions of 2 *Henry IV*'s close exists in Sir Edward Dering's early seventeenth-century adaptation, which, by collapsing *1* and *2 Henry IV* into one play, closes with Henry IV's death and the spectacle of Henry V's coronation, suitably diminished so as not to deform its "tragical-historical" design.[49] While Dering does not entirely erase Falstaff from the close, he much abbreviates the rejection to include only Falstaff's approach to Hal-Henry V, a warning from the Lord Chief Justice, and most of Hal's last speech, ending with this addition:

> Now change our thoughtes for honour and renowne,
> And since the royalty and crowne of Fraunce,
> Is due to us wee'll bring itt to our awe,
> Or breake itt all to peeces. Vanityes farewell
> Wee'll now act deedes for Chronicles to tell.
>
> *(ll. 77–81)*

Dering reads Falstaff's rejection simply as a necessary tying-up of narrative strands; in his finale, Hal's last words, which sound remarkably like Edward IV's in *3 Henry VI* (5.7.45–46), look forward to "Chronicle deeds" and so strongly anticipate *Henry V*, and Hal's perfected princehood, as a sequel. Although Dering's text was never performed, several other performance texts, widely separated in time, also reshape 2 *Henry IV* to conform, in varying degrees, to neoclassical decorum. Barry Sullivan's 1797 2 *Henry IV*,[50] for example, omitted Falstaff's rejection altogether to close with Henry IV's death in the Jerusalem chamber, conceived as a tableau: at the King's death, all exclaim, "The King is dead! Long live the King," three times and, as Henry IV's entourage encircles the dead King's body, Prince Henry kneels to swelling organ music and a slow curtain fall. And in 1951, Michael Redgrave's Shakespeare Memorial Theatre 2 *Henry IV*—part of a second tetralogy conceived to celebrate the Festival of Britain and the first time the *Henry IV* plays had been presented since 1932[51]—also valorized Henry IV's death as "the end." Not only did Redgrave follow the scene with an interval but, by having attendants remove the King's body on a litter to leave an empty stage where lights picked out the painted motif identifying the space as the Jerusalem Chamber and so emphasized how his initial desire for a holy crusade had shrunk to the confines of an empty room.

By decisively separating Hal-Henry IV from Hal-Falstaff, Redgrave's strategy isolates the scenes following Henry IV's death as a separate play-within-the play and so invites a neat rhyme with the close of *1 Henry IV*'s tavern playlet, where Hal's "I do, I will" prefigures Falstaff's banishment (2.4.457). His last act opens at Shallow's inn, lit by moonlight effects that yield, with Henry V's entrance in the ensuing scene, to bright light—"He seems to dazzle," reads the prompt copy. Moreover, Redgrave's staging parallels the new Henry V's entrance with his brothers to Richard II's first entrance in *Richard II*; here, however, Henry's manner of assuming his "majesty"—he does not sit on the throne—contrasts markedly with Richard's ceremonial panoply, a change further underscored by the music, which "strike[s] a new note, the dominant sound of Henry V." Following Hal's rejection of Falstaff and the exit of Prince John and the Lord Chief Justice, supers bring Henry V's banner, helmet, and shield center stage to figure, much as in Dering's finale, the heroic action to follow. By exploring kingship's various images—a divinely anointed ruler, a usurper, a prince coming of age to become the pattern of a Christian King—the Quayle-Redgrave Festival *Henriad* not only recuperated, for its post–World War II spectators, a history of institutional leadership to perpetuate, following a war that had wracked the country, the mythos of England as a unified whole, still powerful and powerfully intact but, in the case of 2 *Henry IV*, closed with an emblematic allusion to, and commemoration of, Britain's recent Allied European victory.

Each of these alternative configurations of 2 *Henry IV*'s narrative economy—Redgrave's perhaps less so than either Dering's or Sullivan's—insists on royal closure. So, of course, does Shakespeare's playtext, but those scenes that articulate the transfer of the crown from father to son and Hal's appearance before his brothers and the Lord Chief Justice (4.4–5; 5.2) are positioned within the narrative in such a way as to interweave the official operations of royal genealogy with Falstaff's Gloucestershire visit (4.3; 5.1) and so resist as well as delay foreclosure and containment. Much as Shrewsbury brings Hal and Hotspur together in ritual combat, Hal's last confrontation with his father enacts a similar rivalry; also as at Shrewsbury, where Hal claimed "Nor can one England brook a double reign" (5.4.65), "proud titles," honor, and doubling are at stake. But neither Hal nor Henry IV is a hero here; instead, that role belongs to the crown, which, in that it codes the genealogical myth of legitimacy, functions much like a mediating character. The struggles for the crown's ownership played out on battlefields and in royal council chambers in Shakespeare's earlier histories are here condensed within a private chamber where the crown, as a stage property that simultaneously joins and separates father and son, is tried on, and with, its past history brought to trial. Indeed, Hal's address to the crown, Henry IV's accusations against his son, Hal's response, and the King's subsequent narrative of guilt, expiation, and advice together constitute a massive set speech, disguised as dialogue,[52] which retells the crown's history from Richard II to Henry IV and imagines Henry V's England first as a "wilderness . . . / Peopled with wolves," and then as Hal's "plain and right . . . possession" (4.5.136–37, 222). Acknowledging his own reign as "a scene / Acting that argument" (4.5.197–98), Henry IV performs a parallel of Richard II's "decoronation": as in *Richard II*'s Parliament scene, a King who faces the end of his rule demystifies the crown's properties and simultaneously reconsecrates its mystic capabilities to transform Henry IV's usurpation of the throne into Hal's lineal right and true succession.

But *Richard II* is not the only playtext that invades this encounter to call history's fictions as well as their tellers into question. The sign systems that work toward idealizing and sanctifying the myth of succession are recoded and dismantled by further Falstaffian echoes of *1 Henry IV*'s Shrewsbury. Just as his father before him had usurped Richard II's crown, so does Hal, who did not take Hotspur's favors at Shrewsbury and who now thinks his father dead, appropriate his crown; as he had done after Gadshill's robbery, he also restores the stolen object to its rightful owner, with advantage. Moreover, when Henry IV awakens from a sleep that counterfeits death to turn, once again, on Hal, his son fabricates a new version of his earlier soliloquy and so again gilds a lie with happy terms to please a father.[53] Read through Shrewsbury's doubling economy, where fictional kings counterfeited true ones and where a surrogate father figure dies and then "riseth up," Henry IV's death is, like those of Hotspur and Falstaff, haunted by theatrical deception as well as by political and familial lies, rumors, and reports surviving as raids on other texts. At the scene's close, Henry IV himself speaks a doubly deceiving pun[54]—"But bear me to that chamber; there I'll lie. / In that Jerusalem shall Harry die" (4.5.239–40). In 2 Henry IV's sliding, rumor-fattened verbal economy, even prophecy, that most reliable tool of chronicle historians as well as playwrights, turns out to be a misreading.

Perhaps the best measure of the extent to which his father's death, tainted as it is by theatricality, threatens to destabilize and subvert Hal's historical legitimacy is that his heir's first use of "this new and gorgeous garment, majesty" (5.2.44) is to revalidate himself as a faithful son. Appearing before his brothers and the Lord Chief Justice, Hal first re-presents himself as his father—"I'll be your father and your brother too, / Let me but bear your love, I'll bear your cares" (5.2.57–58)—and then, by investing the Lord Chief Justice with Henry IV's role—"You shall be as a father to my youth" (5.2.118)—as a son to the law. Here, too, yet another playtext, *The Famous Victories*, which lurks throughout *Henry IV*'s margins, invades the encounter; this time, however, 2 *Henry IV* raids it precisely in order to overturn its popular account of the incident when Hal struck the Lord Chief Justice, erase the antagonism between Hal and just authority, and so represent the new King's relation to the law as a family matter.[55] If, however, Henry V's reconstituted family heals male aggression within the historical plot, it also, by deputizing the King's "workings in a second body" (5.2.90), repositions the Lord Chief Justice, not just as an antagonist to Falstaff's outlaw but as his rival father. So refathered, the new Henry V then articulates the bond between subjects and crown, "raze[s] out / Rotten opinion," washes away his former vanity and turns it to "formal majesty," calls a parliament, and promises that a utopian state will accompany his coming-in. His is the most elaborated promise of "right rule" in Shakespeare's Elizabethan history plays, and the King who speaks it so renowned as a "theme of praise"[56] that no show of homage or obedience need accompany this political tour de force of ideological containment and self-enclosure.

Reordering 2 *Henry IV*'s close as Hackett did, in 1841, makes Henry V's newly reconstituted state its finale, for Hackett cleanses the commonwealth of Falstaff *before* the new King encounters the Lord Chief Justice.[57] His adaptation reverses the narrative order of events and cobbles together a last scene in which, even though he knows of Falstaff's banishment, the Lord Chief Justice expects no grace or favor from the new King but receives both. Oddly, however, Hackett omits all references to Henry's family relationships, either with his brothers or the Lord Chief Justice; rather, his close, in which Henry V anticipates his coronation and proclaims himself the happily-ever-after once and future king, not only celebrates the ascendancy of patriarchal law and justice but, by his early containment of "misrule," manipulates the generic signs of closure, as in the adaptations described earlier, to lead directly to Henry V's perfected model of Christian kingship, and so works toward preserving that ideal intact. But 2 *Henry IV* resists such institutionalized closure: from this point forward, its representational politics articulate a far more tenuous negotiation between the virtuous royal image it has constructed and its clown.

An image of the utopian commonwealth the new Henry V promises his subjects is, of course, already in place, with its own figure of justice, Shallow, who presides over a social space in which "natural" labors, not public reform, are the chief business. In 2 *Henry IV*, spectacle is not the only way in which social contradictions are represented and mastered. Shallow's orchard community throws off echoes of the lived antagonisms that structure daily social life, especially when it must accommodate a visiting Falstaff, welcome primarily because he may be useful: as Shallow says, "A friend i' th' court is better than a penny in purse" (5.1.27–28). Yet amidst the flow of wine and apparent merriment, Silence's Shrovetide songs, with their mention of shrewish wives, serve as one faint sign of Carnival and how much it has shrunk: indeed, in this autumnal milieu, misrule's only function is to recirculate tags of memory, hearsay, and Shallow's personal history as fictions destined for Hal's ears. In another important way, too, Shallow's Gloucestershire is "barren, barren, barren" and so looks away from the Hostess's tavern, where meat is consumed unlawfully and where figures described as denizens of hell are joined by a beadle imaged as "goodman death," to look forward instead to Lent.[58]

Like Henry V's new court, this is an exclusively masculine domain, a shift in the play's gender economy that points backward to its early scenes, where, in a rupture within Carnival itself, Mistress Quickly had herself attempted to bring Falstaff to trial for overconsumption without payment (2.1). Just after Pistol's news that "Harry the Fifth's the man" leads Falstaff to imagine that "the young king is sick for me" and that "the laws of England are at [his] commandment" (5.3.117, 131–33), the potential threats Carnival represents are displaced onto the play's women. Beadles arrest Mistress Quickly and Doll Tearsheet (5.4), who become what Falstaff's earlier presence among them earlier had obscured: disruptive figures of misrule. The first to be demonized as corrupt, set aside and excluded from the commonwealth, they are led off by functionaries of an invisible authority or, as Pistol later says, "hailed thither / By most mechanical and dirty hand" (5.5.35–36). In Shakespeare's Jacobean history play, *Henry VIII*, unruly women, some of whom, unlike Doll, *are* pregnant, also threaten to overrun the stage and taint the royal image: there, however, their presence is only reported, not dramatized, and it is the presence of the infant Elizabeth I who, in keeping with the masque's strategies of legitimation, transforms holiday to holy-day. But 2 *Henry IV*, where Carnival has figured the commonwealth, with royal history at play in its margins, insists on visibly controlling and mastering the unruly female body. When he first appeared in 1 *Henry IV*, Falstaff had asked, "shall there be gallows standing in England when thou art king? and resolution thus fubbed as it is with the rusty curb of old father antic the law?" (1.2.54–56). In this initial representation of what Henry V's exchange of "public manners" for "princelie honors" and the Lord Chief Justice's "foremost hand" means, it seems, indeed, as if there will.

Henry V's royal entry, the occasion of Falstaff's rejection, is the most fully dramatized of any coronation in Shakespeare's histories. Here, especially in Falstaff's rejection, it is easy, particularly given present-day conventions of psychological character, for the representation to, so to speak, read its readers and spectators, invite their empathetic involvement, and urge them to perform moral work.⁵⁹ Even those, however, who read this confrontation between king and clown as evidence of how power reconstitutes itself from its opposite accord character and role a social significance. For these closing events can also be read, not in terms of a naturalistic fusion of character and role, but through the codes and sign systems they put into play and the ways they continue to be invaded by other texts. In terms of the King's entry, these differ, depending on whether one consults Quarto or Folio. Quarto's doubled procession—an initial entry that follows the women's arrests with the brief image of the royal train passing over the stage, after which Falstaff and his crew enter, and then a later entrance for the King and his train (K₄ʳ; L₁ᵛ)—not only stresses Falstaff's late arrival but replaces the marginalized female figures of misrule with an image of the King's centrality. In contrast, Folio's single, delayed entry (TLN 3247–49), which emphasizes the omniscience of a power that extends to the state's underlings, funnels all meaning toward the single meeting of king and clown. In both dynamics, however, political and social antagonisms are reasserted and folded up in a spectacle that is coded, at one level of social meaning, in terms of costume. Resplendently attired, the King and his train enter to a Falstaff whose haste has not permitted him to order "new liveries"; "stained with travel and sweating with desire," he and his fellows make "a poor show" in their "marvellous foul linen." (5.5.13; 5.1.31). As one of a number of sign systems linked to theatrical disguise, perhaps its most resonant parallel occurs, in another comedy that also ends with a sermon on obedience, as a similar emphasis on dress in *The Taming of the Shrew*, where Petruchio's fantastical wedding clothes code his "unruly" nature and Kate's new cap and gown her "reformation" (3.2; 5.2).

Like other moments in the play, this meeting is invaded by previous texts, especially by *1 Henry IV*'s "play extempore" (2.4), where Falstaff argued against his banishment, here reprised, and overturned, as Falstaff's ascending series of invocations—"King Hal," "my royal Hal," "most royal imp of fame," "my sweet boy," "my King," "my Jove," "my heart"—names him again and again, recirculating his past and present roles, just as he had named himself repeatedly at the Boar's Head. Here, however, a transformed Hal sees only an "old man" with unbecoming manners—sees, in fact, the clown for what he is, "a fool and jester." Moreover, his sermon throws off echoes of his father, who much earlier had banished Worcester "for I do see / danger and disobedience in thine eye" (*1 Henry IV*, 1.3.15–16) and who, in his first appearance as King in *Richard II*, pardoned a rebel son whose mother knelt before him in a pageant of obedience he then referred to as "The Beggar and the King" (5.3.80). Now the unhistorical figure is regendered as the ambiguously sexed clown. And although this newly Lenten Henry V advises Falstaff to "leave gourmandizing" (5.5.54), he himself will shortly consume France and, repeating his father's history, not only usurp another's crown but, in order to assert his mastery, project the experience of submission and defenselessness onto the bodies of Harfleur's women just as, here, that is displaced onto the body of the clown.

Finally, as at Shrewsbury, the clown's last words work to create another fiction of himself: a Falstaff who will repay Justice Shallow what he owes and "be as good as [his] word" (5.5.86). Just as Falstaff had pretended deafness in his initial confrontation with the Lord Chief Justice (1.2.63), the law refuses him a hearing. Indeed, at this point the play seems oddly incomplete in terms of making legal decisions concerning its figures of misrule, Doll and Quickly as well as Falstaff; it seems to be a temporary banishment "until their conversations / Appear more wise and modest to the world" (5.5.101–2). As the playtext's final words look ahead to rumors of the French war, it circles back to echo Rumor's opening Prologue. Insofar as the stage is now inhabited only by figures who represent royal authority in its absence, the close imagines a state run by deputies, built, perhaps, in one last echo of Shrewsbury, on counterfeits of power.[60] Such an image situates the close of *2 Henry IV* as similar to *Measure for Measure*, an example of the disguised ruler play where a duke deputizes another to serve in his place while he masquerades in a moral disguise, only to appear at the end and, after revealing himself as authority's "true" image, dispense the law. In 2 *Henry IV*'s close, however, the man who has England's laws at his command and the King's brother represent the center and the margins of a power that, in spite of and because of its theatrical self-disguisings, has become panoptical.

ﻼﻀ

The closing images of Terry Hands's 1975 Royal Shakespeare Company 2 *Henry IV*[61] condense the spectacle of rule into a carefully controlled emblematic design in which, as in the close of his *1 Henry IV*, a series of replacements articulates the play's re-formed social and class distinctions. Stagehands draw a huge white carpet over the bare boards of the stage to frame Falstaff's rejection within an abstract "snowscape" further coded by a cluster of bare branches suspended upstage center and golden rushes, strewn on the white groundcloth at downstage center, to juxtapose Falstaff's barren beggary against Hal's new royalty. As the patterned shadows of Shallow's inn give way to hard, brilliant light, a tone picked up in the bright trumpets announcing Henry V's entrance, a travel-stained tavern crew enters first, Falstaff in a carpetbag cloak, red leggings, and baggy boots, and forms a ragged line, stage left, with Falstaff furthest downstage. Wearing pure white cloaks blazoned with scarlet Crosses of St. George, Westmoreland, Clarence, Gloucester, and John enter with the Lord Chief Justice, in scarlet robes and a golden chain of office, to stand in a rigidly ordered column, stage right, with the Chief Justice opposite Falstaff across an empty central aisle. Even before Henry V enters, Hands's choices of mise-en-scène, costume, and blocking separate institutionalized power from its parodic counterparts to predict that the cost of idealizing a king depends on such hierarchical division within the kingdom.

When the new King enters, the nobles kneel, and Falstaff crosses the boundary between nobles and commons to confront a "Jove" dressed and masked in golden armor, an emblematic figure of hedged divinity—unapproachable, austere, wearing the glittering symbols of his power like a shield (fig. 14). Ignoring Falstaff, he continues to move downstage; in place of his request that the Lord Chief Justice speak to "that vain man" and the Chief Justice's warning to Falstaff, both of which are cut, the Chief Justice and Henry's brothers rise to form a barrier that encloses Falstaff's followers and so further isolates and intensifies the exchange between Henry V and Falstaff. When he at last replies to Falstaff's appeals, Henry removes his golden mask, and Falstaff, falling to his knees at Henry's command, remains there until the King exits, followed by the Chief Justice and his brothers. Rising slowly, he stands at center, replacing the deus ex machina–like Hal, isolated even from his companions, who encircle his figure briefly before they are herded offstage by officers at the Chief Justice's silent command. Then, in an echo of Henry's ceremonial entrance, Falstaff walks slowly up the central aisle between the impassive figures of Prince John and the Lord Chief Justice, pausing to stand under the bare branches as a raven croaks: relegated to the past's upstage space, he watches his lawful opposite take over his own central position. By cutting Prince John's comments on the King's "fair proceeding" as well as the Lord Chief Justice's reply, Hands silences any spoken judgment on Falstaff's future; as though unwilling to exclude him, this staging suspends his figure, poised for the exit that will, as Prince John talks of the coming war in France, deny him a place in the next play, except as others remember him.

In that 2 Henry IV gives its "last words" to the King's surrogates, who sustain his power even in his absence, it gestures toward imagining the present-day cultural formation of constitutional monarchy, in which royal display becomes a momentary pageant and royal policy a ministerial business. Certainly the words of Prime Minister Margaret Thatcher, speaking at Harrogate in March 1982, bridge nearly four centuries to recirculate the issues behind Falstaff's "unpleasant" but "necessary" expulsion:

> Over the past two decades you and I have watched all our standards steadily and deliberately vilified, ridiculed, and scorned. For years there was no riposte, no reply. The time for counter-attack is long overdue. We are reaping what was sown in the Sixties—a society in which the old virtues of discipline and self-restraint were denigrated. There are those who wish to undermine institutions and values on which we depend; those who call for extra Parliamentary action and the sacking of judges and Chief Constables:—these are the men and women who are guilty of eroding the respect for the law and values by which society lives.[62]

This excerpt from her speech appeared, among other texts, in the souvenir program for the Royal Shakespeare Company's 1982 Henry IVs, the plays chosen to open the company's new theater at London's Barbican Centre. Fifty years earlier, in 1932, the Shakespeare Memorial Theatre at Stratford had staged the Henry IV plays for a similar theatrical celebration; on both occasions, mise-en-scène designed to show off the technological assets of a new theater—realistically conceived set elements, pageantry, and processions—worked toward rep-

resenting "Elizabethan England" as a timeless theatrical as well as social text.⁶³ Perhaps partially in response to the theatrically historic
occasion, director Trevor Nunn enclosed both plays between two
rhyming processional stage images that, in equating royal authority
with theatrical spectacle, functioned as choral convocations of the theatrical world or as, respectively, a prologue and epilogue of assembly.

In 2 *Henry IV*'s close, the entire cast, grouped around two of the
"rooms" built on movable stage-trucks and placed opposite one another to create a diagonal corridor between them, assembles to watch
the procession.⁶⁴ As rush-strewers prepare the way, Pistol holds up a
T-shirt emblazoned with *Si fortuna me tormenta, spero contenta* and
chants *Obsque hoc nihil est* as an aggressive football slogan—two
anachronisms connecting Pistol's own anachronistic figure to present-
day political and social demonstrations⁶⁵—and Falstaff, looking offstage for the procession, hurries downstage to position himself directly
in its path. Preceded by a crucifix-bearer as well as by Gloucester, Clarence, and Prince John and followed by the Lord Chief Justice, Bardolph, and Poins, Henry V enters, wearing the heavily embroidered
ceremonial white cope Henry IV had worn in the opening of *1 Henry
IV*, his face a blank, unreadable mask. Once the King steps from the
coronation procession to address Falstaff, he regains expressiveness,
even choking back a sob, straining to smile when he moves toward
Falstaff, but then drawing back on "When thou does hear I am as I
have been, / Approach me, and thou shalt be as thou wast." After asking the Lord Chief Justice "to see performed the tenor of my word,"
he pauses as though to enforce it or as though he may say more—a
moment made especially ambiguous by this Hal's rebellious indifference toward both his father and Falstaff. When the procession continues, he stands alone for a moment before the crowd encompasses him
to exit with him stage right; Poins, in a newly splendid short cloak,
marching proudly at its tail end, looks back over his shoulder to flip
Falstaff a triumphant grin.⁶⁶ Those remaining onstage—Falstaff, Shallow, Pistol, and Bardolph—form a central group of spectators, now
isolated from the ceremony: staring after Henry, Falstaff laughs—as
though, in Robert Cushman's words, "this were one more inexplicable
practical joke."⁶⁷ As the Lord Chief Justice and Prince John return with
officers who surround Falstaff's cronies, Falstaff at first attempts to
hide behind a post but then crosses to the Lord Chief Justice; summarily dismissed, he follows an officer offstage as Pistol breaks from the
group and, brandishing his T-shirt, shouts his final line as he is dragged
off, with the others, upstage left. Wearily, the Lord Chief Justice turns
to an elated and self-satisfied Prince John before the stage clears com-

pletely to make way for the returning procession, which fills the entire space with an image almost like that which opened Part One: now, however, only one monk, carrying the cross, walks behind the King who, like his father before him, seems uneasy in majesty's garment and has become a smiling mechanism of authority, flanked by his subjects and official representatives, but, unlike his father, as yet unaccompanied by any choral anthem of praise.

In figuring 2 *Henry IV*'s close as a reprise of Henry IV's image of power, Nunn's finale holds up an ideological mask that accords with the play's suggestions that the son becomes the father to represent succession as an instance of *plus ça change, plus c'est la même chose*. But, at least in its Folio configuration, Shakespeare's playtext directs an exit for Prince John and the Lord Chief Justice, leaving an empty stage—a staging Nunn observed when he codirected the *Henry IV* plays with John Barton and Clifford Williams in 1966 and one that realizes the double absences of both King and Clown.[68] In 1982, Nunn rereads that emptiness as a panoptical view of authority: aristocracy and the populace united in one processional image to represent "England." Such an image, connecting theatrical history, especially the traditions of Victorian stage spectacle,[69] to national history and attaching a final panoply of unity to the play, comfortably and reassuringly suits the anniversary occasion. It also, however, sharply hints at the contradictions masked by this image of containment. There is little sense, as Nunn's 2 *Henry IV* ends, that Henry V has accepted kingship; instead, he seems to be inhabiting its robes only for the purposes of the coronation ceremony. However strong the appeal of this final spectacle, it is hard to forget that it has been achieved at the expense of the richly detailed sense of life characteristic of Nunn's performance text, which, at the close, hollows out one mode of theatrical representation and replaces it with another. To the extent that such foreclosure exposes authority itself as empty theatrical celebration, Nunn's close reads as a faked Epilogue for a play that exposes power itself as suspect, subject to telling itself lies as well as to the rumors and misinterpretations of its subjects.

With *Henry V* yet to come in the *Roses* cycle, the close of Bogdanov's 1987 2 *Henry IV* interrogates Henry V's newly acquired power rather differently.[70] After the slowed, quiet domesticity of Shallow's isolated orchard community, where space swims away into the upstage dark behind downstage benches, wheelbarrows, and baskets of apples, the stage suddenly seems compressed, purposely cramping Henry's coronation procession into a space too small to encompass a Falstaffian body. The tavern crew pushes on two platform trucks from either side of the stage, framing a central aisle for what will be Henry V's upstage center processional entrance. All have banners and flags, one carries a huge Union Jack, and Bardolph passes out tiny Union Jacks to all, including Falstaff, attired in his red-jacketed uniform, his chest ablaze with medals (earned at Shrewsbury and at Gaultree?), a tiny bowler with a Union Jack hatband, like those in Oxford Street souvenir shops, on his head. To Handel's "Coronation March," the nobles, in coronation robes, enter and form double lines, reframing the central aisle; Henry V follows, resplendent in red ermine-trimmed robes. Moving from upstage to downstage, Falstaff pops in and out between the ranked nobles, calling out to Hal from among them, as though playing hide-and-go-seek before kneeling, downstage left, his back to the audience, and, finally, taking off his hat (fig. 15). The rejection comes quickly: bitterly annoyed at Falstaff's interruption of his ceremony, Henry V turns away and exits upstage center, the other nobles following. Almost immediately, the rest of the tavern crew deserts Falstaff as well, making the rejection doubly brutal, and this Falstaff hardly believes that he will be sent for soon at night. The Lord Chief Justice and Prince John come on with bobbies, who at first hold back from arresting Falstaff and then, according him some dignity by not touching him, indicate that he is to follow them. As Falstaff walks slowly upstage to exit, he stops beside John and the Lord Chief Justice, both of whom look away. Now empty except for these two figures, the stage seems unexpectedly still until, as they turn to go, loud music blares out "We're in the army" to figure the absent Henry V's coming war.

The loss that Nunn's staging masks with spectacle Bogdanov reads as a rhyme with the ending of his *1 Henry IV*, which also anticipates *Henry V*. In *1 Henry IV*, Falstaff's "corpse" occupied the same downstage left position as his living body does here; this time, however, Hal refuses Falstaff a sword of justice just as, in the Shrewsbury battle, Falstaff had refused him a dagger of lath and, appearing later with Hotspur's body, had made Henry IV doubt his son's newly reformed valor. While throughout *2 Henry IV* Falstaff functions as its central narrative voice—a guise Bogdanov exploits by doubling the actor as *Henry V*'s Chorus—this close firmly denies his ability to speak either for himself or for the play. For from the point at which he kneels, his back to the audience, he never turns around to face it again: no longer a speaking subject, his presence is recorded in *Henry V* only as the subject of hearsay, his name finally forgotten by Fluellen (4.7.43–45). Hal's new subjects—his brother and his surrogate father—affirm the King's will and authority as their own; no alternative voice contests what Bogdanov's *Henry V* will reveal as the authoritarian beginnings of an imperialist regime, represented here as the offstage sound of a popular military song, heralding the questionable project of mobilizing an entire country for war. To the extent that this close reproduces a trace of future history, which will transform Agincourt into the Falklands in *Henry V*, Bogdanov provides a different sort of false epilogue, one which reappropriates Shakespeare's cultural authority to serve a situation that many read as a present-day counterfeit of Britain's lost imperial power.

2 *Henry IV*, of course, includes a real Epilogue—probably the most underperformed of all Shakespearean closural signs. Indeed, Bridges-Adams's 1932 Shakespeare Memorial Theatre 2 *Henry IV* is one of the few recorded times the Epilogue has been spoken within this century, or for that matter, since Shakespeare's day.[71] Since the production opened on Shakespeare's birthday, with the Prince of Wales in attendance, performing the Epilogue—in an abridged version of its Folio configuration, which ends with the speaker kneeling "to pray for the Queen"—may have been intended to pay homage to the author's "complete text" as well as to end the play with royal compliment, a strategy lost on Prince Edward, who left the theater at 1 *Henry IV*'s interval.[72] While the Epilogue receives editorial attention, most readings of the play also, like the Prince, leave it behind. Certainly its Folio placement on a separate page containing colophon devices that further detach it from the play proper identifies its occasional nature;[73] many conjecture that Heminges and Condell included it in Folio primarily because it reads the Oldcastle disclaimer into published record. Although the Cambridge editors find it difficult to believe that the Epilogue was spoken while the Oldcastle matter was still dangerous,[74] Gary Taylor's argument for returning "Shakespeare's treasonable heresy" to 1 *Henry IV* by restoring Falstaff's name to Oldcastle suggests otherwise. Suppressing Oldcastle's name from 1 *Henry IV* certainly occurred in response to displeased reactions of "personages descended from his title" as well as from others who honored his memory, and 2 *Henry IV*'s Epilogue calls precise attention to the fact that Falstaff is Oldcastle in Part One and Falstaff in Part Two: "Where, for any thing I know, Falstaff shall die of a sweat, unless already 'a be kill'd with your hard opinions, for Oldcastle died martyr, and this is not the man" (Ep., 25–28).[75] Curiously, however, the Epilogue does and does not apologize; rather, it tells a displaced story of censorship, substitution, and replacement that both allays historical rumor (the Oldcastle controversy) and incites fresh theatrical rumor (a new Falstaff play). Embedding this phantom story in an epilogue, which almost by definition

contains some form of apology for the play,[76] wraps it in the most secure of all closural conventions, making what it says both highly noticeable and nearly invisible. Exercising the ambiguity that is the province of all rumor, the play refuses to say which.

Situating 2 *Henry IV*'s Epilogue within such a topical matrix describes only one facet of its controversial double nature. Taken alone, any one of its three paragraphs would serve as the traditional apology for the play; together, they seem, like the lady, to protest too much and so suggest a structure that, while scripted, remains flexible, open to the improvisational skills of its speaker. Even its scripted versions differ, primarily in giving variant placement to the Oldcastle apology and the prayer for the Queen. While Quarto (L_2^v) places the prayer at the end of the Epilogue's first paragraph and delays the Oldcastle apology until just before the speaker's final "good night," Folio follows the Oldcastle apology with the prayer, so that the last phrases read, "my tongue is weary, when my legs are too, I will bid you good night; and so kneel down before you: but (indeed) to pray for the Queen" (TLN 3348–50). Moreover, Folio's order makes the Epilogue conform to an older sense of ending, closing with prayer and subjection—one mocked as early as 1596, when the final speaker of Harington's *The Metamorphoses of Ajax* declares: "I will neither end with sermon nor with prayer, lest some wags liken me to my L. [ ] players, who when they have ended a bawdy comedy, as though that were a preparative to devotion, kneel down solemnly, and pray all the company to pray with them for their good Lord and master."[77] At least in Folio, the syntax of the Epilogue's last phrases can suggest that the Oldcastle apology as well as praying for the Queen may indeed be similar, ultimate jokes that frame the traditional ending jig: the first has made the speaker's tongue "weary"; the gesture of kneeling may, given the often communal nature of the jig, which spectators might perform on their own, not even happen. If so, then 2 *Henry IV*'s Epilogue is at once the play's most perfectly subversive and perfectly submissive gesture, one that uses an outdated theatrical convention to announce publicly that its text contains no treason and that makes a promise, to one royal spectator, that may go unfulfilled.

One reading of the Epilogue explains its multiple configurations by labeling its first paragraph an "authorial" address surviving from a court performance and by assigning its second and third paragraphs to a speaker who is also a dancer. On the Elizabethan stage, a principal actor—a Puck, a Rosalind, a Prospero, in examples from Shakespeare's own practice—delivers the epilogue; in 2 *Henry IV*'s Elizabethan configuration, the obvious choice is Falstaff as impersonated by

Will Kemp, who was famous for his dancing skills. Indeed, the opening lines of the second paragraph—"If my tongue cannot entreat you to acquit me, will you command me to use my legs?" (Ep. 15–16)—invite spectators to overturn his banishment and so recuperate Carnival's parodic inversion of authority: he even promises to "dance out of your debt" and so earns pardon and, perhaps, escapes prison. His reappearance not only makes good on Falstaff's promise to Shallow (and himself)—"I shall be sent for soon at night" (5.5.90–91)—but also, by providing him with an afterhistory, ties up loose narrative ends to resolve the playtext's ambiguities (whether Falstaff receives "competence of life," is "very well provided for," or is carried off to the Fleet) through the convention of the clown's final appearance, which accords him an existence beyond the play. Falstaff's reappearance in the jig, of course, would not only give his Shrewsbury resurrection a final reprise but also restore comedy's conventional structure, which, at least as theorized by Sidney, insists on keeping kings and clowns in separate domains.[78] Like Puss-in-Boots, the Carnival King of Misrule can look at the King only within a Saturnalian context where both play roles: finally, his powerful presence is safely enclosed, contained, by theatrical magic, within secure, ultimately closural conventions.

But epilogues are often not what they appear to be, and, like so many verbal structures in the *Henry IV* plays, this one says one thing and does another. Indeed, Falstaff/Kemp promises that "If you be not too much cloyed with fat meat, our humble author will continue the story, with Sir John in it, and make you merry with fair Katherine of France. Where, for anything I know, Falstaff shall die of a sweat, unless already 'a be killed with your hard opinions" (Ep., 22–27). The syntax here seems just flexible enough to imagine, on the one hand, a dangerous liaison between Falstaff and the French Princess and, on the other, in keeping with the clown's shifting gender, to fold a masculine into a feminine guise. Certainly, as Steven Mullaney points out, *Henry V*'s Katherine inherits, and rehearses over and over again, in her language lesson on the English body, the "gross terms" of a "strange tongue" that Falstaff and Hal, among *Henry IV*'s persons, have put into play. Indeed, this would seem to be one final instance of the return of what 2 *Henry IV* has tried, with Falstaff's banishment, to repress: the transformational prodigality embedded in the roles and tongues of carnival's marginal culture.[79] Here, too, following the suggestions of gender transference, is the prophesy that Falstaff may "die of a sweat"—not, perhaps, just the "lard sweat" of fattened Carnival but that of plague or venereal disease. With this reference to bodily disease, Falstaff/Kemp predicts, at the close, a further metamorphosis for his character, one that figures him much like Hélène Cixous' image for the female body confiscated and demonized by male systems of representation: "the uncanny stranger on display—the ailing or dead figure, which so often turns out to be the nasty companion, the cause and location of inhibitions."[80] If this topples 2 *Henry IV*'s Epilogue forward toward a late twentieth-century configuration perhaps alien to its Elizabethan audiences, it is also possible that they, too, would recognize, in this final sign of the play's fluid gender economy, a trace of the old, familiar image of feminine misrule.

In that it recuperates and re-presents the oppositional energies of the Henry IV plays within a theater of conventions, the ending of La Compagnia del Collettivo, Teatro Due di Parma's *Enrico IV*—the third play in a trilogy comprising *Hamlet* (nostalgia for dialectics), *Macbeth* (absence of dialectics), and *Henry IV* (recuperation of dialectics)—serves as a postmodern epilogue.[81] Ignoring the bardic mythology that surrounds the *Henry IV* plays with romantic reconstructions of a sixteenth-century royal holiday world, the members of the Parma collective chose to see themselves as subjects in a timeless conflict of power and to juxtapose diverse and contradictory acting styles— Noh and Samurai ceremonies, naturalism, vaudeville, improvisational street theater—in an emblematic cross-cultural montage of "strange tongues" that leaps from event to event, resolving their disassociation by the presence of the actor who plays the Prince and who oscillates between functioning inside his role and standing outside it, a cynical and ironic commentator. At the close, Hal walks alone, to the accompaniment of "Thus Spake Zarathustra," toward the scarlet curtains marking the upstage area of the rectangular playing space; crowned, he wraps his father's medallioned robe around him and assumes a fashion model's pose—an androgynous figure who, perhaps, waits to be admired and photographed. Directly opposite him, downstage, Falstaff, dressed in the black suit of the stereotypical Mafia patriarch, seats himself at a café table. The rest of the tavern followers mist the stage with water from spray bottles as Falstaff shakes a huge champagne bottle, calling out to *Il Principe*, " 'Rico, hey, 'Rico!" urging Hal to join him. Immobile, the new King sings "I know thee not, old man" to Mr. Peachum's cynical betrayal song from Brecht's *Threepenny Opera*.[82] Falstaff cries out, writhes, and collapses in his chair; Doll enters, looks at him, picks up a champagne glass, and dashes it to the floor. She crosses upstage to the King, trying, but failing, to plead with him. As the lights go down abruptly, the tune of Gene Raskin's "Those Were the Days" echoes in the darkening space.[83] Ultimately, this exhilarating dislocation of signs has its origins in an equally confrontational dialectic between texts—Holinshed, Daniel, *The Famous Victories* among them—as well as between royal power and its topsy-turvy opposite. In the twentieth century as in the sixteenth, the hegemony of one over the other means Falstaff's death. Here, his only Epilogue is a shattered glass, a woman's mimed appeal, and a song-without-its-words that imagines, nostalgically, the way we were. The ending of 2 *Henry IV* does not try only its Clown and its King: it tries all its beholders. In La Compagnia del Collettivo's *Enrico IV* particularly, it also tries the play, imagining closure as the space where multiple texts cross and exchange vows—or lies—with one another.

Creation of a docile

pop.

The Taught not to

Think for itself

"A FULL AND NATURAL CLOSE, LIKE MUSIC": *HENRY V*

This battle may be a mirror and glass to all Christian princes to behold and follow, for King Henry neither trusted in the puissance of his people, nor in the fortitude of his champions, nor in the strength of his barded horses, nor yet in his own policy, but he put in GOD (which is the cornerstone and immovable rock) his whole confidence hope and trust.

—Edward Hall, *The Union of the Two Noble and Illustrious Families of Lancaster and York*

Agincourt is one of the most instantly and vividly visualized of all epic passages in English history. . . . Visually it is a pre-Raphaelite, perhaps better a Medici Gallery print battle. . . . It is a school outing to the Old Vic, Shakespeare is fun, *son et lumière*, blank verse, Laurence Olivier in armour battle; . . . It is also a story of slaughter-yard behavior and of outright atrocity.

—John Keegan, *The Face of Battle*

F OR THE sixteenth-century chronicler, Agincourt is a miraculous "mirror and glass," King Henry shining at its center as he leads the English from the jaws of defeat to a promised land, much like Moses freeing the Israelites from Egyptian bondage. But for the twentieth-century military historian, the mythologized narrative preserved in patterns of sound, light, and color, and glorified by art, Shakespeare, and Laurence Olivier is only one side of Agincourt's history: the other is a tale of bloody manslaughter.[1] Similarly, critical narratives as well as theatrical representations have fractured *Henry V*, the most generically flexible of Shakespeare's histories, more or less along its fault lines to view its king either as the chroniclers' "blazing comet" King of Desire or as the prisoner-killing warmonger, and so have read the play as a nationalistic pageant-drama or, especially at times of national or world crisis, as an ironic critique of successful military endeavor.[2]

Almost invariably, however, empowering one side of the dialectic empties the other, much like Richard II's "golden crown . . . / That owes two buckets" (*Richard II*, 4.1.184–85). And even Norman Rabkin's attractive image of complementarity—*Henry V* as "rabbit" and "duck"—insists on a coherent, intentional opposition that, he claims, is perceived and synthesized by the play's "best" audience, with the help of the Epilogue, as "the inscrutability of history"³—a view of the play that throws considerable interpretive weight on its spectators as well as on its ending.

That ending poses a nexus of formal as well as ideological problems, but these have to do less with the "inscrutability of history" than with the inscrutability of comedy or, perhaps more appropriately, with a rupture within that genre that derives in some part from the play's sources. For the materials *Henry V* draws on—chronicles, comic-popular history, and Shakespeare's own *Henry IV* plays—map out contradictory accounts: whereas Hall and Holinshed for the most part idealize Henry as the perfect, and perfectly mythologized, Christian King, *The Famous Victories*, by setting Henry apart from Dericke, John Cobler, and the other soldiers, records instead the gulf between master and man, ruler and subject, a perspective that Shakespeare's *Henry IV* plays also, though with far greater complexity, address. A unique example of what Rosalie Colie calls *genera mixta*,⁴ *Henry V* opposes these discourses, flaunts their contradictions, and attempts to fuse them by positioning the King at the center of both an aristocratic and a "base, common and popular" narrative. And that division, sustained and enforced by the play's representational economy (at least until Agincourt) not only works, simultaneously, to mystify and demystify his figure—one might say, with Leonard Tennenhouse, to redistribute the King's Two Bodies⁵—but also calls into question the ideology that supports kingship. This double vision of the King and his French war also extends to Chorus who, on the one hand, invites readers and spectators to perform imaginative work that assumes their investment in such a project and, on the other, by calling attention to the purely theatrical nature of the enterprise, equates the King's own abilities and success with the insufficiencies of the stage that contains him and so exposes his achievements as ephemeral, aesthetic constructs put at his obedient service by the idealizing strategies of the theater itself.⁶ As prismatic as the theatricalized images of Queen Elizabeth, *Henry V* also uses, as Tennenhouse argues, comedy's strategies of disguise and inversion to consolidate royal authority and to seek audience approval for "this star of England [and] his sword / By which the world's best garden he achieved" (Ep., 6–7).⁷ And nowhere do the several images of King Henry exhibit more strain and shatter, so to speak, the "royal captain" (4 Cho., 29) from the man "whose senses have but human conditions" (4.1.100–101) than in *Henry V*'s double or, given Chorus's Epilogue, triple close.

To read each of these endings in turn, as I want to do, is, of course, to intensify the fissures in the play's own representational politics—ruptures that are most obvious as the narrative moves from Agincourt and its immediate aftermath (4.1–4.8) to Chorus's description of Henry's triumphant London welcome and then back to France to dramatize, first, the Fluellen-Pistol quarrel over the leek (5.1) and, finally, the alliance, through marriage, of England and France (5.2), concluding with the Epilogue. In exploring this closural territory, I want to focus especially on how *Henry V* engages with and recirculates the contradictory comic myths that shape the King's "blood brotherhood" and so seek to authorize both his popular and royal genealogies as well as, through a shift in gender economy, to mediate between them. And, as elsewhere in this study, how *Henry V*'s performance texts come to terms with its proto-Brechtian form, and how they attempt either to read its disjunctures or to mask the anxieties they display, records the history of a more specific "local" Shakespeare.

In *Henry V*, all thoughts lead to Agincourt, which, as Chorus insistently reminds the play's readers and spectators, is located on an English stage. For the purposes of this particular dramatic fiction, geography itself is in disguise, which functions to displace England's "intestine division" and so to work through the nationalist separatism that had plagued England during Henry IV's reign, a historical factionalism marked by magnate revolt that the play condenses in Macmorris's question, "What ish my nation?" (3.2.113), as well as further displays through the figures of social and linguistic difference dividing the Scottish, Irish, Welsh, and English captains. For the historical as well as the fictional King Henry, who claims, "No king of England, if not King of France" (2.2.193), foreign war represents a peaceful solution, sanctioned by God, which will not only restore unity to England but, by resolving conflict between Christian kings, achieve the unity of Christendom. Called by Lydgate "the prince of peace," the historical Henry, according to one report, said on his deathbed that he had desired to build again the walls of Jerusalem.[8] And *Henry V* indeed reproduces the dramatic equivalent of this massive ideological unification project in its final images of comic community: the first unites Henry with his men to create, from national difference, the illusion of a "band of brothers" (4.3.60); the last, Henry's marriage to Katherine, unites England with France in "love and fair alliance" and "Christian-like accord" (5.2.329, 337). At the level of the historical plot, Henry wins Agincourt's battle against great odds and establishes, through possession of a woman, his title to France; at the level of Shakespeare's history the play brings a satisfying triple resolution to a narrative begun with *Richard II* and extended in the *Henry IV* plays. Through bloodshed, it ratifies Henry V's dynastic line and proves his descent from his lion-hearted ancestor, Edward, the Black Prince; through French conquest, Henry achieves his father's dream of a Christian crusade, atones for his "fault," and unifies his kingdom; and through Henry's pious insistence that God won the battle, he reconnects himself to the mystifying force of divine right that was Richard II's special province.

Paying homage both to Henry's legendary chronicle self and his dramatic origins in the *Henry IV* plays, *Henry V*'s project rests, as Shakespeare's earlier histories do, on blood-proofs. Here, however, the issue of multiple, competing heirs to the English throne, which set the earlier histories in motion, takes on a new guise and so calls into question not Henry's right to the English throne but, so to speak, his originating authority, which is played out through a series of jokes involving tokens of symbolic exchange. From its opening scenes forward, *Henry V* repeatedly insists that King Henry is not Hal: proof of his miraculous conversion comes, first, from the Bishop of Canterbury (1.1.26–69) and, much later, from Fluellen (4.7.40–44); only the Dauphin, in presenting him, through an ambassador, with tennis balls, and the Boar's Head remnants, who remember his "humors and careers," recall his earlier revelling spirit (1.2.25–54; 2.1.122). The play mobilizes both dissenting opinions to forge Henry's dazzling, though equally contradictory, new image. The Dauphin's gift steels Henry's resolve and sets up an antagonism between England and France that opposes one male heir to another and so generates the play's almost exclusively male gender economy. Indeed, the Salic law—"No woman shall succeed in Salic land" (1.2.39)—that justifies Henry's claim to the French throne (and that also applied to Elizabeth I and James I) is also, as Peter Donaldson writes, "the law of the English stage."[9] And the Boar's Head "swashers," led by a Pistol who goes to France "to suck, the very blood to suck" (2.3.51), function largely, as in the *Henry IV* plays, to undermine Henry's heroic rhetoric of the English royal body, as when they mock his "Once more unto the breach" (3.1.1; 3.2.1–49) and when the corrupt Pistol accepts a ransom of two hundred crowns from le Fer just after Henry has, once again, refused to ransom his own royal body (4.3.90–125; 4.4). But perhaps most significantly, when, on Agincourt Eve, King Henry, disguised as the Welsh "Harry le Roy," encounters

Pistol, he goes unrecognized. Together with his order for Bardolph's execution (3.6.95–109), this is the most obvious sign that Henry V has indeed turned away from his tavern past and that the play dramatizes not the return of the repressed Hal but, instead, generates for its King a new comic-popular genealogy, a process of rejuvenation that stands in oblique relation to Henry's later image as the heir and savior of France—precisely the terms with which his father forged his own claim to the English throne.[10]

Agincourt and its aftermath bring King Henry's "rebirth"—that is, the rebirth of his theatrical as well as his royal body—into sharp focus. The Battle of Agincourt is, at the level of language, a battle over bodies: over who may die and who may be ransomed, over prisoners taken and then killed.[11] Even Richard II's body, "interred anew" by Henry and washed with "contrite tears," figures here; and when Princess Katherine rehearses her English, she catalogues the Anglo-French body through which, much later, Henry will lay claim to France (3.4). If *1 Henry IV*, in Shrewsbury's battle, figures the king through doubles who march in his coats, *Henry V* duplicates the King's Two Bodies rather differently to reread them from the point of view of Williams, Court, and Bates, who risk their own bodies in the king's service. The encounter, which begins as Henry's attempt to prove blood-brotherhood with his soldier-subjects and so to mediate their notions of the justice of war, the responsibilities of monarch and subjects, and issues of obedience, ends in short-tempered words and a symbolic exchange of gloves between Henry and Williams that, much like the Dauphin's gift of tennis balls, anticipates a future quarrel. In a reading of "Upon the King" (4.1.216–70), the secularized version of Gethsemane that directly follows this feudal gesture, Jonathan Dollimore and Alan Sinfield detail Henry's strategies for remystifying kingship, obedience, and "the ideological coherence of the state," and point to how his conversation with Williams as well as the soliloquy accord the king a priestly function.[12] And surely Henry's divine disguise anticipates that of the later *Measure for Measure*'s Duke, Vincentio, who, in putting on a friar's robes, positions himself as a heavenly overseer who offers advice to subjects facing death and monitors his surrogate's uses and abuses of power. Indeed, the "old fantastical Duke of dark corners" (4.3.154–55) in his doubled guise of secular and religious authority bears considerable resemblance to "a little touch of Harry in the night" (4 Cho., 47), especially insofar as both rulers use subjects' bodies in order to legitimate their own power. But the equivalent of *Measure*'s "head for maidenhead" exchange[13] is played out, in *Henry V*'s comedy of male bonding, through Henry's later juggling act with gloves and crowns,[14] where what is at stake is not just the King's promise, in his St. Crispin's Day speech, that "he to-day that sheds his blood with me / Shall be my brother" (4.3.61–62), but the theatrical bloodline of his body as well as his relegitimation as a "good father."

Just before this occurs, however, *Henry V* sets England's idealized "happy few" in high relief. When Henry learns of his victory from Montjoy, the French herald calls particular attention to an unfortunate loss of hierarchical difference:

> I come to thee for charitable licence,
> That we may wander o'er this bloody field
> To book our dead and then to bury them,
> To sort our nobles from our common men—
> For many of our princes, woe the while,
> Lie drowned and soaked in mercenary blood.
> So do our vulgar drench their peasant limbs
> In blood of princes.
>
> (4.7.66–73)

To mix commoners with princes, if not (as Fluellen would put it) "expressly against the law of arms" (4.7.1–2), confuses class and rank, mingling royal with "vulgar" blood. In making Montjoy the spokesman for recuperating the feudal distinctions that the war has erased, *Henry V* seems to oppose a French feudal aristocracy to Henry's homosocial ideal, which flirts with imagining England as a proto-democratic or, more accurately, a fraternal state.[15] But the next stage of Agincourt's aftermath calls that fantasy into question. At first, however, Fluellen, by figuring the King as both royal and common, relocates his heritage in a move that gestures toward suppressing Hal's tavern past. After Henry names the battle Agincourt, Fluellen brings up his likeness to his great-uncle, Edward the Black Prince, reminds him that "all the water in Wye cannot wash your majesty's Welsh plood out of your pody," and proclaims himself proud to be Henry's countryman—"so long as your majesty is an honest man" (4.7.93–109). The comradeship initiated by Fluellen also establishes the leek as one more symbolic object—like the glove that Henry exchanged with Williams, which he now gives to Fluellen, to be worn in one's "Monmouth cap" (or crown)—and positions Fluellen as a surrogate-double for Harry le Roy, the Welsh King of England, whose honesty, and whose own blood brotherhood, are immediately put to trial.

At almost precisely this point in its narrative, *Richard II*, in the scenes concerning the Aumerle conspiracy (5.2; 5.3), dramatizes a trial of faith that reinstates the social contract between king and subject.

Similarly, Henry's elaborately doubled glove trick represents another version of "The Beggar and the King" that tests the truth of subjects' oaths, discovers "treason" (recalling the earlier betrayals of Cambridge, Scroop, and Grey, 2.2), and turns it to obedience. In making Fluellen fight his battles, just as his subjects have fought his wars, the episode not only plays out the issues Williams raised on Agincourt Eve but results in a further exchange: for the glove and royal crowns he gives to Williams, Henry takes from him the soldierly behavior that he later uses, again as a sort of disguise, for wooing the French princess. To so read the glove trick is, of course, to be entirely complicit with containing Henry's fears concerning his subjects' disobedience as well as with affirming the egalitarian promises of St. Crispin's Day. But even this new myth of brotherly origins does not so easily erase Hal's dramatic past. A number of contradictions press into and are rethought in the encounter, from echoes of Gadshill, where Hal and Poins stole crowns, to Henry's later rejection of Falstaff. Obliquely, too, by confirming his kinship with Fluellen, whose insistence on discipline and honesty sounds rather like Henry IV, Henry erases the enmity between the Welsh Owen Glendower and his father that had led to Shrewsbury. Although 1 Henry VI's Joan of Arc had no difficulty in recognizing a king regardless of his disguise (1.2), in Henry V's comedy of power, the ruler's subjects do and do not know the King. When Williams, who continues to speak the language of the band of brothers rather than that of the abject subject, claims that whatever "abuses" the disguised Henry suffered are his own fault, his voice indeed sounds at least as authentic as that of the King. Yet by accepting the "honor" Henry offers and refusing Fluellen's twelve pence, he affirms that the King, not the Welsh captain, is the appropriate giver of crowns. In this curiously ambivalent trick of comic leveling, Henry's loyalty test works not only to reestablish a common origin for the aristocratic body—a construct as important for the mythologizing of King Harry as his atonement for his father's sin—but, in recirculating the feudal distinctions of rule, manages to reconstitute, so to speak, the patriarchal body of the King and his state.

Henry V now exchanges this oddly skewed brotherly fantasy for another and again contrasts, through listing the dead, a French "royal fellowship of death" that reproduces a Great Chain of Classes—princes, nobles, barons, lords, knights, esquires, gallant gentlemen, and mercenaries—with an English brotherhood of name and nation (in the case of the Welsh Davy Gam) owing fealty to God. Finally, the King who had earlier claimed for all who fought with him at Agincourt, "Be he ne'er so vile, / This day shall gentle his condition"

(4.3.62–63), replaces the image of a fraternal, egalitarian state with a "largess universal, / Like the sun" (4 Cho., 43) sanctioned by doubled fathers. Like the closing images of the earlier histories, this one surrounds a newly authorized King with a community of subjects. Unlike them, however, Henry V's Agincourt ending figures its "happy few" as a communal body, masters and men joined together in remembering dead heroes and in pseudosacramental union. Oddly reminiscent of 2 Henry IV's first "full" close, where Hal appears as King to reassure his brothers and name the Lord Chief Justice his surrogate father, these reaffirmations of praise and thanks, by locating Henry V's homosocial fantasy in relation to the sacred, also counter any potential resistance to the perfectly mythologized narrative of this family romance called Agincourt.[16]

Or so it would seem. For in providing what might be called twin codas to Agincourt—Chorus's description of Henry's triumphal London entry and the Fluellen-Pistol quarrel (5.1), both of which precede the final scene in the French court (5.2)—Henry V offers alternate readings of that history. Dr. Johnson's grumpy Aristotelianism would reverse the two and so dismiss "all the comic personages . . . of the history of Henry the Fourth and Fifth" before the last chorus.[17] Such tidiness has some appeal, and certainly Johnson's reordered play would continue Henry V's characteristic pattern in which the "base, common, and popular" clowns undermine the heroic gestures of aristocratic rhetoric. But to so rewrite Henry V's narrative strategy is also to rewrite its deliberate rupture between historical and comic-popular materials and so to reread its engagement with Elizabethan as well as dramatic history. In Shakespeare's representational strategy, which follows Agincourt's celebratory close with Chorus's speech describing an Augustan welcome for a conquering Caesar come home from a foreign land to win English hearts, Henry's Agincourt victory floats out into the Elizabethan social reality to figure his triumph as that of Essex, identified as "the general of our gracious empress" (5 Cho., 30), returning from Ireland after having suppressed Tyrone's nationalist rebellion. Essex had, of course, been associated with Bolingbroke, Henry's father, and still other parallels tied him to Henry: both had escaped domestic troubles with foreign wars, both had laid siege to Rouen, and both sought to remobilize chivalric ideals and so transform the nation's politics.[18] As it turned out, Essex's Irish expedition was as unsuccessful as his later honor revolt, perceived as a threat to Queen Elizabeth's waning power in the final years of her reign. But in 1600, when Henry V was first performed, English spectators could, in anticipating Essex's victorious return, also be invited to think of him as someone whose power rivaled that of the Queen. Indeed, for those who figured Elizabeth as an image of misrule, the processional entry of an "imperial" and suitably masculine hero would be most welcome.[19] Yet even though Chorus's approbation gestures toward extending Agincourt's homosocial fantasy into a more historically local fantasy of male rule, his prologue also makes it clear that Essex is not Henry, whose welcome affords "much more, and much more cause" (5 Cho., 34) for celebration. Indeed, by disguising Essex as Henry, *Henry V* not only masks any potential subversion of Elizabeth's own "masculine" rule but further protects itself through the alienating convention of the narrator. Finally, any connection between Chorus's glowing, doubly "historical" finish to Agincourt and Essex's public exhibitions of military and chivalric power, which were, after all, sanctioned by the Queen, can be considered merely the result of a spectator's own "imaginary forces."

If Chorus's report mobilizes Henry's achievement to allude to a contemporary Elizabethan figure and to invite comparisons between written and future history, Pistol's encounter with Fluellen and his leek, in borrowing closural signs from *1* and *2 Henry IV*, looks in a different direction to reframe Agincourt's victory with particularly suggestive reminders of the ahistorical figure most invested in Henry V's dramatic history. On one level, the scene reopens the division among the English that the play, through Henry's agency, has sought to dispel and thus critiques the authenticity of the "band of brothers"; on another, it reasserts the difference between honor and cowardice, between Hotspur and Falstaff, that animated *1 Henry IV*'s close and firmly expels, as that play hesitated to do, the grotesque body capable of subverting the law of the fatherly state. Most significantly, however, Fluellen beating Pistol with his symbolic leek and then forcing him to eat what he hates as punishment for his insults against the Welsh nation reworks Falstaff's banishment from *2 Henry IV* as ethnic carnivalesque, not royal policy. Certainly Pistol's last words, based in part on Dericke's return to England in *The Famous Victories* and on Falstaff's similarly positioned soliloquy in *1 Henry IV* (5.4.158–61), not only link him rather precisely with Falstaffian lies but identify him with the disbanded soldiers accused of similar thieveries and pretense that Elizabethan proclamations recognized, and condemned, as a threat to social order.[20] In one of its most contradictory moves, *Henry V* seems, on the one hand, to attach enough significance to the threat Pistol represents to displace this last reprise of Boar's Head away from Agincourt's close and so to insulate the "band of brothers" as a fiction untainted by discord; on the other, it invites comparisons between Pistol's status as what James Shapiro calls a "small-time mystifier and small-time thief"²¹ and the more global mystifications and thievery of King Henry's imperial French enterprise, soon to be further played out in the confines of the French royal family.

ॐ

Like *Richard II*, which, at least in one of its late Elizabethan theatrical configurations, was used by Essex's followers to mirror, and so to energize, particular political concerns, *Henry V* becomes, in the theater, a tabula rasa for its culture's current prerogatives. That this occurs with any of Shakespeare's histories is central to my argument, but *Henry V*'s ability to serve its culture's needs and speak its nation's history makes it distinctly unusual. I want to begin with the nineteenth century,²² for it is there, as actor-managers transformed *Henry V* into historically accurate "speaking pictures" that, Bottom-like, translated Sidney's teaching and delighting into an educational project to serve a public hungry for historical knowledge, that the play, and Shakespeare as national poet, take on the semblance of "historical truth." Following a tradition begun by Macready, who commissioned Clarkson Stanfield in 1839 to design grand panoramas for Henry's "Roman" London entry, as well as for the voyage of the English fleet to Harfleur and its siege and for the English and French camps at Agincourt, Charles Kean's 1859 *Henry V* staged the King's victorious return to London as a spectacular recreation of "eyewitness" accounts. Aided by five hundred to six hundred supernumeraries, this pictorial pageantry not only reproduced the entire social configuration but included a Hymn of Thanksgiving ("supposed to be as old as A.D. 1310") sung by a Chorus of fifty, together with Mrs. Kean (the famous Ellen Tree) reciting Chorus in the character of Clio, the Muse of History.²³ Kean viewed such aesthetic-archaeological reconstructions as a service to imperialism— evidence that grand moments from the historical past could and did figure in England's present national superiority; moreover, he assumed not only that Shakespeare's play represented historical truth but that Chorus spoke with its authentic voice. Indeed, like earlier actor-managers, Kean read Chorus literally, as Shakespeare's apology for the lack of effects in his theater: rectifying that absence with opulent illustrations based on meticulous research did not, he claimed, permit "historical truth to be sacrificed to mere theatrical effect" but instead supplied, through the wonders of reconstructed spectacle, what Shakespeare himself would have done with similar resources. The prevalent Victorian opinion that if man could understand history and the past he could understand himself, Michael Booth argues, gave Kean's historical spectacles a cachet of respectability they might not otherwise have had. Indeed, for him as well as for his later theatrical heirs, presenting history truthfully by showing it on the stage was, to quote Beerbohm Tree, "not the least important mission of the modern theater."[24]

Nearly a century later, a remarkably similar combination of Kean's missionary fervor as well as his commitment to panoramic spectacle lay behind Laurence Olivier's 1944 film of Henry V. Olivier himself writes, "I had a mission; . . . my country was at war; I felt Shakespeare within me, I felt the cinema within him. . . . I felt myself to be an agent of his imagination."[25] Dedicated to "the Commandoes and Airborne Troops of Great Britain, the spirit of whose ancestors it has been humbly attempted to recapture," Olivier's Henry V represented an especially timely vision of an England "peopled with heroes"—and with one hero in particular, the king, through whom the people acquire an ideal identity.[26] Certainly the film depends, as Dudley Andrew writes, on the notion that "at the core of history . . . is the power of the great man, a power of self-mastery generating crowd mastery and the mastery of the future."[27] And Olivier's cuts remove all that contradicts this perfect mythic image.[28] Gone are the threats, including the references to rape, that Henry voices to the Governor of Harfleur, together with the executions of Cambridge, Scroop, and Grey for treason as well as the mention of Bardolph's execution and the King's order to kill the French prisoners. The glove trick also disappears: no quarrel taints Henry's compassionate relationship with his subjects to counter the patriotic-moral work of Agincourt Eve. Filmed in a series of crosscut close-ups, subjects and king appear to share an intimate exchange that not only links the spectator with both but reveals Henry as a confident and charismatic presence rather than, as in Shakespeare's play, a ruler anxious to prove the justice of his war.[29] In Olivier's scene, Williams has only a single line; it is Court, played by an Irish boy in his teens, who voices Williams's probing questions about Henry's war and then lies down to sleep while the others debate the King's promises to risk his own body before leaving Henry alone. Spoken in solemn reverence, "Upon the King" not only figures Olivier's Henry as all Englishmen questioning, as World War II draws to a close in Europe, their own survival but stresses the point, as he speaks of his subjects, by having the camera pull back to reveal the sleeping Court beside him. Henry speaks of the cares of kingship as he strokes the boy's head, an image that contradicts and overcomes his willingness to risk human life to show a King who is a gentle, nurturing father. And later, as Henry sees the body of an English boy killed by the French and held toward the camera to show his throat cut, he challenges the Constable of France to single combat, the last honorable, as well as bloodless, duel in Olivier's reshaped fantasy of blood brotherhood.

The boy's blood is indeed the only evidence of what Keegan calls Agincourt's "slaughter-yard behavior and outright atrocity." Shot on location in Ireland, the battle's deep-space images and sharp montage—what Andrew calls "expansive cinema"[30]—contrast markedly to the film's studio sets, which alternate between the high artifice of images borrowed from the *Très Riches Heures* of Jean, Duc de Berri and scenes staged in front of "realistic" rear projections or backdrops. Indeed, Olivier's Agincourt serves as a set piece that substitutes a balletically choreographed historical realism for the contemporary European war to prefigure not only England's victory but that of Western civilization. When, at the battle's end, Henry reads the list of the dead, William Walton's score stops, as though to create a space for the film's spectators to add the names of their own dead; then, accompanied by an anthem, Henry mounts his white horse to lead the army out of the English camp and, through a series of dissolves, the film finally locates this procession within the Duc de Berri's miniature world, where a cut to a snowy village landscape brings the February illustration from *Très Riches Heures* to life: Pistol flirts with village women inside a house; three boys sing carols; a couple goes to church. Only momentarily does the Pistol-Fluellen quarrel, played as pure slapstick and as a last homage to the flourish and panache of Robert Newton's Pistol,[31] interrupt these images of restored social harmony. And it is Pistol, not Williams, who receives "crowns" for his performance: just before Gower walks off with Fluellen, he throws a coin offscreen; in the next shot, Pistol catches it in his helmet and then walks directly toward the camera to speak his farewell before disappearing into a barn, from which he emerges with a pig under one arm and a cockerel in his hand, runs up the hill, and is gone.

If Shakespeare's *Henry V* excludes Pistol from Agincourt's "band of brothers," in Olivier's film he is its most canny survivor, snatching French commodities in short supply in wartime Britain, yet, while celebrating his grotesque body, the film finally deflects any potential threat he poses by placing him within the Duc de Berri's distanced, painterly spaces. Moreover, returning to that pictorial reality for the leek quarrel as well as for Henry's later wooing of Katherine encloses the two events through which Englishmen in 1944 could connect themselves and their material conditions to their cultural heritage (Henry's dark night of the soul and the battle itself) within a glowing world of artifice that celebrates and makes a spectacle of the achievements of medieval and High Renaissance civilization (language, painting, and theater) which a second Great War threatened to destroy. And, although the later French scenes of Olivier's *Henry V* open up some fissures in its self-validating, nationalistic project, it is also true, as Andrew writes, that "seldom has cinema participated in a more massive ideological undertaking. Seldom has it seemed, both historically and aesthetically, more worthwhile."[32]

In 1975, threats of reduced funding replaced those of war as the Shakespeare Memorial Theatre in Stratford celebrated its centenary with Terry Hands's Royal Shakespeare Company productions of *1* and *2 Henry IV*, *Henry V*, and *The Merry Wives of Windsor*. But instituting a new tetralogy was far less important than the analogy between a "band of brothers" snatching hard-won victory from the French and the company's enterprise of seizing theatrical triumph from Arts Council budget cuts.[33] Overall, Hands envisioned *Henry V*, rather traditionally, as the completion of an emotional education begun in the *Henry IV* plays that set Henry the task of joining an England made up of disparate nations. Not only, then, did the soldiers' scenes consistently emphasize the local differences within Henry's army, but it was not until after Henry's talk with Williams, Court, and Bates, his reevaluation of the relation between "self" and ceremony, and his confession of his father's "fault" in the prebattle prayer that he earned, so to speak, royal as well as rhetorical authority. To further point the earlier failures of Henry's military rhetoric, it is only in the St. Crispin's Day speech, delivered not as a set piece to the audience but as an intimate address to his assembled men, that the army becomes welded into a unit that could win a battle. Given this particular interpretive strategy, the glove trick marks a crucial stage in Henry's project, and indeed Hands stages the quarrel betweeen Fluellen and Williams over the glove as a noisy brawl that includes Gloucester and Clarence as well as the commoners and that Henry breaks up with an amused "How now, what's the matter?" Then, to soften Williams's eventual acceptance of his position in feudal history, Henry removes the purse from the glove and, on "wear it for an honor in thy cap," taps Williams on each shoulder with the purse as though to knight him.[34] And just as this gestures toward erasing the distinctions between monarch and plain soldier to make good on Henry's promise to "gentle" those of "vile" condition, when he reads the lists of the dead, lingering over each name, the onstage army, nobles and commons together, clusters in a kneeling circle around a King who is father as well as brother (fig. 16). Carrying forward these images of full-stage community, the later Fluellen-Pistol quarrel also has an onstage audience. Accompanied by jaunty music, all the soldiers enter, whistling, and attach wires to the ground cloth so that it can be flown and then transformed into an overhead canopy for the following scene. Like Chorus, who is also present, they assist the play's theatricality, serving as its technical crew, much like circus workers preparing to hoist the tent.[35] With Pistol's humiliation turned into a public spectacle, it is not just Fluellen but the entire "band of brothers" who, in expelling him from their community, reinstate a parody of the larger royal hierarchy, with Fluellen at its center.

Less insistent on wresting *Henry V* into either a political or an aesthetic unity, Adrian Noble's 1984 Royal Shakespeare Company performance text[36] instead focused firmly on the play's dialectical approach, an emphasis supported in the souvenir program, which featured, in place of the usual snippets of critical opinion, the contradictory views of historians, printed in columns titled "Hero-King" and "Scourge of God" and, in addition, devoted the rest of the space to excerpts from "The History of the Battle of Agincourt" written by an anonymous priest who accompanied the 1415 expedition to France.[37] Implicitly, this arrangement acknowledges the traditional critical dialectic, but with an important difference: by supplying "eyewitness history" that the play's representational economy suppresses, the program not only becomes complicit with Chorus but, in suggesting the gap between several sorts of historical writing, calls his seemingly authoritative perspective into question.[38] Indeed, in Noble's *Henry V*, the events of Agincourt Eve explictly counter Chorus's reassuring picture of "a little touch of Harry in the night." As the glove trick is set up, Henry and Williams are both short-tempered, close to blows; Kenneth Branagh, the production's Henry, writes that "the 'Upon the King' soliloquy emerges because of the terrible certainty of what Williams has said. There will never be any real contact between him and other men however he may persuade them of the rightness of particular acts. They will never have any real desire or inclination to understand him or what he does. It's the confirmation that he will be forever utterly alone."[39] When, after the battle, Montjoy requests permission to bury the French dead, he speaks to a Henry who kneels, face to the ground, near the dead boy, who has been carried onstage by Fluellen. Surprised by Henry's "I know not if the day be ours or no," Montjoy replies, "The day is yours"; and when Henry falls down and rolls over on his back, some of the men move toward him, but Exeter motions them to stand back. Recovering, but still on the ground, Henry asks the name of the castle and, close to physical and mental collapse, rises to name the battle. When Fluellen reminds him that he is both the King and a Welshman, Henry embraces him so that Fluellen now holds not the dead boy but the living boy-king in his arms, an image that underscores the relation between Welsh King and officer, the "disciplines of war" and its cost in human life. And because the glove trick is later played out simply as a joke that all, including Fluellen, share rather than, as in Hands's *Henry V*, a sign of social levelling, it is this earlier image of the bond between the King's body and those of his subjects that condenses the figure of "blood-brotherhood."

Indeed, Noble's *Henry V* delays any further image of English union until the reading of the lists. Henry reads the French names slowly and then hands the paper to Montjoy, who stands apart from the central grouping, on "Here was a royal fellowship of death." As he goes on to name the English dead, the men draw closer to him, and a momentary silence formalizes their acknowledgment of God's victory before a *Te Deum*, begun offstage, is taken up by the soldiers as they exit. After Exeter and then Fluellen leave, Henry remains kneeling by the boy's body as Chorus enters and pulls a white curtain across the stage, masking the two figures. With heavy irony, he marks the distances traveled from Blackheath back to France, the "bruised helmet" and "bended sword" and, in describing London's citizens "Like to the senators of th' antique Rome," flings his own cape, togalike, over his shoulder. As the spotlight dims on Chorus's mockeries, the curtain behind him is backlit to form a scrim that reveals "true things": a Mother Courage–like figure who places lighted candles beside the bodies scattered on Agincourt's field. Then bright front lighting cuts this vision off, and the leek quarrel is played as an especially bitter vaudeville front-curtain act, which ends with a burst of savage anger from Gower and with Pistol's soliloquy, delivered as though he has no choices left. As he concludes, the scrim dividing upstage battlescape from downstage playing area is again backlit to reveal the woman moving among the candlelit dead. Through the scrim, Pistol and the woman exchange a look, making an implicit equation between the figure moving among the dead and the dead Nell Quickly, between the man who will brag of his wounds and the woman who obsessively searches the battlefield for evidence of life among the dead. True to the dialectical conception behind this *Henry V*, the contradictory signs distributed among these three scenes, each played successively closer to the audience, do not reach synthesis but are kept deliberately separate, their disjunctures enforced by shifts in rhetorical and acting styles as well as by markedly different representational strategies. Finally, the upstage area, transformed into the field of the dead, seems to dominate the stage, as though that image has erased—or absorbed—all the others.

Whereas both Hands and Noble stage Agincourt's ending as a tableau with an elegiac coda and then exploit both Chorus's last prologue and the Pistol-Fluellen encounter to reassert the play's theatricality, Michael Bogdanov's 1988 English Shakespeare Company *Henry V* strongly emphasizes the cost of the victory Henry attributes to God and then, by splitting Chorus's prologue, not only gestures in Dr. Johnson's direction but uses the leek quarrel to further comment on Henry's war. In Bogdanov's staging, the boy's death is the war's most expensive loss: his flag-draped corpse on the cart of war that traces through all the *Henry* plays centers the composition of an exhausted group of soldiers listening to Henry read the list of the dead, his voice breaking as he comes to "Davy Gam, esquire." While an Elizabethan spectator familiar with Shakespeare's chronicle sources, and especially with Welsh history, might recognize the name of Dafyyd Gam, whose family had remained loyal to Henry IV during the Glendower (Glyn Dwr) rebellion, for a present-day audience, the reference is lost: "Davy Gam" can become, in a sense, any one of Agincourt's hitherto "unknown soldiers."⁴⁰ Bogdanov's performance text further commemorates Davy by giving him a funeral procession: as Henry calls for *Non Nobis* and *Te Deum* and Chorus walks on to begin the anthem, Williams takes it up, and King and subjects together begin a slow, wandering upstage exit, in which sound both counters and supports image to further qualify Agincourt's victory. And Chorus's presence also colors that victory, for Bogdanov's *Henry V*, in which the actor who had played Falstaff in *1* and *2 Henry IV* also plays Chorus, is indeed a play "with Sir John in it," a doubling that brings additional resonances to the representational moves that precede *Henry V*'s finale.

Bogdanov uses the first twelve lines of Chorus's prologue to introduce the leek scene: a downstage bench where Fluellen and Gower sit, the sounds of screaming gulls and a life preserver handed out from offstage that Chorus positions at the end of a stage-right gangplank sketch its shipboard location and so suggest the army's return to England. After speaking, Chorus stays in the stage-right shadows, where a small table with a brandy bottle and snifter recall (and upgrade) Falstaff's drinking habits—an Alistair Cooke–like presenter of Masterpiece Theatre classics, commodified for public viewing. Pistol enters, sees Fluellen and Gower, and attempts to sneak off but is brought back and forced to eat a small scallionlike leek before Fluellen pulls a much larger and more threatening one from his pocket. Shrugging off his humiliation in the soliloquy, Pistol snatches the life preserver, a sign of his self-interest and ability to survive; as he is about to go, Chorus comes forward, points to the bench, and says, with gentle irony, "Pistol, you might as well take that, too"—and, with a grin that acknowledges his past connection to Falstaff as well as his willing complicity with the play's theatricality, he does. Obliquely, Bogdanov's joke traces a connection between Pistol's stolen life preserver and Henry's later theft of the Dauphin's title; his Falstaffian Chorus seems to license both: abetting the first, he participates in the second. After Pistol leaves the stage, he then describes Henry's London entry and his return to France and, as stage hands bring on a council table and surround it with chairs, Chorus exchanges his tuxedo jacket for morning dress to take Burgundy's role at the Treaty of Troyes where, in this new guise, he will envision France as an unnatural, husbandless garden. Here, Henry will woo and win a Princess; the Kings of England and France will conclude a political and familial alliance; and, with God's blessing, "all things shall be peace" (*A Midsummer Night's Dream*, 3.2.377).

"There shall be from hens forth for ever more and shall follow Pees, Tranquillity, Good Accord and Commune Affection and stable friendship and steadfast between the same roialmes and her subjects before sayd."[41] The language of the Treaty of Troyes, quoted almost verbatim in Lydgate's *Siege of Thebes*, outlines an almost impossible dream. Yet in Henry V's time, bringing love out of hate—a major theme of Gower's *Confessio Amantis* as well as Lydgate's *Siege of Thebes*—was considered the appropriate role for earthly as well as heavenly kings: both Bromyard and Gower use the figure of King David and his harp to define the King's skill in tuning the instrument's jangling strings, his subjects, into harmony. It was a model the historical Henry V took seriously, and indeed, as Maurice Keen argues, peace was the most important commodity Henry suggested that he could bring to France, and also the most difficult to achieve.[42] *Henry V* also takes Henry's kingly ideal seriously, especially in its final scene, which might rather accurately be titled *The Dream of the Treaty of Troyes*, in that it writes the finale of Henry's history in figures of harmony that mark what appears to be a radical shift in the play's gender economy, and so gestures toward rewriting Agincourt's family romance. Except for Katherine's language lesson (3.4), *Henry V*'s representational economy anticipates neither this particular cluster of generic signs embedded in a sociosymbolic resolution nor the particular dissolve of voices that articulates it,[43] which, by interweaving a number of texts, masks history to remake cultural myth. For although *The Famous Victories* supplies a ground plan for both Henry's wooing and the peace treaty, *Henry V*, by appropriating structures and iconography from the consummately inclusive finale of *A Midsummer Night's Dream*, imposes another template on those events.

Dream achieves narrative closure first through Titania and Oberon's newly figured harmony, and then as the lovers wake, restored to one another to have their marriages sanctioned by Theseus's reordered law of the father (4.1); *Henry V* reaches, at Agincourt, a similar resolution of the issues that have driven its narrative. Yet each play continues beyond narrative closure to refill the textual space of rebeginning with a series of closural celebrations. Both withhold the resolution of the "base, common, and popular" comedy until the major issues in the narrative proper have been settled, and both preface their finales with a clown scene that prefigures the kind of community each achieves: while in *Dream* (4.2), Bottom, by returning to his fellows to brag of his dream, makes their play, and the class oppositions and harmonies it engenders, "go forward," in *Henry V*, as Pistol returns to swagger in England, his absence makes possible the construction of an exclusively aristocratic social model. In both plays, too, the close articulates an idealized vision of generative and social bonds[44] and then, through Puck's Epilogue in *Dream* and Chorus's in *Henry V*, reveals that vision as a pattern owing its integrity only to theatrical representation. In *Dream*, the final scene dramatizes the only incomplete strand in the play's narrative, the mechanicals' play, which becomes the centerpiece of the close. But in *Henry V*, the final scene functions not as a play-within-the-play but as a play-*after*-the-play that inverts *Dream*'s relationships between figure (the mechanicals' play) and ground (Theseus's court). There, the Pyramus and Thisbe tragedy articulates a confrontation between texts and genres, an image of tragedy-that-might-have-been transformed by its actors into a performance that turns tragedy to comedy. In *Henry V*'s revision of *Dream*, genres and texts also confront one another in a similar mingle: details taken from chronicle accounts of the Treaty of Troyes are reshaped and encompassed within a fairy-tale playlet that appropriates patriarchy's erotic disguises as well as the royal "feminine mystique" of the earlier comedy to serve Henry's myth.

Like Oberon in *Dream*'s forest community, Henry's function in the French court is to transform Burgundy's Titania-like vision of a natural world gone awry, wasted and unfruitful, through the site of a woman's body into the "best garden of the world" (5.2.36). As Leonard Tennenhouse observes, "Shakespeare personifies the power of the French nation in the French princess";[45] for Henry, who substitutes "plain soldier" for the more courtly guise of a lover, courtship becomes another Agincourt. Indeed, France's king (the exact opposite of *Dream*'s blocking parental figure, Egeus) perfectly expresses Henry's martial-erotic perspective by joking that he turns French cities "into a maid; for they are all girdled with maiden walls that war hath never entered" (5.2.308–9). By husbanding Katherine, Henry possesses the unhusbanded garden of France: it is she who transforms, and so naturalizes, Agincourt's comedy of male bonding to turn it toward the generative social ideal associated with romantic comedy.[46] However, Katherine also represents, in *Henry V*'s newly regendered political economy, a commodity of exchange in what turns out to be, so to speak, another version of the glove trick. For Henry gains not just a wife but a new father, who, at Exeter's specifically pointed request, will address him, in the two formal languages of diplomatic exchange, as "Nostre très cher fils Henri, Roi d'Angleterre, Héritier de France" and "Praeclarissimus filius noster Henricus, Rex Angliae et Haeres Franciae." By the terms of the Treaty of Troyes, King Charles agreed that, on his death, "the crown and kingdom of France with all its rights and appurtenances shall pass to and perpetually abide with the said Henry our son and his heirs"[47]—language that envisions the crown as private property and that, at the level of a figure, Henry's glove trick and reward of crowns anticipates. Curiously, Henry's new relation to France is never, in *Henry V*, spoken in English: just as Katherine becomes subject to Henry in being "unnaturally subjected by his language," so too does the play represent Henry's concession—the difference between his earlier claim, "No king of England, if not King of France," and his new title, "Heir of France"—in a language he claims to understand only imperfectly.[48]

If *Henry V* seems, here, to deflect attention from Henry's compromise concerning the Plantagenet claim to France as well as from how the language of the treaty reflects the male bonding that has sustained its martial plot, the play seems equally anxious to forget that the French King's use of his crown disinherits the Dauphin, whose gift of tennis balls earlier seemed to position him as Henry's opposite. Although neither Quarto nor Folio calls for the Dauphin's presence in *Henry V*'s final scene, neither specifically excludes him: he might be among Quarto's "Lordes" (G_4^v) or part of Folio's "French Power" (TLN 3269). If present, he does not speak; but, in that this is what Philip C. McGuire calls an "open silence,"[49] his response to hearing language which replaces him with an English "fils" and "Héritier de France" can, in performance texts (such as Bogdanov's, described below), generate considerable strain in what is otherwise a perfectly negotiated comic close. At least that is the case in Quarto, where, after the French King agrees to Exeter's request, Henry asks for, and is granted, Katherine's hand and claims that the marriage will "end our hatred by a bond of love" (G_4^v; G_4^r). Folio, however, not only prolongs the close with further speeches from France, Henry, and Queen Isabel but makes what can seem a needless repetition of comic signs serve the realpolitik of the historical treaty. Indeed, two in particular—France's charge to Henry, "Take her, fair son, and from her blood raise up / Issue to me," and Henry's request that Burgundy take an oath "for surety of our leagues" *before* he speaks his wedding vows (TLN 3338–39; 3362–63)—emphasize Henry V's diplomatic skill in claiming France through his heirs and in requiring individual oaths from its nobility that would buttress the terms of the treaty.[50] Yet while these negotiations later made it possible for Henry VI to claim descent from two royal houses, Valois and Plantagenet, both of which carried the blood of Saint Louis in their veins, it was not long before the Burgundian French, the most patriotic of its noble factions, found legal loopholes that made it possible to abrogate the Treaty of Troyes.[51]

If, however, these traces circulate figures of "unnatural" treason and the consequent loss of France through the play's close, they are rather carefully wrapped within other signs of "natural" comic perfection. Largely because it represents a closural voice unique to the histories, the most intriguing of these is Queen Isabel's blessing of the marriage bed (5.2.343–52).[52] Like Titania and Oberon's shared final "Song" of consecration in *A Midsummer Night's Dream* (5.1.390–411), which seeks to deflect the "blots of Nature's hand" from the bridal beds, Isabel's speech invokes similar protections—from "ill office, or fell jealousy"—for the couple as well as for the allied kingdoms for which their marriage is the emblem. Just as marriage is the drama's image for generating the future, so is it the chronicler's image for social and political harmony. The marriage between Richmond and Elizabeth, considered the most significant by the chroniclers for healing England's dynastic conflict and uniting the kingdom, though alluded to in *Richard III*'s epiloguelike final speech, "comes true" at *Henry V*'s close, not as a promise spoken by a deus ex machina successor but as the center of a full political and presentational reality. In so representing succession, *Henry V*'s fantasy finale not only transcends the mystic utopian vision of a united England with which *Richard III* closes but floats out to "naturalize" the Elizabethan social reality, where Elizabeth's own claim to England's throne rested, as did that of her eventual successor, James VI of Scotland, on the legitimacy of female succession.[53] Unlike *Richard III*, where Richmond's final couplet pays her ambiguous homage, *Henry V* makes no such references to the Queen who had refused marriage and who had not as yet named her heir. Rather, it completes its "full and natural" close by imagining a realm where doubly legitimate heirs ensure succession and, as a last homage to *A Midsummer Night's Dream*, by combining the threats of Puck's

"Now the hungry lion roars" (5.1.360–79) and the apology of "If we shadows have offended" (5.1.412–27) to sustain and, then, to undermine its own "insubstantial pageant." Finally, *Henry V's* narrative as well as transactional closural figures take on the play's overall doubleness to reify—one last time, and then again, and again—the dialectic of genres through which it interrogates its own dismantlings and mystifications of history.

Henry V's Epilogue encloses this final visionary scene firmly within the boundaries of the play and so prevents readers as well as spectators from supplying what the scene prompts: the familiar "happily-ever-after" resolution of romance. Having throughout invited both readers and spectators to "work" their imaginary forces, Chorus here withdraws that invitation and closes off interpretive options to reread the play through a saturated, overdetermined formal sonnet that calls attention to the transitory nature of mythologized representations such as those shown on "our stage."[54] A model of enclosure, it figures in miniature the history of Shakespeare's histories:

> Thus far with rough and all-unable pen
>   Our bending author hath pursued the story,
> In little room confining mighty men,
>   Mangling by starts the full course of their glory.   4
> Small time, but in that small most greatly lived
>   This star of England. Fortune made his sword,
> By which the world's best garden he achieved,
>   And of it left his son imperial lord.   8
> Henry the Sixth, in infant bands crowned king
>   Of France and England, did this king succeed,
> Whose state so many had the managing
>   That they lost France and made his England bleed,   12
> Which oft our stage hath shown—and, for their sake,
> In your fair minds let this acceptance take.
>
>   *(Ep., 1–14)*

Given the emphasis, in *Henry V's* last scene, on a newly observed gender economy, perhaps one of the most noticeable features of this sonnet is how it, like the play and its conditions of Elizabethan representation, conforms to Salic Law: although Henry may claim France from the female, the final convention of his play excludes any mention of women, and sketches succession exclusively in terms of a male gender economy. Indeed, the sonnet's organization frames, in the two central quatrains, the reigns of both Henrys, father and son, bookending the two with an opening quatrain and a couplet, both of which refer, self-reflexively, to theatrical occasions. The first quatrain repeats the prologue's apologies—"confining mighty men, mangling by starts the full course of their glory"—a line that is itself "mangled" by an extra syllable; the second not only elevates Henry's story to myth but serves as an epitaph similar to the précis Hall gives at the end of each King's reign to recall the monarch's accomplishments and qualities and fix his portrait in memory, containing his "small time . . . greatly lived" in four lines of verse. Although the first two lines of the third quatrain legitimize his heir—unlike Henry, "crowned king / Of France and England"—in the last two, "king" finds a near-rhyme and antithesis in "managing," and "succeed" in "bleed," drawing opposites into a tension that defines the future's loss. And each quatrain is not only perfectly enclosed but has unusual integrity: the only point at which sense "bleeds" over from one internal division to another is when line 13's "which" requires a reader or speaker to attach the couplet's phrases, as though in afterthought, to the final quatrain.

Although the Epilogue seems at first to be a perfectly regularly Shakespearean sonnet, conforming to the expected rhyme scheme (abab / cdcd / efef / gg), a secondary, deviant rhyme scheme is not only equally valid but contributes to and enforces its meaning.[55] The sonnet first suggests this irregularity at line 7 (its midpoint) by an off-rhyme: "achieved" with "lived." Even though the second quatrain perfectly encloses Henry's praiseful epitaph, it also, through the hesitant rhyme, compromises that achievement, and it is this off-rhyme which initiates the secondary rhyme scheme, for the next quatrain's "succeed" and "bleed," though rhyming with each other, also constitute rhymes for "achieved." By abbreviating the "regular" time of the sonnet, this alternative rhyme scheme—abab / cdcd / ecec / ff—further reinforces the "small time" of Henry's reign. Moreover, the successive rhymes of "lived," "achieved," "succeed," and "bleed" draw together two further patterns. First, the rhyme scheme stumbles on "achieved" and continues to break down in the quatrain summarizing Henry the Sixth's succession and the loss of France; second, extending the c rhymes from the second to the third quatrain joins father to son, but further marks the difference between their reigns with a rupture in the sonnet's "time." In these rhythmic irregularities, the sonnet serves as a paradigm of the play's own movement in theatrical as well as historical time, beginning with failure, continuing to success, and moving toward the future before asserting, through the literary construct most characteristic of Queen Elizabeth's reign, that plays themselves are the supreme historical artifice. Finally, Chorus's Epilogue performs for the narrative what it cannot do: read and understand itself.[56] By referring the meaning of *Henry V*'s history to other plays, and to their past re-presentations, the Epilogue also commemorates the order of Shake-speare's historical writing, a chronology that is transformed when, in the First Folio, monarch follows monarch in "correct" succession. Even in its printed form, however, *Henry V* retains this trace of its theatrical chronology, which rings a final witty change both on Shake-speare's sense of ending and on the play's ability to collapse and re-deem time past into time present—more specifically, into the theatri-cal-historical "now" of the English stage.

One of *Henry V*'s later, and perhaps most famous, configurations, Olivier's 1944 film, plays even further with reconnecting its time and place to the conventions of the Elizabethan stage—and does so long before the Epilogue. Continuing the tradition of productions such as Charles Calvert's 1872 *Henry V* at Manchester's Theatre Royal, which closed with a spectacular realization of Katherine and Henry's mar-riage in Troyes Cathedral,[57] Olivier's film also revises Shakespeare's ending to imagine their union. As the French court scene concludes, Henry and Katherine are invested with state robes and crowns: joining hands, they walk toward two thrones framed in the background of the set by ordered columns taken from the Duc de Berri's illustrations. As the camera tracks them, a cut to the King reveals, when he turns to face the camera, the same exaggerated theatrical makeup he wore in the film's opening sequence in the Globe Theatre; then the camera pans right to a boy-actor made up as Katherine before a rapid dolly-back shows both "royal actors" on the stage of the Globe.[58] Peter Donald-son's analysis, however, discovers in the move from one illusionary reality to another a second shift in levels of representation, for the cam-era's dolly-back is really two separate shots, a close up and a track-back to full shot, the first of which shows, not the boy-actor seen dress-ing for his role in the film's opening shots, but a female performer, who offers her sexually coded image to the gaze of the Globe's Elizabethan gallants (as well as that of the film's spectators) with obvious pleasure. Writes Donaldson: "The actress *may* be Renee Asherson, but if so, her make-up, dress and demeanor are far different from those of the de-mure princess of earlier scenes. The eros that is deferred or muted in the wooing scenes is present here, displaced from the decorous diegetic space [of the *Très Riches Heures* court] into the milieu of the theater—the warm response Henry cannot quite get from Katherine as princess is given to the audience by Katherine as player." If the cut, which now reveals two males, standing in the "static, hierarchical positions remi-niscent of formal Elizabethan portraiture," reproduces the homoerotic gender economy of the Elizabethan stage, Olivier's film also provides, in its fleeting image of a "real" woman, a perfected, fully natural close that, like Henry himself, "claims" its legitimacy "from the female." Just as significant, however, is the image of two males, their hands joined together, which reprises Henry, on Agincourt Eve, stroking the sleeping boy-soldier's head to figure, in the film's last moments, the "triumphant, nurturant union of father and son."[59] And this image of union, joined by the Archbishop of Canterbury, who appears between the couple to give his ceremonial blessing, is not just a state wedding but a wedding *in England* where Henry's bride, in her male as well as female guises, appears as his Queen on the Globe's own stage.

To provide further signs of this overdetermined drive for resolution, Olivier not only omits those lines of Chorus's Epilogue that refer to the undoing of Henry's victory but authenticates Chorus as presenter, master of ceremonies, director, and, perhaps, surrogate *auteur* by having the Globe spectators cluster around him, as though approving both his performance and his view of history.[60] And as the camera tilts up to the stage balcony to discover the Bishop of Ely conducting the choir boys in the sacramental anthem that has throughout supported these images joining two presentational realities, two diegetic (and geographical) spaces, and two gender economies, Ely looks up, nods, and the film cuts to the orchestra in the gallery, whose leader directs them to play louder, in homage to the voice of William Walton's score. After a man pulls the playhouse flag down, rolls it up and exits, the film ends with a panoramic tracking shot of Elizabethan London, the Globe Theatre in the foreground, to show, in a last reassuringly timeless "imprint" that displaces the present-day reality of its spectators, an intact, though artificial, city, unharmed by the bomb damage of the Second World War.

In its more recent stage configurations, *Henry V*'s close not only exhibits far less mastery over history but opens out to engage with, not erase, present-day England and so to relocate the play's own contradictory view of history. In Hands's 1975 *Henry V*, for instance, a textured gold canopy floats over the brightly lit French court; costumed in white and gold, Henry and Katherine pose in the center of a downstage grouping, the French flanking Henry, the English Kate, in an image of the "Christian-like accord" between the two kingdoms observed, from the catwalk framing the playing space, by black-clad stagehands. When Chorus comes forward, his black slacks, informal jacket, and turtleneck identify him as one of these "commoners" to further offset the brilliance of the period tableau, on which the lights dim, as though obeying his evocation of the fading world of "this star of England." And the music sounding under his Epilogue is the *Te*

Deum sung by Fluellen at Agincourt's close, played pianissimo on woodwinds and changing to full brass as he concludes, in a final reminder of the connection between Henry and the Welsh captain and of Agincourt's "band of brothers" that signals, with the military sound of the last chords, the wars to come.[61]

If, within the contexts of the Royal Shakespeare Theatre's economic circumstances and the centenary year, Henry V's achievement merges, in Hands's production, with the company's tour-de-force Brechtian minimalism in a joint celebration of theatrical power, Adrian Noble's 1984 *Henry V* makes spectacle, not sound, reveal the doubt and strain of Henry's French wars. His performance text situates the French court in front of a white scrim hung at midstage, setting off the black velvet robes of the French and the maroon capes of the English, worn over pale grey velvet doublets. As he speaks his last oaths, Henry takes Kate's hand at center stage and, with the others grouped in an informal circle around them, they pose, briefly spotlit (fig. 17), and Chorus walks in front of them. Now only his solitary figure occupies the spot light, while the others become silhouetted "walking shadows" as, again, the scrim is backlit to reveal Agincourt's battlefield, its candles flickering in the half-light (fig. 18). In Noble's staging, past, present, and future history occupy the stage simultaneously, outlining historical cause and effect in terms of actors' presences in space: just as, in this image, that event literally lies behind Henry and Katherine's union, so does their bethrothal kiss betray England's future. When Chorus, on his last line, extends his arms as though inviting spectators, one last time, to share responsibility for the play, he also seems, as Irving Wardle writes, to be asking them to "acknowledge complicity in the play's nationalistic prejudice."[62] And when the production transferred from Stratford to London, the scrim, now inscribed with the names of those killed at Agincourt, linked the Royal Shakespeare Company's stage with Washington's recently dedicated Vietnam Veterans' Memorial to measure Agincourt's war in terms of present-day anxieties concerning imperial idealism, its shows of power and their cost in human life.

Bogdanov's 1988 *Henry V* invites spectators to see that war as an imperialistic enterprise mounted by a Henry who has mobilized an entire country to serve a deeply personal need to prove himself to his father as well as to right Henry IV's usurpation of the English throne. Ranked chairs frame a central council table behind which hangs a large blue banner with the French fleur-de-lys, replacing the Cross of St. George that had identified the similarly set opening scene as the English court. Here, Burgundy, played by the production's Falstaffian

Chorus, is the central figure: the French King and Henry sit at his right and left, respectively—the French in morning dress, Katherine and the Queen in black, and Henry wearing the red jacket and blue trousers of nineteenth-century military uniform but not his crown, which is positioned on the table, as though it were the final prize in yet another glove trick. Left alone, Henry and Katherine sit in chairs on opposite sides of the stage during the wooing scene, and both seem more aware of their political roles than of any mutual attraction. As the French and English lords return, seat themselves, and report on the settlements, Henry formally asks for, and is granted, her hand; then, as he gives Katherine a ceremonial kiss, the Dauphin rises angrily from his chair, knocking it over much as Hotspur and as Henry himself had done when both were lectured by Henry IV (1 Henry IV, 1.3; 3.2), and runs offstage (fig. 19).[63] Annoyed at this interruption in the negotiation, Henry breaks away from Katherine to stand far down right. It is the Queen who brings the couple together and leads them back to center stage, where, in the final tableau, they face one another, their hands joined as Chorus rises, walks slowly upstage of their figures, now bathed in half-light, and, standing in a spotlight, speaks the Epilogue sonnet. As the lights come down in a slow fade, crashing chords accompany "God save our gracious Queen, long live our noble Queen" while the sounds of gunfire and grenade explosions begin to play through the anthem to invite connections between the promised historical future voiced by Chorus and more recent reminders of the gains, and losses, of England's—and the West's—foreign aggressions. If Hands and Noble confine any potential critique of Henry V's dynastic imperative to Chorus's speech and the final stage image, Bogdanov's Henry V, by reading the coming marriage as the last crucial move in Henry's imperialist strategy and by not only calling attention to the Dauphin's disinheritance but also to the political functions of three women—Katherine, Queen Isabel, and (in the anthem) Queen Elizabeth II—embeds signs of that critique within the narrative, eroding its potential harmony well before the Chorus reminds spectators that the theater may only show, but not necessarily rewrite, its culture's prerogatives.

In its Elizabethan guise, Henry V addresses its own contemporary present less explicitly, mediating its conflicts and contradictions through a final ruse of theatrical disguise.[64] Positioned firmly at the play's center, King Henry stands, like Elizabeth, at the mythic core of the kingdom, the focus of the metaphor linking stage and world to express royal power. But unlike Henry, Elizabeth would not have the good fortune to establish a clear succession, a dynastic line, or a title to France. In one reading, then, *Henry V*'s final scene embodies a nostalgic vision of what might have been for England as, during the final years of her reign, the kingdom waited for an heir to be named. The Epilogue, however, erases any possibility that the play's last scene implicates the reigning Queen and refers closure, with extreme policy, to another fiction. And with its last couplet, the playtext circles back, like a dog snapping at its own tail, to affirm, finally, what the closural signs of all Shakespeare's Elizabethan histories have implied but never, until now, made explicit: that what completes or, perhaps more accurately, succeeds represented history is, quite simply, another history play. It is a gesture that acknowledges how completely these plays, and their various theatrical configurations, absorb—and re-place—the social text that gives them life.

CHAPTER 8

UNCOMMON WOMEN AND OTHERS:
HENRY VIII'S "MAIDEN PHOENIX"

Come over the borne, Bessy
Come over the borne, Bessy
Sweet Bessy, come over to me;
.   .   .   .

I am thy lover fair,
Hath chose thee to mine heir,
And my name is merry England.

—William Birch, *"Come Over the Borne, Bessy"*

ON 14 JANUARY 1559, the day before her coronation, Elizabeth Tudor, "richly furnished, and most honorably accompanied," rode in an open litter from the Tower through the City of London to Westminster, witness to a resplendent pageant, one of many in which she would be doubly inscribed, presented and re-presented. At Gracechurch Street, she saw a "gorgeous and sumptuous arch" spanning the street, covered with red and white roses and divided into three levels. On the lowest, two children, representing Henry VII, enclosed in a wreath of red roses, and his wife Elizabeth, enclosed in one of white, sat under one cloth of state, holding hands, "with the ring of matrimony perceived on the finger." Two more children, representing Henry VIII and Anne Boleyn, posed on the middle level, where the banked red and white roses converged and surrounded their figures, above which were written their names and titles. At the top, amid mingled white and red roses, stood a single child representing Elizabeth herself—"now our most dread Sovereign Lady, crowned and apparalled as the other Princes were." "Furnished" with Latin sentences concerning unity and peace, this tableau vivant, as the presenter's verses made clear, celebrated "The Uniting of the Two Houses of Lancaster and York."[1]

For the Princess whose birth had disappointed her father's wishes for a male heir and whose childhood was marked by shifts in favor and power—she was proclaimed illegitimate by an Act of Parliament, imprisoned in the Tower by her half-sister Queen Mary, considered a potential traitor and heretic—the moment embodied an extraordinary rise of Fortune's wheel, of "the coming on of time." When the procession reached the Little Conduit in Cheapside, she herself said, in reference to the figure emblematized there, "Time hath brought me hither." Here, too, she smiled, on hearing one say, "Remember old King Henry the Eighth."[2] "Prayers, wishes, welcomings, cries, tender words": every sign in this expressive pageant honored the new Queen, legitimized her succession, and connected her, through blood ties, to a remembered moment of union and peaceful promise. "To succeed happily through a discreet beginning . . . to have a good eye that there be no innovations, no tumults or breach of orders": Sir Nicholas Throckmorton's advice to the new Queen voiced the hopes of a realm exhausted by the disorders of Henry VIII's last years, Edward VI's minority, Mary's unsettled reign, domestic division along religious lines, and threats of continental war.[3]

First performed in 1613, ten years after the accession of Elizabeth's successor, James I, *Henry VIII* replicates and reinscribes within its close not only the blessings and graces retrospectively associated with Elizabeth's fortunate reign but also a similar cluster of present and represented monarchs inhabiting royalty's "master fiction."[4] In both the Gracechurch pageant and the close of Shakespeare's play, in each staging of royal power, Time collapses into an eternal ideological present in which monarch faces monarch, closing the "wide gap of time" (*The Winter's Tale*, 5.3.154). "King," asserts the doctrine of the King's Two Bodies, "is a Name of Continuance."[5] Variously described as Tudor propaganda, as transcendental culmination, and as purely occasional in its allusions to King James and his newly married daughter, Princess Elizabeth, the past Queen's namesake, that close, like the play itself, eludes generic explanation. Although Folio positions *Henry VIII* as Shakespeare's final history, its later readers have been less sure of its status. The play, with its highly original collaboration of historical-tragical-pastoral signs, can seem as radically flexible as Hamlet's cloud: a camel, a weasel, a whale, or all three simultaneously. In that it draws on historical materials, it is history; in that a series of *de casibus* falls pattern its narrative strategy, it verges toward tragedy; in that features associated with masque override tragic signs to reinterpret historical process, it has strong affinities with Shakespeare's "last plays."[6] Read from the prospect of the close, however, this peculiar generic hybrid exists solely for generation: its purpose is to produce a child—not just another (however extraordinary) Marina or Perdita but a unique female child, an "honorary male" who will become a sovereign Prince of England.

In all accounts of the play, even that of Sir Henry Wotton, who thought it "sufficient in truth . . . to make Greatness very familiar, if not ridiculous,"⁷ this "right royal" project works to expose the full social text of monarchical power in order to disclose how, by insisting on its charismatic nature, that power reconstitutes itself. Like Shakespeare's Elizabethan histories, *Henry VIII* centers on legitimizing succession; unlike them, however, the king's own right, though challenged, is never at issue. Indeed, as Leonard Tennenhouse argues, Henry's body represents a "living icon," a repository of meaning and value;⁸ for those like Buckingham or Cardinal Wolsey who stand close to the royal center as for the Gentlemen who observe how "mightiness meets misery" (Pro., 30), the only desirable or possible power is his.⁹ And Henry stands, at times quite literally, above all; whether seen or merely spoken of, his prerogatives, though they may be called into question, consistently prevail. Rather quickly, *Henry VIII*'s first half sweeps away Buckingham and Wolsey—the one a potential contender for the crown, the other an ambitiously powerful rival. Both, as Tennenhouse points out, are figures who, in Shakespeare's Elizabethan histories, represented threats to royal power and so were as central to the conflicts shaping the earlier plays' narrative strategies as to their politics.¹⁰ In *Henry VIII*, however, such conflicts are marginal to Henry's, and the play's, obsession with replicating himself. Instead, what conflict there is centers on women—that is, on their relation to Henry. Although in the earlier histories women play crucial roles in bearing the burdens of succession, only in *Henry VIII* do they become such spectacular sites, so to speak, for contesting and confirming royal authority. To read *Henry VIII* through "the Queen's part" reveals what might be called an early Stuart *Richard II*, a play which not only deposes a rightful Queen but crowns two others and, finally, through a sacramental procession, restores male rule. And, also somewhat like *Richard II*, this *Henry VIII* has several guises, varying not between one written text and another but between one performance text and another. None, to be sure, omits Katherine's trial, the analogue to Richard II's abdication, where she refuses to be judged in the matter of the divorce by any authority other than Rome (2.4). Rather, in the theater, the major difference between one *Henry VIII* and another has to do with how each re-presents the history of its Queens' bodies and whether it is Anne's coronation procession (4.1) or Elizabeth's christening (5.5) that closes the play.

In its Folio form, *Henry VIII*'s narrative strategy interweaves Katherine's fall from royal favor with Anne's rise, leaving no doubt that what occupies the King's conscience is less "the marriage with his brother's wife" than, as Suffolk puts it, that "his conscience / Has crept too near another lady" (2.2.15–17). Rather schematically, the playtext juxtaposes Henry's first two wives, not once but twice: first, Anne, protesting that "By my troth and maidenhead, / I would not be a queen" receives the title of Marchioness of Pembroke (2.3.23) and, in the following scene, Katherine, at her most queenly, protests her wifely obedience (2.4); then double ceremonies stage Anne's coronation procession and Katherine's vision of "a blessed troop" (4.1; 4.2.87). In *Henry VIII*'s gender economy, the making and unmaking of wives, queens, and mothers eroticizes Anne's body and, so to speak, beatifies Katherine to reproduce, however ambiguously, the familiar whore/virgin dichotomy—or, in this case, the difference between a "quean" and a "queen." Each time she appears, Anne is the object of the desiring male gaze. To Henry, at Wolsey's masque, she is "a dainty one," a kissable commodity (1.4.94); to the Lord Chamberlain, who muses that "from this lady may proceed a gem / To lighten all this isle" (2.3.78–79), she holds fertile promise; and to the Third Gentleman, reporting the coronation itself, "she is the goodliest woman / That ever lay by man" (4.1.69–70). Indeed, both the procession and the reported coronation position Anne as a site of visual pleasure within a kind of early Stuart pornography; voiceless, she is defined only by her relationship to an absent King and by men who "speak" her body even as they tell of what has passed, is passing, and is to come.[11] Prefaced by reminders of Buckingham's trial for treason and Katherine's divorce and illness, the procession crosses the stage, its "sight of honor" giving way to the Third Gentleman's report of the noisy coronation spectators—among them "Great-bellied women / That had not half a week to go" who, "like rams / In the old time of war" (4.1.76–78) overpower the crowd, battering their way into royal space, making of themselves a spectacle that threatens to displace state cermonial with carnival. Not only do these details presage Anne's "divorce," her future execution for supposed adultery and treason, but they also allude, somewhat diplomatically, through the pregnant women, to Henry's delay in crowning Anne until she had proved capable of childbearing. Moreover, the carnival liberty of warlike wives, fused into a collective Amazonian body, points toward the feminine "misrule" sometimes associated with Elizabeth's reign:[12] to the Third Gentleman's eyes, "all were woven / So strangely into one piece" (4.1.80–81) that no man could recognize his own wife.

What can easily be forgotten is that Henry himself, though absent, presides as the carnival King of Misrule and that the comment glances at his apparent inability to tell one pregnant wife from another—at least until she bears a living male heir. Just as state spectacle authorizes the inversions of this abbreviated antimasque, so too, in the ensuing scene, does a more rarified "royal form," the pastoral of the masque proper, articulate Katherine's "assumption."[13] As the sick Katherine meditates on "celestial harmony," six "personages" dressed in white robes and wearing golden vizards appear to her, carrying palms (tokens of victory and triumph) and bays (tokens of joy); they curtsey to her and, three times, hold flower garlands over her head as though to crown her (4.2.82.s.d.). In the court masque, such pastoral conventions customarily express the most benign aspects of the ruler's power; in *Henry VIII*, they cut two ways to suggest, on the one hand, that this royally inspired Platonic vision represents Henry's sanctification of Katherine and, on the other, that she submits, even in imagination, to the *form* associated with sovereign power.

However contradictorily, Katherine's vision endows her abjection with meaning and value: among those swept away as threats to Henry's genealogy, she is the only one to whom the King sends messages, the only one who actively orchestrates her own death, in a nexus of figures that fold outward to embrace past and future Queens. Obediently commending herself as well as her daughter, the future Queen Mary, to the King's attention, she wishes to be "used with honor":

> Strew me over
> With maiden flowers, that all the world may know
> I was a chaste wife to my grave. Embalm me,
> Then lay me forth. Although unqueened, yet like
> A queen, and daughter to a king, inter me.
>
> *(4.2.168–72)*

Both the elliptic allusion to the Catholic Mary and the absence of any reference to Anne Boleyn measure *Henry VIII*'s tactful diplomacy, its awareness that it addresses a society where the Protestant James I occupies a throne recently vacated by the Queen some viewed as Anne Boleyn's bastard, responsible for the execution of another Catholic Queen, Mary of Scotland, James's mother. Equally suggestive, Katherine's emphasis on wedded chastity positions her in relation to the ideal norm for Renaissance women, a norm that restructured gender relations to diminish the power accorded to women by traditions of courtly love and doubly circumscribe them as dependent upon both a husband and a prince.[14] Katherine, in defining herself as "maiden," "wife," "queen, and daughter to a king," also figures Elizabeth's own particularly powerful strategies of self-definition, her sense of herself as England's Virgin Queen, the state's chaste bride.[15] Positioned in their original order, Anne's coronation procession and Katherine's vision not only serve *Henry VIII*'s gender economy but expose the central contradictions of Henry's sexual and political manuevering. It is hardly accidental, in this play, that Katherine's virginlike purity displaces Anne's sexualized body to sweep away erotic carnival with the image of a saintly Queen-Mother. In the structural juxtaposition of these two scenes, *Henry VIII* condenses the danger and pleasure of feminine power, and subjects both to Fortune, Time, and timing.

That this composite figuring of women has, in the theater, articulated closure writes an equally contradictory footnote to women's history as well as to male desire and male artistic practice. Eighteenth-century producers considered *Henry VIII* a tragedy that failed to maintain interest following the disappearance of its two "star" performers, Wolsey and Katherine.[16] The entire fifth act, including the churchmen's plot against Cranmer and his reinstatement by Henry, which figures the "birth" of the Church of England as occurring simultaneously with Elizabeth's offstage birth, as well as her christening, were thought unnecessary additions to an otherwise complete structure. Although Bell's widely used 1773 acting edition retains the conversation just before the coronation procession in which the two Gentlemen mention Katherine's "business" (4.1.22–35) and so makes her the subject of the play's "last words," prevailing theatrical practice absorbed them by staging Anne's coronation, in dumb show, as a spectacular finale. In 1727, the year of George II's accession, for instance, the coronation was such a success at Drury Lane that it was performed as an afterpiece to all other plays in the repertory as well as to pantomimes, apparently in order to make a "close-up" representation of something like George II's own ceremony widely available.[17] If in *Henry VIII*, Anne's coronation functions as a substitute wedding in which state ceremony authorizes Henry's sexual desire, here its theatrical performance becomes another kind of substitute—a curiously anomalous regendering in which George II perhaps replaces Anne in spectators' imaginations, but one which also, like the original, offers an image of power that "makes Greatness familiar."

Herbert Beerbohm Tree's 1910 *Henry VIII* also followed the tradition of omitting the church council proceedings, Cranmer's history, and Elizabeth's christening. Originally, however, Tree had intended to stage the scene where Henry hears of Elizabeth's birth as well as the christening spectacle (5.1; 5.4–5.5). But his plan to adhere to Prologue's "two short hours"—a phrase underlined and annotated in the prompt copy, "The play must be played swiftly . . . and the waits quite short"—meant cutting both.[18] Two other prompt copy notations reveal a particular, perhaps particularly Victorian, view of *Henry VIII* and its authorship. The foreword, after mentioning droit du seigneur, comments: "And so the injustice of the world is once more triumphantly vindicated, royal adultery is blessed by the court or Bishops, while minor poets sing in unison their blasphemous paeans—the fool enters weeping in black." Reversing *Henry VIII*'s representational strategy, Tree positioned Katherine's "unqueening" before Anne's coronation, staged as a full coronation in Westminster Abbey, including an anthem composed by Edward German. After the dimly lit scenes detailing Wolsey's fall and Katherine's assumption, the brilliant light and lavish display of Anne's coronation made a dazzling contrast. Although Stanley Bell's stage manager's book lists 88 persons onstage, the costume plot requires 119 costumes, and a photograph of the scene shows 122 actors and supernumeraries massed in position. Yet in spite of its full realization, reviewers found the spectacle disappointing. One called it a "historical peepshow"; another claimed he had seen better processions in musical comedy—a "higgledy-piggledy, rollicking" crowd in "no apparent order," "a sort of march past at a fancy dress ball."[19] But given the prompt copy note condemning royal adultery, Tree's raggedy procession and unruly, carnivalesque crowd may well have been deliberate, a way to reveal how such ceremonial facades mask "the injustice of the world." If so, reviewers clearly expected, in the year of George V's accession and in anticipation of his own coronation the following year, a "swelling scene" designed to recuperate and reconstitute royal ideology and patriarchal prerogative. After all, following Victoria's triumphant though attenuated reign, the ceremony itself, and its central male, mattered more than an object lesson on domestic fidelity or, for that matter, connecting the new King to a Tudor past that looked forward to the birth of another, equally powerful, Queen.

Tree's intended final image was to have done just that. In order to join offstage and onstage spectators together as communal celebrants for the christening, all on stage were to turn their backs to the audience as, in a (perhaps) more ordered spectacle, Elizabeth was held aloft for the cheering populace. In 1910, such a "sight" might well have worked, as it undoubtedly did for some Stuart spectators in 1613, to recall, variously, a fortunate or threatening image of female rule. Nearly three decades later, with another Princess Elizabeth the heir apparent, *Henry VIII* once again regained its "Tudor-Stuart" form to close with Elizabeth's christening.[20] But these mid-twentieth-century performance texts also rewrote Shakespeare's Tudor body politics, especially in relation to Anne's "state" body. Ben Iden Payne's 1938 Shakespeare Memorial Theatre production, for instance, eliminated

Anne's coronation, as did Robert Atkins's 1945 Stratford *Henry VIII*, which prefaced Katherine's "assumption" with the Three Gentlemen's reports of the procession and ceremony[21]—a strategy of nonrepresentation that not only denies Shakespeare's contradictory, composite figuring of women's public and private bodies but confines all state spectacle to Elizabeth's christening, where it marks the passage of theatrical iconography from one sovereign to another.

More radically, in place of the coronation procession, Tyrone Guthrie's 1949 Shakespeare Memorial Theatre *Henry VIII* substitutes a mime between Anne and the Old Lady, who later reports Elizabeth's birth.[22] Here, Anne skips onto the stage, sees her throne, and sits on it; horrified, the Old Lady shakes a fist at her, but Anne ignores her, puts on a large brooch, and looks eagerly toward the King's throne; then, frightened by a solemn peal of bells, she runs to embrace the Old Lady. Guthrie's invention rewrites the earlier scene between the two, in which the Old Lady, somewhat like *Othello*'s Emilia (4.3), would "venture maidenhead" for a title while Anne demurs, and in which their exchange tips "queen" toward "quean." To be sure, the original scene does close, after Anne has been named a Marchioness, with her premonition—"It faints me / To think what follows" (2.3.103–4)—but Guthrie's mime even more strongly prefigures her future history to position her, not as the eroticized center of a symbolic spectacle of state, but, like Katherine, as a potentially tragic figure. And since Guthrie also eliminated the masquers' "blessed troop" to instead have the seated Katherine sway as though in a dream, hold out her hands toward the audience, and finally rise to reach out toward the invisible world she imagines, his representational strategies diminish *Henry VIII*'s emphasis on celebrating the bodies of its three queens, according each a "coronation" that, though in very different ways, turns each into a site of spectacular visual pleasure.

Nearly seventy-five years after Tree's disorderly "historical peepshow," Howard Davies's 1983 Royal Shakespeare Company *Henry VIII*,[23] by simultaneously exploiting and undermining royal theatrics, opens a different window onto Anne's coronation procession. As the two Gentlemen speak their prologue commentary, they set roped barriers far downstage, just as they had done for Buckingham's execution procession (2.1), marking off the royal enclosure and further separating offstage spectators from their own, more privileged position at the fringes of power. In preparation for the coming ceremony, servants brings on tailors' dummies draped with coronation robes and a large prop table with maces, staves, and crowns; while the minor functionaries assemble, a Gentleman reads the scene's stage directions from a

"Tudor" clipboard while others check to make sure everything is in place. The central participants—Anne, Dorset, Suffolk, the Duke and Duchess of Norfolk, and several ladies in waiting—enter hastily, as though late for the occasion; helped into their robes and organized into a loose procession by anxious dressers, they toast each other with hastily gulped glasses of wine, assume appropriate smiles, move downstage toward the audience, and then, accompanied by a trumpet flourish, leave the stage. On a stage quite suddenly empty of bustling anticipation, all look after them before, their tasks completed, the servants are quickly dismissed while the Gentlemen continue their gossip. By revealing the backstage preparations behind this "actorly" political show, Davies's representational strategies not only reveal class and rank distinctions applicable in Stuart as in twentieth-century Britain but, in giving the scene Brechtian distance, deconstruct majesty's spectacle to expose its "hollow crown." Here, Henry V's "idol Ceremony" turns into a "dress-up" pageant for the nobility, who construct public selves to honor a queen who is herself represented as a construction. In Stuart spectacles of power as in late twentieth-century "media opportunities," theatrical metaphor both encompasses the ruler's body and compels the beholder's gaze. Said Queen Elizabeth herself, "We princes, I tell you, are set on stages, in the sight and view of all the world duly observed." And James's own *Basilikon Doron* expresses a similar view: "A King is as one set on a stage, whose smallest actions and gestures, all the people gazingly do behold."[24]

Punctuated throughout with such staged constructions, rhetorical as well as visual spectacles of rule, *Henry VIII* devotes its final narrative moves to constructing Elizabeth and re-constructing Henry's absolute power. The play opens with Norfolk's report of the "embracement" of "two suns of glory" at the Field of the Cloth of Gold, positioning Henry as one of two heroic central actors in glittering feudal ceremonies reminiscent of medieval romance—"fierce vanities" planned by Wolsey to "[buy] a place next to the king" (1.1.6, 10, 54, 66); it closes, this time with a represented ceremony, to position him as the future Queen Elizabeth's father. Henry's presence at his daughter's christening, which rewrites history,[25] is only one sign of *Henry VIII*'s closural insistence on perfect familial and generational relations. But such perfection is itself a construction, the result of Henry's providential centrality, and it is not without contradictions. For what cannot be represented—Elizabeth's birth—the play substitutes a series of swift reversals of Fortune's wheel: threats to the Queen's life, Henry's luckless game of chance, and Cranmer's potential fall at the hands of the bishops. Finally, Henry himself discovers that Anne has borne, not a male, but a female heir. In a curious, though surely not accidental, coincidence, the "birth" of the Church of England occurs simultaneously with Elizabeth's own,[26] and it is that event, not the undesired daughter, that accords Henry godlike status and permits him to resolve the bishops' opposition to Cranmer: "As I have made ye one, lords, one remain: / So I grow stronger, you more honor gain" (5.3.80–81). A "happy winner" in religious politics and still a charismatic royal actor, Henry is, however, not central but tangential to *Henry VIII*'s final, refashioned "embracement" of "suns of glory," which figures a female infant's body as a fertile site of virtues capable of generating an "imperial" Britain.

The last of *Henry VIII*'s collapsed masques, each of which "reads" a woman's body as a text, this one moves toward royal epiphany through an antimasque filled with carnivalesque inversions—an even more radically contradictory substitute for Elizabeth's christening than was the Church of England's "birth" for her "coming in." Whereas the play's earlier reporters on the ceremonies of greatness have been "gentlemen," here a Porter and his Man, occasionally interrupted by the insistent offstage voice of one who belongs to the larder, record the sight of "rude rascals" (5.4.9) who threaten to flood onto the stage, break down the royal enclosure, and, indeed, destroy the barriers separating one London space from another to transform the entire city into a "liberty"—a "Parish Garden" for bear- and bull-baiting or a "Moorfields to muster in" (5.4.2, 31). Made up of those who stand at the greatest distance from power and gape at its ceremonies—"slaves," watchers of executions, "the limbs of Limehouse," jailbait, "youths that thunder at a playhouse," "faithful friends o' th' suburbs"—this May Day rabble, "young or old, / He or she, cuckold or cuckold-maker," can barely be kept out (5.4.22–23). And like the crowd battering to see Anne's coronation, this one contains unruly women, laying seige, so the Porter imagines, to see "some strange Indian with the great tool"—a prurient "fry of fornication," bursting with rampant sexuality.[27] "On my Christian conscience," says the Porter, "this one christening will beget a thousand; here will be father, godfather and all together" (5.4.31–34). Nearest the door stands a Bardolph-like fellow with a fiery face and a railing haberdasher's wife whose fashionable "pinked porringer" falls off her head as she shouts for apprentices to join the fray; the Porter even predicts that some of the gang will later be run through the streets and publicly whipped.

This carnival catalogue cuts in a number of ways, and across time. In one reading, it figures Henry's as well as Elizabeth's cultural vitality, counterbalancing his sexuality with traces of her own puzzling composite image, especially insofar as signs of disorderly misrule press into this descriptive display. In another reading, this crowd of marginal women and men absorbs the rude populist energies and erotic desires of *Henry VIII*'s mighty rulers, which are displaced onto them; in yet another, they figure echoes of civil controversies that rose during the early years of James I's reign. Indeed, the play seems here to document—and bring together within London's city spaces—a fantasy record of the Midlands grain riots a few years before where "Levellers," many of them women, tore down hedge and ditch barriers enclosing land once held in common; of public punishments, such as the Skimmington rides; and of the skirmishes in Stuart London itself in which the city attempted to keep its liberties from Crown control.[28] And the play also moves itself forward from Tudor to Stuart London in another way to figure the multitude expecting festival cakes and ale in honor of Elizabeth's christening as similar to the crowds watching James I's triumphal entry into London's city space; so uncontrollable were they that many of the pageant "scenes" planned by Dekker and Jonson could not be performed.[29] Here, however, the Lord Chamberlain intervenes precisely in order to make such "performance" possible, accusing the Porters of being drunken "lazy knaves" and of letting in prostitutes returning from the christening for their own use. If the comment seems oddly pertinent to Henry, whose Queen Anne was called by some "the Great Whore," his daughter "the Little Whore,"[30] the Porter's excuse also, perhaps, speaks for him: "We are but men," he says, "An army cannot rule 'em" (5.4.70, 72).

In the Elizabethan 2 *Henry VI*, with Jack Cade's rebellion, and in other Stuart plays, notably *Coriolanus*, Shakespeare does not hesitate to represent an unruly crowd, demanding its rights or protesting against royal abuses. But *Henry VIII* confines such inversions to its unusually full narrative-reportorial economy. Violating that distinction, Tyrone Guthrie's 1949 performance text brought marginal misrule onto the Old Vic stage in a noisy, swirling bustle of London citizenry.[31] In the Stuart *Henry VIII*, however, an unruly crowd is already present. Once the Lord Chamberlain threatens the Porters with prison, the two turn on the Globe's "rude" spectators who themselves press too close to the stage enclosure, and even sit on its rails. In this detail at least—though also in its repeated circulation of court news—*Henry VIII* insists on itself as a public play, one that perhaps even extends "ownership" of the aristocratic court masque to a public playhouse, now the home of actors who "belong" to James I and are called the King's Men. And in even more central ways, *Henry VIII* engages with Elizabethan as well as Stuart theatrical politics. Just as it figures the desiring spectators pressing for entrance to Elizabeth's christening as one and the same with the Globe's disorderly audience, so too does it figure the Globe's actors, men who themselves are "of the liberties." On the one hand, some of the King's own men "riot" just offstage, the same men who are "disguised" as nobles and who will shortly accompany the new Princess Elizabeth at her first public appearance—aptly and oddly enough, on the Globe stage, next to Paris Garden. On the other, those onstage protect its boundaries and keep their fellows as well as audience members from the enclosure that has become, for all intents and purposes, a metaphor for royal space. There is perhaps no better image for the theater as a site where the contradictory forces shaping the culture came into sharp focus than this emblem of negotiation between liberty and containment.[32] Yet the emblematic moment passes, as *Henry VIII* now rechannels its representational strategies toward the culmination of its public masque in a rhetorical and visual spectacle that overturns carnival to subdue and disperse its rude energies and, through Cranmer's incantatory prophecy, safely reintegrate them[33]—even those that press toward figuring the "misrule" some associated with Elizabeth—into an idealized royal hierarchy.

As in the close of the Stuart court masque, *Henry VIII* bridges the gap between carnival-antimasque and masque proper with the appearance of a figure who joins both worlds, transforming chaos and vice into ideal order.[34] Like the play's earlier processions, this one prescribes a rigid ceremonial hierarchy that surrounds Elizabeth with city officials, nobles, her two godmothers, and ladies, to position her, as in her later London entry, at the center of a renewed political and, in this case, religious community. In Elizabethan plays as varied as *The Rare Triumphs of Love and Fortune* (1582), *A Looking Glass for London and England* (1590), *Friar Bacon and Friar Bungay* (1589), *Every Man out of His Humour* (1599), and *The Arraignement of Paris* (1581), as well as Shakespeare's own *Richard III*, closure pays tribute to the Queen with flattery and devotion that perpetuate her "invisible visibility" by including her as an imaginative if not an actual witness.[35] *Henry VIII*'s close alludes to such forms, expands their textual and representational space, and imbeds their suggestions of the Queen's redemptive potential in a vision of England's future under Elizabeth's rule. Whereas in Shakespeare's Elizabethan histories, closure dis-closes royal genealogy as a stable force shaping an uncertain future, *Henry VIII*'s ending triples its generational power to frame Elizabeth between Henry VIII and James I and to marry closural features inherited from Elizabethan drama with those of the Stuart masque, enclosing one strategy for asserting royal power with another to reauthorize and transfigure both. By means of a complex "intertextual" process, the play sanctions corporate kingship, insistently coding and recoding its present and re-presented royal bodies with value. Among these, Elizabeth herself becomes a generative text, subject to and the source of an idealized culture and its cultural ideology.

As in *Cymbeline*, where the soothsayer Philharmonius deciphers Jupiter's "text" (5.5.435–51), *Henry VIII* charges a similar "good man" with the office of interpreting Elizabeth's own text. Here, however, he is no ordinary truth-speaker but Cranmer, Archbishop of Canterbury, Elizabeth's godfather and the man whose opinions concerning Henry's divorce made her, if only briefly, a legitimate child. Also as in *Cymbeline*, he speaks following an exchange filled with closural gestures: Elizabeth's text occurs *after* the Garter-King-at-Arms has announced the child's presence, *after* Cranmer has offered prayers for Elizabeth and for Henry, *after* Henry has kissed his daughter and asked God's protection for her, *after* Cranmer pronounces "Amen," *after* Henry has thanked Elizabeth's godparents for their gifts. Indeed, Henry's own "last" words in this series of signs—"I thank ye heartily: so shall this lady, / When she has so much English" (5.5.13–14)—are a joke that masks Elizabeth's lack of voice; and since at this point Cranmer interrupts the King to complete his verse line with "Let me speak, sir," the playtext even suggests that he speaks for her. Located, so to speak, beyond closure, Cranmer's speech is also in several senses beyond time, for not only do the dead Queen's virtues "speak" through Cranmer but his words, "For heaven now bids me," are divinely inspired. Drawing "truth" and authority from Isaiah 11, the first fully developed promise of the Messiah's reign, as well as from other Old Testament references to a universal kingdom of peace and fellowship, Cranmer approaches his subject and his audience, as his sources do, as particular historical entities—"*this* royal infant"; "*this* land"; "few *now* living" (5.5.17, 19, 21)—to position both in relation to a second power of signification.[36] Elizabeth's "coming," if not precisely a virgin birth, analogizes that of the Messiah, her relationship to her kingdom and to her successor figured as a mystical wedding.[37] Whether or not Stuart spectators chose to believe Cranmer's disclaimer—"Let none think flattery" (5.5.17)[38]—the stylistic features of his speech clearly announce it: the closest analogue for Cranmer's parallel phrasing as well as for the additive principle marking his speech is the recently published (in 1611) Authorized Version of the Bible, a resemblance clarified by relineating and repunctuating eight central lines:

All princely graces that mould up such a mighty piece as this is,
With all the virtues that attend the good,
Shall still be doubled on her:
Truth shall nurse her;
Holy and heavenly thoughts still counsel her;
She shall be lov'd and fear'd:
Her own shall bless her;
Her foes shake like a field of beaten corn,
And hang their heads with sorrow.

(5.5.25–32)

If, however, this variant lineation suggests that *hearing* Cranmer's speech may reproduce the cadences of the most famous text associated with James I, its actual lineation, as well as other rhythmic and syntactic features, strains to mask such echoes and accommodate their energies to a different form, a "transfiguration" particularly visible in its central section (emphases added):

All princely graces 25
That mould up such a mighty piece as this *is*,
With all the virtues that attend the good,
Shall still be doubled on *her*. Truth shall nurse *her*,
Holy and heavenly thoughts still counsel *her*;
She shall be lov'd and fear'd: *her* own shall bless *her*; 30
Her foes shake like a field of beaten corn,
And hang their heads with sorrow: good grows with *her*;
In *her* days every man shall eat in safety
Under his own vine what he plants, and sing
The merry songs of peace to all his neighb*ours*. 35
God shall be truly known, and those about *her*
From *her* shall read the perfect ways of hon*our*,
And by those claim their greatness, not by blood.
Nor shall this peace sleep with *her*; but, as when
The bird of wonder dies, the maiden phoenix, 40
Her ashes new create another *heir*
As great in admiration as *her*self,
So shall *she* leave *her* blessedness to one
(When heaven shall call *her* from this cloud of darkness)
Who from the sacred ashes of *her* hon*our* 45
Shall star-like rise, as great in fame as *she was*,
And so stand fix'd.

(5.5.25–47)

Simple diction as well as the building repetition of balanced monosyllabic phrases—"truth shall nurse her"; "her own shall bless her"; "good grows with her"—give the speech a prayerlike calm and so reinforce its theme of peace, associated with both Elizabeth and James.[39] Moreover, these serial elements punctuate a structure that has strong affinities with prose. The rarity of end-stopped lines; the frequent midline syntactic breaks, with syntactic units running across lines; and the dominance of eleven-syllable lines counteract potential end-rhymes (such as "grac*es*" and "*is*" in lines 25–26), force the biblical phrases into new relationships, and resist poetic closure, producing a structure that constantly regenerates its own strategies. Elizabeth herself "appears," either through a pronoun reference or an epithet, in all but four of these twenty-three lines. Of these, five privilege "her" as the terminal word of a line; and lines 35, 37, and 45 end with off-rhymes of "her" ("neighb*ours*," "hon*ours*," "hon*our*"), acoustical echoes that multiply the word's—and Elizabeth's—"closural" force. "Her" also occurs twice as the opening word of a line and twice at a midline break as well as tracing an insistent pattern of internal rhymes elsewhere in the quoted passage. Not only is Elizabeth's presence the inspiration for a speech that is *about* her: she is, quite literally, the alpha and omega of many of its poetic lines, an effect heightened by continuing the variant lineation suggested earlier. Curiously, in lines 28–37 of the original, where the end-rhyme effect dominates, each "her" (or its off-rhyme) makes up the eleventh syllable of the line. According to poetic conventions, the eleven-syllable line ends with an unstressed syllable—what Shakespeare's era as well as ours calls feminine rhyme. But although the off-rhymes for "her" in this passage are indeed unstressed syllables, the terminal "her" in lines 28–30, 32, and 36 must, in order to make sense, receive a stress. And although the usual explanation for the prevalence of eleven-syllable lines in *Henry VIII* is "Fletcher-not-Shakespeare" and weakened poetic inspiration, their presence here as stressed rather than unstressed features seems designed not only to "masculinize" the verse structure by adding "one thing to my purpose [something]"—that is, Elizabeth—but to transform a potentially feminine rhyme to a masculine one.[40] In its play of gendered endings, this "wrenched" rhyme figures the Queen's mysterious, composite image: her female form, her masculine body politic. Furthermore, the passage continues to sustain this play of gendered identity. Although lines 27, 29, and 31 all have ten syllables, and thus stand out from the poetic texture, a cluster of ten-syllable lines (38–39, 41–42), with appropriate masculine rhyme, also accompanies the "birth," so to speak, of Elizabeth's "heir," James I, precisely at the midpoint of the speech. In this sequence, only line 40, which introduces the "maiden phoenix," ends with an unstressed syllable—a poetic politics that, by exchanging unstressed for stressed syllables, suitably feminizes Elizabeth's generative role as "maiden phoenix–mother."

But at the point where James enters Cranmer's text as a "masculine" presence, he is at first figured as Elizabeth's double. In line 41, for instance—"*Her* ashes new create another *heir*"—only the added "i" prevents it from replicating Elizabeth once more, a connection the next line—"As great in admiration as herself"—further supports. And this particular regendering "fixes" James, through the legendary phoenix, the fabulous bird of virtue, within Elizabeth's own mythology. The phoenix, an emblem Elizabeth had appropriated for her own and a common figure for the royal succession as well as for Christ's resurrection, was reappropriated by James I, who drew more specifically than Elizabeth had on its iconographic associations with the renewal of Roman Empire in Britain and the return of a Golden Age.[41] Indeed, Dekker's Nova Arabia Felix Arch for James's triumphal 1603 London entry symbolized England's "new Arabia," a land of peaceful plenty restored by James's presence as the new phoenix, Elizabeth's successor. The next arch, known as Hortus Euporiae or the Garden of Plenty, figured England as a garden state, revivified by the new King's presence.[42] Although *Henry VIII* represents Anne's and Elizabeth's state processions, it also evokes processional memories associated with James. Cranmer's text reproduces, in its references to him, precisely such a succession of emblems, first to figure James as the new phoenix, and then to link him to the pastoral biblical images previously associated with Elizabeth. Just as James inherits Elizabeth's generative and imperial power—"His honour and the greatness of his name / Shall be, and make new nations" (5.5.51–52)—so too does the verse structure emphasize continuity through run-on lines and midline breaks. Indeed, the next verse sentence, which links James to the king of trees, associated with Solomon, the King's chosen archetype,[43] begins and ends in the middle of a line:

> He shall flourish,
> And like a mountain cedar, reach his branches
> To all the plains about him: our children's children
> Shall see this, and bless heaven.
>
> *(5.5.52–55)*

And within that sentence, line 54 contains, not eleven, but thirteen syllables: James's "branches"—"our children's children"—extend past conventional poetic "time" into a future lying beyond Cranmer's text, and the stage.

Spectators at court as well as many in a public playhouse might well have read Cranmer's words as the culmination, if not the close, of Shakespeare's Stuart masque of Princes. In the court masque, similar elaborations of sovereign virtues and allusions to the reigning monarch—"fixed" in the text as well as within the audience—inform its close to assert royal power and incite the ruler to become what he sees, to translate, through his person, the master fiction.[44] This final transformational apotheosis joins the fabular masque world to the contemporary social reality through the royal presence, now recognized as the solution and re-solution of the masque's riddle. "God gave not Kings the stile of Gods in vaine," reads the first line of the sonnet prefacing *Basilikon Doron*, James's manual of kingship; and insofar as Cranmer's text draws on biblical sources of divination, it seems perfectly gauged to negotiate the secular and the sacred and so to express James's desired image of himself as Defender of the Faith. For the players on the stage, within the play, he speaks of the future; for spectators, his words fuse the immediate historical past with the ruler's present. That all—actors and spectators alike—might know better, might recognize the distance between the real King and his imagined self, points the contradictions central to this Mass-like "mystery," this Stuart translation of the King's Two Bodies. For like that doctrine, Cranmer's text fuses one body with another and masks history to make, and re-mystify, cultural prerogatives.[45]

Closing by, with, and on the King, the Stuart masque is not at liberty to interrogate itself or to question the "chosen truth" of what it represents. Instead, it can only mystify the power its conventions assert, even to the extent of politicizing divine inspiration, and so resolve cultural indeterminacy. But *Henry VIII's* "solution" to Cranmer's rhetoric of essentializing power is not, as it would be in the "ideal" masque, James but Elizabeth, and it is Henry, King within the play, who deciphers its message. Indeed, his response to Cranmer's vision of Stuart continuance—"Thou speakest wonders" (5.5.55)—encloses his prophecy within the limits of the dramatic fiction. And when Cranmer continues, he foresees Elizabeth's lengthy reign "to the happiness of England" (5.5.56) and, then, her death: "a most unspotted lily shall she pass / To th'ground, and all the world shall mourn her" (5.5.61–62). Cranmer's text lays to rest the image of Elizabeth as an unruly "woman on top" and absorbs her threatening composite gender into nostalgic, evocative praise that figures her, like Katherine, with attributes of female chastity. But Henry himself never once calls his daugh-

ter by name nor refers to her gender. She is simply "this happy child"—
a "little one" who "gets" his own power, makes him a man, and turns
carnival inversion to "Holy-day." The final image of self-recognition
in the play also belongs to Henry: "when I am in heaven I shall desire
/ To see what this child does, and praise my Maker" (5.5.67–68). As
when he looked down on the churchmen's council to observe their proceedings against Cranmer (5.2; 5.3), it is an image of perfect invisibil-
ity and centrality, of seeing without being seen, that figures kingship
with godlike power. This, too, was James's self-image. Finally, *Henry
VIII* accords Elizabeth a contradictory generative power. By so tripling
its figures of rule, the play both produces and erases Elizabeth to position her, at the close, as the one who connects James I to Henry VIII
and as the one who, like her virginal namesake, bears a "miraculous"
child. Indeed, the play turns the Virgin Queen into what Parliament,
in the early years of her reign, wished her to be: a transition between
two male rulers.[46] Like Shakespeare's Elizabethan histories, *Henry
VIII* ends with succession. But in no history other than *Richard II* does
the close so allusively figure continuance as a paradox and so elusively
articulate the ruler's self-recognition of his own mutability. That occurs only in Shakespeare's other "last" play, *The Tempest*.

And, as in *The Tempest, Henry VIII*'s final closural gesture is an
Epilogue. Yet unlike Prospero's Epilogue, this one hardly seems necessary, for the play has already tripled closure—first with a masquelike
transformation; next with Elizabeth's epitaph; then with Henry's interpretation of both. It is as though *Henry VIII* endows each royal
presence—James, Elizabeth, and Henry—with a separate convention
and deliberately privileges those forms *as forms*, flaunting each one in
turn to interweave Stuart with Elizabethan forms of closure. From
Cranmer's Janus-like prophecy, facing past and future at a poised moment of presence, and Henry's response, the playtext now reframes its
history with an Epilogue, one of the oldest, and also, at this time, a
newly popular terminal convention. And that Epilogue verges on taking a form that reached its highest development during Elizabeth's
reign—a sonnet.

'Tis ten to one this play can never please
All that are here: some come to take their ease
And sleep an hour or two; but those we fear
W' have frighted with our trumpets, so 'tis clear
They'll say 'tis naught: others to hear the city
Abus'd extremely, and to cry 'That's witty,'
Which we have not done neither; that I fear

All the expected good w'are like to hear
For this play at this time, is only in
The merciful construction of good women,
For such a one we show'd 'em; if they smile,
And say 'twill do, I know within a while
All the best men are ours; for 'tis ill hap
If they hold, when their ladies bid 'em clap.

(Ep., 1–14)

Like the opening Prologue, which announces what the play will *not* do and so divorces what follows from other plays and from other perspectives of history, *Henry VIII*'s Epilogue begins with the conventional apology for the play's inability to please and continues to elaborate on what "we have not done" and so glances at spectator-critics' "abusive" playhouse behavior. Then, at its midpoint, the verse "turns" toward "the expected good" and toward gendering its spectators: only "the merciful construction of good women"—and one in particular— will prompt applause, first from the women and then, at their bidding, from "all the best men." Although by no means unique in its references to women spectators, who were, in the early seventeenth century, exerting potential influence on staged representations of women, *Henry VIII*'s Epilogue-"sonnet" does exhibit a noticeably deviant rhyme scheme and structure.[47]

Like Shakespeare's twelve-line Sonnet 126—"O thou, my lovely boy, who in thy power / Dost hold Time's glass, his sickle hour"—it is composed in rhyming couplets. But because it is also all one sentence, that larger syntactic structure overrides both the end-rhymes and any potential internal division into either quatrains or sestets to block the tendency toward closure characteristic of serial couplets. Given the tension between its informal proselike sentence and the potentially enclosural power of the Epilogue, this "sonnet" seems to be formally featured to figure Elizabeth—one possibility for the "such a one" to whom the speaker refers. Not only do the playtext's final syntactic operations analogize the unity associated with Elizabeth's reign; the Epilogue's chained couplets express the mutuality to which the "sonnet" alludes as an agreement between women and men. And like this "sonnet," which refuses to conform to its couplets, Elizabeth herself refused the mutuality of marriage but instead transformed the potential submissiveness of that relationship into a powerful rhetorical strategy that repeatedly articulated her relationship with her subjects in a negotiated language of love. Said one of her subjects, "We did all love her, for she said she loved us, and much wisdom she showed in this matter."[48]

What *Henry VIII*'s Epilogue-"sonnet" figures, so to speak, is indeed a "merciful construction" of Elizabeth that reveals both her inscription within and her independence from the form that had become, in her time as in Shakespeare's, a sign of, if not a synonym for, love within human—and poetic—time.

In the theater, who speaks this Epilogue? Trevor Nunn's 1969 Royal Shakespeare Company performance text, which culminated a season (his first as artistic director) that included *Pericles* and *The Winter's Tale*, eliminated it, thereby stressing the resemblances between *Henry VIII* and the two other plays.[49] At the close, the entire company at the christening, all costumed in white, advances toward the spectators, chanting Cranmer's characterization of rule—"Peace, plenty, love, truth, terror"—as though simultaneously acknowledging their presence at the staged celebration and threatening them with power's attributes, much as, five years earlier, at the close of Peter Brook's production of Peter Weiss's *Marat/Sade*, the inmate-actors had seemed about to take their revolution into the audience.[50] Momentarily, this unsettling challenge to the barrier between stage and audience seems to be "the end," for the company exits slowly and the stage darkens. At the play's opening, a representation of da Vinci's golden figure of Renaissance man inscribed within a circle had straddled the darkened stage, his arms outstretched; now, in the performance text's final image, Henry strides back into that darkness with the infant Elizabeth in his arms and stands, silent, as the lights fade. For Ronald Bryden, Henry "paus[ed] to stare defiantly into the surrounding oblivion where man finds nothing to lean on but his own strength, his power to bring forth children and build hopes for them"; for Harold Hobson, "his face is very strange; it is blanched and weary, and it seems in some inexplicable way to be questioning the future, questioning it in fatigue and apprehension."[51] Certainly omitting the Epilogue and closing on Henry and Elizabeth gives *Henry VIII*'s ending a stronger rhyme with the father-daughter restorations of *Pericles* and *The Winter's Tale* and, by privileging Henry as the play's final "understander," returns power to the play's titular King. But Nunn's substitute "epilogue" also expresses, in Bryden's as well as Hobson's reading, Henry's sense of his own erasure, a detail his last speech implies. And whereas the play's original Epilogue speaks exclusively for and of the play on any occasion of its performance and reception by an audience of gendered spectators, Henry's defiant apprehension echoes the earlier challenge of the chanting spectators in Nunn's staging and invites audiences to examine their own social text, their own "succession," at the end of one decade and the beginning of another.

If Nunn's representational strategies refigure *Henry VIII*'s ending by adding an "open silence"⁵² that continues to tell Henry's story, Howard Davies's 1983 staging strictly observes the playtext's terminal emphasis on conventions rather than on narrative. In Davies's performance text, the stage is stripped to bare, dark boards and backed by a cyclorama of drifting clouds that pattern shadows over the christening scene, its participants all in black, with white touches, like the figures in Dutch genre painting. The central participants in the ceremony—Henry, the woman holding Elizabeth, and Cranmer—occupy stage center; the rest of the crowd, grouped around them, remains in the background. Thus Cranmer's words occupy the space at the center of the social reality and are directed specifically to Elizabeth's spotlit "family," with the others as privileged listener-onlookers. He speaks very softly, as though telling yet another "story" in a performance text that foregrounds the gentlemen's running commentaries on court news equally with the self-consciously fashioned epitaphs of Buckingham, Wolsey, and Katherine. Like Friar Lawrence's recapitulation of the past in *Romeo and Juliet*'s closing scene (5.3.229–69), this rhetorical spectacle opens up a meditative space that invites spectators to reflect on Cranmer's vision of a future that has and has not come true—a vision that is enclosed by, but also escapes, the staged fiction. And just as Henry himself speaks the Prologue, marching onto the bare stage and tearing up papers, strewing them right and left, as though to destroy previous writings of his own story,⁵³ the Epilogue-speaker in Davies's performance text also counters history and, to a lesser extent, convention. She is the woman who has held Elizabeth throughout the christening (fig. 20). Now she gives the child to Henry and steps forward, leaving the final tableau behind, breaking Cranmer's incantatory spell and Henry's quietly spoken thanks to voice the power invested in the playtext's final convention. Her presence figures the "chosen truth" of this *Henry VIII* not simply as the difference between one history and another but as that between one powerful male ruler and another, who has the voice and body of a woman.⁵⁴

At the turn of the seventeenth century, Rosalind told *As You Like It*'s spectators that "It is not the fashion to see the lady the epilogue, but it is no more unhandsome than to see the lord the prologue" (Ep., 1–2). It was, however, fashionable to see the lady, figured as the Queen, *in* the Epilogue, and Davies's staging seems alert to both these closural regenderings and to the Epilogue's direct appeal to women spectators. But whereas Davies's *Henry VIII* seems poised to intervene into present-day cultural debates concerning women, for Stuart audiences, the Epilogue could not, in all probability, fully release such meanings. Nor, given James's restrictive views concerning women,[55] would it be politic to do more than pose the accessibility of such an intervention. Nevertheless, for Stuart as well as for late twentieth-century spectators, such a "construction" can be read as the final sign of the anomalous female phoenix, a closural compliment to the Queen's manly strength and to the surety that an heir would emerge miraculously from the ashes of the sovereign's funeral pyre. Much like Elizabeth's refusal to name her successor, *Henry VIII* specifies no speaker for the Epilogue, remaining silent about who the good woman—"such a one"—it refers to may be. Although I have argued for Elizabeth, the play accords equally "merciful" (and politic) treatment to her mother, Queen Anne, beheaded for adultery and treason, and to the Catholic Katherine. And if the play were performed at court, details of Cranmer's prophecy might be taken to figure James's daughter Elizabeth, newly married to Prince Frederick, the Elector Palatine, a leader of the protestant union in Germany.[56] Even James had no way of knowing, no way of objecting to what seems to be Shakespeare's (and Fletcher's) late contribution to the annual celebrations of the accession of Eliza, Queen of Shepherds, which were held during his reign, a form of acclaim never accorded the anniversaries of his own coming-in. Even for the monarch who figured himself with Solomon's wisdom, to know— and to object—would be to deny the power *Henry VIII*'s "maiden phoenix" accords him as the heir who could make all come true.

If not actually performed before James, *Henry VIII* certainly inscribes his reign and traces of his "imperial" image within its text. At its close, the play negotiates carefully between one successor and another to celebrate, not necessarily the "good women" to whom the Epilogue refers, but the impossibly contradictory construction of one woman, an exception to the Law of Nature, who exceeded her sex. James, who commissioned her Westminster Abbey tomb and, in unexpected homage, had it placed in the north aisle of Henry VII's chapel, also caused to be carved on it an inscription naming Elizabeth "the mother of this her country, the nurse of religion and learning; for perfect skill of very many languages, for glorious endowments, as well of mind as of body, a prince incomparable."[57] And Sir Robert Cecil, Elizabeth's chief minister during the last years of her reign, a man whose political career continued to flourish under James, wrote to her godson, Sir John Harington, after her death:

> You know all my former steps: good knight, rest content, and give heed to one that hath sorrowed in the bright lustre of a court, and gone heavily even on the best-seeming fair ground. Tis a great task to prove one's honesty, and

yet not spoil one's fortune. You have tasted a little hereof in our blessed Queen's time, who was more a man and, in troth, sometimes less than a woman. I wish I waited now in her Presence Chamber, with ease at my foot, and rest in my bed. I am pushed from the shore of comfort, and know not where the winds and waves of a court may bear me.[58]

As in both these tributes, Elizabeth, the "maiden phoenix," framed between her father and her successor, presides over *Henry VIII*'s ending as a countervailing image of historic female power—power which, like that between players and audience, between subjects and prince, depended upon and was articulated as a moment of praise.

"NO EPILOGUE, I PRAY YOU"

"Our virtues / Lie in th' interpretation of the time."
—*Coriolanus*

IN THEIR First Folio address to "the great Variety of Readers," Hemminges and Condell speak of themselves as the author's "Friends," collectors of his writings who "have published them, as where (before) you were abus'd with diverse stolen, and surreptitious copies, maimed and deformed by the frauds and stealthes of injurious imposters, that exposed them: even those are now offered to your view cured, and perfect of their limbs, and all the rest, absolute in their numbers, as he conceived them." In contrast to the earlier privilege accorded to theatrical performance of the plays, Folio, in keeping with the new emphasis on authorial ownership, sought a stable, certain Shakespeare.[1] Yet in this initial editorial project as in later ones, as well as in his critical and theatrical guises, Shakespeare is always (already) performance work. Although each enterprise makes reference to the "True Originall copies"—in itself a variable, ambiguous designation—the results are flexible, mobile, unfixed. In each, too, social meanings, reordered as editorial, critical, or theatrical meanings, reproduce variant histories and so destabilize the notion of a fixed Shakespeare. As Fredric Jameson writes, doing historical work means writing "the history of the situations of the texts, and not some 'history' of the texts themselves."[2]

Although stopping rather than closing would reproduce the formal features of many of Shakespeare's histories, because the plays themselves insist on opening onto future history, it seems appropriate, at this point, to look forward and so to represent my project as a beginning rather than an ending. In gathering an archive of readings that offer a constellation and collision of intellectual and artistic practices, that project attempts to position critical and theatrical discourse in relation to various other cultural texts at work in a given historical moment in order to show how plays and their variant critical and theatrical re-formations participate in the ideological work of managing reality. It is shot through with attractive paradoxes, for meanings that made sense to Elizabethan or Jacobean spectators can, when reified through present-day critical or theatrical practice, remake cultural sense, even when, as in the double ending for Bogdanov's *Richard III*, they seem to be dismantling ancient edifices of meaning.

There are, however, additional hazards to such an enterprise that, as is common in epilogues, perhaps require explanation, if not direct apology. First of all, looking only at closure, however globally conceived or described, does violence to the "integrity" of the playtext by isolating one part or fragment for study and so interrupting notions of synchronicity and even, perhaps, working to disperse, if not dissolve, textuality. Yet such a focus also has its advantages, in that dropping any pretense of complete coverage avoids slipping into totalizing readings and, instead, attempts to reveal "Shakespeare-history" and "Shakespeare-closing" as means of mapping as well as shoring up a particular historical moment.

Such a "system" for doing history contains its own set of restrictions and problems and is shaped by the sources chosen, by access to those materials, by time constraints, and by the selective biases of the writer. Most of the performance texts described here, for example, are "mainstream" Shakespeare; though a few offer access to what might be called an alternative Shakespeare, important work such as the Rustaveli Company's *Richard III* or Ariane Mnouchkine's *Henriad* in Paris for the Théâtre du Soleil is missing, as is any mention of fringe or experimental productions. Just as reconstructing how a particular play was performed and received by Elizabethan or Jacobean spectators may be highly conjectural, presenting and representing more recent performance texts rests on equally selective and contingent evidence. Prompt copies vary widely in their markings and so influence a researcher's ability to recuperate what was seen and heard by spectators at a particular performance. Those for Royal Shakespeare Company productions, for example, change radically from the middle 1960s to the late 1980s: with the advent of computerized light boards and prerecorded sound cues, latter-day prompt copies seldom include such detail; in addition, many lack full notations of actors' positions in stage space as well as significant stage business. Disappointingly, the prompt copies I have seen for Michael Bogdanov's *Wars of the Roses* show cuts but have only slight markings, making it difficult for someone who did not see a performance to recuperate its detail.[3] And other archival materials, such as reviews, interviews, accounts such as John Barton and Peter Hall's introductory materials for their *Wars of the Roses* or Sally Beauman's "production book" for the 1975 *Henry V*, photographs, and video recordings, represent, of course, instances of already mediated discourses.

But as in writing most history, the problems one encounters suggest new questions and challenges. How, for example, do critical and performance readings remake subjects, construct and reconstruct models of identity and models of gender? More particularly, how does critical and performance discourse on "Shakespeare-history" contribute to perpetuating the myth of the "great man," either as a historical presence or as actorly counterpart? How, too, are both discourses bound up with notions of social hierarchy, with class as well as sexual difference? It would be equally fruitful, say, to fix on textual fragments other than those surrounding the close: to write, for instance, the history of the situations of a particular scene or speech in order to reveal how its rhetorical figurings or formal conventions can be understood as what Franco Moretti calls a "field of conflict between psychical and cultural forces."[4] Such further endeavors might well be more insistently and consistently theorized to intersect with semiotics, with psychoanalysis, with reception theory, especially insofar as that can point to how "Shakespeare-speaking" attempts to secure consent to and reconciliation with cultural norms.[5] Because televised Shakespeare reaches more spectators than mainstream Shakespeare or even than Shakespeare in all his summer festival guises, and because the frame set around its reproduction tends to perpetuate the myth of an elitist Shakespeare, its function, particularly as an educational apparatus, needs to be more thoroughly addressed.[6]

In what is commonly thought of as a global information society, Shakespeare has become remarkably adaptable information, capable of serving, on the one hand, a nostalgic desire for direct, transparent access to a historical past and, on the other, as a site for interrogating and intervening in present-day social processes. New "Shakespeares" or, to borrow Ruby Cohn's phrase, "Shakespeare offshoots,"[7] appear regularly—some as abused and surreptitious as those Heminges and Condell lament, put forth by, some would say, equally "injurious imposters." Yet these, perhaps more insistently than their more acclaimed and more richly furnished relatives, serve as fluctuating indicators of particular, materially imbedded social attitudes and practices. To the extent that anatomizing closure in Shakespeare's histories transports readers and spectators beyond the textual limits of the play, it points toward opening up "historical" fissures that, ultimately, can work to change the social text itself. If to write this kind of history is to uncover a parallel history of cultural situations, at least one convention, similar to the resonant metaphor through which late Elizabethan culture linked the stage with its social world, governs both: in each history, "Exeunt" is never a final stage direction.

1. *King John* (John Barton; 1974): Reading John's Will—Richard Pasco (Philip the Bastard); Simon Walker (Prince Henry).

2. *King John* (Deborah Warner; 1988): John's Death—Nicholas Woodeson (John); Jo James (Prince Henry); David Morrissey (Philip the Bastard). The wheel chair, seen in this dress-rehearsal photograph, was later cut.

3. *Henry VI, The Plantagenets* (Adrian Noble; 1988): Joan la Pucelle at the Stake—Julia Ford (Joan).

4. *Henry VI: House of York* (Michael Bogdanov; 1988): Henry VI's death—Andrew Jarvis (Richard Gloucester); Paul Brennen (Henry VI).

5. *Henry VI: House of York* (Michael Bogdanov; 1988): York Family Portrait—Lynette Davies (Queen Elizabeth); Philip Bowen (Edward IV); Andrew Jarvis (Richard Gloucester).

6. *Richard III* (Bill Alexander; 1984): The Coronation—Antony Sher (Richard III); Penny Downie (Queene Anne).

7. *Richard III* (Bill Alexander; 1984): Richard III's Death—Antony Sher (Richard III); Christopher Ravenscroft (Richmond).

8. *Richard III* (Michael Bogdanov; 1988): Richard III's Death—Charles Dale (Richmond); Andrew Jarvis (Richard III).

9. *Richard III* (Michael Bogdanov; 1988): Henry VII's State-of-the-Nation Address—Charles Dale (Richmond).

10. *Richard II* (Anthony Quayle; 1951): Exton Presents Richard II's Body—Harry Andrews (Henry IV); Michael Redgrave (Richard II); William Squire (Exton).

11. *Richard II* (Terry
Hands; 1980); Henry
IV with Richard II's
Body—Alan Howard
(Richard II); David
Suchet (Henry IV).

12. *Richard II* (Mi-
chael Bogdanov;
1988): The Parlia-
ment Scene—Michael
Pennington (Richard
II); John Castle (Bo-
lingbroke).

13. *1 Henry IV* (Michael Bogdanov; 1988): Who Killed Hotspur?—John Dougall (Hal); Chris Hunter (Hotspur); Michael Cronin (Henry IV); Barry Stanton (Falstaff); John Tramper (Prince John).

14. *2 Henry IV* (Terry Hands; 1975); Falstaff's Rejection—Alan Howard (Henry V); Brewster Mason (Falstaff).

15. *2 Henry IV* (Michael Bogdanov; 1987): Falstaff's Rejection—Michael Pennington (Henry V); John Woodvine (Falstaff).

16. *Henry V* (Terry Hands; 1975): Reading the Lists at Agincourt—Alan Howard (Henry V).

17. *Henry V* (Adrian Noble; 1984): The English-French Alliance—Sebastian Shaw (King of France); Cecile Paoli (Princess Katherine); Kenneth Branagh (Henry V).

18. *Henry V* (Adrian Noble; 1984): Chorus's Epilogue—Ian McDiarmid (Chorus).

19. *Henry V* (Michael Bogdanov; 1988): Henry V Disinherits the Dauphin—John Dougall (Henry V); Francesca Ryan (Princess Katherine); Andrew Jarvis (Dauphin).

20. *Henry VIII* (Howard Davies; 1983): Princess Elizabeth's Christening—Richard Griffiths (Henry VIII); Caroline Harris (Lady); Richard O'Callaghan (Cranmer).

NOTES ❧

CHAPTER 1
"CHORUS TO THIS HISTORY"

1. The seminal studies of closure are Barbara Herrnstein Smith, *Poetic Closure* (Chicago, 1968), and Frank Kermode, *The Sense of an Ending* (Oxford, 1967). See also Robert M. Adams, *Strains of Discord* (Ithaca, 1958); David H. Richter, *Fable's End* (Chicago, 1974); Patricia A. Parker, *Inescapable Romance* (Princeton, 1979); Mariana Torgovnick, *Closure in the Novel* (Princeton, 1981); and David F. Hult, ed. *Concepts of Closure*, Yale French Studies, 67 (New Haven, 1984). Although many readings of individual plays touch in some way on the close, for studies that directly address closural features, see Charles J. Sugnet, "Exaltation at the Close: A Model for Shakespearean Tragedy," *Modern Language Quarterly* 38, no. 4 (1977): 323–35; Walter C. Foreman, Jr., *The Music of the Close* (Lexington, Ky., 1978); Zvi Jagendorf, *The Happy End of Comedy* (Newark, 1984); Dennis Kay, " 'To Hear the Rest Untold': Shakespeare's Postponed Endings," *Renaissance Quarterly* (1984): 207–27; T. W. Craik, " 'You That Way; We This Way': Shakespeare's Endings," in *Mirror Up to Shakespeare*, ed. J. C. Gray (Toronto, 1984), 44–54; R. S. White, *Let Wonder Seem Familiar* (Atlantic Highlands, N.J., 1985); Martha Tuck Rozett, "The Comic Structures of Tragic Endings," *Shakespeare Quarterly* 36 (1985): 152–64; Joseph M. Lenz, *The Promised End* (New York, 1986); and Jean E. Howard, "The Difficulties of Closure: An Approach to the Problematic in Shakespearian Comedy," in *Comedy from Shakespeare to Sheridan*, ed. A. R. Braunmuller and James C. Bulman (Newark, 1986), 113–28. For recent studies that address closure in the histories, see John Wilders, *The Lost Garden* (Totowa, 1978); David Scott Kastan, *Shakespeare and the Shapes of Time* (Hanover, N.H., 1982); and Bernard Beckerman, "Shakespeare Closing," *Kenyon Review* 7, no. 3 (1985), especially 79–83.

2. Cf. Leah Marcus, who argues for "a series of 'local' texts varying in ways that correlate with shifts in external circumstances and in the conditions of performance," in *Puzzling Shakespeare* (Berkeley, 1988), 44–45.

3. In Noble's retitled adaptations, *Henry VI* contains material from *The First* and *Second Parts of King Henry the Sixt*; *The Rise of Edward IV* draws on *The Second* and *Third Parts of King Henry the Sixt*; *Richard III, His Death* contains material from *The Life and Death of Richard the Third*. On curtain calls as closure, see Terence Hawkes, "Opening Closure," *Modern Drama* 24 (1981): 356. See also Bert O. States, "Phenomenology of the Curtain Call," *Hudson Review* 34, no. 3 (Autumn 1981): 371–80; and Hawkes, "Telmah," in *That Shakespeherian Rag* (London, 1986), 94–96. For yet another view of distinctions among conventions of performance, rhetorical conventions,

and authenticating conventions, see Elizabeth Burns, *Theatricality* (London, 1972), 28–39, 40–121.

4. For the notion of poetry and drama performing cultural work, see Louis Adrian Montrose, "The Purpose of Playing: Reflections on a Shakespearean Anthropology," *Helios*, n.s., 7 (1980): 51–74. For a broader context, see Robert Weimann, *Shakespeare and the Popular Tradition in the Theater*, ed. Robert Schwartz (Baltimore, 1978).

5. Thomas Heywood, *An Apology for Actors*, ed. Arthur Freeman (New York, 1973), sig. B₅.

6. In attempting to institutionalize the power of Aristotelian Platonic forms, Sidney argues for the redeeming values of ideal forms and sets these against Elizabethan practice in "A Defence of Poetry," in *Miscellaneous Prose of Sir Philip Sidney*, ed. Katherine Duncan-Jones and Jan Van Dorsten (Oxford, 1973), 79–80. For a full discussion of antitheatricality, see Jonas Barish, *The Antitheatrical Prejudice* (Berkeley, 1981). See also Montrose, who relies on Victor Turner's term "anti-structures" to "describe marginal experiences that do not simply invert structural norms but rather temporarily liberate human capacities of cognition, affect, volition, and creativity from their usual constraints, making cultural innovation possible" ("Purpose of Playing," 64). See also Turner, *The Human Seriousness of Play* (New York, 1982).

7. Montrose, "Purpose of Playing," 67–68. Also pertinent here, especially for present-day performance texts, are Bertolt Brecht's concepts of alienation techniques and nonmimetic disunity in theatrical signification. In critiquing the theater apparatus, Brecht insists that theater must produce a spectator/reader who is not interpolated into ideology but who is committed to a dialectic of observation and analysis; ideally, such a process invites the spectator to continue, beyond a performance text's close, to produce meanings, which would eventually result in choice and action. See *Brecht on Theatre*, ed. John Willett (New York, 1964), especially 190, 264.

8. Samuel Johnson, *Johnson on Shakespeare*, ed. Arthur F. Sherbo (New Haven, 1968), 7:71–72.

9. I borrow from Steven Urkowitz's comments in a seminar on "Rethinking the *Henry VI* Plays" at the 1989 Shakespeare Association of America conference.

10. See Wilson, *The Arte of Rhetorique* (1553, 1560), ed. Thomas J. Derrick (New York, 1982), 33–35, 236–40, 364; Puttenham, *The Arte of English Poesie* (1589), ed. Edward Arber, English Reprints (Westminster, 1895), 225. For a classic discussion of Shakespeare's use of rhetorical figuring, see Sister Miriam Joseph, *Shakespeare's Use of the Arts of Language* (New York, 1947).

11. *Aristotle's Theory of Poetry and Fine Art*, ed. S. H. Butcher (New York, 1951): *Poetics*, section 7, p. 31; and Barthes, *S/Z* (1970), trans. Richard Miller (New York, 1974), 52, 72.

12. See T. W. Baldwin, *Shakspere's Five-Act Structure* (Urbana, 1947), 228–51, 294–96. See also Marvin Herrick, *Comic Theory in the Sixteenth Century* (Urbana, 1950), 89–129.

13. Butcher, *Poetics*, section 18, p. 67; Horace, *Ars Poetica*, ll. 189–92, in *Horace on Poetry*, ed. C. O. Brink (Cambridge, 1971); and Seneca, *Epistolae ad Lucilium*, quoted in Kenneth Tynan, *He Who Plays the King* (London, 1950), 186.

14. Ben Jonson, *Timber; or, Discoveries* (1641), in *Elizabethan and Jacobean Quartos*, ed. G. B. Harrison (New York, 1966), 75.

15. J. C. Scaliger, *Poetices Libri Septem* (1561): 14–15, quoted in Baldwin, *Five-Act Structure*, 295.

16. Ben Jonson, *The Magnetic Lady*, Cho., 5.21–36, in *Works*, ed. C. H. Herford, Percy Simpson, and Evelyn Simpson (Oxford, 1938), 6:578.

17. Francis Beaumont, *The Knight of the Burning Pestle*, ed. John Doebler (Lincoln, Neb., 1967); see 5.225–361 for the passages summarized.

18. For readers' convenient reference, I rely throughout primarily on a modern "Complete Shakespeare," *The Complete Pelican Shakespeare*, ed. Alfred Harbage (New York, 1969), for citations, though for some plays (*King John*, for instance) quotations follow another edition. In cases where my readings concern distinctions between Quarto and Folio texts, I cite Quarto signatures and Folio through line numbers (TLN), and modernize spelling. When citing titles and stage directions, however, I do, in order to preserve their emphases, retain the capitalization and italics of the original. When quoting other early texts, such as Dering's adaptation of *Henry IV*, I have retained the original orthography. For Quarto references, see *Shakespeare's Plays in Quarto*, ed. Michael J. B. Allen and Kenneth Muir (Berkeley, 1981); for Folio references, see *The First Folio of Shakespeare*, ed. Charlton Hinman (New York, 1968).

19. The most comprehensive recent study of genre is Alastair Fowler, *Kinds of Literature* (Cambridge, Mass., 1982). But as Michael Rifaterre points out, genre is "a phantom form that exists only in the mind of the reader" ("Systeme d'un genre descriptif," *Poetique* 9 [1972]: 16n). The discussion that follows draws from Fredric Jameson, *The Political Unconscious* (Ithaca, 1981), 106–50; Leonard Tennenhouse, *Power on Display* (London, 1986), 2–16; and Tony Bennett and Janet Woollacott, *Bond and Beyond* (London, 1987), 67.

20. I borrow this phrase from Rick Altman, "A Semantic/Syntactic Approach to Film Genre," *Cinema Journal* 23, no. 3 (Spring 1984): 6–18.

21. See Louis Althusser, "Ideology and Ideological State Apparatuses (Notes toward an Investigation)," in *Lenin and Philosophy and Other Essays*, trans. Ben Brewster (New York, 1971), 162; and Louis Montrose, "Renaissance Literary Studies and the Subject of History," *ELH* 16 (1986): 9.

22. Leonard Tennenhouse, "Representing Power: *Measure for Measure* in Its Time," in *The Power of Forms in the English Renaissance*, ed. Stephen Greenblatt (Norman, Ok., 1982), 140.

23. Herbert Lindenberger claims that one "cannot categorize historical drama as a genre at all, though one can speak of specific forms of historical plays which prevailed at certain moments in history" (*Historical Drama* [Chicago, 1975], ix). See also Tennenhouse, *Power on Display*, and Walter Cohen, who points out the problematic contradictions in considering history plays as

national drama and as class-inflected constructs, in *Drama of a Nation* (Ithaca, 1985), 220–28.

24. For the classical formulation of this view, see Irving Ribner, *The English History Play in the Age of Shakespeare* (Princeton, 1957).

25. Franco Moretti, " 'A Huge Eclipse': Tragic Form and the Deconsecration of Sovereignty," in Greenblatt, *Power of Forms*, 8.

26. Tony Davies, "The Divided Gaze: Reflections on the Political Thriller," in *Gender, Genre, and Narrative Pleasure*, ed. Derek Longhurst (London, 1989), 131.

27. For a full discussion of these issues, see Graham Holderness, *Shakespeare's History* (New York, 1985), 1–39. See also Stuart Hall, who argues that "the meaning of a cultural form and its place or position in the cultural field is not inscribed inside its forms. . . . The meaning of a cultural symbol is given in part by the social field into which it is incorporated, the practices with which it articulates and is made to resonate" ("Notes on Deconstructing 'the Popular,' " in *People's History and Socialist Theory*, ed. Raphael Samuel [London, 1981], 235).

28. See E.M.W. Tillyard, *The Elizabethan World Picture* (1943; reprint, Harmondsworth, 1963). Michael McCanles argues that "the very concept of a 'world picture' is a post-romantic tool of historical synthesis, owing much more to Herder, Kant, and Hegel than to anything that Renaissance thinkers produced. To assume that indeed a wide variety of statements about the cosmos, man, society, religion, and politics, and so on in a given culture is liable to synthesis into an organic whole, is to assume something that Renaissance thinkers were only beginning to discover" (*Dialectical Criticism and Renaissance Literature* [Berkeley, 1975], 248). See also H. A. Kelly, *Divine Providence in the England of Shakespeare's Histories* (Cambridge, Mass., 1970). Wilbur L. Sanders offers a flexible view in *The Dramatist and the Received Idea* (Cambridge, 1968). Robin Headlam Wells summarizes the Tillyard debate in "The Fortunes of Tillyard: Twentieth-Century Critical Debate on Shakespeare's History Plays," *English Studies* 66 (1985): 391–403. Both Robert P. Merrix and M. M. Reese claim that readers miss much without the Elizabethan World Picture, in "Shakespeare's Histories and the New Bardolators," *Studies in English Literature* 19 (1979): 179–96, and " 'Tis My Picture; Refuse It Not,' " *Shakespeare Quarterly* 36 (1985): 254–56.

29. See Holderness, *Shakespeare's History*, 31. For discussions of humanist historiographical practice, see Donald J. Wilcox, *The Development of Florentine Humanist Historiography in the Fifteenth Century* (Cambridge, Mass., 1969); and Richard Lanham, *The Motives of Eloquence* (New Haven, 1976).

30. See, for instance, Marie Axton, *The Queen's Two Bodies* (London, 1977); Matthew H. Wikander, *The Play of Truth and State* (Baltimore, 1986), especially 11–49; and Steven Mullaney, *The Place of the Stage* (Chicago, 1988).

31. Cf. Montrose, who draws on Raymond Williams's formulations: " 'Interrelations between movements and tendencies both within and beyond a spe-

cific and effective dominance'; these include the residual and emergent, oppositional and alternative values, meanings and practices which are always creating potential spaces from which the dominant can be contested, and against which it must be continuously redefined and redefended" ("Renaissance Literary Studies," 10–11).

32. Axton, *Queen's Two Bodies*, x. Axton's study contextualizes the history plays in relation to other texts that debate and/or polemicize issues pertinent to succession. A number of studies explore how the drama corresponds to or challenges other constructions of political reality. In addition to those already cited, see Jonathan Goldberg, *James I and the Politics of Literature* (Baltimore, 1983), and essays in the following collections: *Alternative Shakespeares*, ed. John Drakakis (London, 1985); *Political Shakespeare*, ed. Jonathan Dollimore and Alan Sinfield (Manchester, 1985); *Shakespeare and the Question of Theory*, ed. Patricia Parker and Geoffrey Hartman (London, 1985); *Literary Theory/Renaissance Texts*, ed. Patricia Parker and David Quint (Baltimore, 1986); and *Shakespeare Reproduced*, ed. Jean E. Howard and Marion F. O'Connor (London, 1987).

33. See Holderness, *Shakespeare's History*, 14–39, and Axton, *Queen's Two Bodies*, 88–115.

34. I borrow Clifford Geertz's phrase from *Local Knowledge* (New York, 1983), 146. Until fairly recently in Britain—probably the mid-1960s, though I cannot locate precise documentation—performances at the Royal Shakespeare Theatre in Stratford either began or ended with singing the national anthem, a practice that coincides with such final compliments. The Shakespeare Centre Library contains a wide variety of settings, the most recent a Raymond Leppard arrangement, taken from the earliest known source of the melody, circa 1740, which was first used at the Royal Shakespeare Theatre for the 1960 season and was also played in 1961 and 1962.

35. Marcus, *Puzzling Shakespeare*, 43.

36. Peter Brook, "Style in Shakespearean Production," in *The Modern Theatre*, ed. Daniel Seltzer (Boston, 1967), 256; see also 251.

37. See, for instance, John Russell Brown, *Free Shakespeare* (London, 1974) and *Discovering Shakespeare* (London, 1981), and Bernard Beckerman, "Explorations in Shakespeare's Drama," *Shakespeare Quarterly* 29 (1978): 133–45.

38. T. S. Eliot, "Four Elizabethan Dramatists," in *Elizabethan Essays* (New York, 1964), 15–16.

39. Helene Keyssar, "I Love You. Who Are You? The Strategy of Drama in Recognition Scenes," *PMLA* 92 (1977): 304. On measuring the "adequacy" and "authenticity" of staged performances, see Jonas Barish, "Shakespeare in the Study; Shakespeare on the Stage," in *Theatre Journal* 40 (1988): 33–47. See also Stephen Orgel, "The Authentic Shakespeare," *Representations* 21 (1988): 1–26.

40. Maynard Mack, *"King Lear" In Our Time* (Berkeley, 1972), 4.

41. Harry Berger, Jr., "Text against Performance in Shakespeare: The Ex

ample of *Macbeth*," in Greenblatt, *Power of Forms*, 51–56, 73, 77–78. See also Berger's "Text against Performance: The Gloucester Family Romance," in *Shakespeare's "Rough Magic*," ed. Peter Erickson and Coppélia Kahn (Newark, 1985), 210–29. For one critique of Berger's methods, see Richard Levin, "The New Refutation of Shakespeare," *Modern Philology* 83 (1985): 123–41. See also Berger's "Bodies and Texts," *Representations* 17 (1987): 144–66, in which he considers the "basic structural forces and cultural changes of which [the debate over performances and readings] is a superficial symptom." Berger reconsiders his position in *Imaginary Auditions* (Berkeley, 1989).

42. See, for example, Stuart Hall, "The Rediscovery of 'Ideology': Return of the Repressed in Media Studies," in *Culture, Society, and the Media*, ed. M. Gurevitch, T. Bennett et al. (London, 1982), 56–90; and "The Toad in the Garden: Thatcherism among the Theorists," in *Marxism and the Interpretation of Culture*, ed. Cary Nelson and Lawrence Grossberg (Urbana, 1988), 48–49.

43. For an analysis of Bogdanov's ending, see my "Absent Bodies, Present Voices: Performance Work and the Close of *Romeo and Juliet*'s Golden Story," *Theatre Journal* 41 (1989): 341–59.

44. Harry Berger, Jr., "Psychoanalyzing the Shakespeare Text: The First Three Scenes of the *Henriad*," in Parker and Hartman, *Shakespeare and the Question of Theory*, 210–29. For a position similar to my own, see Anthony B. Dawson, "*Measure for Measure*, New Historicism, and Theatrical Power," *Shakespeare Quarterly* 39 (1988): 328–41, especially 339–41.

45. For an extended argument of these issues, see my "Parallel Practices, or The *Un*-Necessary Difference," *Kenyon Review* 7, no. 3 (1985): 57–65.

46. Material in this paragraph draws from my "Absent Bodies, Present Voices." Marcus also mobilizes these features of *Hamlet* and *Dream* in an argument parallel to my own, *Puzzling Shakespeare*, 46–50.

47. For a full discussion, see Joel B. Altman, *The Tudor Play of Mind* (Berkeley, 1978). See also Axton, *Queen's Two Bodies*, ix, and Thomas Heywood's account of how, when *The History of Friar Francis* (1593–1594) was performed at King's Lynn, it prompted a woman spectator to confess that seven years earlier she had poisoned her husband as had the play's protagonist in *An Apology for Actors*, sig. G_1^v–G_2^r.

48. See, for example, the title page for the 1595 quarto of *The True Tragedy of Richard Duke of York . . . (3 Henry VI)*, which describes a play "sundry times acted by the Right Honorable the Earl of Pembroke his servants" (Allen and Muir, *Shakespeare's Plays in Quarto*).

49. For a pertinent discussion of intellectual property, see Joseph Lowenstein, "The Script in the Marketplace," *Representations* 12 (1985): 101–14.

50. In borrowing Philip C. McGuire's use of "playtext," I affirm the important distinction between kinds of texts that he makes in *Speechless Dialect* (Berkeley, 1985), xix–xxv.

51. The term derives from Richard Schechner, who refers to performance

texts as theatrical events that grow primarily from rehearsal and laboratory work and, at times, are supported only by a minimal printed text. I appropriate his usage, then, to refer to the result of a process that begins with a (usually) cut version of an existing playtext. See Schechner's discussion in "Collective Reflexivity: Restoration of Behavior," in *A Crack in the Mirror*, ed. Jay Ruby (Philadelphia, 1982), 39–81. See also Schechner, *Performance Theory* (1977; reprint, New York, 1988), and Turner, *Human Seriousness of Play*. For pertinent work on semiotic rather than anthropological approaches to performance, see Keir Elam, *The Semiotics of Drama and Theatre* (London, 1980) and *Shakespeare's Universe of Discourse* (New York, 1984), and Patrice Pavis, *Languages of the Stage* (New York, 1982). In a sense, I have synthesized the two approaches, though as I attempt to trace cultural patterns by mobilizing "signs" within particular performance texts, I have not absorbed those signs into the rather rigorous systems Elam and Pavis use. For yet another related approach, see David Bevington, *Action Is Eloquence* (Cambridge, Mass., 1984).

52. McGuire, *Speechless Dialect*, 127; see also 125–26, 136, 139–40, 146–49.

53. On Prologues and Epilogues written especially for court performances, see E. K. Chambers, *The Elizabethan Stage* (Oxford, 1923), 1:224; for their political character, see 3:361–62. See also Clifford Leech, "Shakespeare's Prologues and Epilogues," in *Studies in Honor of T. W. Baldwin*, ed. Don Cameron Allen (Urbana, 1958), 150–64. For the jig, see C. R. Baskervill, *The Elizabethan Jig and Related Song Drama* (Chicago, 1929).

54. Berger, "Gloucester Family Romance," 228.

55. For a useful critique of tetralogy thinking, see Mary Thomas Crane, "The Shakespearean Tetralogy," *Shakespeare Quarterly* 36 (1985): 282–99.

56. A conversation with Philip C. McGuire helped me formulate these ideas.

57. For an extended argument, see my "Kiss Me Deadly; or The Des/Demonized Spectacle," in *Othello: New Perspectives*, ed. Virginia M. Vaughan and Kent Cartwright (Cranbury, N.J., 1990).

58. See Montrose, "Purpose of Playing." On the notion of performance work, see Jerome J. McGann, *The Beauty of Inflections* (Oxford, 1985), especially 95–96 and 114–20.

59. Except for *1 Henry VI*'s position in that order. See Stanley Wells and Gary Taylor et al., *William Shakespeare: A Textual Companion* (Oxford, 1987), 217–18, and Gary Taylor, "Shakespeare and Others: The Authorship of *1 Henry VI*," forthcoming in *Medieval and Renaissance Drama in England*.

60. Some elements of a production do not, of course, remain constant but are adapted to different theatrical spaces and varied casting; when pertinent, I note such changes. On reading paintings, see Svetlana Alpers, "Describe or Narrate? A Problem in Realistic Representation," *New Literary History* 8 (Autumn 1976): 15–41, and *The Art of Describing* (Chicago, 1983). See also Michael Fried, *Absorption and Theatricality* (Berkeley, 1980).

61. I borrow Clifford Geertz's term from "Thick Description: Toward an

Interpretive Theory of Culture," in *The Interpretation of Culture* (New York, 1973), 3–30.

CHAPTER 2
FASHIONING OBEDIENCE: *KING JOHN*'s "TRUE INHERITORS"

1. Milne's poem appears in *Now We Are Six* (New York, 1927), 2–6.

2. All citations are from *King John*, ed. Robert Smallwood (Harmondsworth, 1974).

3. On *King John*'s date and its relationship to *Troublesome Raigne*, see Smallwood, *King John*, 9–11. For a dissenting opinion that positions *King John* as the earlier of the two plays, see E.A.J. Honigmann's Arden edition (1954; reprint, London, 1973), xliii–lviii. Critical consensus places *King John* between the two so-called tetralogies; see, for example, Virginia M. Vaughan, "Between Tetralogies: *King John* as Transition," *Shakespeare Quarterly* 35 (1984): 407–21. For other recent arguments, see Sidney Thomas, " 'Enter a Sheriffe': Shakespeare's *King John* and *The Troublesome Raigne*," 98–100, and the exchange of E.A.J. Honigmann, Paul Werstine, and Sidney Thomas in *Shakespeare Quarterly* 38 (1987): 124–30. For a discussion of cultural constraints on both chronicle material and plays, see A. R. Braunmuller, "*King John* and Historiography," *ELH* 55 (1988): 309–22.

4. See Bernard Beckerman, *Shakespeare at the Globe* (New York, 1962), 36. Although Beckerman's statement of the Elizabethan dramatic convention that "the last lines of a play, excluding Epilogues and songs, be spoken by the ranking figure" sounds too pat, it nonetheless holds true.

5. Honigmann compares G. D.'s *Briefe Discoverie of Doctor Allens Seditious Drifts* (London, 1588), sig. R₃ᵛ with Matthew 12:25, Mark 3:24, and Luke 11:17 (*King John*, 147n). See also Douglas Wixson, who argues that 1590s propaganda pamphleteering constitutes one source and shapes a series of "open form" debates put together by the audience, in " 'Calm Words Folded Up in Smoke': Propaganda and Spectator Response in Shakespeare's *King John*," *Shakespeare Studies* 14 (1981): 111–27. For a summary of *King John*'s engagement with succession issues, and topical allusions to Spain and to Protestant polemics, see John Loftis, *Renaissance Drama in England and Spain* (Princeton, 1987), 72–82.

6. Fredric Jameson, "The Ideology of the Text," in *Situations of Theory*, vol. 1 of *The Ideologies of Theory*, Theory and History of Literature, no. 48 (Minneapolis, 1988), 33–34.

7. See, for example, John Dover Wilson, *King John* (Cambridge, 1936), lx.

8. In "Cato," *Guilty Men* (London, 1940), 48, quoted in Holderness, *Shakespeare's History*, 179.

9. E.M.W. Tillyard, *Shakespeare's History Plays* (London, 1944); Lily B. Campbell, *Shakespeare's Histories* (San Marino, 1947). See also J. L. Simmons, who sees the play as a fairly "strict construction" of the Tudor myth, in "Shakespeare's *King John* and Its Source: Coherence, Pattern, and Vision," *Tulane Studies in English* 17 (1969): 53–72, especially 71, on the ending. For

a discussion of Tillyard's "Elizabethan World Picture" as a constitutive reproduction of history, see Holderness, *Shakespeare's History*, especially 192–200.

10. The phrase is Michael Manheim's, in *The Weak King Dilemma in the Shakespearean History Play* (Syracuse, 1973), 186. For similar positions, see Adrien Bonjour, "The Road to Swinstead Abbey: A Study of the Sense and Structure of *King John*," *ELH* 18 (1951): 253–74; James L. Calderwood, "Commodity and Honour in *King John*," *University of Toronto Quarterly* 29 (1959–1960): 341–56; William Matchett, "Richard's Divided Heritage in *King John*," *Essays in Criticism* 12, no. 3 (1962): 231–53; and Gunnar Boklund, "The Troublesome Ending of *King John*," *Studia Neophilologica* 40 (1968): 175–84.

11. See, for instance, Alexander Leggatt, "Dramatic Perspective in *King John*," *English Studies in Canada* 3 (1977): 15; Kastan, *Shakespeare and the Shapes of Time*, 51–54; and Larry S. Champion, "The 'Un-end' of *King John*: Shakespeare's Demystification of Closure," in *King John: New Perspectives*, ed. Deborah T. Curren-Aquino (Newark, 1989), 173–85.

12. Honigmann provides a summary of the parallels in the play and the views of Tudor commentators in *King John*, xxix, xxv–xxx.

13. Roger Wendover, *Chronica Sive Flores Historiarum*, ed. H. O. Coxe (London, 1841–1844), 1:1–2, quoted in John R. Elliott, "Shakespeare and the Double Image of *King John*," *Shakespeare Studies* 1 (1965): 64.

14. The following summary draws on Elliott, "Shakespeare and the Double Image," and Virginia M. Vaughan, "*King John*: A Study in Subversion and Containment," in Curren-Aquino, *King John*, 62–75.

15. I borrow the phrase from Marcus, who uses it in a slightly different sense (*Puzzling Shakespeare*, 28).

16. See Elliott, "Shakespeare and the Double Image," 71. See also John R. Elliott, Jr., "Polydore Vergil and the Reputation of King John in the Sixteenth Century," *ELN* 2 (1964): 90–92.

17. See Axton, *Queen's Two Bodies*, 110–11. See also Matchett, who identifies *King John*'s main theme as "who should be King of England and thus what constitutes a right to the throne," in "Richard's Divided Heritage," 231–53. John Blanpied argues that "Shakespeare . . . depolemicizes the issue of regal legitimacy, the question being not a legal one between 'right' and 'strong possession,' but a dramatic one of what constitutes strong possession" in *Time and the Artist in Shakespeare's English Histories* (Newark, 1983), 279.

18. Sigurd Burckhardt refers to the " 'test-case' purity" with which the issues are argued at Angiers, in *Shakespearean Meanings* (Princeton, 1968), 125. For a classical, and thorough, discussion of the succession issue and its myths, see Ernst H. Kantorowicz, *The King's Two Bodies* (Princeton, 1957).

19. See Vaughan, "*King John*," 70.

20. See Paul Johnson, *Elizabeth I* (London, 1976), 10–12.

21. My understanding of women's roles draws from Phyllis Rackin, "Patriarchal History and Female Subversion in *King John*," in Curren-Aquino, *King John*, 76–90; see especially 85. For the notion of the play as a male project, see

Naomi Scheman, "Missing Mothers/Desiring Daughters: Framing the Sight of Women," *Critical Inquiry* 15, no. 1 (1988): 87.

22. See Holinshed 168/1/5, reproduced in Geoffrey Bullough, *Narrative and Dramatic Sources of Shakespeare* (London and New York, 1962), 4:33.

23. Equating Arthur with England constitutes a perfect example of how the history play invests in a process of magnification. For a full discussion of such instances, see Lindenberger, *Historical Drama*, 54–94.

24. See Holinshed 160/2/51, reproduced in Bullough, *Narrative and Dramatic Sources*, 4:26. R. L. Smallwood points to such use of an unhistorical character who tempts spectators and readers to rewrite history as a "splendid exploitation of the possibilities of the history play," in "Shakespeare Unbalanced: The Royal Shakespeare Company's *King John*, 1974–75," *Deutsche Shakespeare-Gesellschaft West* (1976): 94. For comparisons to Falstaff, see also Robert C. Jones, "Truth in *King John*," *Studies in English Literature* 25 (1985): 397–417, especially 397–402.

25. See, for example, Harold C. Goddard, *The Meaning of Shakespeare* (Chicago, 1951), 146.

26. On the Bastard's composite, puzzling role, see, among others, Julia C. van de Water, "The Bastard in *King John*," *Shakespeare Quarterly* 11 (1960): 137–46.

27. See Jonathan Dollimore, "Subjectivity, Sexuality, and Transgression: The Jacobean Connection," *Renaissance Drama*, n.s., 17 (1986): 53–81, especially 57–58.

28. The relations between Carnival and theater have pre-Bakhtin and post-Bakhtin phases. For the former, see C. L. Barber, *Shakespeare's Festive Comedy* (Princeton, 1959); for the latter, see Mikhail Bakhtin, *Rabelais and His World* (1965), trans. Hélène Iswolsky (Cambridge, Mass., 1968), and Michel Foucault, *Surveiller et punir: Naissance de la prison* (Paris, 1975). See also *The Reversible World*, ed. Barbara A. Babcock (Ithaca, 1978). On the relations between Carnival and theater, see Michael D. Bristol, *Carnival and Theater* (London, 1985). See also Peter Stallybrass and Allon White, *The Politics and Poetics of Transgression* (Ithaca, 1986).

29. See, for instance, the Chevrolet "Heartbeat of America" television commercials, initially screened in 1987, or those for Coca-Cola or McDonald's. For one analysis of such phenomena, see Judith Williamson, *Decoding Advertisements* (London, 1978), 40–70. For an analysis of "subject" as a term, see Paul Smith, *Discerning the Subject* (Minneapolis, 1988).

30. I draw the notion of downward displacement from Jonathan Dollimore, "Transgression and Surveillance in *Measure for Measure*," in Dollimore and Sinfield, *Political Shakespeare*, 72–87.

31. Other Shakespearean histories also exploit the midplay death of a rightful King or his surrogate as a narrative rebeginning to produce, as in *Richard II*, a sense of double narratives. Cf., for instance, Simmons, who argues that Arthur's death constitutes the crux of both *King John* and *Troublesome Raigne* ("Shakespeare's *King John*," 66).

32. By the terms of the *Liber Regalis*, the order of service for the coronation oath used from Henry IV to Elizabeth I, a ruler swore to uphold the laws with justice and mercy. Thus the ruler was bound by the law of the land; the oath was essentially a contract between the monarch and the people (*English Coronation Records* [London, 1901], 91–95 [Latin; trans. on 118–20]). Richard II and Edward II both lost thrones on the ground that they had violated this oath.

33. One implication here is that *King John* cannot stand on its own but requires the impetus of another text to energize both the debate over its narrative structures and that over its issues, including what sort of cultural work each accomplishes.

34. For the notion of underrepresentation, see Howard Felperin, " 'Tongue-tied Our Queen?' The Deconstruction of Presence in *The Winter's Tale*," in Parker and Hartman, *Shakespeare and the Question of Theory*, 3–18.

35. On the notion of monarchomachs, see Franklin L. Ford, *Political Murder from Tyrannicide to Terrorism* (Cambridge, Mass., 1985), 150–57.

36. Tillyard claims that "Shakespeare huddles together and fails to motivate properly the events of the last third of his play" (*Shakespeare's History Plays*, 215, 232). Later critics also judge the play in relation to notions of "ideal" form: see, for example, Jones, "Truth in *King John*," 414; Simmons, "Shakespeare's *King John*," 66; Manheim, *Dilemma*, 155; and Robert Ornstein, *A Kingdom for a Stage* (Cambridge, Mass., 1972), 96, 98, 101.

37. Matchett also notes the similarity ("Richard's Divided Heritage," 251).

38. Cf. Etienne Balabar and Pierre Machery, "On Literature as an Ideological Form," in *Untying the Text*, ed. Robert Young (London, 1981), 89.

39. Marlowe's *Edward II* rivals this bleakness: at the close, the new King presents Mortimer's head to his father's "murdered ghost," enclosed in a hearse. He speaks not of how discovering traitors will save the realm, not of God's punishments and rewards, not of renewed commitment and order, but of his own failure to prevent treason. In its visual emblems alone—a hearse, a severed head, a weeping King—the close represents kingship's vulnerability, not its strengths. See *Edward II*, 5.6.93–102, in *Drama of the English Renaissance*, ed. Russell A. Fraser and Norman Rabkin (New York, 1976). Jonathan Reeve Price provides an insightful summary of the "definitive" indefinitions of *King John*'s closing scenes in "*King John* and Problematic Art," *Shakespeare Quarterly* 21 (1970): 28. In that both address issues involving the rights of rulers and how they are chosen, *Titus Andronicus* and *King John* have intriguing similarities. Although *King John*'s close relies heavily on narrated reports while *Titus* commits to overrepresentation in the bloodbath finale, in both plays a child represents the hopes for the future. Indeed, in *Titus*, the possibility exists that two children—Aaron's child and Young Lucius—share that position, thus renewing one of the play's central oppositions. Both also rely on closural features reminiscent of morality endings; the Folio addition to *Titus*'s ending (TLN 2705–8; Pelican, 5.3.201–4) further enforces "moral closure." *Titus* also frames its main action between opening and closing scenes that ad-

dress the succession issue. And in the closing scene, Marcus evokes a free-floating unity (5.3.67–76) comparable to, though constructed differently from, that which the Bastard speaks in *King John*.

40. I allude here to Lawrence Grossberg's term for postmodern cultural "commodities" such as rock and roll as "spectacles of affective empowerment," in "Is There Rock after Punk?" *Critical Studies in Mass Communication* 3, no. 1 (1986): 51–58. Roy Strong connects Elizabeth I's cult with Victoria's: both women were imperialists who stood at the center of national historical mythologies; both ages were obsessed with romance, and appropriated medievalism and related, or reappropriated, its figures to contemporary social change. Strong's view of how Victorian paintings of historical subjects were read applies equally to reading stage representations (*Recreating the Past* [London, 1978], 152–54).

41. For a brief overview of *King John*'s stage history, see Harold Child's summary in Wilson, *King John*, lxiii–lxxix. For accounts of selected productions, see George C. D. Odell, *Shakespeare from Betterton to Irving* (New York, 1920), especially Charles Kemble (2:169–73), and Macready (2:229–32). For a facsimile prompt copy of Macready's 1842 revival, see *William Charles Macready's King John*, ed. Charles H. Shattuck (Urbana, 1962); the volume also contains information on Charles Kean's 1846, 1852, and 1858 revivals. See also Michael R. Booth, *Victorian Spectacular Theatre, 1859–1910* (London, 1981), 44–45. In a study of critical response to nineteenth-century productions, Eugene M. Waith argues for looking at the emotional power of *King John* rather than considering the play as a pattern of political ideas in *"King John* and the Drama of History," *Shakespeare Quarterly* 29 (1978): 192–211. See also Edward S. Brubaker, "Staging *King John*: A Director's Observations," in Curren-Aquino, *King John*, 165–72.

42. See *"King John* at Her Majesty's Theatre," *Lady's Pictorial*, 30 September 1899. My thanks to Barbara A. Kachur for sharing materials on Tree's production. Prompt copy and other materials in the Beerbohm Tree Collection, the University of Bristol Theatre Collection.

43. Souvenir program in the Beerbohm Tree Collection, the University of Bristol Theatre Collection. Tree's *King John* was recorded on film and was, in fact, the first filmed Shakespeare. For an account, see Robert Hamilton Ball, *Shakespeare on Silent Film* (London, 1968), 21–23, 29, 303–4. Initially, Ball read one shot as representing the "Magna Charta" scene; a later essay acknowledges his error. See "Tree's *King John* Film: An Addendum," *Shakespeare Quarterly* 24 (1973): 455–59. My thanks to Sue Williams for calling my attention to this reference.

44. See Wilson, who argues that Shakespeare and his contemporaries "regarded the [Magna Charta] . . . as the treasonable innovation of a rebellious nobility." The "myth" of the Charter did not become "an accepted cornerstone of English political philosophy until the Hanoverians had acknowledged the Whig successors of John's barons as partners in the Constitution" (*King John*, xi–xii). That *King John* verges on formulating a notion of the state that

does not depend on Kings hints at its subversive potential; that it withdraws from such an extreme position to affirm a theory of the state refashioning subjects in obedience remains faithful to the Tudor stress on the parliamentary rights of English subjects. See Martin Carnoy, *The State and Political Theory* (Princeton, 1984), 114–15. One effect of the emphasis on Parliament in Tudor political mythology was to de-emphasize the significance of the Magna Charta, which focused on—indeed, grew out of—*differences* between sovereigns and subjects.

45. For dissenters, see, for instance, William Archer, "The Theatre—*King John*," *World*, 27 September 1899; "Her Majesty's Theatre—*King John*," *Daily Telegraph*, 21 September 1899. For advocates of the dumb show, see "The Drama—Her Majesty's Theatre," *Queen, the Lady's Newspaper and Court Chronicle*, 30 September 1899; "*King John* at Her Majesty's Theatre," *Times*, 21 September 1899; and Malcolm Watson, "Her Majesty's Theatre—*King John*," *St James Gazette*, 21 September 1899. See also Barbara A. Kachur, *Herbert Beerbohm Tree: Shakespearean Actor-Manager* (Ph.D. diss., Ohio State University, 1986), 510–12.

46. On the late nineteenth-century taste for spectacle, see Booth, *Victorian Spectacular Theatre*, 1–29. See also Martin Meisel, *Realizations* (Princeton, 1983), 29–30.

47. *Treasure Trove*, 29 October 1900, quoted in Booth, *Victorian Spectacular Theatre*, 14. For accounts of Tree's Her Majesty's productions and Edwardian taste, see Douglas M. Berry, "Her Majesty's Playhouse: The Relationship of Playhouse Design and Audience," *Theatre Studies* (1979/1980–1980/1981): 135–51; and Ralph Berry, "The Aesthetics of Beerbohm Tree's Shakespeare Festivals," *Nineteenth-Century Theatre Research* 9 (Summer 1981): 23–51.

48. *Evening News*, 21 September 1899; both quotes appear in Kachur, *Herbert Beerbohm Tree*, 507, 523.

49. Prompt copy; my description draws on Kachur, *Herbert Beerbohm Tree*, 507–9.

50. Tree, program note; *Pelican*, 30 September 1899, quoted in Kachur, *Herbert Beerbohm Tree*, 466, see also 530–31.

51. Prompt copy at the Shakespeare Centre Library.

52. "English John," *Birmingham Post*, 17 April 1957.

53. *Observer*, 21 April 1957.

54. "Second Innings," *Sunday Times*, 21 April 1957.

55. "History Brought to Life by This 'King John,'" *Stratford-upon-Avon Herald*, 19 April 1957.

56. The tag is from Robert Cushman's title, "King Barton's 'John,'" *Observer*, 24 March 1974. Prompt copy at the Shakespeare Centre Library. References are primarily to the Stratford version; some changes were made when the production was transferred to London's Aldwych Theatre. I rely throughout on Miriam Gilbert's description of a 1974 Stratford performance and on Smallwood, "Shakespeare Unbalanced."

57. Barton, program note. See also Michael L. Greenwald, *Directions by Indirections* (Newark, 1985), 128–29. Friedrich Dürrenmatt's 1968 adaptation of *King John* also made connections to current political concerns. On the relationship between Shakespeare's *King John* and Dürrenmatt's version, see Rudolf Stamm, "*King John—König Johann*: Vom Historienspiel zur politischen Moralität," *Shakespeare Jahrbuch West* 106 (1970): 30–48.

58. The most recent had been the Royal Shakespeare Company's own 1970 Theatregoround production, directed by Buzz Goodbody, which opened during the General Election campaign at a time when the nation was equally cynical about politics.

59. Barton, program note. For an extended critique of Barton's principles of justification, see Smallwood, "Shakespeare Unbalanced," 79–99. See also Greenwald, *Directions by Indirections*, 128–35.

60. Cf. Edward Bond's prolegomenon, "A Note on Dramatic Method," in Bond, *The Bundle* (London, 1978), vii–xxi.

61. I borrow "creative vandalism" from the title of Jonathan Dollimore's comments on Howard Barker's rewriting of Thomas Middleton's *Women Beware Women*, printed in a text that served as the program: "Middleton and Barker: Creative Vandalism" (London, 1986). Dollimore argues that Barker's reworking (primarily a newly written ending) may, "if we share the view of those historians and critics who have recently discovered in the conflict and crisis of Jacobean drama a prefiguring of the English Revolution of 1642 [be] perversely faithful to the play's originating history, its context, though only by violating the text itself." Cf. Stephen Greenblatt's more totalizing argument: "We are free to locate and pay homage to the [*Henry IV*] plays' doubts only because they no longer threaten us. There is subversion, no end of subversion, only not for us" ("Invisible Bullets: Renaissance Authority and Its Subversion" [1981], reprinted in Greenblatt, *Shakespearean Negotiations* [Berkeley, 1988], 65). For important counterarguments, see Moretti, " 'A Huge Eclipse,' " 7–40; and Christopher Pye, "The Sovereign, the Theater, and the Kingdome of Darkness: Hobbes and the Spectacle of Power," *Representations* 8 (1984): 85–106.

62. Smallwood, "Shakespeare Unbalanced," 98.

63. The first was John's at the beginning of the opening scene; the second for Arthur at the end of the second scene; the third for John in Barton's equivalent of *King John* 4.2. The fifth coronation was for Lewis in Barton's scene 13 (*King John* 5.2); the sixth for Prince Henry at the close.

64. Smallwood, "Shakespeare Unbalanced," 90–91.

65. *Doctor Faustus* was included both in the 1974 Stratford repertory and in the 1975 London season.

66. And so functions much like the three scholars in *Doctor Faustus*, 5.1.332–50. From the playtext in Fraser and Rabkin, *Drama of the English Renaissance*, vol. 1.

67. Perhaps in homage to the reported coincidence of Shakespeare's birth

and death on the same day. See Samuel S. Schoenbaum, *William Shakespeare: A Compact Documentary Life* (Oxford, 1977), 24–26, 28.

68. Irving Wardle, "Good and Evil, Doubly Projected in Stratford's New *King John*," *Times*, 21 March 1974.

69. This emphasis was even stronger by the time the play reached the Aldwych: there, Arthur and Henry were played by the same actor, and John's will was "rolled and torn into a paper crown to add an extra touch of mockery to the coronation" (Smallwood, "Shakespeare Unbalanced," 98).

70. Smallwood, "Shakespeare Unbalanced," 98.

71. Since, according to the chronicler, the historical Prince Henry came to rule in October, Barton's choice to set the ending at Christmas, and to quote Milne's "King John's Christmas" in the program note, suggests that the connections may have been in his mind.

72. Robert Cushman called it "a play about everything" (*Observer*, 24 March 1974); in Gordon Parsons's view, "Barton's play is a baggy monster, uncomfortably mixing dramatic styles and languages" (*Morning Star*, 22 March 1974). For some in the critical community, however, Barton's choices made readable and pertinent connections between John's politics and their own. See, for instance, the *Oxford Mail* (21 March 1974), whose reviewer called the play "a parable for our own times." And the *Daily Mail*'s (22 March 1974) critic noted that "Emrys James's sly, cynical and witty John debating the pros and cons of waging war with his laconic neighbor, Philip of France, reminds one of nothing so much as our present party leaders deciding whether or not to throw the country into the turmoil of another General Election or yo-yo in and out of Europe."

73. Michael Billington, *Guardian*, 21 March 1974, and "Commodity Prices," *Guardian Weekly*, 30 March 1974.

74. Barton, Aldwych program note.

75. "Snakes 'n' Ladders," *Independent*, 12 May 1988. See also Irving Wardle, "Days of Reckoning," *Times*, 12 May 1988; Michael Billington, "Plain John," *Guardian*, 12 May 1988; Michael Coveney, *Financial Times*, 12 May 1988; Michael Ratcliffe, "Decoy-Fox," *Observer*, 15 May 1988; John Peter, "How to Make a Play for Failure," *Sunday Times*, 15 May 1988; and Alan Dessen, "Exciting Shakespeare in 1988," *Shakespeare Quarterly* 40 (1989): 205–7.

CHAPTER 3
ENCLOSING CONTENTION: *1, 2, AND 3 HENRY VI*

1. *King Henry VI, Part 1*, ed. Andrew S. Cairncross (London, 1962), xlii; Kastan, *Shakespeare and the Shapes of Time*, 23–26; and Wilders, *Lost Garden*, 19.

2. Speaking of "design" permits critics to note various patterns of repetition that hold the plays together. For example, Wolfgang Clemen notes patterns of anticipation in *English Tragedy before Shakespeare*, trans. T. S. Dorsch (New York, 1961), 51–55; Larry S. Champion details broken oaths, murders, be-

trayals, omens, and prophecies in *Perspective in Shakespeare's English Histo-ries* (Athens, Ga., 1980), 50; E. W. Talbert notes the repetition of a rising figure at the ending in *Elizabethan Drama and Shakespeare's Early Plays* (Chapel Hill, 1963), 174; John D. Cox draws analogues with medieval drama in "*3 Henry VI*: Dramatic Convention and the Shakespearean History Play," *Comparative Drama* 12, no. 1 (1978): 42–60; and Roger Warren outlines reversals of expectation in " 'Contrarieties Agree': An Aspect of Dramatic Technique in 'Henry VI,' " *Shakespeare Survey* 37 (1984): 75–83.

3. Describing the limits and formal modifications of the *Henry VI–Richard III* tetralogy, Cairncross comments: "Each play suffers to some degree as a unit because it has, where appropriate, to (a) prepare for its successors, and look back to its predecessors; (b) stop somewhere in a continuous, still incomplete, or only partially complete action; (c) carry on the general theme; (d) duplicate general material for the sake of the exposition in the individual play" (*King Henry VI, Part 1*, xlii, lii).

4. Robert Y. Turner's title—*Shakespeare's Apprenticeship* (Chicago, 1974) —reflects this position.

5. Emrys Jones evokes the model of Senecan tragedy in *The Origins of Shakespeare* (Oxford, 1977), 267–72; Ribner that of the morality history in *English History Play*, 100–104. O. B. Hardison, Jr. terms all the history plays "a secular equivalent to the sacred cycle of the Middle Ages," in *Christian Rite and Christian Drama in the Middle Ages* (Baltimore, 1965), 290. Connecting these plays to divine or salvation history models, however, makes ending ultimately unknowable by extending it beyond time, referring it to cosmic, eternal patterns. Cf. Kastan, who argues that no such extension occurs (*Shakespeare and the Shapes of Time*, 46–47). For the relation to romance histories, see Paul Dean, "Shakespeare's *Henry VI* Trilogy and Elizabethan 'Romance' Histories: The Origins of a Genre," *Shakespeare Quarterly* 33 (1982): 34–48. For connections to epic, see David Riggs, *Shakespeare's Heroical Histories* (Cambridge, Mass., 1971).

6. For a condensed summary of these operations, see Jonathan Dollimore, *Radical Tragedy* (Sussex, 1984), 9–19, 27–28, 197–203.

7. For a summary of the traditional debate over authenticity and order, see Cairncross, *King Henry VI, Part 1*, xxviii–xxxvii. *The Complete Works*, ed. Stanley Wells and Gary Taylor (Oxford, 1986), places *1 Henry VI* after *2* and *3 Henry VI*, gives the latter plays their Quarto titles, *The First Part of the Contention* and *The True Tragedy*, and attributes *1 Henry VI* to "William Shakespeare and Others."

8. Edward Hall, *The Union of the Two Noble and Illustrious Families of Lancaster and York* . . . (1548); reprint, (London, 1809), facsimile title page.

9. Hall, *Union*, 1–2.

10. The quoted phrases are from Hall, *Union*, 1–2.

11. For a full discussion of this myth, see Kantorowicz, *King's Two Bodies*.

12. The phrase is Sir Thomas More's (*The History of King Richard III*, ed.

Richard S. Sylvester [New Haven, 1976], 83). Both Hall and Holinshed incorporate More's *History* in their own accounts.

13. Performed before some other audience, the play would have violated Elizabeth's own edict of 16 May 1559 "forbidding plays which touched on religion or politics, . . . [these] being no meet matters to be written or treated upon but by men of authority, learning, and wisdom, nor to be handled before any audience but of grave and discreet persons" (quoted in Thomas Sackville and Thomas Norton, *Gorboduc; or Ferrex and Porrex*, ed. Irby B. Cauthen, Jr. [Lincoln, Neb., 1970], xii).

14. See Norman Rabkin, "Stumbling toward Tragedy," in Erickson and Kahn, *Shakespeare's 'Rough Magic,'* 29–31.

15. Altman argues that "Sackville and Norton have actually written two tragedies—a demonstrative tragedy of moral error . . . and a tragedy of fate" (*The Tudor Play of Mind*, 249–59). See also Jones, *Origins*, 124–25. On *Gorboduc* and ideology, see Mark Breitenberg, "Reading Elizabethan Iconicity: *Gorboduc* and the Semiotics of Reform," *English Literary Renaissance* 18 (1988): 194–217.

16. *Gorboduc*, in Fraser and Rabkin, *Drama of the English Renaissance*, vol. 1. Cf. the dumb show that opens act 1: "First the music of violins began to play, during which came in upon the stage six wild men clothed in leaves, of whom the first bare in his neck a fagot of small sticks, which they all, both severally and together, assayed with all their strengths to break; but it could not be broken by them. At the length, one of them plucked out one of the sticks and brake it; and the rest, plucking out all the other sticks one after another, did easily break them, the same being severed; which being conjoined, they had before attempted in vain. After they had this done, they departed the stage, and the music ceased. Hereby was signified that a state knit in unity doth continue strong against all force, but being divided is easily destroyed; as befell upon King Gorboduc dividing his land to his two sons, which he before held in monarchy, and upon the dissension of the brethren to whom it was divided."

17. Moretti reads more assurance in the ending: "the play concludes with the clear suggestion that the army of aristocrats will vanquish [the Duke of Albany]" (" 'A Huge Eclipse,' " 8).

18. On relations between *Gorboduc* and the Elizabethan succession, see Gertrude Catherine Reese, "The Question of the Succession in Elizabethan Drama," *University of Texas Studies in English* 22 (1942): 59–85. See also Mortimer Levine, *The Early Elizabethan Succession Question, 1558–1568* (Stanford, 1966), especially 38–44; and Axton, *Queen's Two Bodies*.

19. Although these examples focus selectively on representations of civil war, they nevertheless represent closural strategies common to any number of pre-Shakespearean as well as contemporary plays. Dates are from *Annals of English Drama 975–1700*, ed. Alfred Harbage, revised by Samuel S. Schoenbaum (London, 1964).

20. See Natalie Zemon Davis, "Women on Top: Symbolic Sexual Inversion

and Political Disorder in Early Modern Europe" (1975), reprinted in Babcock, *Reversible World*, 147–90. See also David Underdown, *Revel, Riot, and Rebellion* (Oxford, 1985), 102–11.

21. David Bevington explains the play's conservative bias by arguing that the author's topical motive was to glorify "Elizabeth's merciful handling of both her Catholic enemies and the restive peasantry" (*Tudor Drama and Politics* [Cambridge, Mass., 1968], 236–38).

22. See Montrose, "Purpose of Playing," 51–53.

23. For the origins and development of the history play as a form, see Ribner, *English History Play*, and Jones, *Origins*. Cairncross assumes that Shakespeare's need to develop Hall's plan generated various modifications of dramatic form, especially noticeable at the close (*King Henry VI, Part I*, xlii). But surely the point is not that Shakespeare *needs* to reproduce Hall but that he *chooses* to do so.

24. My formulations draw from several essays in Hult, *Concepts of Closure*: D. A. Miller, "Balzac's Illusions Lost and Found," 164–65; Thomas M. Greene, "The End of Discourse in Machiavelli's 'Prince,'" 57–71; and Gabrielle Schwab, "The Dialectic of Opening and Closing in Samuel Beckett's *Endgame*," 191–202.

25. Hayden White, "The Value of Narrativity in the Representation of Reality," *Critical Inquiry* 7 (1980): 20. See also Louis O. Mink's response to White in the same issue, "Everyman His or Her Own Annalist," 777–83.

26. On narrative and the erotic, and the desire of narrative to generate new narrative, see Barthes, *S/Z*, 88–90.

27. *Pierce Pennilesse His Supplication to the Divell*, quoted from *Works*, ed. R. B. McKerrow (1904; reprint, Oxford, 1958), 1:212.

28. Geoffrey Bullough argues that Shakespeare began with Henry VI's reign rather than with Richard II's because of "a certain topicality in the circumstances which allowed the dramatist to imply parallels between the war in France in the first half of the fifteenth century and that in the fifteen-nineties." Among others, Essex, Willoughby, Vere, and Norris went to France to put increasing pressure on the Spanish armies in the Netherlands. They were recalled because of lack of funds. Bullough suggests that it was topical, at a time when complaints that the government was insufficiently supporting the forces fighting in France, to present a play in which failure was attributed to lack of support from home and to dissension among the nobles ("Disorder and Misrule in Shakespeare's Early Histories," *Literary Half-Yearly* 21 [1980]: 82–97). This connection bears to some extent on Shakespeare's double ending, which deflects attention from Talbot's defeat in France and shows Charles paying allegiance to the English monarch, followed by Margaret's marriage. Other topical references position it among post-Armada plays that rework its events; these include John Lyly's *Midas* (1589 or 1590), and Robert Wilson's *The Three Lords and Three Ladies of London* (1590) and *The Cobbler's Prophecy*. For a discussion, see Bevington, *Tudor Drama*, 187–211.

29. For the pioneering study against previous disintegrationists, see Here-

ward T. Price, *Construction in Shakespeare*, University of Michigan Contributions to Modern Philology, 17 (Ann Arbor, 1951). See, for example, S. C. Sen Gupta, *Shakespeare's Historical Plays* (London, 1964), 63; Thomas Marc Parrott, *Shakespearean Comedy* (1949; reprint, New York, 1962), 209–10; and Tillyard, *Shakespeare's History Plays*, 162–68.

30. I draw here as well as in what follows from Marcus's fine discussion in *Puzzling Shakespeare*, 63–69.

31. For an analysis of Joan's potential subversions, see Marina Warner, *Joan of Arc* (New York, 1981), 96, 105–8, 117, 143–45. See also Lisa Jardine, *Still Harping on Daughters* (Sussex, 1983), 105–6, 156–59. Gabriele Bernhard Jackson positions Joan in relation to several topical historical roles in "Topical Ideology: Witches, Amazons, and Shakespeare's Joan of Arc," *English Literary Renaissance* 18 (1988): 40–65. On Queen Elizabeth's Amazonian image, see Winfried Schleiner, "*Divina virago*: Queen Elizabeth as an Amazon," *Studies in Philology* 75 (1978): 163–80.

32. Marcus, *Puzzling Shakespeare*, 68. I am also indebted to a conversation with Carol Rutter.

33. On witchcraft, see Keith Thomas, *Religion and the Decline of Magic* (1971; reprint, Harmondsworth, 1973), 515–680. For Elizabeth's association with demons, see Sir John Harington, *Nugae Antiquae* 1:165; and Johnson, *Elizabeth I*, 223–24. See also Marcus, *Puzzling Shakespeare*, 81.

34. See Patricia-Ann Lee, "Reflections of Power: Margaret of Anjou and the Dark Side of Queenship," *Renaissance Quarterly* 39 (1986): 183–217. See also Irene Dash, *Wooing, Wedding, and Power* (New York, 1981), 159–93; and Phyllis Rackin, "Anti-Historians: Women's Roles in Shakespeare's Histories," *Theatre Journal* 37 (1985): 329–44.

35. At later hearings about the historical Joan's 1431 trial, witnesses report that she was sexually abused; each placed the attempted rape after she recanted and before she withdrew her statement. If indeed her English guards did rape her, they did so at a time when she admitted to being false, to having lost faith; in order "to lay hands on her body, they needed her word that its magic powers had run out" (Warner, *Joan of Arc*, 106–7).

36. Marcus, *Puzzling Shakespeare*, 72–74, 88.

37. Hall, *Union*, 204.

38. Knox argues against women governors in *The First Blast of the Trumpet Against the Monstrous Regiment of Women* (1558), ed. Edward Arber (London, 1878). For a fine discussion of female rulers, see Carole Levin, "Queens and Claimants: Political Insecurity in Sixteenth-Century England," in *Gender, Ideology, and Action*, ed. Janet Sharistanian (New York, 1986), 41–66.

39. Dean positions the Margaret-Suffolk material in relation to similar love triangles in so-called romance histories such as *Friar Bacon and Friar Bungay, James IV, Fair Em, George a Greene*, and *Edward III* (" 'Romance' Histories," 39–43).

40. Johnson, *Elizabeth I*, 109–43, especially 109–12.

41. See Wells and Taylor, *William Shakespeare: A Textual Companion*, 177.

42. Thomas Gataker, *Marriage Duties Briefely couched together* (London, 1620), 9–10, quoted in Susan Dwyer Amussen, *An Ordered Society* (Oxford, 1988), 47.

43. *Thomas Platter's Travels in England, 1599*, trans. Clare Williams (London, 1937), 181–82, quoted in Amussen, *An Ordered Society*, 48. See also Edward Chamberlayne, *Angliae Notitia; or The Present State of England: Together with Divers Reflections upon the antient State thereof*, 2d. ed. (London, 1669), 461.

44. Although Dee was traditionally represented as a magician-astrologer, Johnson argues that he was "an experimental and theoretical scientist of outstanding originality." For Elizabeth's relationship with Dee, see Johnson, *Elizabeth I*, 221–24.

45. The language comes from sixteenth-century proceedings of defamation cases brought by women against other women. See Amussen, *An Ordered Society*, 97, 101–3; and, on women's relations with their husbands, 121–23.

46. Cairncross conjectures possible censorship in order to explain the differences between Quarto and Folio, here and elsewhere (*King Henry VI, Part 2*, xxv–xxvii).

47. A number of readers note the marred succession. See, for example, Edward I. Berry, *Patterns of Decay* (Charlottesville, 1975); Mark Rose. *Shakespearean Design* (Cambridge, Mass., 1972), 126–33.

48. In Folio, it is Somerset's head (TLN 303).

49. On the relations between Cade's rebellion and the carnivalesque, see Stephen Greenblatt, "Murdering Peasants: Status, Genre, and the Representation of Rebellion" (1983), reprinted in *Representing the English Renaissance*, ed. Stephen Greenblatt (Berkeley, 1988), 23–25. See also Bristol, *Carnival and Theater*, 89–90.

50. I draw the notion of recording from Greenblatt, "Invisible Bullets," 21–65. Bevington argues that by not reproducing, from the chronicle account, the rebels' demands, *2 Henry VI* purposefully undermines and ridicules Cade (*Tudor Drama*, 239–40). The list makes claims against "diverse of his council, lovers of themselves, oppressors of the poor commonality, flatterers to the king and enemies to his honor, suckers of his purse, and robbers of his subjects, partial to their friends, and extreme to their enemies, for rewards corrupted, and for indifference, nothing doing" (Hall, *Union*, 220). Contrary to Bevington, it would seem that Cade's attacks on the nobility include rather than exclude most of these practices.

51. Writing about the demonizing of deviancy in *Measure for Measure*, Dollimore makes a point that is equally pertinent here: "In fact we need to distinguish, as Christopher Hill does, between this mob element, little influenced by religious or political ideology but up for hire, and the 'rogues, vagabonds and beggars' who, although they 'caused considerable panic in ruling circles . . . were incapable of concerted revolt' " ("Transgression and Surveillance," 80). Also important is that the rebellion's leaders here are not outcasts or vagabonds but workingmen with roles central to England's economy—especially

Cade and Smith the Weaver, whose professions sustain the wool trade. See Richard Wilson, " 'A Mingled Yarn': Shakespeare and the Cloth Workers," *Literature and History* 12, no. 2 (Autumn 1986): 164–80.

52. Bevington argues that the Say incident suggests that "the agrarian commons . . . are no longer capable of distinguishing good aristocrats from bad, and turn their particular wrath on Lord Say, who is Duke Humphrey's successor in the play as a man of flawless integrity" (*Tudor Drama*), 240. Before condemning Say, Cade admits to being moved by his well-spoken self-defense; if, however, he is to maintain power, the situation requires Say's execution. To some extent, the class rebellion reproduces systems of repressive authority in not being able to afford moral distinctions.

53. Cf. 3.1.6–182, where Gloucester is accused of being insolent and deceitful, of flattering the commons, of instigating his duchess to frame Henry's fall, of levying taxes and staying soldiers' pay and thus losing France, of devising strange tortures for offenders, and of false swearing. Intriguingly, the references to learning glance specifically at Henry himself: "This King Henry was of a liberal mind, and especially, to such as loved good learning, and them whom he saw profit, in any virtuous science, he heartily favored and embraced, wherefore he first helped his own young scholars to attain to discipline, and for them he founded a solemn school at Eton . . . in the which he hath established an honest college of sad priests, with a great number of children which be there, of his cost frankly and freely taught the erudity of Cambridge, called the King's College, for the further erudition of such as were brought up in Eton which, at this day so flourisheth in all kinds, as well of literature, as of tongues, that above all other, it is worthy to be called the Prince of Colleges" (Hall, *Union*, 304).

54. Dollimore, "Transgression and Surveillance," 85.

55. Just as, in the later *Henry V*, the French campaigns become an excuse used by those in power to deflect attention from domestic troubles (1.1).

56. For other Quarto-Folio distinctions concerning Cade, see Stephen Urkowitz, "Rewriting Shakespeare?/Shakespeare Rewriting? 2 and 3 *Henry VI* (1594, 1595, 1623)," unpublished paper, Shakespeare Association of America conference, 1989. My thanks to Urkowitz for sharing his work.

57. "The Sentence of the High Court of Justice upon the King [27 January 1649]," in *The Puritan Revolution*, ed. Stuart E. Prall (London, 1969), 192. David Kastan argues that the representation of Kings on stages generated conditions that made it possible to execute Charles I in " 'Proud Majesty Made a Subject': Shakespeare and the Spectacle of Rule," *Shakespeare Quarterly* 37 (1986): 459–75.

58. York in fact literally replaces him, entering with his army as Iden exits with Cade's body (5.1). Berry sees York as Cade's reductio ad absurdum (*Patterns of Decay*, 46).

59. For a reading of the textual issues, see Steven Urkowitz, " 'If I Mistake in Those Foundations Which I Build Upon': Peter Alexander's Textual Analy-

sis of *Henry VI*, Parts 2 and 3," *English Literary Renaissance* 18 (1988): 246–49.

60. Sherbo, *Johnson on Shakespeare*, 7:597.

61. For a discussion of 2 and 3 *Henry VI*'s textual history, see Cairncross, *King Henry VI, Part 3*, xiii–xxxii. On the relation between the Octavo and later texts, see Wells and Taylor, *William Shakespeare: A Textual Companion*, 197–99.

62. Letter from Sir Robert Cecil to Sir John Harington, 1603, in *Nugae Antiquae*, 1:345. For an analysis of the historical Margaret and Margaret's representation in Shakespeare's plays, see Patricia-Ann Lee, "Reflections of Power."

63. For the notion of the vendetta, see Coppélia Kahn, *Man's Estate* (Berkeley, 1981), 59–62. See also Berry, *Patterns of Decay*; Ronald S. Berman, "Fathers and Sons in the *Henry VI* Plays," *Shakespeare Quarterly* 13 (1962): 494–97; Don M. Ricks, *Shakespeare's Emergent Form* (Logan, Utah, 1968), 64; and, on the trilogy, C. L. Barber and Richard P. Wheeler, *The Whole Journey* (Berkeley, 1986), 93–102. Cf. the strictures in the 1571 *Homilie against Disobedience and Wylfull Rebellion*.

64. Cf. Hall: "This conflict was in manner unnatural, for in it the son fought against the father, the brother against the brother, the nephew against the uncle, and the tenant against his lord" (*Union*, 256). See also *Gorboduc*, 5.2.180–233.

65. For the relationship between this scene and the two that frame it, see Rose, *Shakespearean Design*, 32–34.

66. Michael Neill compares the mirroring process in which the mother, in responding to the child, gives him back an image of himself and thus generates the basis for an identity. Neill argues that Richard, as dramatist and star performer, narcissistically plays roles and makes up "a false self to be the object of his consuming need for love," "Shakespeare's Halle of Mirrors: Play, Politics, and Psychology in *Richard III*," *Shakespeare Studies* 8 (1976): 99–129.

67. "I am come amongst you as you see, at this time, not for my recreation and disport, but being resolved, in the midst and heat of the battle, to live or die amongst you all, to lay down for my God, and for my kingdom, and for my people, my honour and my blood, even in the dust." The speech, which exists as a transcription by her chaplain, Dr. Lionel Sharp, was first printed in *Cabala: Mysteries of State and Government in Letters of Illustrious Persons* (London, 1654) and is quoted in Johnson, *Elizabeth I*, 320. For excerpts from Elizabeth's speeches in the Queen's manuscript version, see Allison Heisch, "Queen Elizabeth I: Parliamentary Rhetoric and the Exercise of Power," *Signs* 1 (1975): 31–55.

68. Hall reports that Henry VII sued to the pope to have Henry VI canonized but later dropped the matter because it was too costly (*Union*, 304). For the notion of opposed faces of monarchy, see Walter Benjamin: "In the baroque the tyrant and the martyr are but two faces of the monarch. They are the necessarily extreme incarnations of the princely essence. As far as the tyrant is

concerned, this is clear enough. The theory of sovereignty which takes as its example the special case in which dictatorial powers are unfolded, positively demands the completion of the image of the sovereign, as tyrant" (*The Origins of German Tragic Drama*, trans. John Osborne [London, 1977], 69). In pointing to the absolute self-determination associated with the tyrant, Benjamin's formulation describes Macbeth as well as Richard III.

69. Whereas the previous two plays delay generating the usurper fully (although he may earlier, as in *2 Henry VI*, announce his intent) until the final moments, *3 Henry VI* places that point further back in the narrative (3.2.123–95), a choice that permits full irony to this succession of comic signs.

70. At the probable time *3 Henry VI* was written and performed, the Queen was, of course, well past childbearing age.

71. Cf. Hall: "Because they had no enemies . . . [they] exercized cruelty against their own selves: and their proper blood embrued and polluted their own hands and members" (*Union*, 303).

72. The pertinent lines from *Dream* are as follows: "And the blots of Nature's hand / Shall not in their issue stand. / Never mole, harelip, nor scar, / Nor mark prodigious, such as are / Despised in nativity, / Shall upon their children be" (5.1.398–403). See also Louis Adrian Montrose, "Shaping Fantasies: Figurations of Gender and Power in Elizabethan Culture," *Representations* 1 (1983): 61–94.

73. From Elizabeth's Tilbury speech, quoted in Johnson, *Elizabeth I*, 320.

74. All three *Henry VI* plays have, of course, been individually produced, often in successive years, by repertory companies committed to staging "Shakespeare's Complete Works." However, even in such formats, tetralogy thinking prevails, for *Richard III* inevitably follows: the Oregon Shakespeare Festival, for example, staged all four plays in consecutive years from 1975 to 1979.

75. Not precisely true, for the San Francisco Repertory Company staged them in 1903 (Sally Beauman, *The Royal Shakespeare Company* [Oxford, 1982], 32–33). In 1889, Osmond Tearle presented *1 Henry VI*, primarily so that he could play Talbot. His performance text ends with a tableau formalizing the English-French peace treaty, concluding on a note of national prosperity to rewrite *1 Henry VI* as a forerunner of *Henry V*. Prompt copy at the Shakespeare Centre Library.

76. Sir Barry Jackson, "On Producing *Henry VI*," *Shakespeare Survey* 6 (1953): 51–52. Douglas Seale directed.

77. For the complete text, see John Barton in collaboration with Peter Hall, *The Wars of the Roses* (London, 1970). Prompt copy at the Shakespeare Centre Library.

78. Although not without precedent, as in the Quarto and Octavo titles for *2* and *3 Henry VI* as well as that for the 1619 combined text, *The Whole Contention between the Two Famous Houses, Lancaster and York*, Barton's title reflects a consciously modern historical unit. In titling individual plays, however, he conforms to the sixteenth-century chroniclers' natural division into Kings' reigns and to Shakespeare's own example. On ten occasions only,

the three were presented as a trilogy—a total playing time of nine hours and fifty-five minutes (Greenwald, *Directions by Indirections*, 55).

79. For an analysis of Barton's language, see my "*The Wars of the Roses*: Scholarship Speaks on the Stage," *Deutsche Shakespeare-Gesellschaft West Jahrbuch* (1972): 170–84.

80. Hall and Barton met at Cambridge in 1950 where Tillyard was a fellow at Jesus College and university lecturer when his *Shakespeare's History Plays* was first published in 1943.

81. Barton and Hall, *Wars*, x.

82. For Kott's reading of the histories, see Jan Kott, *Shakespeare, Our Contemporary*, trans. Boleslaw Taborski (1964); reprint, (New York, 1974), 3–55. Alan Sinfield puts *Wars* into a broader political context of what he calls "culturism," in "Royal Shakespeare: Theatre and the Making of Ideology," in *Political Shakespeare*, 158–81; for *Wars*, see especially 160–63. For an earlier appropriation of the *Henry VI* plays, see John Crowne's *The Misery of Civil War* (1681); Matthew H. Wikander discusses its adaptational politics in "The Spitted Infant: Scenic Emblem and Exclusionist Politics in Restoration Adaptations of Shakespeare," *Shakespeare Quarterly* 37 (1986): 340–49.

83. And, in terms of box office, the least popular of the three. Barton conjectures that because it had an unfamiliar title, audiences assumed that it was the most reworked (Barton and Hall, *Wars*, xvii).

84. See Scheman, "Missing Mothers/Desiring Daughters," 87. Repositioning the marriage achieves the formal integrity some of *1 Henry VI*'s critics, Cairncross among them, have wished for. See *King Henry VI, Part 1*, xlviii–lii.

85. Barton and Hall, *Wars*, xix.

86. See Sinfield, "Royal Shakespeare," 161.

87. F. R. Benson's restructuring chose a different, though equally conclusive, end point. The only extant prompt copy for his productions, that for *2 Henry VI* (1899), ends with Cade's escape from London and York's reconciliation with Henry (*2 Henry VI*, 4.8). Although Benson's ending does preserve the compromised resolution that characterizes closure in each of Shakespeare's *Henry VI* plays, his strategy seems designed to mask Cade's threat and to protect and enforce Henry's authority rather than his weakness. Presumably, his reworked *3 Henry VI* opened with some version of the St. Albans battle. Prompt copy at the Shakespeare Centre Library.

88. Cf. *Richard III*, 1.1.5–8: "Now are our brows bound with victorious wreaths, / Our bruised arms hung up for monuments, / Our stern alarums changed to merry meetings, / Our dreadful marches to delightful measures."

89. Barton and Hall, *Wars*, xii–xiii.

90. Ibid., xxiv.

91. Ibid., xiv.

92. Barton writes, "The long period during which I have lived with the texts, in the rehearsal room, and in performance, leaves me increasingly doubtful whether the *Henry VI*s are wholly by Shakespeare. More crucially, I believe

that the form in which they have come down to us in the Folio represents the adaptation and partial revision of some earlier texts . . . undertaken by Shakespeare to make them part of a cycle which was completed by his *Richard III*" (Barton and Hall, *Wars*, xiii).

93. Prompt copies at the Shakespeare Centre Library. Two articles have been helpful in interpreting prompt copy evidence: Homer D. Swander, "The Rediscovery of *Henry VI*," *Shakespeare Quarterly* 29 (1978): 146–63, and David Daniell, "Opening Up the Text: Shakespeare's *Henry VI* Plays in Performance," in *Themes in Drama 1: Drama and Society*, ed. James Redmond (Cambridge, 1979), 247–78. See also G. K. Hunter, "The Royal Shakespeare Company Plays *Henry VI*," in *Renaissance Drama*, n.s. 9, ed. Leonard Barkan (1978): 91–108.

94. Quoted in Swander, "Rediscovery," 149–50.

95. Quoted in Swander, "Rediscovery," 148. Hands's performance texts do not include any of the Quarto variants noted earlier; the New Penguin edition was used for the prompt copy.

96. For example, the Dauphin in *1 Henry VI* and Cade in *2 Henry VI* were doubled, and one actor played a number of minor roles throughout—Falstaff, Woodville, Sheriff, Mayor, Whitmore, Iden, and Hastings.

97. As with *Wars*, all three parts were presented on the same day several times during the run, both in Stratford and in London. In addition, rather than presenting *Richard III*—which Hands had twice directed, therefore bringing to the *Henry VI* project an informed awareness of its relationships to the others—the company broke the tradition of offering that play as the obvious conclusion of a tetralogy. Instead, they implicitly created a new tetralogy by reviving Hands's 1975 *Henry V* in the same season's repertory. Alan Howard played both Henry V and Henry VI. Hands comments: "I think that the son is truly the son of Henry V, and in a sense should be played by the same actor. . . . The boy who develops has all his father's vision finally, and perception of what should be done, but lacks his father's physicality and the ability to carry it out by war, by the system that exists. That practicality in *Henry V*—the ability to use the system to improve the system—is something that Henry VI just doesn't possess" (quoted in Swander, "Rediscovery," 156).

98. Quoted in Swander, "Rediscovery," 150.

99. Michael Billington, referring both to the bridge and the bare, empty stage space, called Farrah's set design "the aircraft carrier stage" (*Guardian*, 15 July 1977).

100. Cf. staging conventions in the Noh drama, where upstage positions represent the past, midstage positions the present, and downstage the future.

101. Both quotations are from Daniell, "Opening Up the Text," 270–71.

102. Daniell, "Opening Up the Text," 271.

103. Contradicting what I read as an effort to generate a conclusive ending for *3 Henry VI*, both Irving Wardle (*Times*, 15 July 1977) and B. A. Young (*Financial Times*, 15 July 1977) wished for *Richard III* to complete the tetralogy. Wardle felt that Hands's performance text ended inconclusively: "the

piece gathers in irrepressible momentum toward the missing finale"; he found the lack especially frustrating because Anton Lesser's Richard seemed so promising.

104. Quoted in Swander, "Rediscovery," 149.

105. In a September 1988 interview, Bogdanov said that he thought the places to break the plays were fairly obvious.

106. Bogdanov had staged *The Henrys* (*1* and *2 Henry IV* and *Henry V*) in 1987; *Richard II*, the *Henry VIs*, and *Richard III* were added to the 1987 *The Henrys* in 1988. See Michael Bogdanov and Michael Pennington, *The English Shakespeare Company* (London, 1990).

107. See Pierre Bourdieu, *Distinction*, trans. Richard Nice (Cambridge, Mass., 1984), 22–26.

108. Since the production was still playing in London in early 1990, I have not been able to examine prompt copies, nor can I report further on Wood's abbreviated stay with the company. See, however, William Shakespeare, *The Plantagenets* (London, 1989), and Noble's Introduction, vii–xv.

109. See Meisel, *Realizations*, 29–30.

110. Coveney, *Financial Times*, 24 October 1988; Ratcliffe, *Observer*, 30 October 1988.

111. Richard Edmonds, "A Haunting, Horrifying Marathon," *Birmingham Evening Mail*, 24 October 1988.

112. Hilary DeVries, *Christian Science Monitor*, 3 June 1988.

113. From Bogdanov's comments made in a September 1989 interview.

114. Quoted in *Festival Focus*, publicity materials for Chicago's International Theatre Festival, 1988.

115. As in Jameson's title, "Postmodernism, or The Cultural Logic of Late Capitalism," *New Left Review* 146 (July–August 1984): 53–92; for material quoted, see 58, 65–66, 68.

116. See Fredric Jameson, "On Magic Realism in Film," *Critical Inquiry* 12, no. 2 (Winter 1986): 303.

117. Jameson, "Postmodernism," 68, 75.

118. Prompt copy at the offices of the English Shakespeare Company. In January 1989, *House of Lancaster* was one of several that were available.

119. Cf. Stephen Orgel's comments on effeminization in "Nobody's Perfect: Or Why Did the English Stage Take Boys for Women?" *South Atlantic Quarterly* 88, no. 1 (Winter 1989): 7–29.

120. Hall, *Union*, 204.

121. Wardle, "National Family at War," *Times*, 24 October 1988.

122. DeVries, *Christian Science Monitor*, 3 June 1988.

123. Robert Gore Langton, "The Plantagenets," *Plays and Players* 422 (November/December 1988): 36.

124. Michael Billington, *Guardian*, 23 March 1987.

125. Michael Billington, "Bloodstains over Eden," *Guardian*, 24 October 1988.

126. John Peter, "Outright Winners in the Game of Politics," *Sunday Times*, 30 October 1988.

127. Bourdieu, *Distinction*, 3.

128. Stewart McGill, "Battle on Waterloo Road," *Plays and Players* 425 (March 1989): 16.

CHAPTER 4
"THE COMING ON OF TIME": *RICHARD III*

1. For the quote from More, see *History*, 83. On the relations between kingship and playing, see Kastan, "Proud Majesty Made a Subject," 459–75. For a different view of subversion, see Greenblatt, "Invisible Bullets," 21–64.

2. For a pertinent discussion of More, see Stephen Greenblatt, *Renaissance Self-Fashioning from More to Shakespeare* (Chicago, 1980), 11–73. See also Elizabeth Story Donno, "Thomas More and Richard III," *Renaissance Quarterly* 35 (1982): 401–47.

3. My title echoes Brecht's *The Resistible Rise of Arturo Ui*, in which Ui is compared to Richard III in the introductory prologue to the play and which contains a scene (scene 6) where Ui takes speech and movement lessons from a Shakespearean actor. First performed in 1941, Ui is clearly meant to be Adolph Hitler. Bertolt Brecht, *Collected Plays*, ed. Ralph Manheim and John Willett (New York, 1976), vol. 6.

4. Prompt copy at the Shakespeare Centre Library. I borrow, and revise, the description of Alexander's performance text from my "Parallel Practices," 63.

5. Alexander's interval point reflects an unusual choice. Most prompt copies I have examined—Royal Shakespeare Company 1953, 1963, 1970, and 1980—observe the interval after 3.7, as did Adrian Noble's *Richard III, His Death* for the Royal Shakespeare Company's 1988 *Plantagenets*. Michael Bogdanov's 1988 *Wars of the Roses' Richard III* positioned the interval to follow Hastings's (onstage) execution, his throat slit by Ratcliffe (3.4).

6. For the significance of such mockery, see Bakhtin, *Rabelais and His World*, 303–67. For Alexander's coronation scene, see also Antony Sher, *Year of the King* (London, 1985), 214–15; R. Chris Hassel, "Context and Charisma: The Sher-Alexander *Richard III* and Its Reviewers," *Shakespeare Quarterly* 36 (1985): 630–43; and S. P. Cerasano, "Churls Just Wanna Have Fun: Reviewing *Richard III*," *Shakespeare Quarterly* 36 (1985): 618–29.

7. The function of this speech as both Prologue and opening soliloquy and its relationship to conventions familiar from the morality play and from Marlowe's *Jew of Malta* require no further rehearsal. But the speech also draws on several conventions of ending: a recapitulation of the past wars that Richard contrasts to a weak and "feminized" time of peace and, perhaps, a trace remembrance of Hall's eccentric closural feature, the description of the King that ends each chronicle reign. Since physical descriptions of Richard occur elsewhere in both the chroniclers' accounts and Shakespeare's play, I do not mean to turn *Richard III*'s unique opening strategy into an epigraph-epitaph or to

stress the equation with Hall but simply to suggest that, like the *Henry VI* plays, this one conflates signs of ending with those of beginning.

8. On Elizabethan spectacle, see, for instance, Stephen Orgel, *The Illusion of Power* (Berkeley, 1975). The notion of cultural production driven by images or simulacra constitutes one of the focal points in the debate on defining postmodernism. See Andreas Huyssen, "Mapping the Postmodern," *New German Critique* 33 (1984): 5–52; and Fredric Jameson, "Postmodernism," 53–92.

9. From *A Speech, as It Was Delivered in the Upper House of the Parliament to the Lords Spiritual and Temporal, and to the Knights, Citizens and Burgesses There Assembled*, Monday, 19 March 1603, in *The Political Works of James I*, ed. Charles Howard McIlwain (1616; reprint, Cambridge, Mass., 1918), 271.

10. Indeed, James I fashioned himself after Richmond to the extent that he gave orders that he be buried in his tomb (David M. Bergeron, *Shakespeare's Romances and the Royal Family* [Lawrence, Kans., 1985], 41, quoting Antonia Fraser's biography of James).

11. Cf. Johnson, *Elizabeth I*, 1–2. For a discussion of the pamphleteers, such as Edward Gosynhill (*The Schole house of Women*, 1541) and John Knox (*The First Blast of the Trumpet Against the Monstrous Regiment of Women*, 1558), who railed at women's faults and at their inability to govern, see Joan Gadol Kelly, "Early Feminist Theory and the *Querelle des Femmes*, 1400–1789," in *Women, History, and Theory* (Chicago, 1984), 65–109.

12. For an account of James I's representational strategies, see Goldberg, *James I*, especially 17–55, 85–112.

13. Such retextualizings tend to be distributed into two polar camps and a growing middle ground. For Tillyard, *Richard III*'s "main end is to show the working-out of God's will in English history . . . [and] to complete the national tetralogy"; in his view, Richmond's speech represents Shakespeare's "official self" (*Shakespeare's History Plays*, 208, 214). Kott's totally opposite, though equally transparent, vision sees the operations of a ruthlessly deterministic machine of state power inhabited first by Richard and then by Richmond (*Shakespeare, Our Contemporary*, especially 9–11). A. P. Rossiter, however, argues that *Richard III* is not contained by the Tudor ideal and that an "overall system of paradox is the play's unity . . . [and this] is revealed as a constant displaying of inversions, or reversals of meaning," in "Angel with Horns: The Unity of *Richard III*," in *Angel with Horns and Other Shakespeare Lectures*, ed. Graham Storey (New York, 1961), 20. Rossiter's view is supported and extended by Wilbur Sanders and A. L. French, though none of the three fully explores the implications of what might be called unsatisfactory providentialist closure: Sanders, *Dramatist and the Received Idea*, 72–120; French, "The World of *Richard III*," *Shakespeare Studies* 4 (1968): 25–39. Nicholas Brooke attempts to account for the problem in formal terms, pointing to how Shakespeare's play not only accommodates two essentially comic structures but requires them, mounting a dialectic between history and tragedy as radically contrasted ideas of value in *Shakespeare's Early Tragedies* (London, 1968),

50–52. Kastan labels *Richard III* a romance in *Shakespeare and the Shapes of Time*, 132–33. More recently, Barber and Wheeler extend Rossiter's notion of geological fault to view this pull in two directions as a stress in the play that exchanges "fully-dramatized, secular, family-based determinants of action for ritual and sacred, ceremonial causality" (*Whole Journey*, 115). See also Richard P. Wheeler, "History, Character and Conscience in *Richard III*," *Comparative Drama* 5 (1971–1972): 301–21; Kristian Smidt further explores Rossiter's notion of "geological faults" in *Unconformities in Shakespeare's History Plays* (Atlantic Highlands, N.J., 1982).

14. I make no attempt to place these variants within a full bibliographical context. For a cogent and convincing rebuttal of the bases of modern editorial practice, which has disordered *Richard III*'s two texts into one "eclectic, synthetic assembly," conflating Folio and Quarto versions, see Steven Urkowitz, "Reconsidering the Relationship of Quarto and Folio Texts of *Richard III*," *English Literary Renaissance* 16 (1986): 442–46. Urkowitz offers a "model of *Richard III* as a work in progress, an early state in the Quarto, a later state in the Folio" (458).

15. Barber and Wheeler, *Whole Journey*, 123.

16. Perhaps even more curiously, critical discourse on these scenes refuses this potentially feminized attachment, preferring to remain under Richard's spell—or that of Richmond's promise—so that the majority read the women's presences as a reactive mechanism that deepens the role of curse and prophecy or, in the case of the second wooing scene (4.4), as a digressive parallel to Richard's wooing of Anne. See also Marcus, *Puzzling Shakespeare*, 94.

17. Elsewhere in the scene (TLN 2471–85), Folio stresses both the family bonds and the hierarchical relations among the women and so points the reversal of their positions of power.

18. Prompt copy at the Shakespeare Centre Library.

19. See Barton and Hall, *Wars*, scene 66. *Wars* cut the later conversation between Stanley and Christopher Urswick concerning Stanley's willingness to support Richmond but also mentions the difficulty of his position, since Richard holds his son hostage (4.5). Another result of the new coda is that it prevents the scene from ending with Elizabeth's plea and so stresses male action and feminine helplessness.

20. Prompt copies at the Shakespeare Centre Library.

21. Prompt copy at the Shakespeare Centre Library.

22. Barber and Wheeler, *Whole Journey*, 105. "We have seen the historical Richard inventing witches in fastening on the Queen and Mistress Shore his sense that he is bewitched. Shakespeare invents Margaret as a real woman to play this witch's role" (105).

23. Cf. Harold F. Brooks, " 'Richard III': Unhistorical Amplifications: The Women's Scenes and Seneca," *Modern Language Review* 75 (1980): 722. Brooks reads this scene, as well as Anne's wooing (1.2), as an expansion of Seneca's *Troades*: he works out a system of correspondences between the women in Seneca's playtext and Shakespeare's that equates the Duchess of

York with Hecuba, Queen Elizabeth with Andromache, Edward with Astyanax, Anne with Polyxena, and Iphigenia and Margaret with Helen of Troy. He also mentions *Hercules Furens* and *Hippolytus* as specific influences (725–37).

24. In the scene's initial sequence, the women's litany against Richard, Quarto and Folio again describe slightly different dynamics. Quarto (I_3^v; I_4^r) stresses the separation of Queen Elizabeth and the Duchess of York, each locked in her own thought, suppressing the Duchess's voice to focus on Elizabeth's woes. Folio (TLN 2780–2829), however, not only weights their verbal power equally but heightens its antiphonal patterning by alternating regularly between the two, by increasing Margaret's punctuating asides, and by emphasizing a progression in their thought that moves from the specific to the general, from private to public woes. What develops from the women's recital of their losses has been read by Madonne M. Miner as women aiding women, enabling them to cope with their situation and, eventually, to successfully counter Richard's use of women as currency, a success Miner ascribes to their "humanity," in " 'Neither Mother, Wife, nor England's Queen': The Roles of Women in *Richard III*," in *The Woman's Part*, ed. Carolyn Ruth Swift Lenz, Gayle Greene, and Carol Thomas Neely (Urbana, 1980), 48, 52.

25. Cf. Barber and Wheeler, *Whole Journey*, 86, 102–13. Although at first resisting the idea that what Richard did derived from "being hated by Mom," Antony Sher finally based his 1984 Richard on precisely that relationship. See *Year of the King*, 129–30. See also Miner, " 'Neither Mother, Wife, nor England's Queen,' " 51.

26. Indeed, such exclusion defines the shape of what is included. Cf. Babcock, *Reversible World*, 15.

27. Citations are from the version of *Richardus Tertius* reproduced in Bullough, *Narrative and Dramatic Sources*, 3:311–12; see also 236–37. See also R. Chris Hassel, Jr., *Songs of Death* (Lincoln, Neb., 1987), 72.

28. Citations are from *True Tragedy*, scenes xiii–xv, reproduced and summarized in Bullough, *Narrative and Dramatic Sources*, 3:330–34. Bullough labels *Richardus Tertius* an analogue and *True Tragedy* a probable source.

29. Hall, *Union*, 391. See also Ralph A. Griffiths and Roger S. Thomas, *The Making of the Tudor Dynasty* (New York, 1985), 89–109.

30. Hall, *Union*, 406. In allying her behavior to that of all women, Hall voices a common assumption. See, for example, Linda Woodbridge, *Women and the English Renaissance* (Urbana, 1984), especially 281–82, and Catherine Belsey, *The Subject of Tragedy* (London, 1985), 184–91.

31. Elizabeth's hesitations in decision making became legendary; see, for example, Johnson, *Elizabeth I*, 134–38.

32. Hall's Richard "abstained both from the bed and company of [Anne]," complaining of her "infortunate sterility and barrenness"; he sought to approach Elizabeth only after Anne's death, even then deferring the matter "because all men, and the maiden herself most of all, detested and abhorred this unlawful and in manner unnatural copulation" (*Union*, 407). Given Richard's habit of displacing his own faults onto others, especially women, as well as the

play's stress on generation, that Shakespeare did not exploit the hint about Anne's sterility may be designed to protect the reigning Queen Elizabeth I's failure to provide an heir. For a rebuttal of the hearsay that it was Elizabeth's own sterility that caused her to avoid marriage, see Johnson, *Elizabeth I*, 109–13.

33. In a discussion of Fletcher's *Love's Cure*, Jonathan Dollimore points out that Vitelli "presents masculine desire as spectacle, . . . narcissistically demanding confirmation of an audience even as he also conceives his masculinity as spontaneous, autonomous desire" ("Subjectivity, Sexuality, and Transgression," 75). Richard, too, requires confirmation, from a largely female audience.

34. The first of these variants is also pertinent, since it seems designed to further adjust the chronicler's perspective of Elizabeth as forgetting her sons' murder. While Quarto provides only three brief references to the murder (K_2^v; K_2^r; K_3^r; cf. Pelican, 4.4.220–21, 271–73, 384–85), the Folio-only passage (TLN 3001–14) not only gives Elizabeth a sustained speech centered on them but also endows her with Margaret-like language. Antony Hammond claims that because the speech takes up Margaret's tone, it is out of place (*King Richard III* [London, 1981], 334n). But this is precisely the point: Elizabeth has asked Margaret to teach her how to curse, and this speech demonstrates the result, and the powerlessness, of such words at this point in the action.

35. Emrys Jones argues similarly that this "time loop" in the narrative concerns the only dimension of time not tainted by Richard's presence, what he finally swears by in order to appease Elizabeth—"the time to come" (*Origins*, 224–25).

36. In the gallery at Whitehall, Elizabeth I concluded a speech that was intended to forestall legislation concerning the succession with these words: "And so I assure you all that, though after my death you may have many stepdames, yet shall you never have a more natural mother than I mean to be unto you all" (quoted in Johnson, *Elizabeth I*, 134).

37. In comparison, Hands retained thirty-six lines (1970) and forty (1980); Alexander used twenty-six lines.

38. For Hall's justification, see Barton and Hall, *Wars*, xxii.

39. Barton and Hall, *Wars*, scenes 71 and 74.

40. Certainly Stanley's delay conforms to historical fact; recent historians describe his last-minute intervention on Richmond's behalf as the crucial factor that lost Bosworth's battle for Richard. See Griffiths and Thomas, *Making of the Tudor Dynasty*, 159–65. For a descriptive reconstruction of the battle, see D. T. Williams, *The Battle of Bosworth, 22 August 1485* (Leicester, 1973).

41. In addition to the variants I discuss, in Quarto, Buckingham's penultimate line, "Come, sirs, convey me to the block of shame," suggests an ironic awareness of illegality similar to Richard II's at the end of the Parliament scene: "O, good! Convey? Conveyers are you all, / That rise thus numbly by a true king's fall" (*Richard II*, 4.1.317–28). In Folio, Buckingham's "Come, lead

me, officers, to the block of shame" (TLN 3400) suppresses that potential irony.

42. Prompt copies at the Shakespeare Centre Library.

43. More, *History*, 96.

44. Judith H. Anderson, *Biographical Truth* (New Haven, 1984), 105–6.

45. For more substantive (voiced) proof of Richmond's legitimacy, it is necessary to reach back to Henry VI's prophetic blessing of the young Richmond (*3 Henry VI*, 4.6.68–76).

46. In representing the battle as a single, continuous scene, both Quarto and Folio privilege a simultaneity denied by present-day editorial practice, which divides the play's last sequence into discrete scenes. For a pertinent discussion of doubling, see Neill, "Shakespeare's Halle of Mirrors," 99–130.

47. Quarto (L$_3$^{v}; L$_3$^{r}) positions Richmond's as well as Richard's requests for ink and paper at the end of their preliminary orders to their men; while Richmond invites his officers into his tent, Richard orders Ratcliffe and the others to leave him. Folio, however, in repositioning Richmond's request for ink and paper and the three subsequent lines concerning his battle plan to follow his initial order to Sir William Brandon to bear his standard (TLN 3458–65), deepens the sense of community among Richmond and his soldiers. Cf. Pelican, 5.3.19–79.

48. On these references, see R. Chris Hassel, Jr., "Last Words and Last Things: St. John, Apocalypse, and Eschatology," *Shakespeare Studies* 18 (1986): 25–40.

49. Quarto and Folio prescribe different orders for the Ghosts' entrances: while Quarto's order (L$_4$^{v}; L$_4$^{r}; M$_1$^{v}) seems random, Folio (TLN 3561–3625) positions the Ghosts in the order in which they were killed. Since neither text indicates that each Ghost exits after speaking, the impression is of a steadily accumulating weight of past history.

50. For readings placing this speech in a psychological context, see Berry, *Patterns of Decay*, 98–101, and Barber and Wheeler, *Whole Journey*, 110. In a discussion of kinship, Keith Wrightson argues that, although surnames were passed patrilineally, the kinship system was not patrilineal but ego-centered, "pivoting on the individual who traced kin outwards from himself" (*English Society, 1580–1680* [New Brunswick, N.J., 1982], 46). Although Wrightson's discussion focuses on local communities and not on royal kinship relations, his findings seem equally pertinent to Richard's ego-centered sense of self.

51. For a discussion that positions both battle orations within the context of handbooks on military oratory, see R. Chris Hassel, Jr., "Military Oratory in *Richard III*," *Shakespeare Quarterly* 35 (1984): 53–61. Hassel concludes that Richmond's speech conforms precisely to the advice given in such manuals for heroic speeches and that, by comparison, Richard's speech is poorly constructed as well as dull.

52. Some editions elide this sign, changing "mother" to "brother"; for a rationale, see Hammond, *King Richard III*, 326n.

53. In contrast, Quarto's stage direction calls for a continuous rush of action

and omits the Flourish: "Alarum, Enter Richard and Richmond, they fight, Richard is slain then retreat being sounded. Enter Richmond, Derby, bearing the crown, with other Lords, etc." (M₃ᵛ). In an analysis of *Richard III*'s two-phased structure, Alan C. Dessen conjectures a staging of this fight stressing its morality elements (*Shakespeare and the Late Moral Plays* [Lincoln, Neb., 1986], 53–54).

54. William Hazlitt, *Complete Works*, ed. P. P. Howe (1930–34; reprint, New York, 1967), 5:182. James H. Hackett's prompt copy records the directions for the fight: "Fights furiously back and forth—in turning loose [*sic*] balance, falls on his knee and fights up—in turning receives Richmond's thrust—lunges at him feebly after it—clenchy is shoved from him—stagger—drops the sword—grasps blindly at him.—Stagger backward and falls head to R. H.— turns upon R side—writhes, rests on his hands—gnashes his teeth at him (L. H.)—as he utters his last words—blinks and expires rolling on his back" (from the facsimile prompt copy of *Richard III*, ed. Alan S. Downer [London, 1959]). Hackett uses the 1822 Oxberry edition, Colley Cibber's adaptation, in which Richard dies with these words: "But let one spirit of the First-born Cain / Reign in all bosoms, that each heart being set / On bloody Actions, the rude Scene may end, / And darkness be the Burier of the Dead" (5.9.17–20).

55. Leigh Hunt's description of Kean's death said: "The crowning point was the look he gave Richmond, after receiving the mortal blow. . . . He stood looking the other in the face, as if he was already a disembodied spirit, searching him with the eyes of another world; or as if he silently cursed him with some new scorn, to which death and its dreadful knowledge had given him a right" (*British Stage and Literary Cabinet* 4, no. 35 [November 1819]: 55). And even when the Richard III is Shakespeare's rather than Cibber's, the spectator remains fixed on the physical and imaginative reality of the actor's performance. James Agate, writing of Robert Atkins's Richard (Old Vic, 1923), praises the lord who, in offering Richmond the crown, "bent his head as he did so towards the dead body of Richard. 'You lost,' that gesture seemed to say, 'but you were the bigger man!' " (*The Contemporary Theatre, 1923* [1924; reprint, New York, 1969], 77–78).

56. For Cibber's text, see Christopher Spencer, *Five Restoration Adaptations of Shakespeare* (Urbana, 1965), 275–344. For a compilation of details from various performance texts, see *Richard III*, ed. Julie Hankey, Plays in Performance (Totowa, N.J., 1981), 247–50. See also the brief stage history in Hammond, *King Richard III*, 71.

57. For a reading of the entire film, see Jack Jorgens, *Shakespeare on Film* (Bloomington, 1977), 136–47. John Gielgud plays Clarence and Ralph Richardson Buckingham; somewhat disturbingly, Olivier's casting permits him to "kill" his two great rival actors.

58. Hall, *Union*, 421.

59. The opening credits read: "The history of the world, like letters without poetry, flowers without perfume, or thought without imagination, would be a dry matter indeed without its legends, and many of these, though scorned by

proof a hundred times, seem worth presenting for their own familiar sakes."
The inscription silently acknowledges More, Cibber, and others, as well as,
perhaps, appeasing members of the Richard III Society.

60. See Barton and Hall, *Wars*. Prompt copy at the Shakespeare Centre Library.

61. Trewin, *Birmingham Post*, 21 August 1963.

62. Levin, *Daily Mail*, 21 August 1963.

63. Less conventionally, in a reading that undermines Richmond's claims
for peace and union, Jan Kott describes a 1960 Warsaw performance text
that gave the ending an even more deterministic slant. Jacek Woszczerowicz,
playing Richard as a clown who saw the world as a gigantic buffoonery, was
finally butchered like a pig. "Rows of bars are lowered from above. Henry VII
speaks of peace, forgiveness, justice. And suddenly he gives a crowing sound
like Richard's, and, for a second, the same sort of grimace twists his face. The
bars are being lowered. The face of the new king is radiant again" (*Shakespeare, Our Contemporary*, 55). Sturua's 1979 performance text for the Rustaveli Company visualized the fight as a symbolic struggle for the land itself:
Richard's and Richmond's heads poked through holes in a huge painted map
of England as they lunged at each other with enormous swords, and Richard
died, finally, away from the map, dispossessed. In yet another symbolic staging, the Richmond in Michael Bogdanov's 1979 Young Vic production, who
was costumed as a leftist guerilla leader, brought on a real pig's head, placed
it on a stand, and halved it with a cleaver. See Hankey, *Richard III*, 248–49.

64. Prompt copy at the Shakespeare Centre Library.

65. Wardle, *Times*, 16 April 1970.

66. Prompt copy at the Shakespeare Centre Library. I draw from Miriam
Gilbert's description of a December 1980 performance.

67. Prompt copy at the Shakespeare Centre Library.

68. Alexander's original notion was to have the full cast onstage at the close,
setting up a structural rhyme with the coronation (Sher, *Year of the King*, 234).

69. With all knowledge transformed into bits of information, it therefore
potentially can be reconstructed in a new order that erases the "historical moment" and instead absorbs it into a seamless "present time" where all is simultaneously present. See Schechner, "Collective Reflexivity," 55.

70. See Meisel, *Realizations*, 29–30.

71. *Calendar of Letters, Dispatches, and State Papers of England and Spain*
(London, 1862), 11 January 1500.

72. I reproduce the Arden punctuation, which more closely resembles Folio,
rather than that in Pelican, which includes five exclamation points and does
not separate the penultimate and final lines of the speech with a period.

73. In his exhaustive commentary, Wolfgang Clemen notes that *Richard III*
purposefully isolates the opposition between Richard and Richmond and the
replacement of one with the other by rearranging the conventional closural
signals associated with tragedy. Rather than directing a final crowd scene, ending with a ceremonial funeral march, the play substitutes the Ghosts' earlier

appearance, displacing these elements but retaining their potentially closural function. Other features are suppressed or, like the epitaph for the dead, occur only in truncated form: "the bloody dog is dead," a partial line that, in echoing Margaret's label for Richard, constitutes one final sign of her presence, eerily voiced by Richmond (*A Commentary on Shakespeare's Richard III*, trans. Jean Bonheim [London, 1968], 200–203, 235.

74. White, "The Value of Narrativity in the Representation of Reality," in *On Narrative*, ed. W.J.T. Mitchell (Chicago, 1981), 20.

75. For this detail (which I missed), my thanks to Lynda E. Boose and Samuel Crowl.

CHAPTER 5
"IF I TURN MINE EYES UPON MYSELF": *RICHARD II*

1. Elizabeth was not unaware of the pattern that connected her to Richard II as a monarch whose "unprofitable counsellors" led to his fall "from the high glory of fortune's wheel into extreme misery and miserable calamity." As early as 1578, her kinsman Sir Francis Knollys predicted her overthrow unless she gave up her favorite, Leicester, and subjected her will and affections to good counsel, for "who will not rather shrinkingly . . . play the parts of King Richard the Second's men then to enter into the odious office of crossing her Majesty's will? . . . And then King Richard the Second's men will flock into court apace, and will show themselves in their colors" (Thomas Wright, *Queen Elizabeth and Her Times* [London, 1838], vol. 2, part 1, 75–76, quoted in Campbell, *Shakespeare's Histories*, 173). For an account of other texts that drew further analogies between the Queen's policies and those during Richard's reign deemed "inconvenient" and "insolent" by chroniclers, see Campbell, 170–91. More recently, E. W. Ives explores the connections between Shakespeare's play and the Essex rebellion in "Shakespeare and History: Divergencies and Agreements," *Shakespeare Survey* 38 (1985): 19–35.

2. For these facts as well as a discussion of the controversy over whether the performed play was or was not Shakespeare's, see *King Richard II*, ed. Peter Ure (London, 1954), lvii–lxii. Chambers reports that "up to a point, players had a fairly free hand even with contemporary events. . . . They might mock at foreign potentates, if they did not, as was sometimes the case, embarrass Elizabeth's diplomacy in so doing." Chambers refers to performances, one in Brussels and one in Antwerp, late in Elizabeth's reign (1598), in which she was mocked at a dumbshow. It was not until 1624 that James I's anger provoked a "standing order against the representation of any 'modern Christian King' " (*Elizabethan Stage*, 1:327).

3. The entire conversation is printed in John Nichols, *The Progresses and Public Processions of Queen Elizabeth* (London, 1823; reprint, New York, 1966), 3:552–53. Lambarde's recent biographer reads the incident as revealing Elizabeth's need to confide in somone and as a sign of Lambarde's loyalty to the Queen (Wilbur Dunkel, *William Lambarde, Elizabethan Jurist, 1536–1601* [New Brunswick, 1965], 178). In a letter to James VI dated 30 April

1601, Elizabeth responds to his congratulations for having survived a revolt in which some historians have implicated him: "And where they have congratulated us from you [on] our happy prevention of the late treasonable attempts, the suppression whereof, praised be God, fell out to be only *opus unius diei*, we do accept in very good part that kind office from you, and requite you with this good wish, that the like may either never befall you or at least be as easily passed over; that being utterly extinguished in twelve hours which was in hatching diverse years" (*Letters of Elizabeth and James VI of Scotland*, ed. John Bruce [London, 1849], 136). For an important "alternative" reading of the traditional narrative, see Leeds Barroll, "A New History for Shakespeare and His Time," *Shakespeare Quarterly* 39 (1988): 441–64.

4. "Queen Elizabeth is the chosen and beloved of God, which from heaven, by his providence over her . . . He hath demonstrably shown. . . . The which denieth his duty to the visible God, his Prince and Sovereign, cannot perform his duty to God invisible" (*A Sermon*, quoted in Mervyn James, "At a Crossroads of the Political Culture: The Essex Revolt, 1601," in *Society, Politics, and Culture: Studies in Early Modern England* [Cambridge, 1986], 445–46).

5. A proclamation issued by Elizabeth in 1559 orders that no plays be permitted "wherein either matters of religion or of the gouernaunce of the estate of the common weale shalbe handled or treated, beyng no meete matters to be wrytten or treated upon, but by menne of aucthoritie, learning and wisedome, nor to be handled before any audience, but of graue and discreete persons" (quoted in Chambers, *Elizabethan Stage*, 4:263).

6. James, "At a Crossroads," 452.

7. For a full discussion of these pageants, see Roy Strong, *The Cult of Elizabeth* (London, 1977), 129–63.

8. See Strong, *Cult of Elizabeth*, especially 14–55.

9. Walter Bourchier Devereux, *Lives and Letters of the Devereux, Earls of Essex, in the Reigns of Elizabeth, James I, and Charles I* (London, 1853), 2: 99; letter dated 12 May 1600.

10. James, "At a Crossroads," 452–53. See also Richard C. McCoy, " 'A Dangerous Image': The Earl of Essex and Elizabethan Chivalry," *Journal of Medieval and Renaissance Studies* 13, no. 2 (1983): 313–29.

11. Quoted in Devereux, *Lives and Letters*, 2:89.

12. For the classical discussion of the problem of divine right in relation to Shakespeare's *Richard II*, see Kantorowicz, *King's Two Bodies*, 24–41.

13. See Holderness, *Shakespeare's History*, 64.

14. Devereux, *Lives and Letters*, 1:501. Cf. Bolingbroke's words in *Richard II*, 2.3.113–36; 3.1.22–27. For Carlisle's answering warning, see 4.1.114–49.

15. From *A Journal of All that Was Accomplished by Monsieur de Mausse, Ambassador in England from King Henry IV to Queen Elizabeth, A.D. 1597*, trans. G. B. Harrison (London, 1931), 114, quoted in James, "At a Crossroads," 444. For a full discussion of the "tension between the male self-assertiveness of honour, and the fact of female rule," see James, 442–46. In *Richard II* performance texts such as that for the Shakespeare Memorial Theatre in

1951, where Richard is represented as distinctly effeminate, the dynamic of this gender myth continues to be put into play. For a discussion of "gender identity," see Dianne Ferris, "Elizabeth I and Richard II: Portraits in 'Masculine' and 'Feminine' Princes," *International Journal of Women's Studies* 4 (1981): 10–18.

16. James, "At a Crossroads," 417, 455–59.

17. See, for example, Tillyard, *Shakespeare's History Plays*, 244–64; John Palmer, *Political Characters of Shakespeare* (1945; reprint, London, 1961), 65–117; Ribner, *English History Play*, 155–92; M. M. Reese, *The Cease of Majesty* (New York, 1961), 225–59; Brooke, *Shakespeare's Early Tragedies*, 107–37; Sanders, *Dramatist and the Received Idea*, 158–93; James Winny, *The Player King* (New York, 1968), 48–85; Ornstein, *Kingdom for a Stage*, 102–24; Moody E. Prior, *The Drama of Power* (Evanston, 1973), 139–82; and Manheim, *Dilemma*, 53–65 .

18. For readings that explain the loss of a particular "world" of resonant correspondences, either through aestheticizing Foucault's notions of order or by focusing on metadrama or issues of language and genre, see Wilders, *Lost Garden*, 82–86, 106–9, 135–37; James L. Calderwood, *Metadrama in Shakespeare's Henriad* (Berkeley, 1979), 10–29; Joseph A. Porter, *The Drama of Speech Acts* (Berkeley, 1979), 11–51; Marion Trousdale, *Shakespeare and the Rhetoricians* (Chapel Hill, 1982), especially 66–73; and H. R. Coursen, *The Leasing Out of England* (Washington, D.C., 1982), 15–98.

19. See, for instance, Greenblatt, introduction to *Power of Forms*, 4, and Jonathan Dollimore, "Introduction: Shakespeare, Cultural Materialism, and the New Historicism," in Dollimore and Sinfield, *Political Shakespeare*, 8.

20. "At the Play—*King Richard II* at His Majesty's Theatre," *Lady's Pictorial*, 19 September 1903. For a full description of Tree's production, see Kachur, *Herbert Beerbohm Tree*, 531–60.

21. Prompt copy in the Beerbohm Tree Collection, the University of Bristol Theatre Collection.

22. I borrow Ure's phrase (*Richard II*, lxxix). A. P. Rossiter calls the last acts a "ragged, muddled end" ("Angel with Horns," 29).

23. For a fine discussion of the scene, see Holderness, *Shakespeare's History*, 60–65. See also Wilders, *Lost Garden*, 109; Kastan, " 'Proud Majesty,' " 471; and Alexander Leggatt, "A Double Reign: *Richard II* and *Perkin Warbeck*," in *Shakespeare and His Contemporaries*, ed. E.A.J. Honigmann (Manchester, 1986), 129–32.

24. Richard was consistently seen as a type of Christ in the civic ceremonies associated with his reign; when he entered London for the first time as King, for example, a triumphal pageant prefigured his soul's future entry into Celestial Jerusalem. See Gordon Kipling, "Richard II's 'Sumptuous Pageants' and the Idea of the Civic Triumph," in *Pageantry in the Shakespearean Theater*, ed. David M. Bergeron (Athens, Ga., 1985), 888–93.

25. See note 5 above.

26. For a summary of the issues, see *King Richard II*, ed. Andrew Gurr

(Cambridge, 1984), 8–9 and 175–76. David Bergeron argues, from negative evidence, that the deposition scene was not written until after 1601 ("The Deposition Scene in *Richard II*," *Renaissance Papers*, 1974 (1975): 31–38.

27. Only ten copies of Q4 (1608) survive; each has the 160-line addition. Of these, three have no title page, six have the original title page, and one has a new title page, which reads "with the new additions of the Parliament Scene, and the deposing of King Richard as it hath been lately acted etc." See Barroll, "New History," 449n.

28. Not so, however, in the case of other plays, as Leah Marcus has recently conjectured for *King Lear* and *Measure for Measure*. See *Puzzling Shakespeare*, 148–59, 165–202.

29. See, for example, Steven Urkowitz, *Shakespeare's Revision of King Lear* (Princeton, 1980), and the essays in *The Division of the Kingdom*, ed. Gary Taylor and Michael Warren (Oxford, 1983).

30. See note 27 above. On the abdication, see *Richard II: The Variorum Edition*, ed. Matthew W. Black (Philadelphia, 1955), 369–77, and John Jowett and Gary Taylor, "Sprinklings of Authority: The Folio Text of *Richard II*," *Studies in Bibliography* 38 (1985): 151–200.

31. Gurr provides a good review of Shakespeare's use of Holinshed (*King Richard II*, 84–91). For a more detailed examination, see Matthew H. Black, "The Sources of Shakespeare's *Richard II*," in *Joseph Quincy Adams Memorial Studies*, ed. James G. McManaway, Giles E. Dawson, and Edwin E. Willoughby (Washington, D.C., 1948), 199–216. See also Bullough, *Narrative and Dramatic Sources*, 3:353–82.

32. The law derived from a 1352 statute. See "Calendar of the Contests of the *Baga de Secretis*," in *Fourth Report of the Deputy Keeper of the Public Records*, Appendix 2 (London, 1843), 293, quoted by Kastan, " 'Proud Majesty,' " 473.

33. I appropriate Marcus's phrase (*Puzzling Shakespeare*, 28). Cf. Dr. Johnson: "Part of the addition is proper, and part might have been forborn without much loss" (*Johnson on Shakespeare*, 7:446). My discussion draws from Holderness, "Shakespeare's History: *Richard II*," *Literature and History* 57 (1982): 2–24; Axton, *Queen's Two Bodies*; Leonard Tennenhouse, "Strategies of State and Political Plays: *A Midsummer Night's Dream, Henry IV, Henry V, Henry VIII*," in Dollimore and Sinfield, *Political Shakespeare*, 109–28, an argument Tennenhouse furthers in *Power on Display*, 76–81. For a treatment of *Richard II* as dialectic, see Susan Wells, *The Dialectics of Representation* (Baltimore, 1985), 36–44.

34. Johnson, *Elizabeth I*, 424–31.

35. The 1972 Masterpiece Theatre presentation, *Elizabeth R*, dramatizes the famous performance and (unhistorically) shows Essex among those present; as the actor playing Richard comes to the lines that deprive him of his crown, he dries in his role.

36. Certainly Samuel Daniel's *Civil Wars* imagines deposition as death: describing Richard's entrance to abdicate, Daniel refers to him as "Intomb'd in

his own, and others' blame." See second book, stanza 109, in *Complete Works*, ed. Alexander B. Grosart (London, 1885; reprint, New York, 1963), 2:93.

37. Scott McMillin discusses the images of seeing in this scene and the next in "Shakespeare's *Richard II*: Eyes of Sorrow, Eyes of Desire," *Shakespeare Quarterly* 35 (1984): 40–52.

38. Tree's 1903 performance text staged this processional entry, complete with mob, just as he had also interpolated the Magna Charta signing into *King John* (Booth, *Victorian Spectacular Theatre*, 129).

39. Raphael Holinshed, *Holinshed's Chronicles* (1587; reprint, New York, 1965), 3:3–4.

40. Holinshed, *Chronicles*, 3:4.

41. These much-maligned scenes have often been omitted in performance on the grounds that they interrupt and delay its tragic progression and contain awkward verse. Harley Granville-Barker, writing to John Gielgud in 1937 (who omitted them from his 1937 and 1952 performance texts), describes them as an "excited interlude between the slow . . . farewell between Richard and the Queen and the slow, philosophical death scene." Quoted in *Richard II: Critical Essays*, ed. Jeanne T. Newlin (New York, 1984), 137, 141. John Russell Brown, *Shakespeare's Plays in Performance* (Baltimore, 1966), 129–45, is their kindest critic, and Ornstein, *Kingdom for a Stage*, 124, their most severe detractor. Leonard Barkan views them as farce in "The Theatrical Consistency of *Richard II*," *Shakespeare Quarterly* 29 (1978): 5–19, as does Sheldon P. Zitner in "Aumerle's Conspiracy," *Studies in English Literature* 14 (1974): 239–57. James Black treats them as antimasque in "The Interlude of the Beggar and the King in *Richard II*," in Bergeron, *Pageantry in the Shakespearean Theater*, 104–13; Harry Berger, Jr. reads them as an elaborate psychoanalytic fable in "Textual Dramaturgy: Representing the Limits of Theatre in *Richard II*," *Theatre Journal* 39 (1987): 135–55. See also Joan Hartwig, *Shakespeare's Analogical Scene* (Lincoln, Neb., 1983), 113–34.

42. Natalie Zemon Davis notes that "Renaissance rhetorical theory does not include asking pardon among its figures for ending" (*Fiction in the Archives* [Stanford, 1987], 205). Davis also calls attention to Cynthia Herrup's work in progress on royal pardons in early modern England, a project that may well bear on this scene (187).

43. For relations between ballad discourse and plays, see Bruce Smith, "Some Lists, Some Sums, and a Summary," unpublished paper read at the 1989 Shakespeare Association of America conference. See also Bernard Capp, "Popular Literature," in *Popular Culture in Seventeenth-Century England*, ed. Barry Reay (New York, 1985), 198–243.

44. See James, "At a Crossroads," 443–44.

45. Another, fleetingly "local," reading of the Groom, which risks an out-of-fashion topicality, might figure him as connected with one of Elizabeth's courtiers, the Master of the Horse—an office held first by Robert Dudley, Earl of Leicester, and later by Robert Devereux, Earl of Essex. Like much else about

the play, this somewhat irresponsible association cuts two ways—either as "a sign of love" or, to the Queen's detractors, a curiously skewed emblem of favoritism. Either, or both, would serve a Richard figured as Elizabeth. But such readings would surface only to particular eyes and, perhaps, only for those spectators at the February 1601 performance, where Essex himself was not present. Such circumstances aside, *Richard II* voices its most politic statement concerning loyalty through the Groom: "What my tongue dares not, that my heart shall say" (5.5.97).

46. Kastan summarizes neatly: "Exton conceives of his deed as an act of closure. . . . But the death of Richard II does not end much more than Richard's life. The historical process continues, and, indeed, it is Richard's murder itself that opens up the play's ending" (*Shakespeare and the Shapes of Time*, 49).

47. Philip C. McGuire discusses *Richard II*'s strategies of delay and entry and exit patterns in "Choreography and Language in *Richard II*," in *Shakespeare: The Theatrical Dimension*, ed. Philip C. McGuire and David A. Samuelson (New York, 1979), 61–84. In an analysis of Richard's "antic disposition," Lois Potter shows how his speech patterns are echoed by Exton and carried through in the formal gestures surrounding the close ("The Antic Disposition of Richard II," *Shakespeare Survey* 27 [1974]: 39–41).

48. Holinshed, *Chronicles*, 3:62. For a reading that complements my own, see Christopher Pye, "The Betrayal of the Gaze: Theatricality and Power in Shakespeare's *Richard II*," *ELH* 55 (1988): 575–98.

49. "The Night of the Play," *Nottingham Guardian*, 26 March 1951.

50. Anthony Quayle, foreword to J. Dover Wilson and T. C. Worsley, *Shakespeare's Histories at Stratford, 1951* (London, 1952), ix.

51. Wilson and Worsley, *Shakespeare's Histories*, 4. See also Beauman, *Royal Shakespeare Company*, 203–9.

52. Anthony Quayle, program note.

53. Quayle, program note.

54. *Tribune*, 6 April 1951.

55. *Birmingham Gazette*, 26 March 1951.

56. Wilson and Worsley, *Shakespeare's Histories*, 43.

57. Prompt copy at the Shakespeare Centre Library. Such cuts reflect traditional practice; see note 39 above.

58. Cf. Grossberg, "Is There Rock after Punk?" 51–58; Huyssen, "Mapping the Postmodern," 5–52; and Jameson, "Postmodernism," 53–92.

59. *Times*, 26 March 1951. Since the national anthem was played at the beginning of each performance, that "theme" was indeed stated, though not, perhaps, carried through (to the reviewer's satisfaction) by the staged representation that followed it.

60. For an analysis of Quayle's project as a reactionary venture, see Holderness, *Shakespeare's History*, 203–13; although I agree with his assessment, I try to set my own analysis slightly apart from his.

61. Barton's performance text is exceptionally well documented. See, for instance, Timothy O'Brien, "Designing a Shakespeare Play: *Richard II*,"

Shakespeare Jahrbuch West (1974): 111–20; J. E. Stredder, "Dramatic Representation in Shakespeare's *Richard II*," *Sydney Studies in English I* (1975–1976): 32–45; Stanley Wells, *Royal Shakespeare: Four Major Productions at Stratford-upon-Avon* (Manchester, 1977), 65–80; Miriam Gilbert, "*Richard II* at Stratford: Role-Playing as Metaphor," in McGuire and Samuelson, *Shakespeare*, 85–101; and Greenwald, *Directions by Indirections*, 117–27.

62. Prompt copy at the Shakespeare Centre Library. My description draws from Gilbert, "*Richard II* at Stratford," 91, and Wells, "John Barton's *Richard II*," 80.

63. In Richardson's playing but not Pasco's (Wells, "John Barton's *Richard II*," 80).

64. Wells, "John Barton's *Richard II*," 80.

65. Gilbert, "*Richard II* at Stratford," 100.

66. Michael Billington, *Guardian*, 4 November 1980. In the repertory, *Richard II* was paired with *Richard III*, converting the two plays, with Alan Howard playing both title roles, into what Irving Wardle called "a compressed epic" (*Times*, 4 November 1980).

67. Prompt copy at the Shakespeare Centre Library.

68. Performance at the Auditorium Theatre, Chicago, Illinois, 13 May 1988.

CHAPTER 6
"LET THE END TRY THE MAN": *1* AND *2 HENRY IV*

1. See A. C. Bradley, "The Rejection of Falstaff," 1902; reprinted in *Henry the Fourth, Parts I and II*, ed. David Bevington (New York, 1986), 81, 96.

2. Quoted in Juan Cobos and Miguel Rubio, "Welles and Falstaff," 1966; reprinted in *Chimes at Midnight*, ed. Bridget Gellert Lyons (New Brunswick, N.J., 1988), 261.

3. For discussions of Welles's film, see Jorgens, *Shakespeare on Film*, 106–21; Samuel Crowl, "The Long Goodbye: Welles and Falstaff," *Shakespeare Quarterly* 31 (1980): 369–80; and Dudley Andrew, *Film in the Aura of Art* (Princeton, 1984), 152–71.

4. Sherman H. Hawkins reviews, judges, and extends the two-century-old debate over the plan, structure, and aesthetic unity of the plays, which ranges from Dr. Johnson and Malone to Harold Jenkins, in "*Henry IV*: The Structural Problem Revisited," *Shakespeare Quarterly* 33 (1982): 278–301. See also Calderwood, *Metadrama in Shakespeare's Henriad*, especially 111–16, and Berry, *Patterns of Decay*, 109. Giorgio Melchiori posits an "original" one-part play (based on *The Famous Victories*) comprising *1* and *2 Henry IV* and *Henry V*, rejected because of the Oldcastle controversy and later divided into three ("Reconstructing the *Ur-Henry IV*," in *Essays in Honour of Kristian Smidt*, ed. Peter Bilton, Lars Hartveit, Stig Johansson, and Arthur O. Sandved [Oslo, 1986], 59–77).

5. Bradley, "Rejection of Falstaff," 97.

6. See, for instance, Barber, *Shakespeare's Festive Comedy*, 214–16; Greenblatt, "Invisible Bullets," 265; Holderness, *Shakespeare's History*, 88–95;

Bristol, *Carnival and Theater*, 180–83, 204–7; Barber and Wheeler, *Whole Journey*, 198–217; Tennenhouse, *Power on Display*, 83–84; and Steven Mullaney, "Strange Things, Gross Terms, Curious Customs: The Rehearsal of Cultures in the Late Renaissance," in Greenblatt, *Representing the English Renaissance*, 82–89.

7. Quoted in Cobos and Rubio, "Welles and Falstaff," 262.

8. Mullaney, "Strange Things," 87.

9. Prompt copy in the Beerbohm Tree Collection, the University of Bristol Theatre Collection.

10. Because Tree played Falstaff, he probably remained onstage, since common stage practice licensed actor-managers' presences at significant moments, especially at curtain, regardless of the playtext's stage directions. Whether or not his presence undercut the embrace between father and son is impossible to gauge. Although 5.5 was apparently returned at a later time (perhaps for the 1906 production), a second, less thoroughly marked, prompt copy for this production also highlights the Battle of Shrewsbury conceived as a spectacular tableau.

11. For example, in Anthony Quayle's 1951 Shakespeare Memorial Theatre production; prompt copy at the Shakespeare Centre Library.

12. Prompt copy at the Shakespeare Centre Library.

13. Richard Helgerson, *The Elizabethan Prodigals* (Berkeley, 1977). See also Mullaney, "Strange Things," 83.

14. In reading the substitutions and replacements in these character relations, I draw from V. I. Propp, *Morphology of the Folktale* (1928); reprint, trans. Laurence Scott (Austin, 1958); A. J. Greimas, "Elements of a Narrative Grammar" (1969), reprinted in *Diacritics* 7 (1977): 23–40; and Barthes, *S/Z*. See also my "Falstaff: History and His Story," *Iowa State Journal of Research* 53, no. 3 (1979): 185–90. For an analysis based on René Girard's concept of sacred mythic difference, see Laurie E. Osborne, "Crisis of Degree in Shakespeare's *Henriad*," *Studies in English Literature* 25 (1985): 337–59. On morality elements, see Dessen, *Shakespeare and the Late Moral Plays*, 55–90.

15. On Falstaff's "curiously feminine sensual abundance," see Kahn, *Man's Estate*, 72. See also Valerie Traub, "Prince Hal's Falstaff: Positioning Psychoanalysis and the Female Body," *Shakespeare Quarterly* 40 (1989): 456–74. On the *Henriad* as an Oedipal narrative, see Ernst Kris, "Prince Hal's Conflict," *Psychoanalytic Quarterly* 17 (1948): 487–506. See also Richard Wheeler, *Shakespeare's Development and the Problem Comedies* (Berkeley, 1981), 158–67.

16. Marcus also notes the connection (*Puzzling Shakespeare*, 94).

17. See Tennenhouse, *Power on Display*, 83–84.

18. On the Oldcastle connection, see Alice Lyle Scoufos, *Shakespeare's Typological Satire* (Athens, Oh., 1979). See also *Henry the Fourth, Part I*, ed. David Bevington (Oxford, 1987), 3–10. Gary Taylor argues for returning Oldcastle's name to the playtext ("The Fortunes of Falstaff," *Shakespeare Survey* 38 [1985]: 95–100). Holderness positions the Oldcastle controversy in rela-

tion to *The True and Honourable History of the Life of Sir John Oldcastle* and to Puritan risings (*Shakespeare's History*, 107–12).

19. *Almond for a Parrat* (1590); *Apology for Actors* (1612); both quoted in David Wiles, *Shakespeare's Clown* (Cambridge, 1987), 11.

20. See Wiles, *Shakespeare's Clown*, 116–20.

21. I borrow Beverle Houston's apt phrase, "Power and Dis-Integration in the Films of Orson Welles," *Film Quarterly* 35 (Summer 1982): 2.

22. Sidney, *A Defence of Poetry*, 77. On the clown's "disorder," see David Scott Kastan, " 'Clownes Should Speake Disorderlye': Mongrel Tragicomedy and the Unitary State," unpublished paper, Shakespeare Association of America, 1989.

23. Holinshed, *Chronicles*, 521/1/74, reproduced in Bullough, *Narrative and Dramatic Sources*, 4:191.

24. Sidney, *A Defence of Poetry*, 77.

25. See Holinshed's report of Hal coming to his father strangely attired (538/2/74, reproduced in Bullough, *Narrative and Dramatic Sources*, 4:193).

26. Holderness, *Shakespeare's History*, 122. See also Gerard H. Cox, " 'Like a Prince Indeed': Hal's Triumph of Honor in *1 Henry IV*," in Bergeron, *Pageantry in the Shakespearean Theater*, 133, 135–47; and Derek Cohen, "The Rite of Violence in *1 Henry IV*," *Shakespeare Survey* 38 (1985), especially 82.

27. Holinshed, *Chronicles*, reproduced in Bullough, *Narrative and Dramatic Sources*, 4:191.

28. Daniel, *Civil Wars*, 4:110–11, reproduced in Bullough, *Narrative and Dramatic Sources*, 4:214.

29. See, for instance, Edward Pechter, "Falsifying Men's Hopes: The Ending of *1 Henry IV*," *Modern Language Quarterly* 41 (1980): 227–28. See also Barber, *Shakespeare's Festive Comedy*, 204–6; James Black, "*Henry IV*: A World of Figures Here," in McGuire and Samuelson, *Shakespeare*, 173–80; and Calderwood, *Metadrama in Shakespeare's Henriad*, 83–84, 119, 174. In Welles's film, Hal sees breath rising like steam from the kettle of Falstaff's armadillo-like armor, which turns his "Embowelled will I see thee by-and-by" (5.4.108) into a threatening joke.

30. See Stow's account, taken from Walsingham; quoted in Scoufos, *Shakespeare's Typological Satire*, 109.

31. See Wiles, *Shakespeare's Clown*, 120–22.

32. See Holinshed, *Chronicles*, quoted in Bullough, *Narrative and Dramatic Sources*, 4:191.

33. Wiles also notes this (*Shakespeare's Clown*, 123).

34. For a pertinent discussion of counterfeit images, see Sharon Willis, "Disputed Territories: Masculinity and Social Space," *Camera Obscura* 19 (1989): 5–23.

35. See Wiles, *Shakespeare's Clown*, 110–15.

36. Prompt copy at the Shakespeare Centre Library.

37. Hands replaces 5.4.18–19 so that these lines cap Hal's praise of John—

"Before I loved thee as a brother, John, / But now I do respect thee as my soul"—and gives Hal John's "But soft, what have we here?"

38. In Michael Edwards's 1984 *1 Henry IV* at Santa Cruz, Hal "avoided the simple notion that Hal returns to the role his father offered him—deliberately refusing . . . to resolve the many-sided, partly contradictory aspects of the part 'into an overall theory about Hal.' " See Mary Judith Dunbar, "Shakespeare at Santa Cruz," *Shakespeare Quarterly* 35 (1984): 477.

39. The prompt copy at the Shakespeare Centre Library provides practically no directions for the close. I rely on notes taken at an August 1982 performance. See also R. L. Smallwood, "*Henry IV, Parts 1 and 2* at the Barbican Theatre" (1983; reprinted in Bevington, *Henry the Fourth, Parts I and II*, 423–30). Tree's 1895 production also opened with a procession accompanied by a Gregorian chant (prompt copy in the Beerbohm Tree Collection, the University of Bristol Theatre Collection).

40. See Smallwood, "*Henry IV, Parts 1 and 2*," 425.

41. Quoted in an interview with Michael Mullin, "On Playing Henry IV," *Theatre Quarterly* 7, no. 27 (1977): 31.

42. My account combines details from a June 1987 performance in Toronto and a May 1988 performance in Chicago. In a September 1988 interview, Bogdanov indicated that his rearranged ending indeed drew from Welles's film, which he much admires.

43. See Calderwood, *Metadrama in Shakespeare's Henriad*, 118; and Hawkins, "*Henry IV*," 289–90, 292–94. On narrating conventions in modern histories, see Paul Hernadi, *Interpreting Events* (Ithaca, 1985), 18–20, 30–32. On Rumor as an allegory of Henry's usurpation, see Richard H. Abrams, "Rumor's Reign in *2 Henry IV*: The Scope of a Personification," *English Literary Renaissance* 16 (1986): 467–95. For a semiotic analysis, see Harry Berger, "Sneak's Noise, or Rumor and Detextualization in *2 Henry IV*," *Kenyon Review* 6, no. 4 (1984): 58–78.

44. See the studies cited in note 6 above.

45. In the history of the Shakespeare Memorial Theatre/Royal Shakespeare Theatre, for example, *2 Henry IV* was produced independently (by F. R. Benson) in 1894, 1898, 1901, 1913, 1914, and 1915, and by Bridges-Adams in 1921 and 1926. Benson produced *1 Henry IV* in 1909, and *2 Henry IV* the following year; in 1905, Benson included both plays in the repertory, as did Bridges-Adams in 1932, a practice that has become a tradition (*Theatre at Stratford-upon-Avon: A Catalogue-Index to Productions of the Shakespeare Memorial Theatre/Royal Shakespeare Theatre, 1879–1978*, ed. Michael Mullin [Westport, Conn., 1980], 138–51).

46. Five quartos appeared between 1598 and 1613. For a recent discussion of these and their relation to Folio, see Bevington, *Henry the Fourth, Part 1*, 85–110.

47. Readings that position the plays as moral histories are Tillyard, *Shakespeare's History Plays*, 264–304, and Dessen, *Shakespeare and the Late Moral Plays*, 91–112. See also Michael Billington's review of Trevor Nunn's 1982

Royal Shakespeare Company production, "There's a Hole in Hal's Bucko," *Guardian*, 11 June 1982.

48. Viewing the play as Falstaff's tragicomic romance with history associates it with plays such as *Friar Bacon and Friar Bungay*, *George a Greene*, and *James IV*, which foreground comedy and romance and use historical events and personages to anchor, enrich, and/or interfere with the basic romance plot. Shakespeare's *Cymbeline* constitutes just such an example. In one sense, however, Parts One and Two can be considered incompatible; repetition constitutes just one feature that argues for their separateness. A reader or spectator could generate *most* of the preceding history of *1 Henry IV* by reading or watching *2 Henry IV*; what would be missing would be Hotspur's heroic action, and the emphasis would rest on Falstaff's history.

49. See *The History of King Henry the Fourth, as Revised by Sir Edward Dering, Bart.*, Folger Facsimile, ed. G. Walton Williams and G. B. Evans (Charlottesville, 1974).

50. Prompt copy at the Shakespeare Centre Library.

51. Prompt copy at the Shakespeare Centre Library. Anthony Quayle directed all the plays except for *2 Henry IV*; he also played Falstaff. For an account of the 1951 cycle, see Wilson and Worsley, *Shakespeare's Histories*. See also Beauman, *Royal Shakespeare Company*, 205–10.

52. See Thomas Cartelli, "Ideology and Subversion in the Shakespearean Set Speech," *ELH* 53 (1986): 1–25. On the entire scene, see Burckhardt, *Shakespearean Meanings*, 162–63, and John W. Blanpied, "Unfathered Heirs and Loathly Births of Nature," *English Literary Renaissance* 5 (1975): 223–30.

53. Cf. William Empson's discussion of links between the sonnets and the plays (*Some Versions of Pastoral* [London, 1935], 85–111). See also Barber and Wheeler, *Whole Journey*, especially 198–219.

54. Among others who note the pun, see Terry Eagleton, *William Shakespeare* (London, 1986), 17.

55. See *The Famous Victories of Henry the Fifth*, scene 4, reproduced in Bullough, *Narrative and Dramatic Sources*, 4:307–10. Nunn's 1982 production staged the scene as an entr'acte interlude between Parts One and Two. Performed as street theater and in farcical knockabout style by members of the company who played minor roles, it functioned as homage to a theatrical text and an acting tradition as well as a kind of theatrical fantasy of the chroniclers' report.

56. Holinshed, *Chronicles*, 583/1/59, reproduced in Bullough, *Narrative and Dramatic Sources*, 4:407.

57. Prompt copy at the Theatre Museum, the Victoria and Albert Museum.

58. See Wiles, *Shakespeare's Clown*, 124–25.

59. See, for instance, Calderwood, *Metadrama in Shakespeare's Henriad*, 100–104; Edward I. Berry, "The Rejection Scene in *2 Henry IV*," *Studies in English Literature* 17 (1977): 201–18.

60. The historical Prince John, of course, became regent in England during Henry's French war.

61. Details are from the prompt copy at the Shakespeare Centre Library and from T. F. Wharton, *Henry the Fourth, Parts 1 and 2: Text and Performance* (London, 1983), 73.

62. For the text of Thatcher's speech, see *Observer*, 28 March 1982.

63. Such stagings are, of course, not original in this century. In 1821, the coronation of George IV provided the occasion for spectacle to be tacked on to Macready's *2 Henry IV*. *European Magazine* reports: "The grand attraction of the evening, however, was not precisely the legitimate drama, as the latter portion of the Play introduced three new scenes of Henry the Fifth's Coronation: first, the processional platform with it's [sic] splendid retinue; next, the magnificent inauguration in Westminster Abbey; and last, and best, the gorgeous banquet in the Hall, with the introduction of the mailed Champion, and the ceremony of his challenge. All these were set forth not only with the taste and grandeur to be expected at Covent Garden, but with almost the regal splendor of the originals. All was light and blazonry, and gold and glory; and we should despair indeed of public curiosity, and of theatrical taste, did we not prophecy a long career to the united attractions of Shakespeare's poetry, and a Coronation's magnificence." Quoted in Galmini Salgado, *Eye-Witnesses of Shakespeare* (New York, 1975), 181–82.

64. Prompt copy at the Shakespeare Centre Library.

65. On Pistol's anachronisms, see Phyllis Rackin, "Temporality, Anachronism, and Presence in Shakespeare's English Histories," *Renaissance Drama*, n.s., 17 (1986): 117–18.

66. Cf. Dr. Johnson, who complains that "Shakespeare certainly lost [Poins] by heedlessness, in the multiplicity of his characters, the variety of his action, and his eagerness to end the play" (Sherbo, *Johnson on Shakespeare*, 7:522).

67. Robert Cushman, "Enter the Barbican," *Observer*, 13 June 1982.

68. Prompt copy at the Shakespeare Centre Library. The production also obeyed Quarto's stage directions for a ceremonial procession passing across the stage just following the rush-strewers' dialogue, returning for the rejection, and exiting after it. C. E. McGee draws intriguing comparisons to Elizabeth's last royal entry ("*2 Henry IV*: The Last Tudor Royal Entry," in *Mirror Up to Shakespeare*, ed. J. C. Gray [Toronto, 1984], 149–58). See also Barbara D. Palmer, " 'Ciphers to This Great Accompt': Civic Pageantry in the Second Tetralogy," in Bergeron, *Pageantry in the Shakespearean Theatre*, 122–23.

69. See Booth, *Victorian Spectacular Theatre*. Nunn's performance text owes an additional debt—especially in Part Two's closely observed tavern scenes—to his own *Nicholas Nickleby* (Royal Shakespeare Company, 1980), also a two-part play.

70. My description combines details from the Toronto (1987) and Chicago (1988) productions.

71. Prompt copy at the Shakespeare Centre Library. Except for Thomas Donovan's 1896 text, where a note indicates "can be omitted," no existing nineteenth-century texts or prompt copies include the Epilogue. In the twentieth century, the Players' Shakespeare (1926), and performance texts by Nu-

gent Monck (1923), Ben Iden Payne (1934), Bernard Hepton (1960), Stuart Burge (1965), William Roberts (1972), and Edward Peyton Call (1974) do include it (William P. Halstead, *Shakespeare as Spoken* [Ann Arbor, 1978]).

72. Beauman, *Royal Shakespeare Company*, 114–20.

73. Other Epilogues are not so separated, in either Quarto or Folio texts.

74. See *King Henry IV, Part 2*, ed. John Dover Wilson (Cambridge, 1946), 215.

75. Taylor notes, "No one seems to have remarked upon the syntactical role of 'for' in this unusual sentence, perhaps because its implications are obvious . . . the immediate change of subject, and the assertion of a causal link between the two statements, makes it seem to me probable that Shakespeare here alluded to the displeasure of some spectators at the original identification of the character as Oldcastle" ("Fortunes of Falstaff," 97).

76. Natalie Zemon Davis notes that "Renaissance rhetorical theory does not include asking pardon among its 'Figures for ending' " and cites Quintilian, who says in his section on the peroration that "some think this part should include prayers and excuses"—which would be for the client, not for the lawyer and his speech (*Fiction in the Archives*, 205n). *2 Henry IV*'s Epilogue seems to juggle with this rhetorical positioning.

77. Harington, *Metamorphoses of Ajax* (1596); see also *A Mad World, My Masters* (1608), 5.2.200: "This shows like kneeling after the play; I praying for my good lord Owemuch and his good countess, our honourable lady and mistress." Such prayers might be combined with one for the sovereign and estates. See Chambers, *Elizabethan Stage*, 1:135, 311.

78. On Falstaff as Epilogue-speaker, see Martin Holmes, *Shakespeare and His Players* (New York, 1972), 47. See also Wiles, *Shakespeare's Clown*, 128–32.

79. Mullaney, "Strange Things," 88–89.

80. Hélène Cixous, "The Laugh of the Medusa," in *New French Feminisms*, ed. Elaine Marks and Isabelle de Courtivron (New York, 1981), 250.

81. My account draws on an August 1983 performance at London's Riverside Studios.

82. In Brecht's play, a trio sung by Peachum, Polly, and Mrs. Peachum—"Concerning the Insecurity of the Human State," the First Threepenny Finale. See Brecht, *Collected Plays*, 177–79.

83. Written in 1962, Raskin's song was adapted from a Russian folk song. The Limelighters first recorded it, but it did not become a popular hit until 1968, with Mary Hopkins's recording. The first two lines of the lyric are "Those were the days, my friend; we thought they'd never end."

CHAPTER 7
"A FULL AND NATURAL CLOSE, LIKE MUSIC": *HENRY V*

1. John Keegan, *The Face of Battle* (1976; reprint, Harmondsworth, 1978), 78.

2. *Henry V* has answered to many names—salvation history, epic, hagiog-

raphy, "implicit tragedy," "ceremonial drama," comedy, failed comedy, romance—each of which attempts to erase the play's contradictions and institutionalize its unity. For a summary of these, see Joanne Altieri, "Romance in *Henry V*," *Studies in English Literature* 21 (1981): 223–40.

3. See Norman Rabkin, "Either/Or: Responding to *Henry V*," in *Shakespeare and the Problem of Meaning* (Chicago, 1981), 33–62.

4. See Rosalie Colie, *The Resources of Kind* (Berkeley, 1973), especially 18–21.

5. Tennenhouse, *Power on Display*, 84.

6. On the relations between the play and its Chorus, see Holderness, *Shakespeare's History*, 136–37, and Peter B. Erickson, " 'The Fault / My Father Made': The Anxious Pursuit of Heroic Fame in Shakespeare's *Henry V*," *Modern Language Studies* 10 (1979–1980): 10–25. See also Anne Barton, "The King Disguised: Shakespeare's *Henry V* and the Comical History," in *The Triple Bond*, ed. Joseph G. Price (University Park, Pa., 1975), 92–117, and Lawrence Danson, "*Henry V*: King, Chorus and Critics," *Shakespeare Quarterly* 34 (1983): 27–43. On Chorus and "authority," see Robert Weimann, "Bifold Authority in Shakespeare's Theatre," *Shakespeare Quarterly* 39 (1988): 411–16. On Chorus in the theater, see Trevor Nunn's comments on the 1964 Royal Shakespeare Company *Henry V*, quoted in Ralph Berry, *On Directing Shakespeare* (New York, 1977), 57–58.

7. Tennenhouse, *Power on Display*, 68–71, 83–85.

8. Lydgate, *Troy Book*, 3:870, in EETS Extra Series, ed. H. Bergen (London, 1906–1912); quoted in G. L. Harriss, "Introduction: The Exemplar of Kingship," in *Henry V: The Practice of Kingship*, ed. G. L. Harriss (Oxford, 1985), 23.

9. Peter S. Donaldson, " 'Claiming from the Female': Gender and Representation in Laurence Olivier's *Henry V*," 4—a chapter in Donaldson's *Shakespearean Films/Shakespearean Directors* (London, 1990). My thanks to Donaldson for generously permitting me to see his work while it was still in manuscript form.

10. Harriss, "Introduction," 1.

11. Cf. Michael Goldman's discussion of theatrical bodies in *Shakespeare and the Energies of Drama* (Princeton, 1972), 3–11.

12. See Jonathan Dollimore and Alan Sinfield, "History and Ideology: The Instance of *Henry V*," in Drakakis, *Alternative Shakespeares*, 216–18. See also Cartelli, "Ideology and Subversion," 5–10.

13. See Jan Kott, "Head for Maidenhead, Maidenhead for Head: The Structure of Exchange in 'Measure for Measure,' " *Theatre Quarterly* 8, no. 31 (Autumn 1978): 18–24.

14. Barber and Wheeler label the glove exchange "military pastoral" in *Whole Journey*, 225–26.

15. I draw here from Lynn Hunt, "The Revolution without Lineage: Freud and the French Revolution," a lecture given at the National Humanities Center, 13 January 1989.

16. Emrys Jones suggests retitling the play *Agincourt* (*Scenic Form in Shake-speare* [Oxford, 1971], 235).

17. See Sherbo, *Johnson on Shakespeare*, 8:562–63. Ornstein echoes John-son's objections: in saying "we prefer the captain with his men to the rough-and-ready wooer because the former is more natural than the latter," he de-romanticizes the play's ending and re-romanticizes male comradeship (*King-dom for a Stage*, 198–99).

18. G. B. Harrison, *The Life and Death of Robert Devereux, Earl of Essex* (London, 1937), 214–15, quoted in Dollimore and Sinfield, "History and Ide-ology," 219.

19. For a discussion of James I's "Roman style," see Goldberg, *James I*, especially 46–54. See also Holderness, *Shakespeare's History*, 141–44, and *Henry V*, ed. Gary Taylor (Oxford, 1984), 7–8. For connections between this narrated entry and civic pageants, see Strong, *Cult of Elizabeth*, 129–63, and David Bergeron, *English Civic Pageantry, 1558–1642* (Columbia, S.C., 1971), especially 70–71, 89–91.

20. See Dollimore and Sinfield, "History and Ideology," 223–24.

21. Shapiro argues that Pistol competes with Henry V as Tamburlaine's heir, in "Revisiting *Tamburlaine*: *Henry V* as Shakespeare's Belated Armada Play," unpublished paper presented at the 1988 Shakespeare Association of America conference.

22. For an earlier use of *Henry V*, see Aaron Hill's 1723 adaptation, which includes a conspiratorial subplot led by Scroop's niece, Harriet, a rival to Katherine. Hill's text was turned into a one-act version called *The Conspiracy Discovered: French Policy Defeated*; the playbill proclaims "(taken from Shakespeare) with a Representation of the Trials of the Lords for High Trea-son, in the Reign of Henry V." The adaptation was almost certainly occasioned by the trial, which began in Westminster Hall on 28 July, of Lords Kilmarnock, Cromarty, and Balmerino for their participation in the Rebellion of '45. See Charles Beecher Hogan, *Shakespeare in the Theatre, 1701–1800* (Oxford, 1952), 199. For the plot details of Hill's text, see Odell, *Shakespeare from Betterton to Irving*, 1:194–95.

23. See Booth, *Victorian Spectacular Theatre*, 52–59, and Odell, *Shake-speare from Betterton to Irving*, 2:355. Productions by John Coleman (1876) and George Rignold (1878–1879) revived Kean's effects; Coleman introduced further tableaux, as well as ballets, in the closing scenes. See Odell, 2:309, and Booth, 30–31.

24. Booth, *Victorian Spectacular Theatre*, 53.

25. Laurence Olivier, *On Acting* (New York, 1986), 275–76.

26. See Tennenhouse, *Power on Display*, 84.

27. See Andrew, *Film in the Aura of Art*, 139.

28. For an analysis of how Olivier's film shaped its perspective, see Harry M. Geduld, *Filmguide to Henry V* (Bloomington, 1973). See also Jorgens, *Shakespeare on Film*, 122–35. For the film script, see *Film Scripts One*, ed.

George P. Garrett, O. B. Hardison, Jr., and Jane R. Gelfman (New York, 1971).

29. My analysis draws on Donaldson, " 'Claiming from the Female,' " 15–18.

30. In contrast, Andrew labels Agincourt Eve "introspective cinema" (*Film in the Aura of Art*, 132–34).

31. The leek scene has a long history of stage business. See A. C. Sprague, *Shakespeare and the Actors* (Cambridge, Mass., 1944), 120–21. Gary Taylor explains the scene in terms of Freud's theory of jokes, in *To Analyze Delight* (Newark, 1985), 128–31.

32. Andrew, *Film in the Aura of Art*, 151. See also Graham Holderness, "Agincourt 1944: Readings in the Shakespeare Myth," *Literature and History* 10 (Spring 1984): 24–45. Anthony Quayle's 1951 tetralogy for the Festival of Britain performed a similar ideological function; see Wilson and Worsley, *Shakespeare's Histories*. And John Dover Wilson comments on Frank Benson's 1914 Stratford Memorial Theatre *Henry V*: "The epic drama of Agincourt matched the temper of the moment, when Rupert Brooke was writing *The Soldier* and the Kaiser was said to be scoffing at our 'contemptible little army' which had just crossed the Channel, so exactly that it might have been written expressly for it" (*Henry V* [Cambridge, 1947], viii).

33. See Sally Beauman, *The Royal Shakespeare Company's Centenary Production of Henry V* (Oxford, 1976), 5–8, 14–15. Prompt copy at the Shakespeare Centre Library.

34. For an account of the rehearsal controversy behind these choices, see Beauman, *Centenary Production*, 210–11n. For a spectator's response, see Taylor, *To Analyze Delight*, 126–28, 157–58.

35. See Beauman, *Centenary Production*, 215–16n.

36. Prompt copy at the Shakespeare Centre Library.

37. According to the souvenir program, this account was translated from Latin by Sir Harris Nicolas in 1832. The historians quoted are John Gillingham, London School of Economics, and J. L. Bolton, Queen Mary College, London.

38. For another director's view of the need to present a "cohesive" vision of history to *Henry V*'s spectators, see Gavin Cameron-Webb, "England's History Versus Shakespeare's History," *On Stage Studies* 5 (1987): 17–31.

39. See *Players of Shakespeare 2*, ed. Russell Jackson and Robert Smallwood (Cambridge, 1988), 103–4. Branagh used a Welsh accent in the night scene and so made it easier for Williams to mistake Fluellen for Henry. Branagh's film of *Henry V*, which derives from this production, was released in New York in November 1989. For Branagh's screen adaptation, see *Henry V* (London, 1989).

40. See Taylor, *Henry V*, 4.8.102, 257n.

41. *Foedera, Conventiones et Litterae*, ed. T. Rhymer, 2d ed., 20 vols. (London, 1727–1735), 9:919; quoted in Harriss, "Introduction," 23.

42. Maurice Keen, "Diplomacy," in Harriss, *Henry V*, 196. See also Harriss, "Introduction," 17.

43. For the idea of a text's dissolve of voices, see Barthes, *S/Z*, 41–42.

44. On *Dream*, see Montrose, "Shaping Fantasies." *Henry V*'s finale also throws off echoes of *The Taming of the Shrew*, of another Kate as well as Henry's "Petruchio-ness"—see especially *Henry V*, 5.2.132–65. Cf. also *The Merchant of Venice*, which attempts to resolve the ideological and sexual differences raised in Venice by returning to Belmont's suburban community.

45. Tennenhouse, *Power on Display*, 69; here and elsewhere, my discussion draws on his. For the contexts of Burgundy's speech, see James C. Bulman, "Shakespeare's Georgic Histories," *Shakespeare Survey* 38 (1985): 37–47.

46. Cf. Coppélia Kahn, who notes that the ending "returns to the simple, idealized male comradeships" and that Henry's soldierly wooing "sets the distance between [Henry and Katherine] on which his manhood depends" (*Man's Estate*, 81). Shapiro reads a debt to *Tamburlaine*'s ending ("Revisiting *Tamburlaine*," 15).

47. Keen, "Diplomacy," 194.

48. Tennenhouse, *Power on Display*, 71. See also Philip C. McGuire, "Seeing *Henry V* 'Perspectively,' " in *The Shakespeare Plays* (Dubuque, 1980), 115–29.

49. For a discussion of such silences in a series of plays, see McGuire, *Speechless Dialect*.

50. Another distinction between Quarto and Folio involves Henry and Katherine's public kiss: Quarto's "Come, give me thy hand" (G_4^r) evades the gesture; Folio, however, calls upon those present to "bear me witness all / That here I kiss her as my Sovereign Queen" (TLN 3347–48). On Quarto as an acting version, see Gary Taylor, "We Happy Few: The 1600 Abridgement," in Stanley Wells and Gary Taylor, *Modernizing Shakespeare's Spelling, with Three Studies in the Text of Henry V* (Oxford, 1979), 72–123.

51. See Keen, "Diplomacy," 193–94.

52. Unique, that is, with the possible exception of *Henry VIII*, at least in one performance text (see chapter 8 below), where a woman spoke the Epilogue. Since its opening stage direction reads "Queene Katherine," Quarto (G_2^v) seems to eliminate Queen Isabel; adding a comma between "Queene" and "Katherine" would, however, restore her. If indeed she is present, then her sustained silence may be Quarto's way of suggesting the future losses Folio's Epilogue makes explicit. Some contemporary performance texts, such as Hands's and Noble's, eliminate her presence entirely. For Hands's rationale, see Beauman, *Centenary Production*, 219n.

53. See Axton, *Queen's Two Bodies*, 112–13. See also Burckhardt, who draws connections to "The Phoenix and the Turtle" (*Shakespearean Meanings*, 178, 201). C. G. Thayer argues that *Henry V* is written for James (*Shakespearean Politics* [Athens, Ohio, 1983], 149).

54. Barber and Wheeler call Chorus "the sonneteer transferred into the theater, asking it to do more than theater can do, as the poet often asks the sonnet

to do more than poetry can do—or laments the impossibility of its doing so" (*Whole Journey*, 218). See also James Calderwood, "*Richard II* to *Henry V*: Poem to Stage," in *Shakespeare's 'More Than Words Can Witness*,' ed. Sidney Homan (Cranbury, N.J.: 1980), 59–60.

55. My reading draws on Philip C. McGuire, "Shakespeare's Non-Shakespearean Sonnets," *Shakespeare Quarterly* 38 (1987): 304–19.

56. I draw from Richard Goodkin's reading of Racine's *Andromache*, "A Choice of Andromache's," in Hult, *Concepts of Closure*, 245–47.

57. For an account of Calvert's production, see Richard Foulkes, "Charles Calvert's *Henry V*," *Shakespeare Survey* 41 (1989): 23–34. George Rignold's 1878–1879 Drury Lane production moved Katherine's language lesson to the beginning of act 5, just preceding the marriage ceremony (Odell, *Shakespeare from Betterton to Irving*, 2:309).

58. See Geduld's description in *Filmguide to Henry V*, 9.

59. Donaldson, " 'Claiming from the Female,' " 11–13, 25.

60. Olivier's Epilogue is reproduced in Garrett, Hardison, and Gelfman, *Film Scripts One*, 134. Some performance texts—Robert Atkins (1934), Milton Rosmer (1943), Glen Byam Shaw (1951), *The Age of Kings* (1961), Edward Peyton Call (1964) and Michael Kahn (1969)—cut the sonnet completely. See Halsted, *Shakespeare as Spoken*, vol. 8. Anthony Quayle's 1951 *Henry V* for the Festival of Britain featured a revised Epilogue, written by Patric Dickinson, in which the original second quatrain breaks off at "By which the world's best garden was achieved" to continue as follows, uniting *Richard II, 1* and *2 Henry IV*, and *Henry V* under a commemorative umbrella that invites a retrospective and nostalgic view of the history they dramatize: "And nourished there the red rose of his blood / Awakened from the self-despising dream / Of tavern victories hallowed by Sir John / He moves in his true measure: so our theme / From Richard's winter builds this summer throne; / Which oft our stage hath shown; and for their sake, / In your fair minds let this acceptance take."

61. Hands's performance text created a structural rhyme between sonnets: its second half opened with the French night scene (3.7), in which the Dauphin mentions the sonnet he has written to his horse; the play concludes with a "real" (English) sonnet. On the music, see Guy Woolfenden's interview in Beauman, *Centenary Production*, 48–49.

62. Irving Wardle, *Times*, 30 March 1984, 15.

63. Bogdanov's staging echoes a closural feature of a number of Shakespeare's playtexts—*As You Like It, The Merchant of Venice, Twelfth Night, Much Ado About Nothing* and, in Folio, *A Midsummer Night's Dream*—in which one figure either refuses to join or is deliberately excluded from the final comic harmony. On *Dream*'s Folio ending, see my "Gaining a Father: The Role of Egeus in Quarto and Folio," *Review of English Studies* 37, no. 148 (Fall 1986): 534–42.

64. Cf. Stephen Greenblatt's discussion of the circulation of social energy in

Shakespearean Negotiations, 1–20. See also Holderness, *Shakespeare's History*, 225.

CHAPTER 8
UNCOMMON WOMEN AND OTHERS: *HENRY VIII*'s "MAIDEN PHOENIX"

1. A full description of this pageant appears in John Nichols's *Progresses and Public Processions*, 1:38–43. See also Sydney Anglo, *Spectacle, Pageantry, and Early Tudor Policy* (Oxford, 1969), 344–59.

2. Nichols, *Progresses and Public Processions*, 1:48, 58. The reporter remarks: "A natural child, which at the very remembrance of her Father's name took so great a joy, that all men may well think, that as he rejoiced at his name whom this realm doth hold of so worthy memory; so in her doings she will resemble the same."

3. Johnson, *Elizabeth I*, 63.

4. I borrow the phrase from Geertz, *Local Knowledge*, 146.

5. Kantorowicz, *King's Two Bodies*, 23, 407.

6. Howard Felperin's title, "Tragical-Comical-Historical-Pastoral," for his chapter including *Cymbeline* and *Henry VIII* aptly expresses this mixture of genres (*Shakespearean Romance* [Princeton, 1972], 177–210). For a range of opinion, see G. Wilson Knight, *The Crown of Life* (1947; reprint, London, 1952), 256–336; Frank Kermode, "What Is Shakespeare's *Henry VIII* About?" *Durham University Journal*, n.s., 9 (1948): 48–55; Paul Bertram, "*Henry VIII*: The Conscience of the King," in *In Defense of Reading*, ed. Reuben A. Brower and Richard Poirier (New York, 1962), 152–73; H. R. Richmond, "Shakespeare's *Henry VIII*: Romance Redeemed by History," *Shakespeare Studies* 4 (1968): 334–49; R. A. Foakes, *Shakespeare: The Dark Comedies to the Last Plays* (Charlottesville, Va., 1971), 173–83; Frederick O. Waage, Jr., "*Henry VIII* and the Crisis of the English History Play," *Shakespeare Studies* 8 (1975): 297–309; Tom McBride, "*Henry VIII* as Machiavellian Romance," *Journal of English and Germanic Philology* 76 (1977): 26–39; John D. Cox, "*Henry VIII* and the Masque," *ELH* 45 (1978): 390–409; William M. Baillie, "*Henry VIII*: A Jacobean History," *Shakespeare Studies* 12 (1979): 247–66; Edward I. Berry, "*Henry VIII* and the Dynamics of Spectacle," *Shakespeare Studies* 12 (1979): 229–46; Frank V. Cespedes, " 'We Are One in Fortunes': The Sense of History in *Henry VIII*," *English Literary Renaissance* 10 (1980): 413–38; Alexander Leggatt, "*Henry VIII* and the Ideal England," *Shakespeare Survey* 38 (1985): 131–43; and Paul Dean, "Dramatic Mode and Historical Vision in *Henry VIII*," *Shakespeare Quarterly* 37 (1986): 175–89.

7. Henry Wotton, letter to Edmund Bacon, *Reliquiae Wottoniae* (1685), 425–26; quoted in Andrew Gurr, *Playgoing in Shakespeare's London* (Cambridge, 1987), 226.

8. Tennenhouse, *Power on Display*, 97.

9. Cf. Geertz's analysis of charisma: "This is the paradox of charisma: that though it is rooted in the sense of being near to the heart of things, of being

caught up in the realm of the serious, a sentiment that is felt most characteristically and continuously by those who in fact dominate social affairs, who ride in the progresses and grant the audiences, its most flamboyant expressions tend to appear among people at some distance from the center, indeed often enough at a rather enormous distance, who want very much to be closer" (*Local Knowledge*, 143–44).

10. Tennenhouse, *Power on Display*, 96–97.

11. For the notion of visual pleasure and the initial theoretical work on the gendered gaze, see Laura Mulvey, "Visual Pleasure and Narrative Cinema" (1975), reprinted in *Feminisim and Feminist Film Theory*, ed. Constance Penley (New York, 1988), 62. Later studies that respond to, extend, or qualify Mulvey's formulations include Teresa de Lauretis, *Alice Doesn't* (Bloomington, 1984); Mary Anne Doane, *The Desire to Desire* (Bloomington, 1987); and Tania Modleski, *The Women Who Knew Too Much* (London, 1988).

12. For a full discussion, see Marcus, *Puzzling Shakespeare*, 51–105. On Elizabeth's Amazonian body, see Schleiner, "*Divina virago*," 163–80. On the women's roles, see Kim H. Noling, "Grubbing Up the Stock: Dramatizing Queens in *Henry VIII*," *Shakespeare Quarterly* 39 (1988): 291–306.

13. On masque conventions, see Stephen Orgel, *The Jonsonian Masque* (Cambridge, Mass., 1965) and *Illusion of Power*. On the relationship between *Henry VIII* and the masque, see Cox, "*Henry VIII* and the Masque."

14. On this restructuring, see Joan Kelly, "Did Women Have a Renaissance?" in *Women, History, and Theory*, especially 30–47.

15. See Johnson, *Elizabeth I*, especially 23–37.

16. See Odell, *Shakespeare from Betterton to Irving*, 2:43–44.

17. Ibid., 1:307–8.

18. Prompt copy in the Beerbohm Tree Collection, the University of Bristol Theatre Collection. The Prologue was spoken by a clown, who entered through the curtains while the house lights were full up; the prompt copy notes, "After Wolsey's fall, he sent his fool to Henry as a gift"—perhaps justifying his appearance, which represents a conscious or unconscious homage to Rowley's *When You See Me You Know Me* (1605). In Rowley's play, Will Summers has a featured role, especially at the close, when he engages in a rhyming match with Henry and Queen Katherine (Parr) as part of a comic finale; see scene 15, lines 3019–94, reproduced in Bullough, *Narrative and Dramatic Sources*, 4:508–10. For a full discussion of Tree's production and its surrounding circumstances, see Booth, *Victorian Spectacular Theatre*, 134–60. Will Barker's Globe Film Company made a film of Tree's *Henry VIII*, released for distribution on 27 February 1911, which played for five weeks in London and six weeks in the provinces. For full details, see Ball, *Shakespeare on Silent Film*, 78–82, 320–22. Seeing the film may have functioned as a substitute for witnessing George V's coronation, held in the same year. All copies of the film were burned in April 1911; *Bioscope* (20 April 1911) records the event and refers to a cartoon of Tree throwing the reels into a furnace.

19. Both reviews are quoted in Booth, *Victorian Spectacular Theatre*, 154, 155.

20. Though later producers eliminated it, Charles Kean's 1855 production was the first to restore Elizabeth's christening, which included a moving panorama of the Lord Mayor's journey from Greenwich to London. See Odell, *Shakespeare from Betterton to Irving*, 2:290.

21. Prompt copies at the Shakespeare Centre Library. Although no printed record suggests it, Iden Payne's, and especially Atkins's, performance texts may well have reduced spectacle because of economic constraints.

22. Prompt copy at the Shakespeare Centre Library. For an account of Guthrie's production, see Muriel St. Clare Byrne, "A Stratford Production: *Henry VIII*," *Shakespeare Survey* 3 (1950): 120–29. St. Clare Byrne found the mime "more real" than the ceremonial spectacle and much admired the substitute scene, 127–28.

23. Prompt copy at the Shakespeare Centre Library.

24. Elizabeth is quoted by J. E. Neale, *Elizabeth I and Her Parliaments* (New York, 1958), 2:119. For James I, see *Political Works of James I*, 43. Present-day rhetorical stagings of power take a slightly different form: for Margaret Thatcher's 1987 campaign, the composer of "Hello Dolly" wrote a song with a refrain that goes, "Thatcher, Thatcher, Thatcher, / Not a man around to match her." On Thatcher's "royal" image, see Marina Warner, *Monuments and Maidens* (New York, 1985), 39–45.

25. See Johnson, *Elizabeth I*, 9–10. On Elizabeth's relation to her father, see Leah Marcus, "Erasing the Stigma of Daughterhood: Mary I, Elizabeth I, and Henry VIII," in *Daughters and Fathers*, ed. Lynda E. Boose and Betty S. Flowers (Baltimore, 1989), 400–417.

26. On this conjunction, see Bertram, "*Henry VIII*," 172; Leggatt, "*Henry VIII* and the Ideal England," 137; and Cespedes, " 'We Are One in Fortunes,' " 433–45.

27. As in *Measure for Measure*, which refers to but does not (except for Mistress Overdone) represent its whores, these "marginal women" are symbolically central. See Dollimore, "Transgression and Surveillance," 85–86. See also Babcock, introduction, to *Reversible World*, 32.

28. See, for instance, Bullough, *Narrative and Dramatic Sources*, 5:456–60, and E. C. Pettet, "*Coriolanus* and the Midlands Insurrection of 1607," *Shakespeare Survey* 3 (1950): 34–42, both cited in Marcus, *Puzzling Shakespeare*, 204. On Skimmington, see Underdown, *Revel, Riot, and Rebellion*, 102–11. See also Peter Burke, *Popular Culture in Early Modern Europe* (New York, 1978), especially 178–204.

29. For these details, see Graham Parry, *The Golden Age Restor'd* (New York, 1981), 3, 21.

30. See Corally Erickson, *The First Elizabeth* (London, 1984), 31. See also Alison Plowden, *The Young Elizabeth* (New York, 1971), 36–40.

31. Prompt copy at the Shakespeare Centre Library. As the christening bells begin to peal, the stage fills with a disorderly crowd and then with a massed procession, flags, and banners waving beside the white and gold canopy covering the Duchess of Norfolk, who carries Elizabeth. Henry is given the child when he enters; as Cranmer comes down from the gallery level to speak the

prophecy, Henry ascends and remains there while Cranmer speaks, descending again to thank the assembled crowd, hand Elizabeth back to the Duchess, and blow his nose. As the procession re-forms, the crowd sings *Gloria patri filio et Spiritus Sancto in saecula saeculorum* as a three-part canon—first sung, then spoken, then whispered, closing with a final whispered "Amen."

32. See, among others, Greenblatt, *Shakespearean Negotiations*, especially 1–20, and Montrose, "Purpose of Playing."

33. See Parry, *Golden Age Restor'd*, 49–50.

34. See Orgel, *Illusion of Power*, especially 40–42. For other strategies of idealization, see O. B. Hardison, Jr., *The Enduring Monument* (Chapel Hill, 1962), especially 30–57.

35. See Leggatt, "*Henry VIII* and the Ideal England," 131–33. See also Wikander, *Play of Truth and State*, 48. Staging the queen was, however, a different matter. Although in the original conclusion of Jonson's *Every Man Out of His Humour* Queen Elizabeth's silent figure, "us'd to a Morall and Mysterious end," cures Macilente of envy by "the verie wonder of her Presence," that ending was later disallowed. For Jonson's original text, the revised conclusion, and his justification, see *Ben Jonson*, ed. C. H. Herford and Percy Simpson (Oxford, 1927), 3:602–4. On this and other stagings of Elizabeth, see Anne Barton, *Ben Jonson, Dramatist* (Cambridge, 1984), 300–320, especially 306.

36. See especially Isaiah 11:1–2, 4–5. See also 1 Kings 4:25; 2 Kings 18:31; Isaiah 36:16–17; and Micah 4:4. R. A. Foakes notes these references in *Henry VIII* (London, 1968), 175n. These biblical events—a unified realm, promised delivery from foreign invasion, and a utopian vision of peace—are especially pertinent to assuaging the fears that haunted the reigns of Elizabeth I and James I. The allegory of England as a vineyard was a familiar one: Roy Strong cites an undated Queen's Day sermon by Edwin Sandys (1585), which uses figures similar to Cranmer's (*Cult of Elizabeth*, 124). For useful discussions of biblical prophecy and poetry, see Robert Alter, *The Art of Biblical Poetry* (New York, 1985), especially 137–62. In contrast to Shakespeare's Protestant emphasis, Calderón's play about Henry VIII, *La cisma de Inglaterra* (1626–1627), closes with a scene that "seems to point unhistorically to the reestablishment of Catholicism in England." See Loftis, *Renaissance Drama in England and Spain*, 17.

37. In comparing the entire scene to the weddings that close the comedies, Foakes notes that Steevens mentions a possible parody of Cranmer's speech in Beaumont and Fletcher's *Beggar's Bush*, 2.1 (*King Henry VIII*, 175n). Even given Fletcher's probable coauthorship, the existence of a parody indicates that the speech was known; writers do not bother to parody unnoticed texts.

38. Cox notes how conventions are modified in order to displace the flattery ("*Henry VIII* and the Masque," 407).

39. It also recalls other pastoral images, such as Henry's disguise as a shepherd at Wolsey's masque, prefiguring his role as shepherd of the Church (1.4), and Katherine's vision of eternity (4.2). For a detailed exploration of the ideology of pastoral and its ability to embody assertions of royal power, see, for

example, Louis Adrian Montrose, "Of Gentlemen and Shepherds: The Politics of Elizabethan Pastoral Form," *ELH* 50 (1983): 415–29.

40. Philip C. McGuire argues that the unstressed syllables that end each line of Sonnet 20 provide additional readerly "pleasure" by adding "one thing" to each of its lines. Thus Sonnet 20 "inverts the process the speaker purports to describe: a person initially created to be feminine is made masculine by the 'addition' of 'one thing' that, the speaker laments, denies him 'pleasure' and is 'to my purpose nothing' " ("Shakespeare's Non-Shakespearean Sonnets," 314–15). For a very different view of the play's feminine endings, see Knight, *Crown of Life*, 258–63.

41. On the phoenix symbol, see Francis A. Yates, *Astrea* (London, 1975), 58–69, and Jardine, *Still Harping on Daughters*, 176–79, 194–95. See also Marcus, *Puzzling Shakespeare*, 88–89. On its association with James, see Parry, *Golden Age Restor'd*, 18.

42. Ibid., 10–17.

43. Ibid., 26.

44. See Orgel, *Illusion of Power*, especially 42–58.

45. The process extends even to present-day audiences. In *Authors Takes Sides on the Falklands* (London, 1982), G. Wilson Knight writes: "I have for long accepted the validity of our country's historical contribution, seeing the British Empire as a precursor, or prototype, of world order. . . . Our key throughout is Cranmer's royal prophecy . . . Shakespeare's final words to his countrymen. This I still hold to be our one authoritative statement, every word deeply significant, as forecast of the world-order at which we should aim," quoted in Hawkes, *That Shakespeherian Rag*, 68.

46. See Allison Heisch, "Queen Elizabeth I and the Persistence of Patriarchy," *Feminist Review* 4 (1980): 49. Tyrone Guthrie's 1953 Old Vic revival, which marked Elizabeth II's coronation, cut all the references to James in Cranmer's speech (prompt copy in the University of Bristol Theatre Collection).

47. On women spectators, see my "He Do Cressida in Different Voices," *English Literary Renaissance* 20 (1990). See also Gurr, *Playgoing in Shakespeare's London*, 55–58, 92–94, 102–4. On deviant sonnets, see McGuire, "Shakespeare's Non-Shakespearean Sonnets."

48. Sir John Harington, *Nugae Antiquae*, 1:83. On Elizabeth's rhetoric, power, and abjection, see Michael Calvin McGee, "The Origins of 'Liberty': A Feminization of Power," *Communication Monographs* 47, no. 1 (March 1980): 23–45. See also McGee, *On Feminized Power*, Van Zelst Lecture in Communication, Northwestern University, May 1985. My thanks to McGee for a copy of this lecture.

49. Prompt copy at the Shakespeare Centre Library.

50. Ronald Bryden describes *Henry VIII*'s close as "a sonorous white hippie mass," "Tudor Scandals," *Observer*, 12 October 1969.

51. Ibid.; Harold Hobson, "A King Afraid," *Sunday Times*, 12 October 1969.

52. I borrow McGuire's term, "open silence," from his *Speechless Dialect*.

53. For an analysis of the souvenir program's emphasis on textuality, see Simon Barker, "Images of the Sixteenth and Seventeenth Centuries as a History of the Present," in *Literature, Politics, and Theory*, ed. Francis Barker, Peter Hulme, Margaret Iversen, and Diana Loxley (London, 1986), 185–86.

54. In Tyrone Guthrie's 1949 *Henry VIII*, the Old Lady spoke both Prologue and Epilogue, after which she herself initiated applause before mingling with the company for the curtain call. A woman also spoke the Epilogue in Guthrie's 1953 Old Vic revival, on the occasion of Elizabeth II's coronation.

55. See, for instance, Kelly, "Early Feminist Theory," 88–91.

56. For the circumstances surrounding the Princess's wedding, an occasion many believe the play addresses, see Foakes, *King Henry VIII*, xxxii–iv. See also Bergeron, *Shakespeare's Romances*, 212, 221–22. Clifford Leech associates the woman with Katherine ("The Structure of the Last Plays," *Shakespeare Survey* 11 [1958]: 19–30).

57. Translation of the Latin inscription on Elizabeth's tomb, quoted by Johnson, *Elizabeth I*, 441.

58. From the text of a 1603 letter from Sir Robert Cecil to Sir John Harington, *Nugae Antiquae*, 1:345.

CHAPTER 9
"NO EPILOGUE, I PRAY YOU"

1. On Folio and "authorizing," see Marcus, *Puzzling Shakespeare*, 1–50.

2. Jameson, introduction to *Situations of Theory*, xxvi.

3. A video recording of Bogdanov's *Roses* was made in early 1989 at Swansea, but whether or not it will be available in the United States is, at this writing, not certain.

4. Franco Moretti, *Signs Taken for Wonders* (1983; reprint, London, 1988), 35.

5. Such work is already under way. See, among others, Sinfield, "Royal Shakespeare"; Graham Holderness, "Radical Potentiality and Institutional Closure: Shakespeare in Film and Television," in Dollimore and Sinfield, *Political Shakespeare*, 182–201; Thomas Cartelli, "Prospero in Africa: *The Tempest* as Colonialist Text and Pretext," in Howard and O'Connor, *Shakespeare Reproduced*; and the essays in Graham Holderness, ed., *The Shakespeare Myth* (Manchester, 1988). See also Lorraine Helms, "Playing the Woman's Part: Feminist Criticism and Shakespearean Performance," *Theatre Journal* 41 (1989): 190–200; and my "Kiss Me Deadly" and "He Do Cressida in Different Voices." On the issues of consent, see Ania Loomba, *Gender, Race, Renaissance Drama* (Manchester, 1989).

6. See Holderness, "Radical Potentiality and Institutional Closure." See also the essays in *Shakespeare on Television*, ed. J. C. Bulman and H. R. Coursen (Hanover, N.H., 1988).

7. Ruby Cohn, *Modern Shakespeare Offshoots* (Princeton, 1976).

INDEX ❧

34126

9.5.96